T0075639

IET COMPUTING SERIES 27

Managing Internet of Things Applications across Edge and Cloud Data Centres

IET Book Series on Big Data – Call for Authors

Editor-in-Chief: Professor Albert Y. Zomaya, University of Sydney, Australia

The topic of Big Data has emerged as a revolutionary theme that cuts across many technologies and application domains. This new book series brings together topics within the myriad research activities in many areas that analyse, compute, store, manage and transport massive amount of data, such as algorithm design, data mining and search, processor architectures, databases, infrastructure development, service and data discovery, networking and mobile computing, cloud computing, high-performance computing, privacy and security, storage and visualization.

Topics considered include (but not restricted to) IoT and Internet computing; cloud computing; peer-to-peer computing; autonomic computing; data centre computing; multi-core and many core computing; parallel, distributed and high-performance computing; scalable databases; mobile computing and sensor networking; green computing; service computing; networking infrastructures; cyberinfrastructures; e-Science; smart cities; analytics and data mining; Big Data applications and more.

Proposals for coherently integrated International co-edited or co-authored handbooks and research monographs will be considered for this book series. Each proposal will be reviewed by the editor-in-chief and some board members, with additional external reviews from independent reviewers. Please email your book proposal for the IET Book Series on Big Data to: Professor Albert Y. Zomaya at albert.zomaya@sydney.edu.au or to the IET at author_support@theiet.org.

Managing Internet of Things Applications across Edge and Cloud Data Centres

Edited by
Rajiv Ranjan, Karan Mitra, Prem Prakash Jayaraman
and Albert Y. Zomaya

The Institution of Engineering and Technology

Published by The Institution of Engineering and Technology, London, United Kingdom

The Institution of Engineering and Technology is registered as a Charity in England & Wales (no. 211014) and Scotland (no. SC038698).

The Institution of Engineering and Technology
Futures Place
Kings Way, Stevenage
Hertfordshire, SG1 2UA, United Kingdom

www.theiet.org

British Library Cataloguing in Publication Data
A catalogue record for this product is available from the British Library

ISBN 978-1-78561-779-9 (hardback)
ISBN 978-1-78561-780-5 (PDF)

Typeset in India by MPS Limited

Cover credit: Just Super/E+ *via Getty Images*

Contents

About the editors

Rajiv Ranjan is the university chair professor for Internet of Things research, co-director of the Networked and Ubiquitous Systems Engineering (NUSE) Group and academic director of the School of Computing, as well as research director of the Newcastle Urban Observatory at Newcastle University, UK. He is an expert in algorithms, resource management models, and distributed system architectures for cloud computing, IoT, and big data. He has developed novel techniques and distributed system architectures to facilitate performance-driven provisioning of multimedia and IoT applications over multiple cloud datacentres. He serves on the editorial board of international journals such as the *IEEE Transactions on Computers*, *IEEE Transactions on Cloud Computing* and *Future Generation Computer Systems*. He is a senior member of IEEE.

Karan Mitra is an associate professor at Luleå University of Technology, Sweden. He received his dual-badge PhD from Monash University, Australia and Luleå University of Technology in 2013. He received his MIT (MT) and a PGradDipDigComm from Monash University in 2008 and 2006, respectively. He received his BIS (Hons.) from Guru Gobind Singh Indraprastha University, Delhi, India in 2004. His research interests include quality of experience modelling and prediction, context-aware computing, cloud computing, and mobile and pervasive computing systems. From January 2012 to December 2013, he worked as a researcher at CSIRO, Canberra, Australia. He is a member of the IEEE and ACM. He serves as an associate editor for ACM Computing Surveys.

Prem Prakash Jayaraman is a professor in Internet of Things and distributed systems at Swinburne University of Technology, Australia. He leads several strategic initiatives, including the Factory of the Future, the Digital Innovation Lab and the Advanced Manufacturing Industry 4.0 Hub at Swinburne. His research area of interest is broadly around distributed systems, particularly IoT, cloud computing, and mobile computing aiming to establish and develop novel techniques and solutions for deploying and provision resilient and interoperable IoT analytics applications across multi-cloud and smart device/edge environments.

Prof. Jayaraman's has received over $18Mil in competitive external research funding from both industry and the Australian Research Council. He has published over 150 papers in several top venues including IEEE Communication and Tutorials, ACM Surveys, Transaction of Cloud Computing, and serves as speciality chief editor, associate editor, and chairs for several high-quality journals and conference such as

Frontiers in Internet of Things, ACM Computing Surveys and IEEE Consumer Communication and Networking Conference. He has been awarded twice Vice Chancellor awards for excellence in industry-based research at Swinburne, two best paper awards at top tier computer science conferences, and one industry award (iAwards 2023) for his pioneering industry-based research.

Albert Y. Zomaya is Peter Nicol Russell Chair Professor of Computer Science and Director of the Centre for Distributed and High-Performance Computing at the University of Sydney. To date, he has published > 700 scientific papers and articles and is (co-)author/editor of >30 books. A sought-after speaker, he has delivered >250 keynote addresses, invited seminars, and media briefings. He was previously Editor in Chief of the IEEE Transactions on Computers (2010–2014) and the IEEE Transactions on Sustainable Computing (2016–2020).

Prof. Zomaya is a decorated scholar with numerous accolades including Fellowship of the IEEE, the American Association for the Advancement of Science, and the Institution of Engineering and Technology. Also, he is a Fellow of the Australian Academy of Science, Royal Society of New South Wales, Foreign Member of Academia Europaea, and Member of the European Academy of Sciences and Arts.

Some of Prof. Zomaya's recent awards include the *Research Innovation Award, IEEE Technical Committee on Cloud Computing* (2021), the *Technical Achievement and Recognition Award, IEEE Communications Society's IoT, Ad Hoc and Sensor Networks Technical Committee* (2022). Prof. Zomaya is a Clarivate 2022 Highly Cited Researcher, and his research interests lie in parallel and distributed computing, networking, and complex systems.

Foreword

Spanning the inter-related fields of Internet of Things (IoT), Edge Computing, and Cloud Computing, this timely and valuable compendium will provide educators, researchers, and developers with the background needed to understand the intricacies of this rich and fast-moving field which requires novel and more efficient solutions to handle a variety of new challenges and open problems.

The chapters provide a good coverage of the important research themes related to the development of methodologies to manage these complex systems and cover a sample of applications to give a flavour of the challenges facing researchers, and what will impact the development of the next generation of applications.

The editors have assembled an excellent team of international contributors to provide a rich coverage of these topics. I am sure that the readers will find this volume useful and a source of inspiration for future research work in this area. This book should be well received by researchers and developers from academia and industry, and it will provide a valuable resource for senior undergraduate and graduate classes.

Prof. Albert Y. Zomaya
Editor-in-Chief of the *IET Book Series on Big Data*

Preface

The Internet of Things which has emerged as a buzz word in the last decade is now transitioning into a main stream technology that current and in the future will underpin every aspect of our lives, societies, industries, and environment. In 2022, broadband IoT (4G/5G) reached 1.3 billion connections with wide-area use cases that require higher throughput, lower latency, and larger data volumes. As per recent reports from McKinsey, by 2025, IoT applications could have $11 trillion impact. Research driven by ambitious use cases and benefiting from innovation areas in components, systems, networking, and web technologies are further driving the development of new and innovation IoT applications.

As IoT applications continue to grow, and emergence of technologies such as edge, 5G/6G, the traditional model of cloud-based processing data processing is no longer scalable and hence needs to shift. Shifting data processing to the edge of the networks can help organisations take advantage of the growing number of IoT devices deployment, improve network speeds, reduce cost of processing, guaranteeing high degree of security, and enhance customer experiences. The scalable nature of edge computing makes it an ideal solution for fast-growing, agile organisation, especially if they are co-located edge and cloud data centres infrastructures.

The future design of the IoT applications will depend crucially on the development of sophisticated edge-cloud platforms and data centres architectures and infrastructure for smart objects, embedded intelligence, and smart networks. Most of the today's IoT application deployment are mainly focused on data collection from sensors, whereas in the future, real-time actuation and smart behaviour will be the key points. Further, research driven by ambitious use cases and benefits from innovations in key areas of systems, networking, and web will change the dimension of future IoT applications and systems in terms of scalability, heterogeneity, complexity, and dynamicity.

The main issue arising in using several computing models to support IoT applications is the management of different physical/virtual infrastructures (e.g., datacentres, edge devices, IoT devices, and gateways) according to specific application/service requirements (e.g., latency, data volume, responsivity, processing delay, etc.). In particular, it is often hard to determine a priori how to deploy the IoT applications into different infrastructures – since resources' availability, system load, and connectivity features can unpredictably change over the time.

Written and edited by an international team of experts in the field, every chapter submitted to the book has been critically evaluated by at least two expert reviewers. The critical suggestions by the reviewers certainly helped and influenced the authors of the individual chapter to enrich the quality in terms of experimentation, performance evaluation, representation, etc. The book may serve as a complete reference for state-of-the-art interdisciplinary computing research in the application lifecycle management for Internet of Things in the paradigm of edge-cloud computing. The chapters in the book address challenges from a distributed system perspective that includes both cyber and physical aspects. Chapters 1, 2, and 3 focus on the resource allocation and offloading challenges in cloud-fog architectures. Chapter 4 focuses on the important topic of developing benchmarking capability for testing and evaluating distributed cloud-edge architectures that support IoT applications. Chapters 5 and 6 introduce smart learning analytics in the context of IoT. Chapters 7 and 12 introduces the area of blockchain and IoT another key emerging area of IoT application that will challenge the edge-cloud paradigm. Chapters 8 and 9 discuss the important area of security and privacy for IoT application in the edge-cloud paradigm while Chapter 10 aims to address the topic of quality in IoT. Chapters 11 and 12 focus on specific IoT use cases and related challenges in deploying them in the edge-cloud paradigm.

In summary, the book aims to bring together and identify key opportunities, challenges and research advances at the intersection of the four paradigms of cloud and edge computing, cyber physical systems, internet of things and big data for future IoT applications. This book offers key insights to researchers, engineers, IT professionals, advanced students, postgraduate students, and lecturers working in the fields of parallel and distributed computing, data mining, information retrieval, cloud, edge and fog computing, and the IoT.

Acknowledgements

We thank the reviewers of the book for their valuable time in providing constructive feedback on the chapters. Their feedback has helped in improving the quality of each chapter and the entire book. The editors would like to thank Ms. Olivia Wilkins, Assistant Editor, The Institution of Engineering and Technology for the editorial assistance and cooperation to produce this important scientific work.

Editors

Prof. Rajiv Ranjan, Newcastle Urban Observatory at Newcastle University, UK
A/Prof. Karan Mitra, Luleå University of Technology, Sweden
Prof. Prem Prakash Jayaraman, Swinburne University of Technology, Australia
Prof. Albert Y. Zomaya, University of Sydney, Australia

Chapter 1

Task offloading using fog analytics

Rakesh Matam[1] and Somanath Tripathy[2]

Fog computing has recently evolved as a promising technology to meet the specific latency and QoS requirements of Internet of Things (IoT) applications. End-devices use fog computing facilities to minimize latency, communication costs, and energy in the cloud-based frameworks. This, however, has many associated challenges, mainly due to the distributed nature of the fog network. As different applications have different QoS requirements, a single framework for task offloading would not be optimal. Thus, the issues in task offloading include the decisions of when, where, and what tasks to offload, as well as how the offloading task be scheduled to minimize latency. Besides that, limited energy, device heterogeneity, and task workload would influence the offloading decision. In view of different application requirements, the objective of task offloading becomes a multi-objective optimization problem. In this work, we first present the impact of various parameters on task-offloading decisions. Subsequently, we analyze the impact of different fog analytics schemes and learning algorithms on task offloading. This study presents the optimal performance criterion for task-offloading decisions using fog analytics. The data collected from multiple fog-nodes at discrete time intervals in a distributed manner is used to select a fog node for task offloading.

1.1 Introduction

Over the past decade, there have been rapid advancements in wireless technologies and embedded systems. Everything or everyone is surrounded by such technologies to make their life easier. To use these technologies to the fullest, most of the physical things are embedded with sensors and communication elements and are being connected to the Internet to improve the quality of life. These things are smart and work as per the requirements of the environment, and the purpose of the entity and generate enormous amounts of data. These things make up the Internet of Things (IoT). Because of the advancements in wireless technologies and IoT more and more devices such as mobile phones, wearable devices, and electronic devices are getting

[1]Department of Computer Science and Engineering, Indian Institute of Information Technology—Guwahati, India
[2]Department of Computer Science & Engineering, Indian Institute of Technology—Patna, India

connected to the Internet. Major applications like Smart Grid, Home Automation, Smart Health Care, etc. are adapting these new technologies instead of the traditional methods to operate. All of these have different requirements in terms of bandwidth, storage, and computation. They generate a huge volume of data that are needed to be stored and analyzed to provide necessary services by improving the working of applications based on the data. Storing, computing, and processing such a huge amount data are not possible for the commodity resources or local resources, hence, Cloud Computing is opted as a preferable method to carry out all the tasks related to IOT applications to simplify the procedures. But Cloud Computing also has a few disadvantages and challenges since the cloud is geographically located far away which results in high communication cost, latency, etc. It also gives significant rise to the carbon footprint, hence, Fog-computing concept has emerged as an alternative to fulfil the dependence on Cloud. It is a decentralized infrastructure initiated by Cisco where applications are located in a layer between devices and cloud which would solve several problems like latency factor by pushing cloud facilities to the edge of the networks and the computation, storage, processing, etc. will be done closer to the device rather than sending it up to cloud which is located far away. This fog layer exists in between the IoT end device layer and cloud creating a three-layer architecture. The first tier consisting of IoT devices is heterogeneous, constrained and has different requirements, processing, computation, and storage capacity. The middle tier which is the fog layer consists of interconnected devices like gateway routers, access points, base stations, cloud-lets, etc. which provide services to the IoT devices similar to cloud but distributed in nature. The third layer is the cloud layer which is connected to the fog layer via fog–cloud interface. The fog layer consists of several fog nodes where each fog node consists of resources to process requests and store data from IoT devices. Each application consists of a primary fog node which determines and processes the requests. Applications with different QoS and different requirements place requests in the fog node and the fog node decides how and when to handle the requests based on the application requirement. Requests those, a fog node that cannot handle on its own due to lack of enough resources is offloaded to another fog node called the secondary fog node or to the cloud to be executed and to overcome the lack of computing power. This process is called task offloading. End users can access short-delay and high-performance computing which is more beneficial for delay-sensitive applications.

1.2   Fog-computing architecture

As mentioned earlier, the fog-computing architecture extends the facilities offered by the cloud by bringing computing, storage, and networking resources, in close vicinity of the nodes that generate data. By doing so, an additional computing layer has been introduced between the cloud and IoT systems, which balances resources by addressing the limitations of cloud. Typically, a three-layered architecture as shown in Figure 1.1 is widely presented in the literature. Here, the bottom layer is comprised of end-user devices. These devices are generally power constrained, with low storage

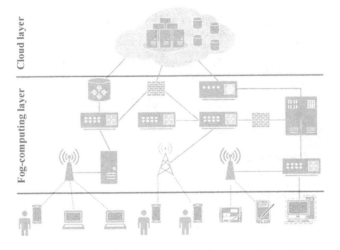

Figure 1.1   Three-layered fog-computing architecture

and processing capabilities, and thus rely on the middle (fog) layer and top (cloud) layer for carrying out their application tasks effectively. Effectiveness is specific to application needs and is aimed at enhanced performance. For example, an oil pipeline whose status is continuously monitored for leakages benefits from fog computing by lowering the latency in reporting abnormal conditions. Several applications related to mobile phones, and IoT make up the bottom layer of the architecture that includes applications like vehicular networks, wireless sensor networks, home automation networks, personal area networks, etc. Tier 2 represents the fog layer, which is comprised of different devices like gateway routers, access points, base stations, micro data center, cloudlets, etc., that are inter-networked. Its services (storage and processing) are made available to EU devices through the fog–things interface, similar to the cloud. But the difference is that the cloud services are centralized, whereas fog layer is distributed in nature. The fog network is highly virtualized that provides services to applications via the fog–things and fog–cloud interface. Tier 3 represents the cloud, and the interactions are via the fog–cloud interface.

The fog-computing layer itself can be organized as six layers based on the functionalities offered to the end-user devices. These include physical and virtualization, monitoring, pre-processing, temporary storage, security, and transport layers as shown in Figure 1.2. The ordering of layers based on functionalities, which may vary depending on the implementation by the fog network. At the lowest level, the fog network aims to connect with all the devices in tier 3 of Figure 1.1 that generate data. This may also depend on the network architecture, and how the gateway nodes are configured if exist. Managing devices requires monitoring of the node's activities like their

Transport layer	Transporting of pre-processed and secured data to the cloud.
Security layer	Encryption/decryption, privacy, and integrity measures.
Storage layer	Data distribution and replication. Storage device maintenance and storage virtualization.
Pre-processing layer	Data analysis, filtering, and data reconstruction.
Monitoring layer	Monitoring of: activities, power, resources, response, and services.
Virtualization and physical layer	Virtual sensors and networks. Things, physical sensors, and sensor networks.

Figure 1.2   Layers in fog-computing architecture

current state, power levels, and task and storage requirements. The physical and virtualization layer and the monitoring layer are closely bound together because of their inter-dependencies. That is, the fog-network connects to these devices and monitors their activities to offer services to applications. For example, a device can be monitored for its energy consumption and power levels to offer task offloading service. Services may differ based on application requirements but the necessary inputs are provided by the monitoring layer. Higher layers like pre-processing and temporary storage are responsible for preliminary analysis, data filtering, and storage of data.

The pre-processing layer can determine what data to be sent to the cloud, thus lowering unnecessary interactions. Further, enabling decision making capabilities at the fog-layer enhances application performance, decreases costs associated with cloud interactions, and improves security.

The storage layer is responsible for storing the data that may be immediately accessed. It acts as a storage space in the short term. For permanent storage, cloud would be preferred. For example, the frequent sensor readings of smart-lights in a building may be temporarily stored in fog, analyzed, pre-processed, and then sent to cloud for storage and data analytics. This cuts down data and communication costs.

The fog-network can also provide security services for applications that lack them. Location privacy and anonymity can be enabled by fog for certain applications like in health care. It can provide different encryption/decryption services, integrity checks, and authentication mechanisms that are computational intensive and cannot be implemented on the device. Implementing these services close to the devices generating data would prevent the side-channel analysis and the misuse by the cloud. Lastly, the transport layer is responsible for transferring the data to the cloud. It can handle different data representations and data-exchange formats supporting interoperability.

The functionalities offered by fog nodes listed above are generic and more specific features can be added or discarded, based on the configuration of the fog-network. Services offered by the fog-network can meet specific application demands of different applications as resources are positioned close to the devices needing them. Thereby, fog-network can offer more context-aware customized services and thus proven to be highly performance centric and cost-effective. For example, a latency-sensitive smart healthcare application can benefit from fog services by processing data locally. As an example, a smart wearable device that reports oxygen saturation and blood-sugar levels of a patient can identify abnormal conditions and alerts the concerned in milliseconds using fog service, which would take hundreds of milliseconds if relied on the cloud. Further, fog can act as interoperability platform for enabling cooperation among different IoT networks with disparate mandates.

1.3 Task offloading

End-user devices depend on fog and cloud computing layers for their computation and storage requirements. Devices typically offload tasks either partially or fully based on the device, or task, application requirements. Device requirements are almost mostly energy centric, i.e., targeted towards conserving energy as the majority of IoT devices are constrained. As each task has an associated cost with it, devices generally make a choice on the place of execution (locally/offload) to minimize this cost. For example, if the cost of processing a task locally is more than the cost incurred to offload, then usually such a task is offloaded. In other words, if the energy needed to process a task locally is higher than the communication cost to fog/cloud for offloading it, then devices prefer to offload. Alternatively, a device might not be capable of processing the task due to the lack of processing/storage or any other task requirements, then a device offloads the task. Lastly, a few applications necessitate task offloading. For example, some applications are latency bound, and only offloading can help in meeting these latency requirements.

1.3.1 Task and task offloading

A task can simply be denoted as a 3-tuple (δ, C, M), where δ represents the data size, C represents computation time (in CPU cycles) required to process the task, and M represents the optional storage space that would be necessary if the results of the task are to be stored on the fog node. Tasks can be further sub-categorized based on other requirements like deadline, where the task needs to be processed within a stipulated time limit. These deadlines can be either hard or soft time limits. Tasks may be prioritized and needs to be handled based on their priorities (e.g. high/medium/low).

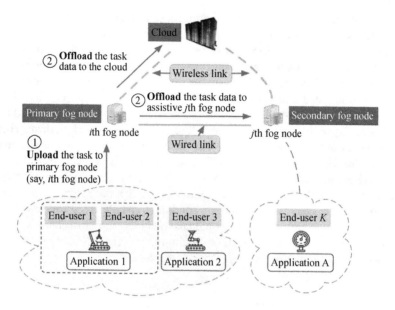

Figure 1.3   Illustration of task offloading in a fog network

Besides that, some tasks may need specific resources like GPU, so as to be handled accordingly.

End-user devices offload their tasks based on their requirements. The logic to determine whether to offload or not may be implemented on the device, or a smart gateway which can be configured to make a decision on behalf of the device based on its status. Most of the existing literature assume the former approach, however, a few works have also considered the later [1]. One of the core functionalities of the fog layer is to handle offloading requests from IoT devices, with each IoT network/application having a designated fog node called primary fog node. Typically, this is the node through which devices/applications access fog-network services. The primary fog node is responsible for handling the offloaded tasks. The primary fog-node node itself may process the task, or offload to other neighboring fog nodes on the fog layer or to the cloud, which is decided from the cost–benefit analysis, and task requirements. This interaction is shown in Figure 1.3.

Herein, the end-user device/application offloads a task to the primary fog-node. As a primary fog node concurrently serves multiple device requests, lack of computing resources at that requested instant or inability to meet task requirements is an expected scenario. To handle this, the fog node further offloads a task to neighboring fog nodes (also called as secondary fog nodes) or to the cloud, based on a cost function. For example, if the latency requirements of a task can only be met by offloading it to the cloud, the primary fog-node does so. Contrarily, if the task is to be offloaded to the secondary fog node(s), the process of such a fog-node selection is an important step in the task-offloading process. The selected fog node not only has to meet the task requirements but also has to incur optimal cost for offloading. Further to make such a selection, a fog node should have a global view of the system to make an offloading decision.

1.3.2 When to offload tasks?

The decision to offload a task by a device (or a fog node) can be motivated by several factors such as lack of resources (computing power or storage space), inability to meet latency requirements/task deadlines, higher energy consumption if the task is processed locally, data dependency, security and privacy issues, etc. Data dependency is when the essential data for processing the task is not available, and it is effective if the fog node gathers the data and processes it. Fog-node selection is a two-step process where the first is to identify a fog node that meets task requirements, and the second to choose a fog node to which the cost of offloading is minimal. Herein, obtaining the status of peer fog nodes on the fog network becomes the core challenge of task offloading. The global view of the system is the collection of individual status of all fog nodes in the network. The status of a fog node is generally defined in terms of computing and storage resources that can be spared for other fog nodes in the fog network. Multiple queuing model-based approaches are employed to represent the current state of a fog node and the resources it can spare for other fog nodes in the fog network. Fog analytics using learning algorithms can predict the availability of resources that facilitate task offloading in the network. In the next section, we highlight such approaches and the way they improve task offloading.

1.4 Fog analytics

Task offloading is one of the core functionalities of fog-computing environment that enables IoT devices to rely on fog-network resources for their varied needs. Therefore, most of the preliminary research in fog computing has been centered around the design of efficient offloading techniques that aim to improve offloading performance in terms of latency, energy consumption, task priorities, security, etc. [1–3]. However, most of these techniques are application specific and aim to optimize one or more of above-mentioned parameters for a specific network scenario. Furthermore, these schemes have to be run by each of the fog nodes to accommodate the changes in network topology and task load. Thus, the majority of the existing task-offloading schemes are not suited to dynamic fog networks. To address these issues, machine-learning algorithms can be used to design intelligent offloading techniques that can adjust to varying network and fog-node conditions.

Analyzing data points related to task offloading on fog-devices has shown to improve the performance of offloading schemes [4–7]. The status of fog network is monitored over time to facilitate optimal scheduling of resources on fog devices that enable better task offloading. It primarily improves the latency in fog-node selection to enable the fog node to process more tasks reducing the offloading burden. The use of efficient machine learning and edge-analytics techniques would increase the capability of a fog node to process more tasks in less time.

1.4.1 Learning approaches for task offloading

1.4.1.1 Unsupervised learning

A fog node offloads a task to a neighboring fog node based on the information gathered about the availability of resources. This information is typically collated by a fog node by exchanging messages and is used to select an optimal fog node. A fog node can learn about the availability of resources by analyzing task-load patterns and resource availability status. Unsupervised learning approaches can be adapted to learn using the data patterns at different fog nodes. Authors in [8] introduced a concept of task caching and offloading that relies on caching of completed tasks and their related data in edge cloud. Tasks are cached on the basis of the popularity of the tasks, size of the content, and required computation capacity of tasks. For example, in mobile devices rendering scene, recognizing and tracking objects are highly popular tasks which need a lot of data transmissions and computation. Task caching and offloading can reduce energy and delay and meet the requirements. Therefore, the authors addressed the challenges of designing an optimal joint task caching and offloading, while considering the heterogeneity of the tasks and limited resources to minimize the total energy consumed by the mobile devices while meeting the delay requirements. In [9], authors discussed about the usage of mobile edge computing in ultra-dense networks to meet the requirements of low latency in such networks. But the distributed computing resources in edge cloud and limited energy in mobile devices make it challenging to offload the task. This is because ultra-dense networks have a much higher density of radio resources and the network contains more number of cells than active users. Hence, authors proposed an efficient offloading scheme by dividing the problem into two sub-problems task placement and resource allocation and solving them. They proposed software-defined network (SDN) technology for task offloading in ultra-dense network as SDN technology can achieve logical centralized control in a distributed network which would allow the controller to collect information on mobile device, edge cloud, and sense network from global perspective. This would help the centralized controller in decision making towards executing the tasks locally or to offload, etc. Thus, the proposed strategy achieved better results and succeeded in minimizing the task duration and saving energy.

1.4.1.2 Supervised learning

Supervised-learning approaches allow fog nodes to learn about load patterns and resource availability based on dynamic data points created through prior interactions. The outcome of these learning approaches is the decision that allows fog nodes to select an optimal offloading fog device. To address this, authors in [10] introduced a concept of service caching and task offloading. Service caching refers to caching application services and its related libraries and databases in the edge server which enables their corresponding tasks to be executed. For example, services like video streaming, social gaming, navigation, augmented reality, etc. Decisions on which services to be cached are made on the basis of the services which can maximize edge computing performance and this decision is made after considering several concepts such as popularity, long-, and short-term performance as the resources are limited in the edge and only limited service can be cached. Hence, the authors in the paper studies service caching in dense cellular network and propose a decentralized algorithm to optimize both service caching and task offloading in such networks thereby minimizing latency under long-term energy consumption constraints. Several authors presented their works on optimizing the task-offloading phenomenon. In [11], the authors have addressed the challenges of when and where to offload the data to perform computing task. The authors have contributed to the optimization with the help of two decision-making models to take optimal decision on when and where to offload task. The authors evaluated the performance using real-world data sets and compared with baseline deterministic and stochastic models. The authors in [12] considered a scenario for offloading task where the user is not located in a fixed position and the user is moving through many mobile edge computing servers deployed at the network edge. Such dynamic conditions (when the user is moving) choose the appropriate time and server, for task offloading. So, in this work, the authors have tackled the decision-making problem and evaluated the performance of their proposed method using real-world data set to reduce the execution delay of task offloading in sequential manner. Small Cell Cloud (SCC) contains Cloud-enabled Small Cells (CeSCs) which works as radio ends for mobile user equipment and provides the advantages of the centralized cloud service to mobile devices. Authors in [13] introduced the concept of implementation of framework for offloading task from user equipment to SCC to examine how the computation of various types and various networking parameters affects the scenario. The authors evaluated the framework by using Augmented Reality app since it requires high level of computation and have a low-latency requirements and evaluations showed results in significant decrease in latency and energy consumption as a benefit of using SCC. In [14], the authors focus on the offloading of task between fog nodes while maintaining low delay. A task offloading network architecture is introduced which contains multiple fog nodes. In the paper, they proposed an analytical framework to offload task to a fair fog node by considering different computing capabilities, parameters like delay, energy consumption, and sustainability of fog nodes. For each fog node, the authors constructed a fairness scheduling metric to calculate which fog node can be considered fair or better to offload the task and then a two-step scheme is followed for the task-offloading job. The first step is to select the best fog node according to fairness metric and second step is to offload the task based on minimum delay rules. The scheduling metric is constructed based on time–energy efficiency of the fog nodes. Hence, the proposed method in this chapter helps in selecting an optimal fog node to offload tasks and minimizes delay and energy consumption. The authors of [15] address the challenges of critical applications which have strict requirements of ultra-reliable and low latency but the design of the proximal mobile edge-computing servers where tasks are offloaded is mostly average-based and cannot cope with ultra-high requirements. Hence, to tackle this problem, the authors proposed a framework for task offloading and resource allocation by considering the statistics of the events of different queue lengths as the queue length is associated with amount of delay. Thereby treating the queue lengths as delay metric, the threshold is set for the queue lengths in the framework and a probabilistic requirement on the threshold is set as a constraint for minimizing power during task computation and offloading. Thus, taking into account the mobility features of user equipment, the authors proposed a timescale framework for association with a server to perform task offloading and resource allocation in a shorter timescale. Hence, the overall motive of the research is to minimize power consumption while allocating resources and task offloading. In [16], the authors propose the concept of implementing learning algorithm for task offloading in a vehicular environment. The authors mention that the vehicular network is dynamic and uncertain since it is not fixed in a definite place. Vehicular edge computing provides computation and resources to vehicles and resources and have fast-changing topologies and varying workloads which serve as the main challenge in designing an optimal task-offloading framework for such networks. Hence, in the paper the authors propose a solution which enables the devices/vehicles to learn the offloading delay performance of their neighboring vehicles while offloading tasks. The authors designed an adaptive learning-based algorithm to minimize the average delay while offloading which works in a distributed manner. The vehicles are classified as either Task Vehicles (TaV) or Service Vehicles (SaV) where TaV needs task offloading and SaV can help execute tasks. The proposed adaptive learning algorithm helps TaV to take task offloading decision individually to reduce average delay.

1.4.1.3 Reinforcement learning

More recently, reinforcement learning approaches have been employed that facilitate fog nodes to learn from the neighboring environment and make offloading decisions. The authors in [17] mentioned about the various delay requirements of the tasks. The end users have limited resources and tasks are offloaded to the primary fog nodes but since the fog nodes also have limited resources, it becomes challenging to handle multiple tasks with different delay requirements of the applications to allocate resources and carry out the task within delay deadline, hence, in such a case, the primary fog node needs to offload the task further to the secondary fog node or the remote cloud to complete the task while considering various other factors. Hence, in the paper, the authors propose a model considering computational and transmission delay of the tasks to optimize the task offloading decision and the amount of data to be offloaded while considering multiple tasks with different delay deadlines. The authors also used a heuristic approach to show that the proposed method guarantees the latency deadline compared to fixed computing resource allocation.

The authors of [18] focus on the application of fog computing in large-scale industries where there are high demand for latency-sensitive applications. In their paper, they discussed about the computation offloading in a fog network where end users offload task to the primary fog node and in case that fog node cannot process the request due to limited computation resources, the task be further offloaded to either a neighboring fog node or the remote cloud. This further offloading of task in both cases has its own challenges. When the task is offloaded to another neighboring fog node, it might incur a burden on that fog node and offloading the task to remote server might suffer from limited communication resources. Hence, to solve the problem, the authors considered the transmission delay from end user to fog node and fog node to cloud, local computation time, and waiting time due to queuing in the fog node. The authors jointly optimized the amount of tasks being offloaded to neighboring fog nodes and communication resource allocation for remote cloud using optimization methods and proposed an optimized and scalable solution to achieve latency deadlines and, hence, minimized the task completion time.

The authors in [19] propose a strategy of computation offloading to minimize the total cost of energy and delay incurred while processing a task per end user. An offloading policy is proposed to find the optimal solution of where and how much task data should be offloaded under energy and delay constraints. The individual computational capability of the fog nodes is considered which mainly affects the task-processing time and total task-processing delay. The authors also focus on to minimize the total system cost calculated as the weighted sum of energy consumption during task offloading.

In [20], the authors mentioned about the intelligent transport system (ITS) which is a growing concept of interest for the future. But ITS has a requirement of low latency and highly reliable data analytics solution for data from various sources within the network and such requirements cannot be fulfilled by the cloud as it has high communication and computation latency. So in the paper, the authors introduced edge analytics architecture for ITS where data is processed at device/vehicle or roadside sensor to overcome the challenges of high latency and low reliability of the remote cloud. The data generated by the vehicles in ITS are heterogeneous in nature and are generated from various types of tasks within the network which again creates a challenge. Hence, the authors proposed deep-learning solutions to process on the data and enable ITS devices with computer vision and signal-processing functions.

Similarly, authors in [21] proposed deep-learning-based IoT edge analytics for intelligent healthcare system to cope with the delay-sensitive healthcare data, the authors of [22] propose deep-learning-based framework for performing edge analytics on various types of videos generated from various sources, the authors of [23] also mentioned about the aspects of implementing deep learning on data analytics and its abilities to reduce human interventions and workloads. In [24], the authors proposed the implementation of deep-learning concept on edge analytics. The authors in this paper mentioned about merging cloud and edge computing for IoT data analytics and propose a deep-learning-based approach for data reduction on the edge and machine learning on the cloud to perform human activity recognition.

The authors in [25] discussed about the problems in intelligent water distribution network which have anomalous behaviors such as leakage and bursts; hence, to address the problems based on such networks, the authors proposed a system that combines a lightweight edge anomaly detection algorithm. The technique was used on the edge analytics data and an efficient localization algorithm based on graph theory to produce a timely and accurate localization result could reduce the communication. The authors in [26,27] proposed edge analytics model that is communication efficient-predictive modeling within the edge network. In [28], the authors discussed about the overview of fog computing in smart grid and analyses its benefits and challenges. Smart grid applications generate immense amount of data from various sources which need timely processing and have low-delay requirement. The authors in [29] stated about the smart meters which play a significant role in a smart grid used for load identification. The authors in this paper proposed an intelligent edge analytics approach to perform the load identification by using the transformation process to extract features of the types of load and passing it through embedded neural network for load identification. Similarly, the authors in [30] mentioned about the big data that are produced by smart grid and edge analytics on advanced metering infrastructure and have used parameter estimation algorithms on AMI data. Previously, the authors of [10,31] discussed about the concept of service caching and task offloading.

1.5 Task offloading using fog analytics

Intelligent task offloading can dynamically schedule the network and fog-computing resources for the next-generation IoT networks. The main aim of such a task-offloading scheme is to first select a list of fog nodes that meet task requirements and then to select an optimal fog node for offloading. Therefore, multiple methods of learning can be employed to achieve task offloading. Especially, for fog node selection when the network and fog-node resources are dynamic, learning algorithms that can work with minimal information, like reinforcement learning or federated learning techniques can be employed. The initial selection of the platform to offload, that is, local computing, fog-network, or cloud can be viewed as a simple classification problem where different parameters like latency, cost, and energy can be used to compute an optimal place for offloading. The intelligent task-offloading algorithm presented in [7] uses the K-nearest neighbors (KNN) algorithm to find the most suitable place for offloading considering the delay requirement and task size of each task. The KNN algorithm is used to calculate the Euclidean distance between each task with cloud server, fog network, and local computing, respectively. When the fog network is selected as a desired platform for offloading, and when multiple tasks are to be offloaded simultaneously, it is important to consider the allocation of computing and storage resources. With network utilization and status of fog nodes being highly dynamic, minor changes in status necessitate the optimization solution to be recomputed, resulting in huge network overhead. Also, fog nodes need to frequently exchange their current status in terms of the resources that they can spare for the fog network to enable the offloading decision. Therefore, employing learning algorithms like reinforcement learning can benefit in the design of task-offloading algorithms. The fog nodes in the network can learn from the environment that comprises of neighboring fog nodes, their interactions and incentive-penalty mechanism employed by the fog network. This approach allows fog nodes to dynamically adapt to changing network conditions and task load of different fog nodes in the network and choose a offloading node.

A typical learning architecture for task offloading is shown in Figure 1.4. Here, the end-devices (ED) offload tasks to the primary fog-nodes to which they are connected. Each fog node implements a learning module (LM) that allows it to interact with the other fog nodes in the environment to learn about their behaviors and task

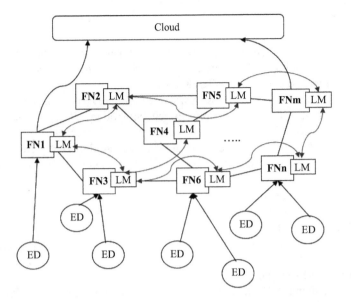

Figure 1.4   Proposed learning architecture for task offloading

load. The learning module that is trained over data gathered through interactions and environment makes a recommendation to the fog node for the choice of offloading location. This simplest model can address the limitations of other static models and also reduces the overhead in computing the optimal location for offloading whenever there is a change in network-topology or task load of fog nodes in the network.

1.6   Discussion and conclusion

Task offloading in a fog-computing environment is a hard problem as it involves determining the current status of all fog nodes, and then choosing an optimal fog node for offloading. This selection is based on parameters like offloading cost, latency, and energy, assuming that multiple fog nodes exist and all such nodes can process the offloaded task. In a dynamic environment like fog network, where the status of fog devices keep changing, a deterministic solution will not have an optimal result. Employing machine-learning techniques to select a fog node for task offloading has been shown to address this problem effectively. In this chapter, we have emphasized on the issues that arise due to task offloading in fog-computing environment and summarized several existing techniques. Later, we presented how analyzing fog-node metrics can help in choosing a fog node for task offloading. We also presented how these schemes can be implemented in a fog network. Different approaches based on supervised, unsupervised, and reinforcement learning techniques are discussed and the effectiveness of mechanisms based on each of these techniques are discussed.

References

[1] Aazam M, Zeadally S, and Harras KA. Offloading in fog computing for IoT: review, enabling technologies, and research opportunities. *Future Generation Computer Systems*. 2018;87:278–289.

[2] Jiang YL, Chen YS, Yang SW, *et al.* Energy-efficient task offloading for time-sensitive applications in fog computing. *IEEE Systems Journal*. 2019;13(3):2930–2941.

[3] Bian S, Huang X, and Shao Z. Online task scheduling for fog computing with multi-resource fairness. In: *2019 IEEE 90th Vehicular Technology Conference (VTC2019-Fall)*; 2019. p. 1–5.

[4] Dadmehr Rahbari MN. Task offloading in mobile fog computing by classification and regression tree. *Peer-to-Peer Networking and Applications*. 2020;13:104–122.

[5] Chen J, Chen S, Luo S, *et al.* An intelligent task offloading algorithm (iTOA) for UAV edge computing network. *Digital Communications and Networks*. 2020;6(4):433–443.

[6] Hao Y, Jiang Y, Chen T, *et al.* iTaskOffloading: intelligent task offloading for a cloud-edge collaborative system. *IEEE Network*. 2019;33(5):82–88.

[7] Cui Y, Liang Y, and Wang R. Intelligent task offloading algorithm for mobile edge computing in vehicular networks. In: *2020 IEEE 91st Vehicular Technology Conference (VTC2020-Spring)*; 2020. p. 1–5.

[8] Hao Y, Chen M, Hu L, *et al.* Energy efficient task caching and offloading for mobile edge computing. *IEEE Access*. 2018;6:11365–11373.

[9] Chen M and Hao Y. Task offloading for mobile edge computing in software defined ultra-dense network. *IEEE Journal on Selected Areas in Communications*. 2018;36(3):587–597.

[10] Xu J, Chen L, and Zhou P. Joint service caching and task offloading for mobile edge computing in dense networks. In: *IEEE INFOCOM 2018—IEEE Conference on Computer Communications*. IEEE; 2018. p. 207–215.

[11] Alghamdi I, Anagnostopoulos C, and Pezaros DP. On the optimality of task offloading in mobile edge computing environments. In: *2019 IEEE Global Communications Conference (GLOBECOM)*. IEEE; 2019. p. 1–6.

[12] Alghamdi I, Anagnostopoulos C, and Pezaros DP. Time-optimized task offloading decision making in mobile edge computing. In: *2019 Wireless Days (WD)*. IEEE; 2019. p. 1–8.

[13] Dolezal J, Becvar Z, and Zeman T. Performance evaluation of computation offloading from mobile device to the edge of mobile network. In: *2016 IEEE Conference on Standards for Communications and Networking (CSCN)*. IEEE; 2016. p. 1–7.

[14] Zhang G, Shen F, Yang Y, *et al.* Fair task offloading among fog nodes in fog computing networks. In: *2018 IEEE International Conference on Communications (ICC)*. IEEE; 2018. p. 1–6.

[15] Liu CF, Bennis M, Debbah M, *et al.* Dynamic task offloading and resource allocation for ultra-reliable low-latency edge computing. *IEEE Transactions on Communications.* 2019;67(6):4132–4150.

[16] Sun Y, Guo X, Song J, *et al.* Adaptive learning-based task offloading for vehicular edge computing systems. *IEEE Transactions on Vehicular Technology.* 2019;68(4):3061–3074.

[17] Mukherjee M, Kumar S, Zhang Q, *et al.* Task data offloading and resource allocation in fog computing with multi-task delay guarantee. *IEEE Access.* 2019;7:152911–152918.

[18] Mukherjee M, Kumar S, Mavromoustakis CX, *et al.* Latency-driven parallel task data offloading in fog computing networks for industrial applications. *IEEE Transactions on Industrial Informatics.* 2019;16(9): 6050–6058.

[19] Mukherjee M, Kumar V, Kumar S, *et al.* Computation offloading strategy in heterogeneous fog computing with energy and delay constraints. In *ICC 2020–2020 IEEE International Conference on Communications (ICC),* pp. 1–5. IEEE, 2020.

[20] Ferdowsi A, Challita U, and Saad W. Deep learning for reliable mobile edge analytics in intelligent transportation systems; 2017. arXiv preprint arXiv:171204135.

[21] Fadlullah ZM, Pathan ASK, and Gacanin H. On delay-sensitive healthcare data analytics at the network edge based on deep learning. In: *2018 14th International Wireless Communications & Mobile Computing Conference (IWCMC).* IEEE; 2018. p. 388–393.

[22] Ran X, Chen H, Zhu X, *et al.* Deepdecision: a mobile deep learning framework for edge video analytics. In: *IEEE INFOCOM 2018—IEEE Conference on Computer Communications.* IEEE; 2018. p. 1421–1429.

[23] Dey S and Mukherjee A. Implementing deep learning and inferencing on fog and edge computing systems. In: *2018 IEEE International Conference on Pervasive Computing and Communications Workshops (PerCom Workshops).* IEEE; 2018. p. 818–823.

[24] Ghosh AM and Grolinger K. Deep learning: edge-cloud data analytics for IoT. In: *2019 IEEE Canadian Conference of Electrical and Computer Engineering (CCECE).* IEEE; 2019. p. 1–7.

[25] Kartakis S, Yu W, Akhavan R, *et al.* Adaptive edge analytics for distributed networked control of water systems. In: *2016 IEEE First International Conference on Internet-of-Things Design and Implementation (IoTDI).* IEEE; 2016. p. 72–82.

[26] Harth N, Anagnostopoulos C, and Pezaros D. Predictive intelligence to the edge: impact on edge analytics. *Evolving Systems.* 2018;9(2):95–118.

[27] Harth N and Anagnostopoulos C. Quality-aware aggregation & predictive analytics at the edge. In: *2017 IEEE International Conference on Big Data (Big Data).* IEEE; 2017. p. 17–26.

[28]   Okay FY and Ozdemir S. A fog computing based smart grid model. In: *2016 International Symposium on Networks, Computers and Communications (ISNCC)*. IEEE; 2016. p. 1–6.

[29]   Sirojan T, Phung T, and Ambikairajah E. Intelligent edge analytics for load identification in smart meters. In: *2017 IEEE Innovative Smart Grid Technologies-Asia (ISGT-Asia)*. IEEE; 2017. p. 1–5.

[30]   Ashok K, Divan D, and Lambert F. Grid edge analytics platform with AMI data. In: *2018 IEEE Power & Energy Society Innovative Smart Grid Technologies Conference (ISGT)*. IEEE; 2018. p. 1–5.

[31]   Li M, Rui L, Qiu X, *et al.* Design of a service caching and task offloading mechanism in smart grid edge network. In: *2019 15th International Wireless Communications & Mobile Computing Conference (IWCMC)*. IEEE; 2019. p. 249–254.

Chapter 2

Resource management in edge and fog computing using FogBus2 framework

Mohammad Goudarzi[1], Qifan Deng[1] and Rajkumar Buyya[1]

2.1 Introduction

The rapid advancements in hardware, software, and communication technologies enable the Internet of Things (IoT) to offer a wide variety of intelligent solutions in every single aspect of our lives. Therefore, IoT-enabled systems such as smart healthcare, transportation, agriculture, and entertainment have been attracting ever-increasing attention in academia and industry. IoT applications generate a massive amount of data which requires processing and storage, while IoT devices often lack sufficient processing and storage resources. Cloud computing offers infrastructure, platform, and software services for IoT-enabled systems, through which IoT applications can process, store, and analyze their generated data in surrogate Cloud Servers (CSs) [1,2]. There are different Cloud Service Providers (CSPs) with a wide variety of services, where each CSP provides a particular set of services such as computing, database, and data analysis in an optimized way. Hence, no CSP can satisfy the full functional requirements of different IoT applications in an optimized manner [3]. As a result, each IoT application can be particularly serviced by a specific CSP or simultaneously by different CSPs, which is often called hybrid cloud computing [3]. Although hybrid cloud computing platform provides IoT devices with unlimited and diverse computing and storage resources, CSs are residing multi-hops away from IoT devices, which incurs high propagation and queuing latency. Thus, CSs cannot solely provide the best possible services for latency-critical and real-time IoT applications (e.g., intelligent transportation, smart healthcare, emergency, and real-time control systems) [4,5]. Besides, forwarding the huge amount of data generated by distributed IoT devices to CSs for processing and storage may overload the CSs [6]. To overcome these issues, edge and fog computing has emerged as a novel distributed computing paradigm.

In edge- and fog-computing environments, the geographically distributed heterogeneous edge servers (ESs) (e.g., access points, smartphones, Raspberry-Pis),

[1]The Cloud Computing and Distributed Systems (CLOUDS) Laboratory, School of Computing and Information Systems, The University of Melbourne, Australia

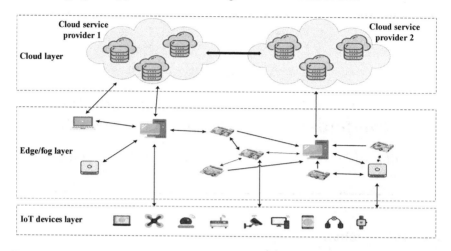

Figure 2.1   Heterogeneous computing environment containing multiple cloud servers, edge/fog servers, and IoT devices

situated in the vicinity of IoT devices, can be used for processing and storage of IoT devices' data. These ESs can be accessed with lower latency, which makes them a potential candidate for latency-critical IoT applications, and reduce the traffic of the network's backbone [7]. However, the computing and storage resources of ESs are limited compared to CSs, so that they cannot efficiently execute computation-intensive tasks. Therefore, to satisfy the resource and Quality of Service (QoS) requirements of diverse IoT-enabled systems, a seamlessly integrated computing environment with heterogeneous edge/fog and different cloud infrastructures is required, as depicted in Figure 2.1.

The computing and storage resources in such an integrated environment are highly heterogeneous in terms of their architecture, processing speed, RAM capacity, communication protocols, access bandwidth, and latency, just to mention a few. Furthermore, there are a wide variety of IoT-enabled systems with various QoS and resource requirements. Accordingly, to satisfy the requirements of IoT applications in such an integrated environment, scheduling, and resource management techniques are required to dynamically place incoming requests of IoT applications on appropriate servers for processing and storage [8]. To develop, test, deploy, and analyze different IoT applications and scheduling and resource management techniques in real-world scenarios, lightweight and easy-to-use frameworks are required for both researchers and developers. There are some existing frameworks for integrating IoT-enabled systems with edge and fog computing such as [8–14]. However, they only focus on one aspect of IoT-enabled systems in edge and fog computing, such as scheduling, implementation of a new type of IoT application, or resource discovery. In this chapter, we provide a tutorial on FogBus2 framework [15] which offers IoT developers a suite of containerized IoT applications, scheduling and scalability mechanisms, and different resource management policies in an integrated environment, consisting of multi-cloud service providers, edge and fog computing servers, and IoT devices. Furthermore, we extend this framework with new resource management techniques such as a new scheduling policy. In addition, new types of IoT applications, either real-time or non-real-time, are implemented and integrated with the FogBus2 framework.

The rest of the chapter is organized as follows: we start with a discussion on the FogBus2 framework, its main components, and respective communication protocols. Next, we describe how to install and run the current functionalities of FogBus2, considering different IoT applications. Finally, we provide a guideline presenting how to develop and integrate new IoT applications and new policies into the FogBus2.

2.2   FogBus2 framework

FogBus2 [15] is a new container-based framework based on docker containers, developed in Python. To enable the integration of various IoT application scenarios in highly heterogeneous computing environments, FogBus2's components can be simultaneously executed on one or multiple distributed servers in any computing layer. This feature significantly helps researchers and developers in the development and testing phases because they can develop, test, and debug their desired IoT applications, scheduling, and resource management policies on one or a small number of servers. Furthermore, in the deployment phase, they can run and test their IoT applications, scheduling, and resource management techniques on an unlimited number of servers.

2.2.1   Main components

FogBus2 consists of five containerized components, namely *User*, *Master*, *Actor*, *Task Executor*, and *Remote Logger*. Among these components, the *User* should run on IoT devices or any servers that directly interact with users' sensory or input data. The rest of the components can run on any servers with sufficient resources. Each of these containerized components contains several sub-components (sub-C) with specific functionalities. Figure 2.2 presents FogBus2's main components and their respective sub-Cs. Since the components of the FogBus2 can run on geographically distributed servers, a *message handler* sub-C is embedded in each component to handle sending and receiving of messages. In what follows, we briefly describe the main functionalities and sub-Cs of each component.

- **User**: This component controls the IoT device's requests for surrogate resources and contains two main sub-Cs, namely *sensor* and *actuator*, alongside with *message handler*. The *sensor* is responsible for capturing and management of raw sensory data and configuring sensing intervals based on IoT application scenarios. Besides, the *actuator*'s main function is collecting the incoming processed data and executing a respective action. The *actuator* can be configured by its users to perform real-time actions based on incoming processed data or periodic actions based on a batch of processed data. Researchers and developers can configure the *sensor* and *actuator* to implement different application scenarios.

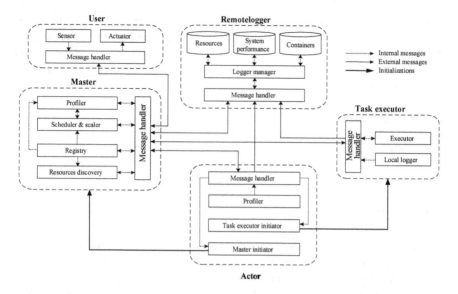

Figure 2.2   FogBus2 main components, sub-components, and their interactions

- **Remote logger**: The main functionality of this component is to collect and store the contextual information of servers, IoT devices, IoT applications, and networking. It contains the *logger manager* sub-C that can connect to different databases, receives logs of other components, and stores logs in persistent storage. By default, the *Remote Logger* connects to databases to store logs, which is easier to manage and maintain. However, logs can be stored in files as well.

- **Master**: In a real-world computing environment, one or multiple *Master* components may exist. This component contains four main sub-Cs, called *profiler*, *scheduler & scaler*, *registry*, and *resource discovery*, alongside with the *message handler*. When the *Master* starts, the *resource discovery* sub-C periodically search the network to find available *Remote Logger*, *Master*, and *Actor* components in the network. If new components can be found in the network, the *resource discovery* advertise itself to those components, so that they can send a request and register themselves in this *Master*. If the *Master* receives any requests for registration or placement requests from IoT devices (i.e., *User* components), the *registry* sub-C will be called. This sub-C records the information of IoT devices and other components and assigns them a unique identifier. Besides, when the incoming message is a placement request from *User* components, it initiates the *scheduler & scaler* sub-C. The *scheduler & scaler* sub-C receives the placement request from the *registry* sub-C, the contextual profiling information of all available servers, and networking information from the *profiler* sub-C. Next, if it has enough resources to run the scheduling policy and its placement queue is not very large (configurable queue size), it runs one of the scheduling policies implemented in the FogBus2 framework to assign tasks/containers of the IoT application on different servers for the execution. According to the outcome of scheduling policy, the *Master* component forwards required information to the selected *Actors* to execute tasks/containers of the IoT application. Currently, three scheduling policies are embedded in the FogBus2 framework, namely Non-dominated Sorting Genetic Algorithm 2 (*NSGA2*) [16], Non-dominated Sorting Genetic Algorithm 3 (*NSGA3*) [17], and Optimized History-based Non-dominated Sorting Genetic Algorithm (*OHNSGA*) [15]. If due to any reason the *Master* component cannot run its scheduling policy, it runs the *scalability* mechanism to forward the placement request to other available *Master* components, or it initiates a new *Master* component on one of the available servers. In the rest of this chapter, we describe how to use current scheduling and scalability policies. Furthermore, we also present how to implement new scheduling and scalability policies and integrate them into the FogBus2 framework.

- **Actor**: The main responsibility of this component is to start different *Task Executor* components on the server on which it is running. To illustrate, available surrogate servers in the environment should run *Actor* component. Then, these *Actor* components will be automatically discovered and registered by one or several *Master* components in the environment. The *Actor* component profiles the hardware and networking condition of the server on which it is running using the *profiler* sub-C. Besides, when a *Master* component assigns a task of an IoT application to an *Actor* for the execution, it calls the *task executor initiator* sub-C which initiates different *Task Executor* components on the server according to different IoT applications. This sub-C also defines the destination to which the result of each *Task Executor* should be forwarded based on the dependency model of the IoT application. Finally, to scale *Master* components in the environment, each *Actor* is embedded with a *master initiator* sub-C. When an *Actor* receives a scaling message from one of the available *Master* components in the environment, the *master initiator* sub-C will be called. This sub-C starts a *Master* component on the server, which can independently serve incoming IoT application requests. In addition, it can be seen that each server simultaneously can run different components (e.g., *Master, Actor, Task Executor*, etc.) and play different roles.

- **Task executor**: IoT applications can be represented as a set of dependent or independent tasks or services. In the rest of this chapter, tasks and services are used interchangeably. In the dependent model, the execution of tasks has constraints and each task can be executed when its predecessor tasks are properly executed. In FogBus2, each *Task Executor* component is responsible for the execution of specific task; i.e., each task or service can be containerized as a *Task Executor*. To illustrate, an IoT application with three decoupled tasks should have three separate *Task Executor* components, so that each *Task Executor* corresponds to one IoT application's task. Considering the granularity level (e.g., task, service) of IoT applications in FogBus2, an application can be deployed on distributed servers for execution. The *Task Executor* consists of two sub-Cs, called *executor* and *local logger*. The former Sub-C initiates the execution of one task and forwards the results to the next *Task Executor* components if the IoT application is developed using the dependent model. It is crystal clear that in the independent model, the results will be forwarded to the *Master* component for the aggregation or directly to the corresponding *User* component. Besides, the *local logger* sub-C records the contextual information of this task, such as its execution time.

2.2.2   Interaction scenario

Considering the FogBus2 framework is in a ready state, Figure 2.3 depicts the inter-action of IoT users with the framework as a sequence diagram. The IoT device runs a specific *User* component for each IoT application, configuring and controlling the sensing interval and aggregation of sensory data. The *User* component sends a placement request to the *Master* component. The *Master* checks the IoT device and requested IoT application, and accordingly assigns it a unique identifier and regis-ters it in its record. Next, the *Master* calls its *scheduling & scaler* sub-C to handle the current placement request. The *scheduling & scaler* sub-C has the contextual information of available *Actors*, *Task Executor* components, IoT application, and the networking condition. Accordingly, it runs the scheduling and scaling policies to find the best possible configuration of constituent parts of an IoT application. Based on the outcome of *scheduling & scaler*, two scenarios may happen. In the first sce-nario, if there exist no available *Task Executor* components to be reused for this new request, the *Master* sends the placement request to the *Actor* components, selected by the scheduling mechanism. Then, the *Actor* components who receive this message initiate corresponding *Task Executor* components on the servers on which they are

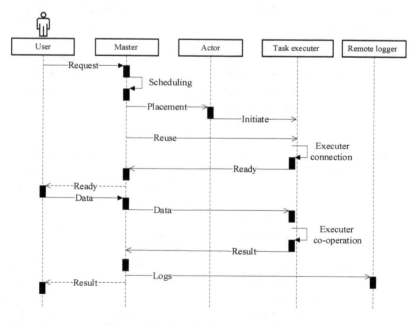

Figure 2.3   FogBus2 sequence diagram

assigned. In the second scenario where there are some corresponding *Task Executor* components in the cooling-off period, the *Master* directly reuses those *Task Executor* components, which reduces the service ready time of IoT application. When all corresponding *Task Executor* components of the IoT application are ready, the *Master* sends a ready message to the *User* component. This message states that the service is ready, and the IoT device can start sending data. Hence, *User* component sends the sensory data to the *Master*, and this component forwards the sensory data to the corresponding *Task Executor* components. After *Task Executor* components finish their execution, the result will be forwarded to the *Master*. Finally, the *Master* component sends the respective logs to the *Remote Logger* component, and also forwards the results to the *User* component.

In addition, if the current *Master* component cannot handle the placement request, the request will be forwarded to other *Master* components in the environment, or a new *Master* component will be initiated on a new server. The rest of the steps for handling the placement request is the same as the above-mentioned process.

2.2.3   Communication protocol

Different components of the FogBus2 framework can communicate together by passing messages. Therefore, understanding the communication protocol of FogBus2 is important, especially for the developers. The communication protocol of FogBus2 is implemented in JSON format and messages contain eight main elements, as depicted in Figure 2.4.

The *source* and *destination* are JSON objects containing the metadata of source and destination of one message, respectively. The *sentAtSourceTimestamp* and *receivedAtLocalTimestamp* elements are embedded to calculate the networking delay. Furthermore, each message can carry any type of information, stored in *data*. Besides there are three other elements, namely *type*, *subType*, and *subSubType*, which are used to categorize messages. There are 10 types of messages in the current version of FogBus2 framework, shown in Figure 2.4, where each *type* can be further divided into 41 *subType* and 5 *subSubType*. Hence, *type*, *subType*, and *subSubType* elements logically provide a hierarchical structure for the categorization of the messages. Due to the page limit, we cannot describe all the messages here; however, the most important messages and their respective description are provided in Table 2.1. Also, code snippet 2.1 presents a sample FogBus2 message used for sending the log information (*type* = *log*) of server resources (*type* = *hostResources*) from an *Actor* component (*source role* = *Actor*) to the *Remote Logger* component (*destination role* = *RemoteLogger*). Accordingly, the message contains the resources information in the *data* element.

2.2.4   Main capabilities

In this section, we briefly describe the main capabilities of the FogBus2 framework.

- **Container-enabled**: All components of the FogBus2 framework, alongside IoT applications, are containerized. Not only does this feature enable fast deployment

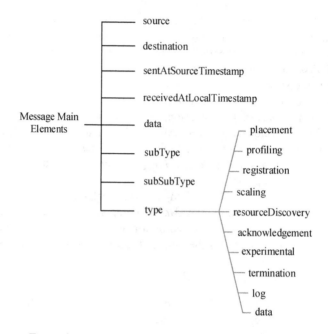

Figure 2.4   FogBus2 communication protocol format

of IoT applications but it also leads to faster deployment of the framework's components. Also, it brings fast portability as the containerized IoT applications and components of the framework can run smoothly on different servers.

- **Multi-platform support**: In a highly heterogeneous computing environment, a wide variety of servers and IoT devices with different platforms (e.g., Intel x86, AMD, and ARM) exist. To fully utilize the potential of heterogeneous servers in the cloud and/or at the edge, the containerized framework should be compatible with different platforms. To achieve this, the FogBus2 framework uses multi-arch images. Such images are built and pushed to registries with multiple variants of operating systems or CPU architectures while the image name is the same for all. Accordingly, pulling images on a server with specific architecture results in a compatible image variant for that server.
- **Scheduling**: Considering available resources of heterogeneous servers and various types of IoT applications with different levels of resource requirements, the scheduling of incoming requests of IoT applications is of paramount importance. As a result, the *Master* component of the FogBus2 framework is embedded with a *scheduler & scaler* sub-C, which is integrated with different scheduling policies. The researchers and developers can either use the integrated policies or can develop their scheduling policies and integrate them with the *scheduler & scaler* sub-C.

Table 2.1 Important communication messages

Sender	Receiver	Type	SubType	SubSubType	Description
Master	Actor	placement	runTaskExecutor	–	Master has finished the scheduling and sends this message in a no-reuse scenario
TaskExecutor	Master	placement	lookup	–	Task Executor requests the address of its children Task Executors (in the dependent model)
Master	TaskExecutor	placement	lookup	–	Master responds to the lookup message of Task Executors
TaskExecutor	Master	acknowledgement	ready	–	Task Executor has received its children's information and uses this message to acknowledge the Master that it is ready
Master	User	acknowledgement	serviceReady	–	When the service is ready and user can start sending sensory data
User	Master	data	sensoryData	–	sensoryData forwarded from the User
Master	TaskExecutor	data	intermediateData	–	Master sends sensory data to Task Executor(s) for processing
TaskExecutor	TaskExecutor	data	intermediateData	–	Task Executor finishes its execution and send intermediate data to other Task Executor(s)
TaskExecutor	Master	acknowledgement	waiting	–	Task Executor asks Master whether it can go into the cool-off period
Master	TaskExecutor	acknowledgement	wait	–	Master asks Task Executor to start its cool off period immediately
Master	TaskExecutor	placement	reuse	–	Master has finished the scheduling and sends this message in reuse scenario
TaskExecutor	Master	data	finalResult	–	Task Executor sends final results to Master
Master	User	data	finalResult	–	Master sends final results to User
Master A	Master B	scaling	getProfiles	–	Master A sends request to get profiles from the Master B
Master B	Master A	scaling	profilesInfo	–	Master B sends profiles to Master B
Master	Actor	scaling	initNewMaster	–	Master asks Actor to initiate a new Master
RemoteLogger	Master	log	allResourcesProfiles	–	This message is sent in response to requestProfiles message of the Master
Master A	Master B	resourcesDiscovery	requestActorsInfo	–	Master A asks Master B the information of Actors registered at Master B for further advertisement
Master B	Master A	resourcesDiscovery	actorsInfo	–	Master B sends its registered Actors' information to Master A
Master	Actor	resourcesDiscovery	advertiseMaster	–	Master advertises itself to Actor
Any components	Any components	resourcesDiscovery	probe	try	Any component receiving probe message should provide its component role, such as Master, Actor, etc. to the sender
Any components	Any components	resourcesDiscovery	probe	result	The response to the probe message received from one component

```
 1 {'data': {'resources': {'cpu': {'cores': 8,   // Message type is log,
         subtype is hostResources. Thus, data contains resources
 2                       'frequency': 2400.0,
 3                       'utilization': 0.052,
 4                       'utilizationPeak': 1.0},
 5                       'memory': {'maximum': 17179869184,
 6                       'utilization': 0.075,
 7                       'utilizationPeak': 1.0}}},
 8 'destination': {'addr': ['127.0.0.1', 5000],
 9                       'componentID': '?',
10                       'hostID': 'HostID',
11                       'name': 'RemoteLogger-?_127.0.0.1-5000',
12                       'nameConsistent': 'RemoteLogger_HostID',
13                       'nameLogPrinting': 'RemoteLogger-?_127.0.0.1-5000',
14                       'role': 'RemoteLogger'},
15 'receivedAtLocalTimestamp': 0.0,
16 'sentAtSourceTimestamp': 1625572932123.89,
17 'source': {'addr': ['127.0.0.1', 50000],
18                       'componentID': '2',
19                       'hostID': '127.0.0.1',
20                       'name': 'Actor',
21                       'nameConsistent': 'Actor_127.0.0.1',
22                       'nameLogPrinting': 'Actor-2_127.0.0.1-50000_Master
         -?_127.0.0.1-5001',
23                       'role': 'Actor'},
24 'subSubType': '',
25 'subType': 'hostResources',
26 'type': 'log'}
```

Code snippet 2.1   An example of FogBus2 message format

- **Dynamic scalability**: The number of IoT devices and incoming requests varies at different times. If the number of incoming requests increases, the framework may become a bottleneck as the queuing time of incoming requests, which require scheduling and processing, increases. Hence, a dynamic scalability mechanism is embedded in the *Master* component of the FogBus2 framework to dynamically scale up the *Master* components as the number of incoming requests increases, which significantly reduce the queuing time of incoming requests from IoT applications. FogBus2 users can use the integrated scalability policy of the FogBus2 or develop their scalability policies.
- **Dynamic resource discovery**: The highly heterogeneous and integrated computing environments, as depicted in Figure 2.1, are considerably dynamic. This indicates that new servers may join or leave the environment due to different reasons. Furthermore, each server may run different components of the FogBus2 framework at a specific time. Hence, the FogBus2 framework offers a dynamic resource discovery mechanism to discover available servers in the environment and the containers they are running. This feature ensures the last-minute information of available servers and their functionalities are always accessible.
- **Supporting different topology models for communication**: IoT applications require different communication models such as client–server and peer-to-peer

(P2P), just to mention a few. Accordingly, to efficiently manage the inter-component communications for different IoT applications, each containerized component of the FogBus2 framework contains a *message handler* sub-C which is responsible for sending and receiving messages to/from other components. Therefore, based on the distributed message handling mechanism of the FogBus2 framework, researchers and developers can implement different communication topology models based on their IoT application scenarios.

- **Virtual private network (VPN) support**: In the highly heterogeneous computing environment, several servers with public and private IP addresses exist. Servers with public addresses can bi-directionally communicate with each other. However, servers with private addresses cannot bi-directionally communicate with servers with public and private IP addresses. As a result, the FogBus2 put forward a P2P VPN script, working based on the Wireguard*, as an optional feature for researchers and developers to set up a VPN among all desired servers. Among the most common VPN tools, the Wireguard has the least overhead, making it a suitable option for IoT applications, specifically real-time and latency-critical ones.

- **Supporting heterogeneous IoT applications**: FogBus2 framework supports various types of IoT applications, ranging from latency-critical and real-time IoT applications to highly computation-intensive IoT applications. Besides, it provides several ready-to-use containerized and modularized IoT applications for its users. Hence, they can simply use the current embedded IoT applications, extend current IoT applications by modifying modules of current IoT applications or integration of new modules or define their desired IoT applications from scratch.

- **Distributed multi-database platform support**: Fogbus2 framework is currently integrated with two different databases. First, it uses the containerized version of MariaDB[†] which is an open-source MySQL-based database developed by the original developers of MySQL. Besides, it is integrated with Oracle autonomous database (AutoDB)[‡] which is an intelligent cloud-based database. AutoDB uses machine learning to automate database tuning, security, backups, updates, and other routine management tasks without human intervention.

- **Reusability**: Containerization significantly helps to reduce the deployment time of IoT applications compared to the traditional deployment techniques. However, as the number of incoming requests from different IoT devices increases, the startup time of containers, serving the IoT requests, may negatively affect the service ready time. Accordingly, the FogBus2 framework offers a configurable cooling-off period for the *Task Executor* components, during which containers keep waiting for the next incoming request of the same type before stopping. This feature significantly helps to reduce the service ready time of IoT applications, specifically when the environment is crowded.

---

*https://www.wireguard.com/https://www.wireguard.com/
[†]https://mariadb.org/https://mariadb.org/
[‡]https://www.oracle.com/au/autonomous-database/https://www.oracle.com/au/autonomous-database/

- **Usability**: FogBus2 offers a default setting for users, by which they can easily run the embedded IoT applications and test the functionality of all framework's components. Besides, users can play with several embedded options to configure IoT applications and the framework's components according to their desired scenario. In the rest of this chapter, we explain the most important options of this framework so that the users can efficiently configure the framework.

2.3   Installation of FogBus2 framework

FogBus2 is a new containerized framework developed by the Cloud Computing and Distributed Systems (CLOUDS) Laboratory at the University of Melbourne. As the FogBus2 framework targets both users and developers, we have provided two ways for building images of docker containers: (1) building from scratch and (2) pulling from docker hub. Accordingly, a straightforward way to install this framework is put forward.

2.3.1   Building from scratch

IoT developers may want to extend and configure the FogBus2 framework and define their applications on top of this framework. Hence, it is required for them to know how to build the images from scratch. In what follows, we describe this process, which is tested on Ubuntu 18.04, Ubuntu 20.04, Ubuntu 21.04, and macOS Big Sur.

1. Prepare the prerequisites:
    (a)   Install python3.9+
    (b)   Install pip3
    (c)   Install docker engine
    (d)   Install docker compose
2. Clone/download the source code of FogBus2 framework from https://github.com/Cloudslab/FogBus2 to any desired location.
3. go to the FogBus2 folder:

```
1 $ cd fogbus2
2 $ pwd
3 /home/ubuntu/fogbus2
```

4. Install the required dependencies:

```
1 $ python3.9 -m pip install -r /containers/user/sources/
    requirements.txt
```

5. Prepare and configure the database:

```
1 $ cd containers/database/mariadb/
2 $ python3.9 configure.py --create --init
```

6. Build all docker images:

```
1 $ pwd
2 /home/ubuntu/fogbus2/demo
3 $ python3.9 demo.py --buildAll
```

The *demo.py* file automatically starts building all docker images to simplify this process. This process may take a long time to complete based on the server on which you are building the images. Besides, after any changes the developers apply to the code, the images should be rebuilt. Moreover, in distributed application scenarios, where different components should run on different servers, the components' images should be created or migrated on/to different servers. To do so, *demo.py* can be configured through command-line options to only build specific images rather than creating all images. Finally, developers who are interested in extending the framework or defining new applications can use this file to understand how to create and configure their images.

2.3.2   Pulling from docker hub

To simply use and test the latest features of the FogBus2 framework, the multi-arch images of different components of this framework are available in the docker hub to be pulled. Although it is a faster and simpler way to run and test the FogBus2 framework and its integrated applications, users who are interested in extending and modifying this framework should build the images from scratch. In what follows, we describe the required steps to install the FogBus2 framework using uploaded images to the docker hub.

1. Prepare the prerequisites:
    (a) Install docker engine
2. Pull the docker images of Master, Actor, User, and RemoteLogger on desired servers using the following commands:

```
1 $ docker pull cloudslab/fogbus2-remote_logger && docker tag
    cloudslab/fogbus2-remote_logge fogbus2-remote_logger
2 $ docker pull cloudslab/fogbus2-master && docker tag cloudslab/
    fogbus2-master fogbus2-master
3 $ docker pull cloudslab/fogbus2-actor && docker tag cloudslab/
    fogbus2-actor fogbus2-actor
4 $ docker pull cloudslab/fogbus2-user && docker tag cloudslab/
    fogbus2-user fogbus2-user
```

3. Install any desired applications by means of pulling respective docker images (i.e., *Task Executor* components) of that application. To illustrate, the following command is put forward:
    (a) Install video-OCR application:

```
1 $ docker pull cloudslab/fogbus2-ocr && docker tag cloudslab/
    fogbus2-ocr fogbus2-ocr
```

The *video-OCR* application consists of one *Task Executor*, called *fogbus2-ocr*. However, there exist other integrated applications, in which each one contains several dependent *Task Executor* components. For such applications, all dependent *Task Executor* components should be pulled for the proper execution of the application.

2.4   Sample FogBus2 setup

In this section, we describe how to configure the FogBus2 framework to run some of the currently integrated applications. We suppose that docker images are properly built or pulled on the servers, and they are ready to use.

Our sample-integrated computing environment consists of six CSs, tagged by A to F, two ESs, tagged by G to H, and a device playing the role of an IoT device, tagged as I. We have used three Oracle Ampere A1 Instances[§][||] and three Nectar instances[¶] to set up a multi-cloud environment. Besides, as ESs, we used Raspberrypi 4B[**] and Nvidia Jetson Nano[††] to set up an edge computing layer with heterogeneous resources. Our CSs have public IP addresses, while ESs do not hold public IP addresses. In this case, to integrate ESs and CSs in the FogBus2 framework VPN connection is required. Consequently, we provide a guideline and a script to simply establish a P2P VPN between all participating servers, either at the edge or at the cloud. It is crystal clear that in case all servers have public IP addresses or all components are running on one server, the VPN is not required. Table 2.2 shows the list of servers, their computing layer, public IP addresses, private IP addresses after the establishment of the VPN connection, and the FogBus2's components running on each server. In the rest of this section, we describe how to set up a P2P VPN, assign private IP addresses to these servers, and how to run FogBus2 components on each server. As a prerequisite, make sure to open the required ports on servers.

```
 1 # Required Ports for FogBus2 Components
 2 REMOTE_LOGGER_PORT_RANGE=5000-5000
 3 MASTER_PORT_RANGE=5001-5010
 4 ACTOR_PORT_RANGE=50000-50100
 5 USER_PORT_RANGE=50101-50200
 6 TASK_EXECUTOR_PORT_RANGE=50201-60000
 7
 8 # Required Port for Wireguard
 9 WG_PORT=4999
10
11 # Required Port for MariaDB Database
12 PORT=3306
```

[§]https://www.oracle.com/au/cloud/compute/arm/https://www.oracle.com/au/cloud/compute/arm/
[||]To reproduce this setup, you can use up to 4 Oracle Ampere A1 instances in always free Oracle Cloud Free Tier.
[¶]ARDC's Nectar Research Cloud is an Australian federated research cloud.
[**]https://www.raspberrypi.org/products/raspberry-pi-4-model-b/https://www.raspberrypi.org/products/raspberry-pi-4-model-b/
[††]https://www.nvidia.com/en-au/autonomous-machines/embedded-systems/jetson-nano/https://www.nvidia.com/en-au/autonomous-machines/embedded-systems/jetson-nano/

Table 2.2 Sample configuration of servers in integrated computing environment

Server tag	Server name	Computing layer	Public IP address	Private IP	Port address	Component role	Environment preparation
A	Oracle1	Cloud	168.138.9.91	192.0.0.1	5000	RemoteLogger, Actor_1	docker and docker-compose
B	Oracle2	Cloud	168.138.10.94	192.0.0.2	automatically assign	Actor_2	docker and docker-compose
C	Oracle3	Cloud	168.138.15.110	192.0.0.3	automatically assign	Actor_3	docker and docker-compose
D	Nectar1	Cloud	45.113.235.222	192.0.0.4	automatically assign	Actor_4	docker and docker-compose
E	Nectar2	Cloud	45.113.232.187	192.0.0.5	automatically assign	Actor_5	docker and docker-compose
F	Nectar3	Cloud	45.113.232.245	192.0.0.6	automatically assign	Actor_6	docker and docker-compose
G	RPi 4B 4GB	Edge	–	192.0.0.7	automatically assign	Actor_7	docker and docker-compose
H	Jetson Nano 4GB	Edge	–	192.0.0.8	5001	Master	docker and docker-compose
I	VM on a Laptop	IoT	–	192.0.0.9	automatically assign	User	Python3.9

2.4.1   P2P VPN setup

We have used the Wireguard to set up a lightweight P2P VPN connection among all servers. In what follows, we describe how to install and configure VPN while all servers run Ubuntu as their operating system:

1.   Install Wireguard on all servers:

```
1 $ sudo apt update
2 $ sudo apt install wireguard
3 $ wg --version
4 wireguard-tools v1.0.20200513 - https://git.zx2c4.com/wireguard-
     tools/
```

2.   Simply configure the wireguard on servers using our auto-generating script:
     (a)   Specify server information on *hostIP.csv*:

```
1 $ pwd
2 /home/ubuntu/fogbus2
3 $ cd config/host/
4 $ cat config/host/hostIP.csv
5 hostname, publicIP
6 oracle1, 168.138.9.91
7 oracle2, 168.138.10.94
8 oracle3, 168.138.15.110
9 nectar1, 45.113.235.222
10 nectar2, 45.113.232.187
11 nectar3, 45.113.232.245
12 rpi-4B-2G,
13 JetsonNano-4G,
14 VM-laptop,
```

     (b)   Automatically generate Wireguard configuration files:

```
1 $ pwd
2 /home/ubuntu/fogbus2
3 $ cd scripts/wireguard/
4 $ python3.9 generateConf.py
5 ...
6 ================================================
7 hostname WireguardIP
8 oracle1 192.0.0.1
9 oracle2 192.0.0.2
10 oracle3 192.0.0.3
11 nectar1 192.0.0.4
12 nectar2 192.0.0.5
13 nectar3 192.0.0.6
14 rpi-4B-2G-4B 192.0.0.7
15 JetsonNano-4G 192.0.0.8
16 VM-laptop 192.0.0.9
17 ================================================
18 [*] Generated Wireguard config for oracle1: /path/to/proj/
      output/wireguardConfg/oracle1/wg0.conf
19 ...
20 ================================================
```

(c)   Copy obtained configuration files to */etc./wireguard/wg0.conf* of each server, respectively.

(d)   Run Wireguard on each server:

```
1 $ sudo wg-quick up /etc/wireguard/wg0.conf && sudo wg
```

3.   Test the P2P VPN connection using *Ping* command and private IP addresses.

4.   If *Ping* command does not properly work, make sure to open the configured Wireguard port on all servers. In FogBus2, the default port of Wireguard is set to UDP 4999, which can be changed from */home/ubuntu/fogbus2/config/network.env*.

```
1 #Install, enable and configure Firewalld
2 $ sudo apt update
3 $ sudo apt install firewalld
4 $ sudo systemctl enable firewalld
5 $ sudo firewall-cmd --state
6 $ sudo firewall-cmd --permanent --zone=public  --add-port=22/tcp
      --add-port=53/tcp --add-port=3306/tcp --add-port=4999/udp --
      add-port=5000-5010/tcp --add-port=5000-60000/tcp
7 $ sudo firewall-cmd --reload
```

2.4.2   Running FogBus2 components

Considering Table 2.2, the FogBus2 components should run on different servers. Also, each server may run several components simultaneously and play different roles, similar to the server *A*. In what follows, we describe how to run these components and provide respective commands.

1.   Starting *RemoteLogger* component:
(a)   Configure database credentials in *containers/remoteLogger/sources/.mysql.env*

```
1 $ pwd
2 /home/ubuntu/fogbus2
3 $ cat containers/remoteLogger/sources/.mysql.env
4 HOST=192.0.0.1
5 PORT=3306
6 USER=root
7 PASSWORD=passwordForRoot
```

(b)   Run *RemoteLogger* component on server *A*

```
1 $ pwd
2 /home/ubuntu/fogbus2
3 $ cd containers/remoteLogger
4 $ docker-compose run --rm --name TempContainerName fogbus2-
      remote_logger --bindIP 192.0.0.1 --containerName
      TempContainerName
```

2. Starting *Master* component on server *H*. The *schedulerName* specifies the name of scheduling policy used by this *Master* component. Hence, in computing environments with multiple *Master* components, each *Master* component can be separately configured to run different scheduling policies:

   (a) On server *H*, configure database credentials:

```
1 $ pwd
2 /home/ubuntu/fogbus2/containers/master/sources/
3 cat .mysql.env
4 HOST=192.0.0.1
5 PORT=3306
6 USER=root
7 PASSWORD=passwordForRoot
```

   (b) Run *Master* component on the server *H*:

```
1 $ pwd
2 /home/ubuntu/fogbus2
3 $ cd containers/master
4 $ docker-compose run --rm --name TempContainerName fogbus2-
      master --bindIP 192.0.0.8 --bindPort 5001 --remoteLoggerIP
      192.0.0.1 --remoteLoggerPort 5000 --schedulerName OHNSGA --
      containerName TempContainerName
```

3. Starting *Actor* components:

   (a) Run *Actor* component on server *A*

```
1 $ pwd
2 /home/ubuntu/fogbus2
3 $ cd containers/actor
4 $ docker-compose run --rm --name TempContainerName fogbus2-
      actor --bindIP 192.0.0.1 --remoteLoggerIP 192.0.0.1 --
      remoteLoggerPort 5000 --masterIP 192.0.0.8 --masterPort
      5001 --containerName TempContainerName
```

   (b) Run *Actor* components on servers *B* to *G* using the above-mentioned command. You need to modify the value of *bindIP* option for each server and use the respective private IP address of that server. For instance, to run the *Actor* component on server *B*:

```
1 $ pwd
2 /home/ubuntu/fogbus2
3 $ cd containers/actor
4 $ docker-compose run --rm --name TempContainerName fogbus2-
      actor --bindIP 192.0.0.1 --remoteLoggerIP 192.0.0.2 --
      remoteLoggerPort 5000 --masterIP 192.0.0.8 --masterPort
      5001 --containerName TempContainerName
```

4. Considering the IoT application, the *User* component can run with different *applicationName* options. The current version of FogBus2 comes with two integrated IoT applications, called *VideoOCR* [15] and *GameOfLifeParallelized* [15], while in the rest of this chapter, we design and implement more IoT applications to describe how to define new IoT applications.

   (a) Run *User* component for *VideoOCR* application on server *I*. The *videoPath* shows the address of input video to feed into VideoOCR algorithm.

```
1 $ pwd
2 /home/ubuntu/fogbus2
3 $ cd containers/user/sources
4 $ python3.9 user.py --bindIP 192.0.0.9 --masterIP 192.0.0.8 --
      masterPort 5001 --remoteLoggerIP 192.0.0.1 --
      remoteLoggerPort 5000 --applicationName VideoOCR --
      applicationLabel 720 --videoPath /path/to/video.mp4
```

   (b) Run *User* component for *GameOfLifeParallelized* application on server *I*.

```
1 $ pwd
2 /home/ubuntu/fogbus2
3 $ cd containers/user/sources
4 $ python user.py --bindIP 192.0.0.9 --masterIP 192.0.0.8 --
      masterPort 5001 --remoteLoggerIP 192.0.0.1 --
      remoteLoggerPort 5000 --applicationName
      GameOfLifeParallelized --applicationLabel 480
```

2.5 Extending FogBus2 framework and new IoT applications

In this section, we describe how to implement and integrate new IoT applications in the FogBus2 framework. Second, we put forward a new scheduling algorithm and demonstrate its integration procedure with this framework.

2.5.1 Implementation of new IoT applications

Every containerized IoT application can be implemented and integrated with the FogBus2 framework. Alongside the implementation of a new IoT application, there are several required steps to follow to implement and integrate the new IoT application with the FogBus2 framework, such as building docker images and defining dependencies between different tasks. In what follows, we describe a straightforward mathematical application, how to implement it, and how to integrate it with the FogBus2 framework.

Figure 2.5 shows a new application to be implemented with the FogBus2 framework. This mathematical application contains three different tasks, called *Part 0*, *Part 1*, and *Part 2*, that can be executed in parallel, and it requires three inputs as *a, b, c*. To integrate this application into the FogBus2 framework, three tasks should be

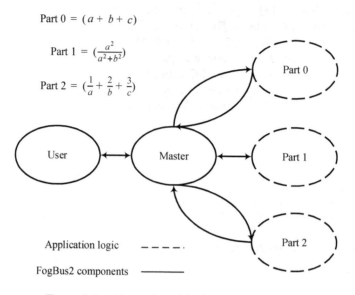

Part 0 = $(a + b + c)$

Part 1 = $(\frac{a^2}{a^2+b^2})$

Part 2 = $(\frac{1}{a} + \frac{2}{b} + \frac{3}{c})$

Figure 2.5   A logical model of a new application

dockerized and prepared to be integrated as *Task Executor* components. Besides, we need a *User* component to receive inputs (using *Sensor* sub-C) and show outputs (using *Actuator* sub-C). The input will be forwarded to the *Master* component of the framework, and this component forwards inputs to corresponding *Task Executor* components based on the outcome of the scheduling algorithm. The following steps demonstrate how to implement and integrate the new application with the FogBus2 framework:

1. Create three python files as three different tasks with the desired naming con- vention. We name these files as *naiveFormula0.py*, *naiveFormula1.py*, and *naiveFormula2.py* which contain the logic of tasks *Part 0*, *Part 1*, and *Part 2*, respectively.

```
1 $ pwd
2 /home/ubuntu/fogbus2
3 $ cd containers/taskExecutor/sources/utils/taskExecutor/tasks
4 $ > naiveFormula0.py
5 $ > naiveFormula1.py
6 $ > naiveFormula2.py
```

2. Edit the corresponding python files of each task and insert the required logic. For each task, a unique identifier *taskID* is required.

(a)   The logic of task *naiveFormula0.py*:

```
1  $ nano naiveFormula0.py
2      from .base import BaseTask
3
4      class NaiveFormula0(BaseTask):
5          def __init__(self):
6              super().__init__(taskID=108, taskName='
   NaiveFormula0')
7
8          def exec(self, inputData):
9              a = inputData['a']
10             b = inputData['b']
11             c = inputData['c']
12
13             result = a + b + c
14             inputData['resultPart0'] = result
15
16             return inputData
```

(b)   The logic of task *naiveFormula1.py*:

```
1  $ nano naiveFormula1.py
2      from .base import BaseTask
3
4      class NaiveFormula1(BaseTask):
5          def __init__(self):
6              super().__init__(taskID=109, taskName='
   NaiveFormula1')
7
8          def exec(self, inputData):
9              a = inputData['a']
10             b = inputData['b']
11             c = inputData['c']
12
13             result = a * a / (b * b + c * c)
14             inputData['resultPart1'] = result
15
16             return inputData
```

(c)   The logic of task *naiveFormula2.py*:

```
1  $ nano naiveFormula2.py
2      from .base import BaseTask
3
4      class NaiveFormula2(BaseTask):
5          def __init__(self):
6              super().__init__(taskID=110, taskName='
   NaiveFormula2')
7
8          def exec(self, inputData):
9              a = inputData['a']
10             b = inputData['b']
11             c = inputData['c']
12
13             result = 1 / a + 2 / b + 3 / c
14             inputData['resultPart2'] = result
15             return inputData
```

    (d)   The return value of *exec* functions in the above-mentioned tasks will be managed by *Task Executor*. If it is none, the return value will be ignored, otherwise, it will be forwarded to next *Task Executor* components based on the specified dependencies among tasks.

3. Configure arguments:

    (a)   Configure *__init__.py*:

```
1  $ pwd
2  /home/ubuntu/fogbus2/containers/taskExecutor/sources/utils/
       taskExecutor/tasks
3  $ nano containers/taskExecutor/sources/utils/taskExecutor/tasks
       /__init__.py
4
5  from .base import BaseTask
6  ...
7  from .naiveFormula0 import NaiveFormula0
8  from .naiveFormula1 import NaiveFormula1
9  from .naiveFormula2 import NaiveFormula2
10 ...
```

    (b)   Configure *initTask.py*:

```
1  $ pwd
2  /home/ubuntu/fogbus2/containers/taskExecutor/sources/utils/
       taskExecutor/tools/initTask.py
3  $ nano containers/taskExecutor/sources/utils/taskExecutor/tasks
       /__init__.py
4
5  from typing import Union
6  from ..tasks import *
7
8  def initTask(taskName: str) -> Union[BaseTask, None]:
9      task = None
10     if taskName == 'FaceDetection':
11         task = FaceDetection()
12     ...
13     elif taskName == 'NaiveFormula0':
14         task = NaiveFormula0()
15     elif taskName == 'NaiveFormula1':
16         task = NaiveFormula1()
17     elif taskName == 'NaiveFormula2':
18         task = NaiveFormula2()
19
20     return task
```

4.   Prepare docker images:
   (a)   Prepare the required libraries:

```
 1 $ pwd
 2 /home/ubuntu/fogbus2/containers/taskExecutor/sources
 3 $ cat requirements.txt
 4
 5 psutil
 6 docker
 7 python-dotenv
 8 pytesseract
 9 editdistance
10 six
```

   (b)   Create dockerfiles: For each of the tasks, a docker file should be created. Considering *NaiveFormula0*:

```
 1 $ pwd
 2 /home/ubuntu/fogbus2/containers/taskExecutor/dockerFiles/
     NaiveFormula0
 3
 4 $ nano Dockerfile
 5
 6 # Base
 7 FROM python:3.9-alpine3.14 as base
 8 FROM base as builder
 9
10 ## Dependencies
11 RUN apk update
12 RUN apk add --no-cache \
13     build-base clang clang-dev ninja cmake ffmpeg-dev \
14     freetype-dev g++ jpeg-dev lcms2-dev libffi-dev \
15     libgcc libxml2-dev libxslt-dev linux-headers \
16     make musl musl-dev openjpeg-dev openssl-dev \
17     zlib-dev curl freetype gcc6 jpeg libjpeg \
18     openjpeg tesseract-ocr zlib unzip openjpeg-tools
19
20 RUN python -m pip install --retries 100 --default-timeout=600
     --no-cache-dir --upgrade pip
21 RUN python -m pip install --retries 100 --default-timeout=600
     numpy --no-cache-dir
22
23 ## OpenCV Source Code
24 WORKDIR /workplace
25 RUN cd /workplace/ \
26     && curl -L "https://github.com/opencv/opencv/archive/4.5.1.
     zip" -o opencv.zip \
27     && curl -L "https://github.com/opencv/opencv_contrib/
     archive/4.5.1.zip" -o opencv_contrib.zip \
28     && unzip opencv.zip \
```

```
29      && unzip opencv_contrib.zip \
30      && rm opencv.zip opencv_contrib.zip
31
32  ## Configure
33  RUN cd /workplace/opencv-4.5.1 \
34      && mkdir -p build && cd build \
35      && cmake \
36          -DOPENCV_EXTRA_MODULES_PATH=../../opencv_contrib-4.5.1/
        modules \
37          -DBUILD_NEW_PYTHON_SUPPORT=ON \
38          -DBUILD_opencv_python3=ON \
39          -DHAVE_opencv_python3=ON \
40          -DPYTHON_DEFAULT_EXECUTABLE=$(which python) \
41          -DBUILD_TESTS=OFF \
42          -DWITH_FFMPEG=ON \
43          ../
44
45  ## Compile
46
47  RUN cd /workplace/opencv-4.5.1/build && make -j $(nproc)
48  RUN cd /workplace/opencv-4.5.1/build && make install
49
50  ## Python libraries
51  COPY ./sources/requirements.txt /install/requirements.txt
52  RUN python -m pip install --retries 100 --default-timeout=600
        \
53      --prefix=/install \
54      --no-cache-dir \
55      -r /install/requirements.txt
56
57  ## Copy files
58  FROM base
59  COPY --from=builder /install /usr/local
60  COPY ./sources/ /workplace
61
62  ## Install OpenCV
63  COPY  --from=builder /usr/local/ /usr/local/
64  COPY --from=builder /usr/lib/ /usr/lib/
65
66  # Hostname
67  RUN echo "NaiveFormula0" > /etc/hostname
68
69  # Run NaiveFormula0
70  WORKDIR /workplace
71  ENTRYPOINT ["python", "taskExecutor.py"]
```

(c) Create docker files for *NaiveFormula1* and *NaiveFormula2* similar to *NaiveFormula0*, as described in step (b).

(d) Create docker-compose files: For each of the tasks, a docker-compose file should be created. Considering *NaiveFormula0*:

```
1  $ pwd
2  /home/ubuntu/fogbus2/containers/taskExecutor/dockerFiles/
       NaiveFormula0
3  $ nano docker-compose.yml
4
5  version: '3'
6
7  services:
8
9    fogbus2-naive_formula0:
10     image: fogbus2-naive_formula0
11     build:
12       context: ../../
13       dockerfile: dockerFiles/NaiveFormula0/Dockerfile
14     environment:
15       PUID: 1000
16       PGID: 1000
17       TZ: Australia/Melbourne
18     network_mode:
19       host
```

(e) Create docker-compose files for *NaiveFormula1* and *NaiveFormula2* similar to *NaiveFormula0*, as described in step (d).

(f) Build docker images: The docker images corresponding to the tasks of new application can be built using the provided automated script (*demo.py*), similar to step (6) in Section 2.3.1.

```
1  $ pwd
2  /home/ubuntu/fogbus2/demo
3  $ python3.9 demo.py --buildAll
```

(g) Verify new docker images:

```
1  $ docker images
2
3  REPOSITORY                TAG       IMAGE ID        CREATED
               SIZE
4  ...
5  fogbus2-naive_formula1    latest    5e9ad6999801    2 minutes ago
               xxx
6  fogbus2-naive_formula0    latest    74cfbb128699    2 minutes ago
               xxx
7  fogbus2-naive_formula2    latest    924d6bc0f281    3 minutes ago
               xxx
8  ...
```

5. Prepare *User* side code:

```
 1  $ pwd
 2  /home/ubuntu/fogbus2/containers/user/sources/utils/user/
        applications
 3  $ nano naiveFormulaParallelized.py
 4
 5  from time import time
 6  from pprint import pformat
 7  from .base import ApplicationUserSide
 8  from ...component.basic import BasicComponent
 9
10
11  class NaiveFormulaParallelized(ApplicationUserSide):
12
13      def __init__(
14              self,
15              videoPath: str,
16              targetHeight: int,
17              showWindow: bool,
18              basicComponent: BasicComponent):
19          super().__init__(
20              appName='NaiveFormulaParallelized',
21              videoPath=videoPath,
22              targetHeight=targetHeight,
23              showWindow=showWindow,
24              basicComponent=basicComponent)
25
26      def prepare(self):
27          pass
28
29      def _run(self):
30          self.basicComponent.debugLogger.info(
31              'Application is running: %s', self.appName)
32
33          # get user input of a, b, and c
34          print('a = ', end='')
35          a = int(input())
36          print('b = ', end='')
37          b = int(input())
38          print('c = ', end='')
39          c = int(input())
40
41          inputData = {
42              'a': a,
43              'b': b,
44              'c': c
45          }
46
47          # put it in to data uploading queue
48          self.dataToSubmit.put(inputData)
49          lastDataSentTime = time()
50          self.basicComponent.debugLogger.info(
51              'Data has sent (a, b, c): %.2f, %.2f, %.2f', a, b, c)
52
53          # wait for all the 4 results
54          while True:
55              result = self.resultForActuator.get()
56
57              responseTime = (time() - lastDataSentTime) * 1000
58              self.responseTime.update(responseTime)
59              self.responseTimeCount += 1
60
61              if 'finalResult' in result:
62                  break
63
64          for key, value in result.items():
65              result[key] = '%.4f' % value
66          self.basicComponent.debugLogger.info(
67              'Received all the 4 results: \r\n%s', pformat(result))
```

6. Define dependencies among tasks of a new application in the database. Considering MariaDB is running on 192.0.0.1 as an example:

   (a) Connect to the database:

```
1 $ mysql -h 192.0.0.1 -uroot -p
2 Enter password:
```

   (b) The *Entry Tasks* contains the root tasks of this application, where the sensory data should be forwarded.

```
1 mysql> SELECT entryTasks FROM FogBus2_Applications.applications
      WHERE name='NaiveFormulaParallelized';
2
3 [
4     "NaiveFormula0",
5     "NaiveFormula1",
6     "NaiveFormula2"
7 ]
```

   (c) The *TaskWithDependency* contains the dependencies among tasks. For each task, we define an array of parents and *children*, representing predecessor and successor tasks.

```
1 mysql> SELECT tasksWithDependency FROM FogBus2_Applications.
      applications WHERE name='NaiveFormulaParallelized';
2
3 {
4 "NaiveFormula0": {
5     "parents": [
6         "Sensor"
7     ],
8     "children": [
9         "Actuator"
10     ]
11 },
12 "NaiveFormula1": {
13     "parents": [
14         "Sensor"
15     ],
16     "children": [
17         "Actuator"
18     ]
19 },
20 "NaiveFormula2": {
21     "parents": [
22         "Sensor"
23     ],
24     "children": [
25         "Actuator"
26     ]
27 }
28 }
```

Table 2.3   The list of all implemented and integrated applications with FogBus2

Application name	Description	Application logic tasks
FaceDetection	Detecting human face from video stream, either realtime or from recorded files.	face_detection
ColorTracking	Tracking colors from video stream, either real time or from recorded files. The target color can be dynamically configured via GUI.	color_tracking
VideoOCR	Recognizing text from a video file. It automatically picks up key frames.	blur_and_p_hash, ocr
GameOfLife Serialized	Conway's Game of Life. The tasks process grids (with different sizes) one by one.	GameOfLife0 to GameOfLife62
GameOfLife Parallelized	Conway's Game of Life. The tasks process grids (with different sizes) in parallel.	GameOfLife0 to GameOfLife62
GameOfLife Pyramid	Conway's Game of Life. The tasks process grids (with different sizes) in a pyramid dependency.	GameOfLife0 to GameOfLife62
NaiveFormula Serialized	A naive formula. Tasks process different parts of formula one by one.	naive_formula0, naive_formula1, naive_formula2, naive_formula3
NaiveFormula Parallelized	A Naive Formula. Tasks process different parts of formula in parallel.	naive_formula0, naive_formula1, naive_formula2

(d)   Considering the FogBus2 framework is running, the *NaiveFormulaParallelized* can be executed using the following command:

```
1 $ pwd
2 /home/ubuntu/fogbus2/containers/user/sources
3
4 $ python user.py --bindIP 192.0.0.9 --masterIP 192.0.0.2 --
    masterPort 5001 --remoteLoggerIP 192.0.0.1 --
```

Table 2.3 presents the list of all applications that have been currently implemented and integrated with FogBus2 framework. The *VideoOCR* and *GameOfLifePyramid* applications were implemented in the main paper, while the *FaceDetection, ColorTracking, GameOfLifeSerialized, GameOfLifeParallelized, NaiveFormulaSerialized,* and *NaiveFormulaParallelized* are implemented and integrated as an extension in this chapter. Due to page-limit, we only described one of these applications (i.e., *NaiveFormulaParallelized*). The required steps for defining and integration of all applications are similar to what is described in this section, while the logic of each application is different.

2.5.2   Implementation of new scheduling policy

One of the most important challenges for resource management in edge and cloud data centers is the proper scheduling of incoming application requests. FogBus2 provides a straightforward mechanism for the scheduling of various types of IoT applications. Different scheduling policies can be implemented and integrated with the FogBus2 framework with different scheduling goals, such as optimizing application response time, energy consumption, the monetary cost of resources, or a combination of any of these goals, just to mention a few. As a guideline, we put forward a new scheduling policy and describe how to integrate it with the FogBus2 framework.

To simplify the process of new policy integration, a *BaseScheduler* class is provided in *containers/master/sources/utils/master/scheduler/base.py*. Users should inherit from *BaseScheduler* class and override the *_schedule* method based on their desired goals. Besides, if the utilization of the current *Master* component, which is responsible for the scheduling of IoT applications, goes beyond a threshold, the new application request should be forwarded to another *Master* component. The *getBest-Master* method handles this process and can be overridden with different policies for the selection of another *Master*. Finally, users, who are interested in augmenting scaling features to their technique, can implement a scaling policy using the *prepareScaler* method. The following steps describe how to define and integrate a new scheduling policy:

1. Navigate to containers/master/sources/utils/master/scheduler/policies and create a new file named schedulerRankingBased.py:

```
1 $ pwd
2 /home/ubuntu/fogbus2/containers/master/sources/utils/master/
     scheduler/policies
3 $ > schedulerRankingBased.py
```

2. Implement the policy in the *schedulerRankingBased.py*. The *_schedule* contains the logic of scheduling policy.

```
1 $ cat schedulerRankingBased.py
2
3 from random import randint
4 from time import time
5 from typing import List
6 from typing import Union
7
8 from ..base import BaseScheduler as SchedulerPolicy
9 from ..baseScaler.base import Scaler
10 from ..baseScaler.policies.scalerRandomPolicy import
      ScalerRandomPolicy
11 from ..types import Decision
12 from ...registry.roles.actor import Actor
13 from ...registry.roles.user import User
14 from ....types import Component
15
16
```

```
17  class SchedulerRankingBased(SchedulerPolicy):
18      def __init__(
19              self,
20              isContainerMode: bool,
21              *args,
22              **kwargs):
23          """
24          :param isContainerMode: Whether this component is running
    in container
25          :param args:
26          :param kwargs:
27          """
28          super().__init__('RankingBased', isContainerMode, *args,
    **kwargs)
29
30      def _schedule(self, *args, **kwargs) -> Decision:
31          """
32          :param args:
33          :param kwargs:
34          :return: A decision object
35          """
36          user: User = kwargs['user']
37          allActors: List[Actor] = kwargs['allActors']
38          # Get what tasks are required
39          taskNameList = user.application.taskNameList
40
41          startTime = time()
42          indexSequence = ['' for _ in range(len(taskNameList))]
43          indexToHostID = {}
44
45          # Ranking of tasks belonging to an application
46          rankedTasksList = self.rankApplicationTasks(
47              indexSequence, **kwargs)
48          indexToHostID = self.tasksAssignment(
49              rankedTasksList, allActors, **kwargs)
50
51          schedulingTime = (time() - startTime) * 1000
52
53          # Create a decision object
54          decision = Decision(
55              user=user,
56              indexSequence=rankedTasksList,
57              indexToHostID=indexToHostID,
58              schedulingTime=schedulingTime
59          )
60          # A simple example of cost estimation
61          decision.cost = self.estimateCost(decision, **kwargs)
62          return decision
63
64      @staticmethod
65      def estimateCost(decision: Decision, **kwargs) -> float:
66          # You may develop your own with the following used values
67          from ..estimator.estimator import Estimator
```

```
68    # Get necessary params from the key args
69    user = kwargs['user']
70    master = kwargs['master']
71    systemPerformance = kwargs['systemPerformance']
72    allActors = kwargs['allActors']
73    isContainerMode = kwargs['isContainerMode']
74    # Init the estimator
75    estimator = Estimator(
76        user=user,
77        master=master,
78        systemPerformance=systemPerformance,
79        allActors=allActors,
80        isContainerMode=isContainerMode)
81    indexSequence = [int(i) for i in decision.indexSequence]
82    # Estimate the cost
83    estimatedCost = estimator.estimateCost(indexSequence)
84    return estimatedCost
85
86 def getBestMaster(self, *args, **kwargs) -> Union[Component,
   None]:
87    """
88
89    :param args:
90    :param kwargs:
91    :return: A Master used to ask the user to request when
   this Master is busy
92    """
93    user: User = kwargs['user']
94    knownMasters: List[Component] = kwargs['knownMasters']
95    mastersNum = len(knownMasters)
96    if mastersNum == 0:
97        return None
98    return knownMasters[randint(0, mastersNum - 1)]
99
100 def prepareScaler(self, *args, **kwargs) -> Scaler:
101    # Create a scaler object and return
102    scaler = ScalerRandomPolicy(*args, **kwargs)
103    return scaler
```

First, we retrieve the information of *user* and all available actors *allActors* (lines 36 and 37). Then, the tasks corresponding to the requested application are retrieved and stored in *taskNameList* (line 39). The *rankApplicationTasks* considers the dependency model of tasks (if any) and satisfies the dependency among tasks while defining an order for the tasks that can be executed in parallel. Several ranking policies can be defined for this method, however, in this version, we consider the average execution time of tasks on different servers as criteria for ranking. Hence, among tasks that can be executed in parallel, the tasks with higher execution time receive higher priority. This eventually helps to reduce the overall response time of the application (lines 46 and 47). Next, *tasksAssignment* method receives the ordered *rankedTasksList* and assigns a proper actor to each task to minimize its execution time (lines 48 and 49). According to the scheduling decision, a *decision* object will be created, storing the ordered list of the application's tasks, the list of server/host mapping, scheduling time, and the cost of scheduling, to be returned (lines 54–59). To illustrate how the execution cost of each task and overall response time of one application can be estimated, a *estimateCost* method is defined (lines 65–84). As mentioned above, the *getBestMaster* and *prepareScaler* also can be defined in *schedulerRankingBased.py*. To reduce the complexity, these methods are working based on random policy.

3. The new scheduling policy can be added to the *schedulerName* options by manipulating the *initSchedulerByName* method of the *containers/master/sources/utils/master/scheduler/tools/initSchedulerByName.py*. There exist names of several scheduling policies currently integrated with the FogBus2 framework. The name of new scheduling policies can be added after the names of existing scheduling policies.

```
1  $ pwd
2  /home/ubuntu/fogbus2/containers/master/sources/utils/master/
       scheduler/tools
3  $ nano initSchedulerByName.py
4
5  def initSchedulerByName(
6          knownMasters: Set[Address],
7          minimumActors: int,
8          schedulerName: str,
9          basicComponent: BasicComponent,
10         isContainerMode: bool,
11         parsedArgs,
12         **kwargs) -> Union[BaseScheduler, None]:
13     if schedulerName == 'OHNSGA':
14         # hidden to save space
15         pass
16     elif schedulerName == 'NSGA2':
17         # hidden to save space
18         pass
19     elif schedulerName == 'NSGA3':
20         # hidden to save space
21         pass
22     # New Added Block
23     elif schedulerName == 'RankingBased':
24         from ..policies.schedulerRankingBased import \
25             RankingBasedPolicy
26         scheduler = SchedulerRankingBased(isContainerMode=
    isContainerMode)
27         return scheduler
28
29     return None
```

4. The *Master* component can be executed using the following command while the *schedulerName* option shows the name of the selected scheduling policy:

```
1  $ pwd
2  /home/ubuntu/fogbus2/containers/master
3  $ docker-compose run --rm --name TempContainerName fogbus2-master
      --containerName TempContainerName --bindIP 192.0.0.8 --
      schedulerName RankingBased
```

2.5.3 Evaluation results

To evaluate the performance of the FogBus2 framework, an integrated computing environment consisting of multiple cloud instances and edge/fog servers is prepared. Table 2.2 depicts the full configuration of servers and corresponding running FogBus2 components.

Figure 2.6 represents the average docker size of FogBus2 components in compressed and uncompressed formats. The compressed docker image size is obtained from the average size of docker images stored in the docker hub for multiple architectures, while uncompressed docker image size is obtained from the average size of extracted docker images on instances. The size of the compressed docker image shows that FogBus2 components are lightweight to be downloaded on different platforms, ranging from few megabytes to roughly 100 MB at maximum. Besides, the uncompressed docker image size proves that FogBus2 components are not resource-hungry and do not occupy the storage. The reason why the image sizes of *User* and *Task Executor* components are not provided is that the docker image sizes of these components heavily depend on the IoT applications.

Figure 2.7 represents the average run-time RAM usage of FogBus2 components in different architectures. It illustrates that the average resource usage of the FogBus2 components on different architectures are low, ranging from 25 MB to 45 MB. Figure 2.8 demonstrates the average startup time of FogBus2 components on different architectures. It contains the amount of time required to start containers until they become in a completely functional state for serving incoming requests. Therefore, the FogBus2 framework only requires a few seconds to enter into its fully functional state. It significantly helps IoT developers in the development and testing phase as they require to re-initiate the framework several times to test and debug their applications.

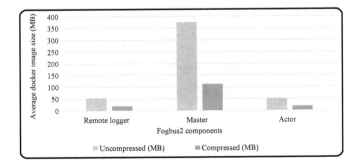

Figure 2.6   Average docker image size of FogBus2 components

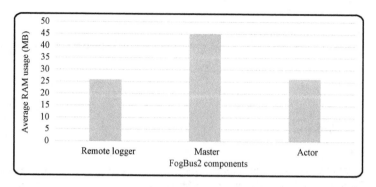

Figure 2.7   Average run-time RAM usage of FogBus2 components

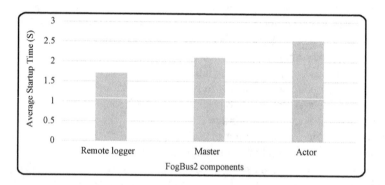

Figure 2.8   Average startup time of FogBus2 components

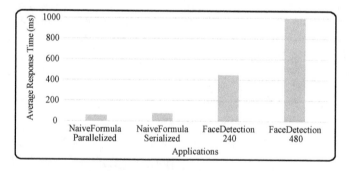

Figure 2.9   Average response time of IoT applications

Furthermore, in the deployment phase, it greatly helps scenarios where scalability is important.

Figure 2.9 depicts the average response time of some of the recently implemented IoT applications in FogBus2 framework.

2.6 Summary

In this chapter, we highlighted key features of the FogBus2 framework alongside describing its main components. Besides, we described how to set up an integrated computing environment, containing multiple CSPs and edge devices, and establish a low-overhead communication network among all resources. Next, we provided instructions and corresponding code snippets to install and run the main framework and its integrated applications. Finally, we demonstrated how to implement and integrate new IoT applications and custom scheduling policies with this framework.

Software availability

The source code of the FogBus2 framework and newly implemented IoT applications and scheduling policies are accessible from the CLOUDS Laboratory GitHub webpage: https://github.com/Cloudslab/FogBus2https://.

References

[1] Hu P, Dhelim S, Ning H, *et al.* Survey on fog computing: architecture, key technologies, applications and open issues. *Journal of Network and Computer Applications*. 2017;98:27–42.

[2] Goudarzi M, Movahedi Z, and Nazari M. Efficient multisite computation offloading for mobile cloud computing. In: *Proceedings of the 2016 International IEEE Conferences on Ubiquitous Intelligence and Computing (UIC)*. IEEE; 2016. p. 1131–1138.

[3] Li Q, Wang Zy, Li Wh, *et al.* Applications integration in a hybrid cloud computing environment: modelling and platform. *Enterprise Information Systems*. 2013;7(3):237–271.

[4] Schulz P, Matthe M, Klessig H, *et al.* Latency critical IoT applications in 5G: perspective on the design of radio interface and network architecture. *IEEE Communications Magazine*. 2017;55(2):70–78.

[5] Goudarzi M, Wu H, Palaniswami M, *et al.* An application placement technique for concurrent IoT applications in edge and fog computing environments. *IEEE Transactions on Mobile Computing*. 2021;20(4):1298–1311.

[6] Mahmud R and Buyya R. Modelling and simulation of fog and edge computing environments using iFogSim toolkit. *Fog and Edge Computing: Principles and Paradigms*. Wiley; 2019. p. 1–35.

[7] Goudarzi M, Palaniswami M, and Buyya R. A fog-driven dynamic resource allocation technique in ultra dense femtocell networks. *Journal of Network and Computer Applications*. 2019;145:102407.

[8] Merlino G, Dautov R, Distefano S, *et al.* Enabling workload engineering in edge, fog, and cloud computing through OpenStack-based middleware. *ACM Transactions on Internet Technology (TOIT)*. 2019;19(2):1–22.

[9]   Tuli S, Mahmud R, Tuli S, *et al.* FogBus: a blockchain-based lightweight framework for edge and fog computing. *Journal of Systems and Software.* 2019;154:22–36.

[10]   Yousefpour A, Patil A, Ishigaki G, *et al.* FogPlan: a lightweight QoS-aware dynamic fog service provisioning framework. *IEEE Internet of Things Journal.* 2019;6(3):5080–5096.

[11]   Nguyen DT, Le LB, and Bhargava VK. A market-based framework for multi-resource allocation in fog computing. *IEEE/ACM Transactions on Networking.* 2019;27(3):1151–1164.

[12]   Bellavista P and Zanni A. Feasibility of fog computing deployment based on docker containerization over raspberrypi. In: *Proceedings of the 18th International Conference on Distributed Computing and Networking*; 2017. p. 1–10.

[13]   Ferrer AJ, Marques JM, and Jorba J. Ad-hoc edge cloud: a framework for dynamic creation of edge computing infrastructures. In: *Proceedings of the 28th International Conference on Computer Communication and Networks.* IEEE; 2019. p. 1–7.

[14]   Noor S, Koehler B, Steenson A, *et al.* IoTDoc: a docker-container based architecture of IoT-enabled cloud system. In: *Proceedings of the 3rd IEEE/ACIS International Conference on Big Data, Cloud Computing, and Data Science Engineering.* Springer; 2019. p. 51–68.

[15]   Deng Q, Goudarzi M, and Buyya R. FogBus2: a lightweight and distributed container-based framework for integration of IoT-enabled systems with edge and cloud computing. In: *Proceedings of the International Workshop on Big Data in Emergent Distributed Environments*; 2021. p. 1–8.

[16]   Deb K, Pratap A, Agarwal S, *et al.* A fast and elitist multiobjective genetic algorithm: NSGA-II. *IEEE Transactions on Evolutionary Computation.* 2002;6(2):182–197.

[17]   Deb K and Jain H. An evolutionary many-objective optimization algorithm using reference-point-based nondominated sorting approach, Part I: solving problems with box constraints. *IEEE Transactions on Evolutionary Computation.* 2013;18(4):577–601.

Chapter 3

Resource management and cloud-RAN implementation for narrowband-IoT systems

M. Pavan Reddy[1] and Abhinav Kumar[1]

Narrowband-Internet of Things (NB-IoT) is a cellular-service-based low-power wide area network technology introduced by 3rd Generation Partnership Project (3GPP). NB-IoT has a design skeleton similar to that of Long-Term Evolution (LTE)/New Radio (NR) and operates on a bandwidth of 180 kHz. The technology co-exists with LTE/NR and can communicate with a large number of IoT devices. Typically, the mobile users operating in the existing LTE deployments require higher data rates and lower latencies, whereas the IoT devices in NB-IoT technology are low-cost, delay-tolerant, and require smaller data rates. Due to these new characteristics of the NB-IoT, the existing legacy LTE resource management techniques are not directly applicable in the context of the NB-IoT. Motivated by this, we consider various resource management techniques for the NB-IoT systems that optimally utilize the limited bandwidth, ensure device fairness and Quality of Service in resource allocation, and minimize the power consumption of the low-cost IoT devices. Through numerical results, we show that the considered techniques significantly improve the network performance. Further, we identify that Cloud Radio Access Network (CRAN) is a suitable candidate for NB-IoT systems and discuss the potential benefits of implementing NB-IoT with CRAN. We also provide up-to-date information about the current NB-IoT standardization activities that may further encourage the readers to explore this domain.

3.1 Introduction

With the advancements in wireless technologies, there has been a rapid increase in the number of connected Internet of Things (IoT) devices. As per Cisco [1], shortly, there will be approximately 14.7 billion connected IoT devices which make 50% of the total connected wireless devices. When compared with the cellular mobile user equipment, these IoT devices have less power consumption, and thus, require lower battery power. They are deployable in remote areas that need a wider coverage area. Typically, these

[1]Department of Electrical Engineering, Indian Institute of Technology Hyderabad, India

devices transmit small chunks of data periodically and are tolerable to relatively larger delays [2,3]. These requirements by the IoT devices are significantly different from the mobile broadband features of the existing cellular technologies, and hence, there was a need for a low power wide area network (LPWAN) technology. To address the issue, 3rd Generation Partnership Project (3GPP) has introduced an LPWAN technology termed as narrowband-Internet of Things (NB-IoT) in its Release 13 specifications [4–6]. The NB-IoT technology aims at providing cellular service to ultra-low-cost devices that are delay tolerant and require smaller data rates. Some of the use cases of the technology include object tracking, smart metering, connected wireless sensors, industrial appliances, environmental monitoring, etc. The 3GPP has enhanced various features of the NB-IoT technology from Release 13 to 16. Further, the standardization of NB-IoT is also expected to evolve and co-exist with long-term evolution (LTE) and new radio (NR) technologies.

As shown in Figure 3.1, the NB-IoT is deployable in three modes of operation, namely, standalone, guardband, and in-band modes. In the standalone mode, NB-IoT operates on any of the existing carriers of the network operator with a minimum bandwidth requirement of 180 kHz. In the guardband mode, it operates in the guard-bands of the existing LTE/NR deployments. In the in-band mode, it co-exists with the LTE/NR and uses 180 KHz of bandwidth in every transmission time interval (TTI). The NB-IoT uses orthogonal frequency division multiplexing (OFDM) and has a design skeleton similar to that of LTE/NR technologies. The key differences as compared to LTE/NR are the availability of only one resource block in the frequency domain, multiplexing of control and data channels across time, and adoption of a large number of repetitions of the data over time to ensure wider network coverage. Due to these new physical layer changes, the existing LTE resource management algorithms are not directly extendable in the context of NB-IoT. Further, the IoT devices have limited bandwidth, and when they operate in in-band mode, they utilize the resources from the LTE/NR systems. Since these available resources are very limited in NB-IoT, the new resource management algorithms should ensure maximum resource utilization. Additionally, the NB-IoT devices are of low cost, and, hence, the algorithms should ensure minimum power consumption to extend the battery life of the IoT devices. Achieving these targets with the new physical layer constraints in NB-IoT is a challenging task. Motivated by this, we consider various resource management algorithms that improve resource utilization, power consumption, and ensure fairness. We evaluate the considered algorithms using system-level simulations and show that they achieve significant improvement in network performance.

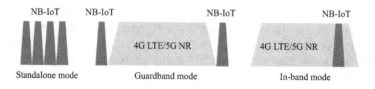

Figure 3.1   Deployment modes of NB-IoT

When NB-IoT co-exists with LTE/NR, the IoT devices and cellular users are connected to the same base station (BS). With this architecture, a rapid increase in the number of connected wireless devices will result in a huge amount of device traffic at the BS. To handle this, the network operators need to install more BSs and serve the dense IoT networks. With legacy radio access network (RAN) structures, this method will increase the capital expenditures (CAPEX), operational expenditures (OPEX), and power consumption. One key solution to address the issue is cloud RAN (CRAN) proposed in [7,8]. In CRAN, the legacy BSs are split into two, namely, base band unit (BBU) and remote radio head (RRH). The RRHs are deployed in each cell-site with the antenna array to carry out signal transmission over the air, whereas the BBUs perform all the base band signal processing procedures. Further, BBUs of multiple cell sites are typically centralized to a single unit, termed as the cloud. With a centralized system like this, the network operators will have the data available from all the cell sites in the cloud. Thus, the network operators can optimize the available resources and transmit power. Further, the operators can easily adapt to the traffic variations in cellular sites in real-time, and thus, improve the Quality of Service (QoS) for each connected device. We identify that the delay-tolerant, smaller data rates, and enhanced coverage requirements of the NB-IoT make it a suitable candidate for implementing it with CRAN. Motivated by the benefits from both the technologies, in this chapter, we present a case of implementing NB-IoT with CRAN.

The key contributions of this chapter are summarized as follows:

- We consider various resource management algorithms to improve the network performance of the NB-IoT systems.
- Through numerical evaluations, we show that proposed algorithms achieve significant improvements in terms of resource utilization and power consumption.
- We explain in detail the architecture of NB-IoT and CRAN, and discuss the benefits of implementing NB-IoT with CRAN.
- We present up-to-date information about the NB-IoT standardization activities that may encourage the readers to further explore the problems identified in this chapter.

The organization of the chapter is as follows. In Section 3.2, we present related work in the literature. The physical layer design of NB-IoT is discussed in Section 3.3. In Section 3.4, we discuss various resource management algorithms and provide numerical evaluations for the same. We discuss the CRAN architecture and benefits of implementing NB-IoT with CRAN in Section 3.5. In Section 3.6, we provide information on the current NB-IoT standardization activities. Section 3.7 presents the conclusion and future research directions.

3.2 Related work

The design rationale, architecture, applicability, and benefits of the NB-IoT have been discussed in [2,3,9–11]. In [12], the authors have discussed the coverage, latency, and battery life analysis of the NB-IoT systems. In [13], uplink scheduling and link adaptation techniques have been proposed for the NB-IoT devices. Various resource management algorithms for control and shared channels of NB-IoT are presented in [9,14–17]. Modeling, simulation, and performance evaluation of NB-IoT systems have been presented in [18–20]. Note that all these works consider the standalone implementation of NB-IoT technology. In [21], the authors have provided performance results from the implementation of NB-IoT with CRAN, and have shown that CRAN is a good candidate for NB-IoT implementation. In [22], a compressive sensing-based CRAN implementation is discussed for LPWAN technologies to improve the IoT devices' battery life. In [23], the authors have discussed the benefits of implementing various LPWAN technologies with CRAN. However, none of these articles consider resource management techniques to improve the network performance of the NB-IoT systems. Thus, in this chapter, we consider various resource management techniques for NB-IoT and provide detailed performance analysis through numerical evaluations.

In [24–26], the authors have presented a comprehensive survey on the CRAN architectures for the cellular networks. An energy-efficient resource allocation scheme for device-to-device communications with CRAN architecture has been presented in [27]. In [28], the authors have proposed various strategies for switching off the BSs in CRAN-based cellular systems to improve the energy efficiency. In [29], the authors have discussed the advantages and disadvantages of cloud-based machine-to-machine communications. In [30,31], various resource allocation techniques and power minimization algorithms have been studied for the CRAN-based cellular architectures. In [32], heterogeneous CRAN architectures have been presented for the cellular networks to improve the spectral efficiency and minimize the power consumption. In [33], various radio resource management techniques have been analyzed for heterogeneous networks, and a comparison of those algorithms has been provided. However, all these works consider CRAN implementation for the existing enhanced mobile broadband services, which require higher data rates and lower latencies. Limited works in the literature [21,22] have jointly considered NB-IoT and CRAN. Thus, in this chapter, we explain the architecture of CRAN and discuss the advantages of implementing NB-IoT with CRAN. Next, we explain the physical layer architecture of NB-IoT in detail.

3.3 NB-IoT physical layer architecture

The NB-IoT has a physical layer design similar to that of LTE/NR. The notion of symbol, subframe, and radio frame is similar to that of LTE/NR systems. The NB-IoT requires a bandwidth of 180 kHz, and thus, effectively, it operates on one physical resource block in every subframe TTI. Similar to LTE/NR, the BS in NB-IoT transmits the synchronization signals termed as Narrowband primary synchronization signal (NPSS) and Narrowband secondary synchronization signal (NSSS) in the downlink. The IoT devices use these synchronization signals to perform cell search and get connected to the BS. As shown in Figure 3.2, NPSS is transmitted by the BS in every fifth subframe, and NSSS is transmitted alternatively on the last subframe

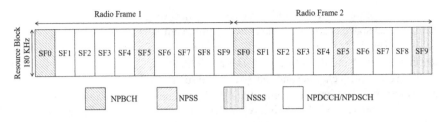

Figure 3.2   Physical layer design of NB-IoT

of every radio frame. Further, there are three physical channels in the downlink, namely, Narrowband physical broadcast channel (NPBCH), Narrowband physical downlink control channel (NPDCCH), and Narrowband physical downlink shared channel (NPDSCH). In case the IoT device successfully gets connected to the BS, it first decodes the NPBCH. NPBCH is transmitted on the first subframe of every radio frame, and carries the essential information required by the IoT device to operate in the NB-IoT network. The actual downlink data intended for an IoT device is transmitted in NPDSCH. However, the device has to know the region over which its data is present in NPDSCH. For this purpose, the BS transmits a payload termed as downlink control information (DCI) in the NPDCCH. DCI carries all the control information required by the IoT device like location of the NPDSCH data, type of modulation and coding scheme being used, and location where it has to transmit the uplink data, etc. Unlike LTE/NR, the control and shared channels in NB-IoT are multiplexed over-time. As shown in Figure 3.2, the subframes that are not allocated to NPSS, NSSS, and NPBCH are available for the NPDCCH and NPDSCH.

To decode the NPDSCH data, the IoT device relies on the DCI transmitted in NPDCCH. However, the BS conveys only the region over which NPDCCH spans and the IoT device has to blindly search the NPDCCH region to decode the DCI payload. This region of NPDCCH is called as search space (R_{max}). Further, to ensure wider coverage, the BS repeats the DCI payload over multiple subframes within the search space. These repetition values (R) are specific to each IoT device and are decided based on the channel conditions observed by the IoT device. Note that the device does not know the repetition (R) with which the BS has transmitted the data, and, hence, it has to try decoding for all possible combinations of repetitions. However, typical IoT devices are of low cost and have minimal battery power. To ensure the long battery life of the IoT devices, 3GPP specifies the following constraints on the repetitions, and, thus, limits the number of blind decoding to be performed by the IoT device [4–6].

$$R_{max} \in \{1, 2, 4, \ldots, 2048\}, \tag{3.1}$$

$$R \in \left\{ R_{max}, \frac{R_{max}}{2}, \frac{R_{max}}{4}, \frac{R_{max}}{8} \right\}. \tag{3.2}$$

From (3.1), the number of subframes in an NPDCCH region can be as high as 2,048 subframes. Given a search space of R_{max} subframes, the IoT device has to try decoding the DCI payload for repetitions satisfying (3.2). Further, the device with repetition requirement of R subframes has to try decoding only at every Rth subframe in the search space [4–6]. This way, only a limited number of blind decodings will be performed by the IoT device. Typically, a low-cost IoT device will require at least 1 ms to perform one blind decoding [14]. Hence, 3GPP specifies an additional 4 ms gap between the control channel and shared channel so that IoT device can complete all the blind decodings. A pictorial representation of the same is presented in Figure 3.3. For the IoT devices D1 and D2 in Figure 3.3, the search space is allocated with $R_{max} = 4$ subframes, and repetitions for each device are $R = 2$ and $R = 1$, respectively. Observe that a 4 ms gap is present between the control and shared channel for each device.

The BS broadcasts the region for NPDCCH and NPDSCH as NPDCCH period (NP), where $NP = R \times G$ and G is a scaling factor. Similar to NPDCCH, the payload in NPDSCH is also repeated based on the channel conditions of the IoT device. The subframes required to transfer the NPDSCH payload and the repetitions required by the payload are represented by N_{SF} and N_{rep}, respectively. The possible values of N_{SF}, N_{rep}, and G, as per [4–6] are as follows:

$$N_{SF} \in \{1, 2, 3, 4, 5, 6, 8, 10\}, \tag{3.3}$$

$$N_{rep} \in \{1, 2, 4, \ldots, 2048\}, \tag{3.4}$$

$$G \in \{1.5, 2, \ldots, 64\}. \tag{3.5}$$

Considering $R_{max} = 4$, $G = 3$, and $R = 12$ subframes, the timing of NPDSCH is presented for two devices in Figure 3.3. Note that similar to downlink, there are control and shared channels in the uplink, namely physical uplink control channel (PUCCH) and physical uplink shared channel (PUSCH), respectively. Readers unfamiliar with NB-IoT physical layer architecture are suggested to read [9,14–16]. Next, we present various resource management techniques for the NB-IoT systems.

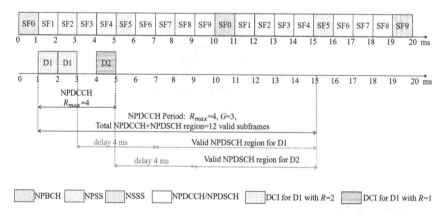

Figure 3.3   Timing diagram of NPDCCH and NPDSCH

3.4   Resource management in NB-IoT

In this section, we initially define performance metrics to evaluate the resource allocation algorithms. We then consider various resource allocation algorithms for the downlink physical channels of NB-IoT. However, all these downlink resource allocation algorithms can be extended to the uplink in a similar fashion.

3.4.1 Performance metrics

3.4.1.1 Resource utilization (χ)

The NB-IoT has limited resources and operates only on one physical resource block in every subframe. Further, while operating in the in-band mode of deployment, it uses the physical resource block from LTE/NR systems. Thus, the time–frequency resources are valuable, and, hence, the allocation algorithm has to improve the resource utilization. In practice, different IoT devices require various combinations of repetition values (R). While performing scheduling at the BS, many of the subframes will be left unallocated because of the 3GPP constraints specified in (3.1)–(3.5). Thus, we consider the resource utilization as a performance metric and define (χ) as follows:

$$\chi = \frac{\text{Number of subframes utilized}}{\text{Number of subframes allocated}}. \tag{3.6}$$

Note that $0 < \chi \le 1$, and higher the value of χ, better will be the resource utilization.

3.4.1.2 Power consumption (η)

The NB-IoT devices are expected to have a battery life of up to 10 years. Thus, the power consumption of the IoT devices is an important factor, and, hence, we have considered it as a performance metric. In NB-IoT, when the BS broadcasts the control and shared channel regions (NP), all the active devices in the system try decoding the region expecting a payload for themselves. However, because of the control channel constraints, a maximum of eight devices can be scheduled in each NP. Note that the control channel region can span over a maximum of 2,048 subframes. Hence, a scheduler should try to schedule as many devices as possible in each NP to reduce the power consumption of the IoT devices. Thus, we define the power consumption of the IoT devices as follows:

$$\eta = \frac{\text{Average number of devices scheduled per NP}}{\text{Maximum number of devices schedulable in an NP}}. \tag{3.7}$$

Note that $0 < \eta \le 1$, and higher the value of η, lower is the battery consumption of the IoT devices. Based on these performance metrics, next, we consider resource allocation algorithms for NB-IoT systems.

3.4.2 Allocation algorithms

In this section, we initially present heuristic and some low-complexity resource allocation algorithms for NB-IoT control channel. We then formulate the resource allocation as an optimization problem to achieve better network performance. Additionally, we consider a joint resource optimization technique that can further improve network performance. Note that all the resource allocation algorithms are explained in the context of NPDCCH. However, with minimal changes, they are directly extendable to the NPDSCH as well.

3.4.2.1   Heuristic algorithm

In the heuristic algorithm, the devices are initially picked in the order of their arrival/priority. In every scheduling attempt, the maximum number of devices is grouped into a search space such that (3.1) and (3.2) are satisfied. When the BS cannot group the next device from the list in the current search space, then it stops scheduling in the current search space. It continues to schedule the next device in a fresh search space and follows a similar procedure again. For easy understanding of the algorithm, consider a set of IoT devices requiring repetitions for control channel as shown in Figure 3.4. For these sets of devices, we present a pictorial representation of the heuristic algorithm in Figure 3.5. Note that, in the first search space with $R_{max} = 8$, there are four vacant subframes. However, because of the constraints in (3.1)–(3.2), the device D4 cannot be scheduled in the same search space. As shown in Figure 3.5, the heuristic algorithm achieves $\chi = 0.708$ and $\eta = 0.291$. Next, we explain sorting-based low-complexity algorithms.

3.4.2.2   Low-complexity algorithms

The problem of scheduling the devices in NB-IoT can be viewed as a bin-packing problem [15]. Sorting is a widely used technique to optimize the bin-packing problems [34,35]. Thus, we consider scheduling algorithms by sorting the IoT devices based on their repetition values R, as follows:

| D1 | D2 | D2 | D3 | D4 | D4 | D4 | D4 | D5 | D6 | D6 | D6 | D6 | D7 | D7 | D7 | D7 |

Figure 3.4   Repetitions required by each IoT device

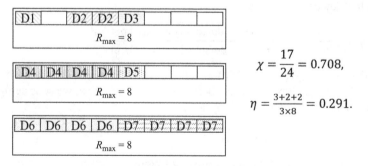

$$\chi = \frac{17}{24} = 0.708,$$

$$\eta = \frac{3+2+2}{3\times8} = 0.291.$$

Figure 3.5   Scheduling of IoT devices with the heuristic algorithm

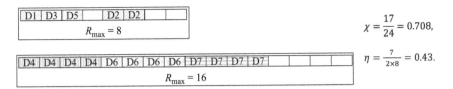

$$\chi = \frac{17}{24} = 0.708,$$

$$\eta = \frac{7}{2 \times 8} = 0.43.$$

Figure 3.6   Scheduling of IoT devices with the Min-R algorithm

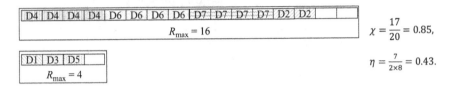

$$\chi = \frac{17}{20} = 0.85,$$

$$\eta = \frac{7}{2 \times 8} = 0.43.$$

Figure 3.7   Scheduling of IoT devices with the Max-R algorithm

Min-R

Initially, all the IoT devices are sorted in the ascending order of their repetition values. Then, the first device from the list is picked, and the other devices are checked if they can be grouped together with this picked IoT device. We continue this procedure and keep adding the devices into the current search space until we can no more add another device. Compared to the heuristic algorithm, this method helps in grouping more number of devices together in a search space. A pictorial representation of the algorithm is presented in Figure 3.6. As shown in Figure 3.6, Min-R algorithm achieves $\chi = 0.708$ and $\eta = 0.43$.

Max-R

In the Max-R algorithm, instead of sorting the devices in the ascending order of their repetitions, the devices are sorted in the descending order. The performance of the algorithm for the same set of examples is presented in Figure 3.7. The sorting helps in achieving better resource utilization, as the Max-R algorithm achieves $\chi = 0.85$. Next, we present an extension of Min-R and Max-R algorithms, where there is no resource wastage.

Min-R relaxed and Max-R relaxed

In the Min-R relaxed algorithm, we follow a procedure similar to that of the Min-R algorithm, but we schedule a device in the search space only if it achieves full resource utilization. In case no device can be grouped with the current device to achieve zero resource wastage, we then schedule only one device in the search space by setting $R_{max} = R$. Similarly, for the Max-R relaxed version, we follow a similar procedure except for sorting the devices in the descending order of the repetitions. We present the pictorial representation of Min-R relaxed and Max-R relaxed algorithms in Figures 3.8 and 3.9, respectively. Both the algorithms achieve full resource utilization ($\chi = 1$).

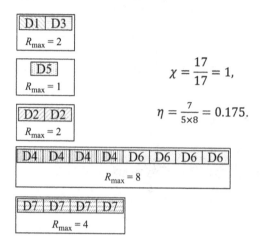

Figure 3.8   *Scheduling of IoT devices with the Min-R relaxed algorithm*

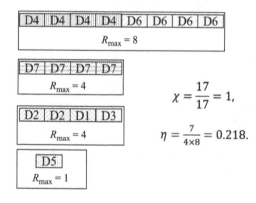

Figure 3.9   *Scheduling of IoT devices with the Max-R relaxed algorithm*

The Min-R relaxed and Max-R relaxed algorithms achieve $\eta = 0.175$ and $\eta = 0.218$, respectively.

Note that compared to the heuristic algorithm, these low complexity algorithms involve sorting of the devices, and, hence, have an additional computation complexity of the order $\mathcal{O}(N \log N)$, where N is the number of active devices. Further, from the above algorithms, it is evident that there is a trade-off between resource utilization and power consumption factors. Based on this observation, we consider an optimization problem for scheduling the devices in the search space.

3.4.2.3   Optimized allocation

We define the objective function as follows:

$$\max_{d_s} \quad [\alpha \chi_s + (1 - \alpha)\eta\}_s], \tag{3.8}$$

$$\text{s.t} \quad (3.1) - (3.2).$$

where s is the search space index, χ_s and η_s are the resource utilization and power consumption metrics for the search space s, d_s is the list of the scheduled devices in the search space s, and $0 \leq \alpha \leq 1$ is an operator defined parameter to achieve various trade-offs between resource utilization and power consumption. When $\alpha = 1$, the objective function tries to achieve maximum resource utilization, when $\alpha = 0$, it tries to achieve better power consumption, and when $\alpha = 0.5$, the algorithm tries to prioritize both the metrics equally. Note that the objective function formulated in (3.8) is an integer linear programming (ILP) problem. With N active devices, the worst-case complexity of the algorithm is of the order $\mathcal{O}(2^N)$. However, there are a wide variety of algorithms available in the literature [36,37] to achieve the solution with much lesser computational complexity. A practical and feasible way of implementing the considered objective function is available in [15,16]. Next, we present a joint optimization problem for scheduling the IoT devices.

3.4.2.4 Joint optimization

In the NB-IoT systems, for every payload transmitted in the shared channel, there is an associated payload in the control channel. Thus, instead of performing standalone resource allocation in each individual channel, implementing a joint resource allocation of NPDCCH and NPDSCH can improve the network performance. We explain the significance of this joint optimization with an example as follows. Consider two IoT devices with a requirement of NPDCCH repetitions $R = \{1, 2\}$, NPDSCH data with $N_{SF} = \{3, 3\}$, and $N_{rep} = \{1, 1\}$. We present the scheduling of the devices with standalone optimization and joint optimization in Figure 3.10. In standalone optimization, initially, a minimum search space length is chosen such that both devices are scheduled. Thus, the algorithm chooses $R_{max} = 4$, and then it decides $G = 3$ to allocate NPDSCH resources. However, in the case of the joint optimization, the algorithm smartly picks $R_{max} = 8$, $G = 1.5$, and, thus, improves the resource utilization.

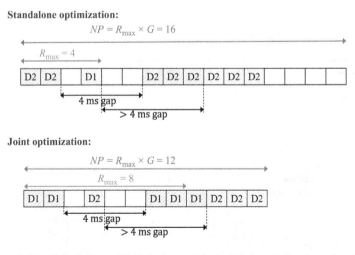

Figure 3.10   Scheduling of IoT devices with the joint optimization algorithm

Similar to (3.8), we formulate the joint optimization problem as follows:

$$\max_{d_s} \quad [\alpha \chi_s + (1 - \alpha)\eta_s], \tag{3.9}$$

$$\text{s.t.} \quad (3.1) - (3.5).$$

The objective function formulated in (3.9) is also an ILP problem, and the complexity of the solving (3.9) in the worst-case scenario is of the order $\mathcal{O}(2^N)$, where N is the number of active devices. A practical and feasible way of implementing the algorithm is available in [15]. Next, we provide a performance comparison of the considered algorithms based on numerical evaluations.

3.4.2.5 Simulation results

For the evaluation of the algorithms, we consider the simulation parameters as presented in Table 3.1. Initially, the IoT devices are dropped randomly in each cell site. As shown in Figure 3.11, each dot represents a device dropped in a cell site. For each device, we then calculate the path loss and received signal power from all the BSs. The devices are associated to the BS from which they receive maximum signal power. In Figure 3.11, a unique color is assigned to each device to distinguish the device-attach to the cell sites. The direction of the BS antenna, line-of-sight, path loss, and channel propagation have a significant impact on the received signal power. Hence, a device dropped in one cell site may get attached to the other cell site as shown in Figure 3.11. We calculate the signal to interference plus noise ratio (SINR) values for each device and assign the repetition requirements based on the channel conditions observed by the device. Note that in practice, the BS relies on the channel conditions feedbacked by the device to assign repetitions. Given these channel conditions of the device, we perform mapping of repetitions based on the link-level physical layer abstractions. Further, we assign the NPDSCH data requirements N_{SF} to each device from a uniform distribution of $\{1, 2, \ldots, 10\}$. We then implemented all the considered resource

Table 3.1   Simulation parameters

Parameter	Value
Bandwidth	180 kHz
BS transmit power	44 dBm
Carrier frequency	900 MHz
Cellular layout	Hexagonal grid, 7 sites, 3 sectors per site
G	$\{1.5, 2, \ldots, 64\}$
Inter-site distance	1,732 m
NB-IoT device location	1,000 devices dropped uniformly in entire cell
NB-IoT mode of operation	Standalone (used in link-abstractions)
N_{rep}	$\{1, 2, \ldots, 2,048\}$
N_{SF}	$\{1, 2, \ldots, 10\}$
R_{max}	$\{1, 2, \ldots, 2,048\}$
UE transmit power	23 dBm

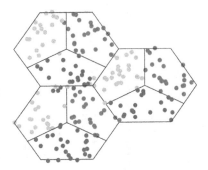

Figure 3.11   Illustration of device drop and association to a base station

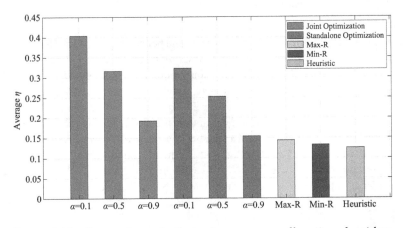

Figure 3.12   Comparison of η for various resource allocation algorithms

allocation algorithms and captured the resource utilization and power consumption from each algorithm. While implementing the optimization problems in (3.8) and (3.9), we have used the MATLAB® built-in function *intlinprog*, and simulated for $\alpha = 0.1, 0.5,$ and 0.9.

In Figure 3.12, we present the comparison of η for various resource allocation algorithms. The Min-R and Max-R algorithms schedule more devices in each NP as compared to the heuristic algorithm. The standalone optimization algorithm with $\alpha = 0.1$ achieves significant improvement in the average number of devices scheduled in the NP. Even when the priority of the objective function is more towards optimizing the resource utilization, i.e., when $\alpha = 0.9$, the algorithm still achieves better η than the low complexity and heuristic algorithms. Further, the joint optimization with $\alpha = 0.1$ schedules more number of devices in an NP and outperforms all the algorithms. Note that when compared to the heuristic algorithm, the joint optimization schedules close to four times more the number of devices in each (NP).

In Figure 3.13, we present the comparison of χ for various resource allocation algorithms. Because of the sorting, the Min-R and Max-R algorithms achieve

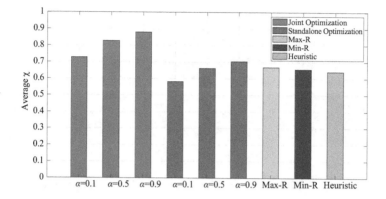

Figure 3.13   Comparison of χ for various resource allocation algorithms

improved resource utilization as compared to the heuristic algorithm. The standalone optimization algorithm with $\alpha = 0.9$ also observes better resource utilization, whereas the joint optimization algorithm significantly outperforms all the algorithms. From the evaluation results, it is evident that there is always a trade-off between the resource utilization and power consumption of the IoT devices. Further, the low-complexity sorting-based algorithms have less computational complexity and achieve reasonably good performance when compared against the heuristic algorithm. Thus, the network operators have to choose the algorithms based on the type of network deployment and the desired performance metrics. Next, we explain the CRAN in detail and discuss the challenges and advantages of implementing NB-IoT systems with CRAN.

3.5   CRAN

In Figure 3.14, we present the legacy RAN architecture, where, the BS has two connected units, namely RRHs and BBUs. The RRH units contain the antenna array and perform the operations like transmission and reception of radio signals, analog and digital conversions, filtering, etc. These RRHs are connected to the BBU using a common public radio interface (CPRI), in the fronthaul link. Typically, the fronthaul is also implemented based on technologies like optical fiber communications, wireless communications, etc. The BBU performs all the base band procedures and is connected to the core network via an Ethernet backhaul connection. This legacy architecture has been used in most of the existing 3G and 4G cellular deployments.

In Figure 3.15, we have presented the CRAN architecture. The key difference in CRAN as compared to the legacy RAN architecture is that all the BBUs are stacked at a centralized place, termed as the cloud. The BBU pool/cloud has all the BBUs interconnected together and communicates with multiple RRHs. With such centralization of the BBUs, the cloud has the information available from all the cell sites, and, thus, the network operators can make optimal decisions to improve the system performance. Furthermore, with the recent advancements, various combinations of

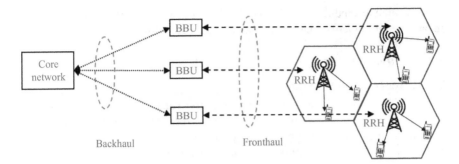

Figure 3.14   Legacy RAN architecture

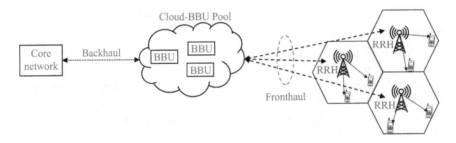

Figure 3.15   CRAN architecture

splits between the centralized and distributed units have been proposed in the literature [38]. These multiple split combinations offer more flexibility for the network operators in the real-time deployments.

3.5.1   NB-IoT with CRAN

Some of the key challenges with the CRAN deployments are the large data rates and minimal latency requirements in the fronthaul links. With the large antenna arrays, beamforming, and advanced coding techniques, the data rates of the users in enhanced Mobile Broadband (eMBB) services have increased significantly. Thus, the fronthaul link between the BBUs and RRHs needs to have a larger capacity to handle these increased data rate requirements. For example, with a 20 MHz carrier, 4×4 antenna configuration, and 32-bit precision of I/Q samples, the fronthaul capacity should be as high as 7.9 Gbps [21]. Similarly, the eMBB and ultra-reliable low latency communications (URLLC) services require low latencies, and thus, the delay between the RRHs and BBUs should be minimal. However, this is not the case with NB-IoT systems, as the devices in NB-IoT are delay-tolerant and require small data rates. Further, the LPWAN technologies like NB-IoT need a wider coverage area. With optimal resource management techniques, CRAN can minimize the inter-cell interference and enhance the cellular coverage. All these factors make the CRAN a much suitable candidate for the NB-IoT technology. We outline some of the key advantages of implementing NB-IoT with CRAN as follows.

3.5.2 Advantages

Interference management

With the CRAN architecture, the network operators can perform joint scheduling and resource allocation for multiple cell sites, and minimize the inter-cell interference. This helps in improving the network capacity as well as the coverage for the IoT devices which is a key requirement for the IoT devices.

Spectrum utilization

Typically, a significant portion of the resource blocks are left unallocated in the real-time LTE/NR networks. With a CRAN architecture, the network operator can identify these unoccupied time and frequency resources and allocate them for the IoT devices.

Optimal BBU resource utilization

With the centralized BBU pool, the network operators can optimize the BBU resources by turning off the BBUs for the cell sites which have minimal traffic load. A common BBU can be assigned for multiple cell sites with such low traffic. This will help in improving the energy efficiency of the cell sites. Further, in the case of a huge traffic load at any cell site, the operators can assign more BBU resources to a single cell site to handle the huge traffic.

Cost reduction

In the case of dense IoT networks, the network operator can install multiple RRHs and connect them to the BBU pool. This way of implementation can significantly reduce the CAPEX and OPEX costs incurred by the network operator. Thus, CRAN offers better scalability of the network. Next, we discuss the standardization activities of NB-IoT in Release-16 and 17 specifications.

3.6 Standardization

In this section, we present the up-to-date information about the current standardization activities of the NB-IoT. In Figure 3.16, we have presented a list of key study items for Release 16 and 17 specifications. In Figure 3.17, we have presented the targeted timeline for the current 3GPP releases.

3.6.1 Release 16

Some of the key work items of the NB-IoT in Release 16 specifications are as follows [39,40]:

Multiple grants within a single DCI

Typically, each DCI payload carries either downlink or uplink scheduling grants. Further, in NB-IoT, based on the channel conditions of the IoT device, the DCI payload is repeated over a large number of subframes in NPDCCH. To reduce this control signaling overhead, scheduling of multiple scheduling grants within a single

RELEASE -16 STUDY/WORK ITEMS:
- **eMBB features:**
  - MIMO enhancements
  - UE power savings in NR
  - NR vehicle-to-everything
  - Study on Non-orthogonal multiple access
  - Integrated access and backhaul
  - NR access to unlicensed spectrum
  - Mobility enhancements
  - Downlink MIMO efficiency for LTE

- **Cellular-IoT:**
  - Enhancements for NB-IoT
  - Enhancements for eMTC
  - NR-Industrial IoT

RELEASE -17 STUDY/WORK ITEMS:
- **eMBB features:**
  - NR MIMO
  - Dynamic spectrum sharing
  - NR vehicle-to-everything
  - NR coverage enhancements
  - Integrated access and backhaul
  - NR sidelink
  - Unmanned aerial vehicles
  - NR extended reality
  - Enhancements for URLLC

- **Cellular-IoT:**
  - Enhancements for NB-IoT/eMTC
  - Industrial IoT
  - Study of IoT over Non-terrestrial networks

Figure 3.16   Key study/work items of Release 16/17 specifications

Figure 3.17   Timeline of current 3GPP releases

DCI is investigated. This new feature can significantly help in minimizing the power consumption of the IoT devices.

Resource block alignment

The NB-IoT is expected to co-exist with the LTE/NR in the in-band mode of operation. Note that the subcarrier spacing is 15 kHz in both NB-IoT and LTE. However, in case of NR, the BS also supports 30, 60, 120, and 240 kHz. When the NB-IoT is operated in in-band mode, if NR operates on a subcarrier spacing other than 15 kHz, the orthogonality feature will be lost. Hence, there is a need for a mechanism to avoid this problem. The network operators can ensure a minimum guard band in between NB-IoT and NR to avoid the orthogonality loss. Additionally, the following issues are identified corresponding to resource block alignment. In the case of LTE/NR operating with 15 KHz subcarrier spacing, to optimize the resource utilization, the BS should align the resource blocks of NB-IoT and LTE/NR. Further, the synchronization signals in NR are transmitted in the synchronization signal block (SSB), which is located at fixed positions in each radio frame. Hence, the network operators should ensure that NB-IoT resource blocks do not overlap with the SSB locations in NR.

Power boosting

To improve the coverage of the NB-IoT systems, power boosting is considered at the BS. The power boosting factor can be specified based on the operating bandwidth of the LTE/NR systems and the NB-IoT carrier location. The BS are required to support a minimum of +3 dB or +6 dB power boosting when the NB-IoT operates in the in-band mode. This power boosting will have significant impact on the coverage of the NB-IoT systems.

Group wake up signaling

To reduce the power consumption of the IoT devices, a group wake up signaling was investigated. In the NB-IoT, all the devices wake up after every discontinuous reception (DRX) cycle and perform the NPDCCH decoding. This leads to an unnecessary power consumption. Instead, a group wake up signaling targeted for a configurable group of devices would help in reducing the power consumption of the devices. In the specified signaling method, each group can configure up to eight devices.

Uplink resources

In the uplink, support for the transmission of the device data in the pre-configured resources in idle mode was investigated. This procedure avoids the time-consuming random access procedures and improves the device battery life.

Link adaptation

As per the Release-13 specifications of the NB-IoT, the channel quality reports are not transmitted by the IoT device. However, enabling these reports can significantly improve the link adaptation and network performance. Apart from these improvements, 3GPP Release 16 activities on NB-IoT also include various other enhancements related to mobility, multi-carrier support, latency improvements, connection to 5G NR core, etc.

3.6.2   Release 17

Some of the key work items of NB-IoT in Release 17 specifications are as follows [41]:

3.6.2.1   Support of NB-IoT over non-terrestrial networks (NTN)

In this work item, the necessary changes required need to be identified to make the NB-IoT work over NTN. Typically, the IoT devices are operated in very remote areas with low or zero cellular connectivity. Some examples of such scenarios include oil harvesting, mining, farming, environmental monitoring, etc. In such scenarios, the satellite connectivity can be used to provide the required coverage. The NB-IoT is considered as a suitable candidate for such NTN communication. The objectives of the work item include investigating the bands of operation, satellite constellation orbits low earth orbit (LEO) and geosynchronous equatorial orbit (GEO), link budget analysis, etc. One key differentiating factor from the typical NB-IoT systems would be the delay in the communication. NTN-based systems observe large delays, and, hence, various NB-IoT features will require modifications like random access procedures, time/frequency adjustment mechanisms, hybrid automatic repeat request (HARQ) procedures, etc.

3.6.2.2   Higher peak data rates

Some industrial applications require higher data rates, and, hence, the support of 16-quadrature amplitude modulation (QAM) is investigated for the downlink and uplink. This modification will further broaden the use cases of NB-IoT.

3.7   Conclusion

In this chapter, we have explained the design of NB-IoT and CRAN in detail. We have considered various resource management techniques to improve the network performance. We have presented low complexity, optimization, and joint optimization algorithms to allocate resources to the devices in the physical layer of NB-IoT systems. We have provided numerical evaluations and compared the performance of proposed algorithms against various metrics. We have shown that the proposed algorithms achieve various trade-offs against the defined performance metrics. Further, we have considered a case of implementing NB-IoT with CRAN, and presented the advantages with the same. In the end, we have provided the information about the current standardization activities in the NB-IoT.

Abbreviations

G	Scaling factor to define the NPDCCH period
N_{SF}	Number of subframes required by NPDSCH payload
N_{ref}	Number of repetitions for NPDSCH payload
$R_{\max}$	Number of subframes for NPDCCH search space
R	Number of repetitions for NPDCCH payload
α	Trade-off parameter
χ	resource utilization factor
η	power consumption factor
3GPP	3rd Generation Partnership Project
BBU	base band unit
BS	base station
CAPEX	capital expenditures
CPRI	common public radio interface
CRAN	cloud RAN
DCI	downlink control information
eMBB	enhanced Mobile Broadband
GEO	geosynchronous equatorial orbit
HARQ	hybrid automatic repeat request
ILP	integer linear programming
IoT	Internet of Things
LEO	low earth orbit
LPWAN	low power wide area network
LTE	Long-Term Evolution
NB-IoT	Narrowband-Internet of Things
NP	NPDCCH period
NPBCH	Narrowband physical broadcast channel
NPDCCH	Narrowband physical downlink control channel
NPDSCH	Narrowband physical downlink shared channel
NPSS	Narrowband primary synchronization signal

NR	New Radio
NSSS	Narrowband secondary synchronization signal
NTN	Non-terrestrial networks
OFDM	orthogonal frequency division multiplexing
OPEX	operational expenditures
PUCCH	physical uplink control channel
PUSCH	physical uplink shared channel
QAM	quadrature amplitude modulation
QoS	Quality of Service
RAN	radio access network
RRH	remote radio head
SINR	signal to interference plus noise ratio
SSB	synchronization signal block
TTI	transmission time interval
URLLC	ultra-reliable low latency communications

References

[1] "Cisco Annual Internet Report (2018–2023) White Paper." Available: https://www.cisco.com/c/en/us/solutions/collateral/executive-perspectives/annual-internet-report/white-paper-c11-741490.html.

[2] Y.-P.E. Wang, X. Lin, A. Adhikary, *et al.*, "A primer on 3GPP narrowband Internet of Things," *IEEE Commun. Mag.*, vol. 55, no. 3, pp. 117–123, 2017.

[3] A. D. Zayas and P. Merino, "The 3GPP NB-IoT system architecture for the Internet of Things," in *Proceedings of ICC Workshops*, 2017, pp. 277–282.

[4] 3GPP, "Physical Channels and Modulation," 3rd Generation Partnership Project (3GPP), Technical Report, 36.211, June 2016.

[5] 3GPP, "Multiplexing and Channel Coding," 3rd Generation Partnership Project (3GPP), Technical Report, 36.212, June 2016.

[6] 3GPP, "Physical Layer Procedures," 3rd Generation Partnership Project (3GPP), Technical Report, 36.213, June 2016.

[7] A. Checko, H.L. Christiansen, Y. Yan, *et al.*, "Cloud RAN for mobile networks—a technology overview," *IEEE Commun. Surv. Tutor.*, vol. 17, no. 1, pp. 405–426, 2014.

[8] "C-RAN: The Road towards Green Radio Access Network. White Paper," Last accessed: June 25, 2021. Available: https://pdfs.semanticscholar.org/eaa3/ca62c9d5653e4f2318aed9ddb8992a505d3c.pdf

[9] P. R. Manne, S. Ganji, A. Kumar and K. Kuchi, "Scheduling and decoding of downlink control channel in 3GPP narrowband-IoT," *IEEE Access*, vol. 8, pp. 175612–175624, 2020, doi:10.1109/ACCESS.2020.3026077.

[10] A. Hoglund, X. Lin, O. Liberg, *et al.*, "Overview of 3GPP release 14 enhanced NB-IoT," *IEEE Network*, vol. 31, no. 6, pp. 16–22, 2017.

[11] J. Gozalvez, "New 3GPP standard for IoT [mobile radio]," *IEEE Veh. Technol. Mag.*, vol. 11, no. 1, pp. 14–20, 2016.

[12]   R. Ratasuk, B. Vejlgaard, N. Mangalvedhe, and A. Ghosh, "NB-IoT system for M2M communication," in *2016 IEEE Wireless Communications and Networking Conference*, pp. 1–5. Piscataway, NJ: IEEE, 2016.

[13]   C. Yu, L. Yu, Y. Wu, Y. He, and Q. Lu, "Uplink scheduling and link adaptation for narrowband Internet of Things systems," *IEEE Access*, vol. 5, pp. 1724–1734, 2017.

[14]   M. P. Reddy, G. Santosh, A. Kumar, and K. Kuchi, "Downlink control channel scheduling for 3GPP narrowband-IoT," in *2018 IEEE 29th Annual International Symposium on Personal, Indoor and Mobile Radio Communications (PIMRC)*, pp. 1–7. Piscataway, NJ: IEEE, 2018.

[15]   M. P. Reddy, A. Kumar, and K. Kuchi, "Joint control and shared channel scheduling for downlink in 3GPP narrowband-IoT," in *2020 International Conference on COMmunication Systems & NETworkS (COMSNETS)*, pp. 476–483. Piscataway, NJ: IEEE, 2020.

[16]   A. Kumar and K. Kuchi, "Design and performance analysis of joint control and shared channel scheduler for downlink in 3GPP narrowband-IoT," *Ad Hoc Netw.*, vol. 114, p. 102440, 2021.

[17]   H. Malik, H. Pervaiz, M. M. Alam, Y. L. Moullec, A. Kuusik, and M. A. Imran, "Radio resource management scheme in NB-IoT systems," *IEEE Access*, vol. 6, pp. 15051–15064, 2018.

[18]   Y. Miao, W. Li, D. Tian, M. S. Hossain, and M. F. Alhamid, "Narrowband Internet of Things: simulation and modeling," *IEEE Internet Things J.*, vol. 5, no. 4, pp. 2304–2314, 2017.

[19]   Y. D. Beyene, R. Jantti, K. Ruttik, and S. Iraji, "On the performance of narrow-band Internet of Things (NB-IoT)," in *2017 IEEE Wireless Communications and Networking Conference (WCNC)*, pp. 1–6. Piscataway, NJ: IEEE, 2017.

[20]   A. Adhikary, X. Lin, and Y-P. Eric Wang, "Performance evaluation of NB-IoT coverage," in *2016 IEEE 84th Vehicular Technology Conference (VTC-Fall)*, pp. 1–5. Piscataway, NJ: IEEE, 2016.

[21]   Y. D. Beyene, R. Jantti, O. Tirkkonen, *et al.*, "NB-IoT technology overview and experience from cloud-RAN implementation," *IEEE Wirel. Commun.*, vol. 24, no. 3, 26–32, 2017.

[22]   J. Liu, W. Xu, S. Jha, and W. Hu, "Nephalai: towards LPWAN C-RAN with physical layer compression," in *Proceedings of the 26th Annual International Conference on Mobile Computing and Networking*, pp. 1–12, 2020.

[23]   A. J. Onumanyi, A. M. Abu-Mahfouz, and G. P. Hancke, "Low power wide area network, cognitive radio and the Internet of Things: potentials for integration," *Sensors*, vol. 20, no. 23, p. 6837, 2020.

[24]   M. A. Habibi, M. Nasimi, B. Han, and H. D. Schotten, "A comprehensive survey of RAN architectures toward 5G mobile communication system," *IEEE Access*, vol. 7, pp. 70371–70421, 2019.

[25]   A. Checko, H. L. Christiansen, Y. Yan, *et al.*, "Cloud RAN for mobile networks—a technology overview," *IEEE Commun. Surv. Tutor.*, vol. 17, no. 1, 405–426, 2014.

[26]   T. O. Olwal, K. Djouani, and A. M. Kurien, "A survey of resource management toward 5G radio access networks," *IEEE Commun. Surv. Tutor.*, vol. 18, no. 3, 1656–1686, 2016.

[27]   Z. Zhou, M. Dong, K. Ota, G. Wang, and L. T. Yang, "Energy-efficient resource allocation for D2D communications underlaying cloud-RAN-based LTE-A networks," *IEEE Internet Things J.*, vol. 3, no. 3, pp. 428–438, 2015.

[28]   F. Han, S. Zhao, L. Zhang, and J. Wu, "Survey of strategies for switching off base stations in heterogeneous networks for greener 5G systems," *IEEE Access*, vol. 4, 4959–4973, 2016.

[29]   N. Xia, H-H. Chen, and C-S. Yang, "Radio resource management in machine-to-machine communications—a survey," *IEEE Commun. Surv. Tutor.*, vol. 20, no. 1, 791–828, 2017.

[30]   K. Wang, K. Yang, and C. S. Magurawalage, "Joint energy minimization and resource allocation in C-RAN with mobile cloud," *IEEE Trans. Cloud Comput.*, vol. 6, no. 3, 760–770, 2016.

[31]   A. Abdelnasser and E. Hossain, "Resource allocation for an OFDMA cloud-RAN of small cells underlaying a macrocell," *IEEE Trans. Mobile Comput.*, vol. 15, no. 11, pp. 2837–2850, 2016.

[32]   M. A. Marotta, N. Kaminski, I. Gomez-Miguelez, *et al.*, "Resource sharing in heterogeneous cloud radio access networks," *IEEE Wirel. Commun.*, vol. 22, no. 3, 74–82, 2015.

[33]   Y. L. Lee, T. C. Chuah, J. Loo, and A. Vinel, "Recent advances in radio resource management for heterogeneous LTE/LTE-A networks," *IEEE Commun. Surv. Tutor.*, vol. 16, no. 4, pp. 2142–2180, 2014.

[34]   P. Hosein, "Resource allocation for the LTE physical downlink control channel," in *Proceedings of IEEE Globecom Workshops*, pp. 1–5, 2009.

[35]   Y. Chen, "Resource allocation for downlink control channel in LTE systems," in *Proceedings of WiCom*, pp. 1–4, 2011.

[36]   F. Rossi and S. Smriglio, "A set packing model for the ground holding problem in congested networks," *Eur. J. Oper. Res.*, vol. 131, no. 2, pp. 400–416, 2001.

[37]   X. Gandibleux, X. Delorme, and V. T'Kindt, "An ant colony optimisation algorithm for the set packing problem," in *International Workshop on Ant Colony Optimization and Swarm Intelligence*, pp. 49–60. Berlin: Springer, 2004.

[38]   V. Q. Rodriguez, F. Guillemin, A. Ferrieux, and L. Thomas, "Cloud-RAN functional split for an efficient fronthaul network," in *2020 International Wireless Communications and Mobile Computing (IWCMC)*, pp. 245–250. Piscataway, NJ: IEEE, 2020.

[39]   3GPP, "Additional enhancements for NB-IoT," 3rd Generation Partnership Project (3GPP), Technical Report, RP 200293, Mar 2020.

[40]   3GPP, "Coexistence between NB-IoT and NR," 3rd Generation Partnership Project (3GPP), Technical Report, 37.824, Jun 2020.

[41]   3GPP, "New Study WID on NB-IoT/eTMC support for NTN ," 3rd Generation Partnership Project (3GPP), Technical Report, RP 193235, Dec 2019.

Chapter 4

Introduction to benchmarking IoT middleware platforms

Shalmoly Mondal[1], Prem Prakash Jayaraman[1],
Alireza Hassani[2] and Pari Delir Haghighi[3]

4.1 Introduction

Internet of Things (IoT) refers to connecting various devices (commonly called IoT devices) over the Internet, which can interact with each other by sending and receiving data. These connected devices in the IoT ecosystem are expected to increase to 75.44 billion by 2025 [1]. This would be a threefold increase from the IoT installed base in 2019 [2]. Collecting these connected devices, a part of the IoT ecosystem, generates enormous data. IoT devices have the capability to monitor the environment, e.g., sensing the temperature of a building (sensing). This data is used by IoT applications to help in making a decision, such as turning on the heater when the temperature drops below a certain threshold (actuation). Hence, IoT aims to potentially resolve issues with minimum or no human intervention. More complex IoT applications use data analytics such as machine learning (ML) algorithms, natural language processing (NLP), and other complex analyses to process the IoT data to produce useful and actionable information that aids decision-making.

The plethora of IoT devices has resulted in an explosion of IoT application development. The significant advances in IoT technology have led to IoT applications being widely used in various scenarios ranging from the smart city [3], smart farming [4][5], to Industrial IoT (IIoT) solutions [6]. Industrial and transportation applications are currently dominating the IoT application areas [7]. For example, the IIoT application [6] aims to improve the productivity of factory workers in a meat processing plant by analyzing data and providing worker-specific predictions. This is achieved by analyzing accelerometer data generated by wearable watch-like IoT devices worn on each wrist by these factory workers. An ML-based activity recognition algorithm is being used to detect the various activities of the meat processing workers, like cutting or

[1]School of Science, Computing and Engineering Technologies, Swinburne University of Technology, Melbourne, Australia
[2]School of Information Technology, Deakin University, Australia
[3]Department of Human Centred Computing, Monash Data Futures Institute, Monash University, Melbourne, Australia

slicing chunks of meat. These activities are then translated to Key Performance Indicators (KPIs) for assessing the performance of individual workers. Another example can be taken of a smart parking application scenario [8], which provides a prediction mechanism for available parking spots by considering factors like the location, weather, and physical attributes of the car.

Smart farming is another area that takes advantage of IoT. There are many added benefits like being able to check soil fertility, analyze crop performance and provide recommendations. Various sensors are used for monitoring the soil fertility, to check the salinity, PH levels, and moisture levels in the soil, which can affect crop production. The data from these sensors can be analyzed to decide if irrigation is necessary and when would be the right time for cultivation. An IoT platform, SmartFarmNet [5] has been developed for smart farming applications which perform crop performance analysis and provide crop recommendations. Another scenario in the farming industry that leverages the benefits of IoT is monitoring the fertility of dairy cattle, which is an important aspect of dairy production. However, the decline in fertility of dairy cows has been a major concern for the dairy industry for a long time. IoT applications can be used for fertility management of dairy cattle [9]. Sensors are attached to the dairy cows, which periodically measure the heat status and notify farmers. IoT applications also find their use in health scenarios. For example, an IoT application can use a smartwatch sensor to predict blood alcohol content (BAC) to avoid drunk driving [10]. The application would be highly beneficial as it can warn its users if they become too intoxicated. Similarly, health vitals from a wearable IoT device combined with an activity recognition algorithm (based on ML) can be used to detect falls in elderly person [11].

As seen from the above examples of the different IoT applications, IoT provides enhanced services to applications connected to the internet using the data generated from the IoT devices. This IoT data can be heterogeneous, e.g., image or time-series sensor data. IoT is also characterized by diversity in various devices, communication, and network protocols. To cope with this diversity, IoT middleware platforms are increasingly being used to manage the devices, and data generated by them, and host IoT applications to facilitate the application development process [12]. The current research trend shows that the market for IoT middleware is expected to reach a value of USD 22.36 billion by 2025 [13]. IoT middleware provides several benefits, including the ability to break silos, manage the integration of data from different application domains, and enable IoT applications to share data between applications. Hence, with such rapid development of IoT applications, IoT middleware platforms are increasingly being used to expedite the application development and deployment process.

The performance of an IoT application depends on the choice of middleware platforms. Traditionally, users deploy IoT applications without sufficient knowledge about the IoT platform they should consider. With so many choices of existing IoT platforms, it is not clear how IoT application developers can make a choice of a platform that suits their needs. Hence, there is a need for a methodology to assess the performance of various IoT middleware platforms and to be able to compare the performance. The aim of this chapter is to give a brief overview of IoT middleware platforms and their significance. We will also discuss the state-of-the-art benchmarking IoT middleware platforms and present the research gaps and challenges. The rest of the chapter is organized as follows. Section 4.2 describes a motivating scenario that highlights the significance of this research. Section 4.3 discusses the evolution of a middleware-based architecture of the IoT ecosystem. Section 4.4 provides an overview of the IoT middleware platforms and presents some commonly used open-source and commercial IoT platforms. Section 4.5 introduces benchmarking and the related work in benchmarking IoT middleware platforms. Section 4.6 discusses the challenges and open issues in the area. Section 4.7 concludes the chapter with a road map for future work.

4.2 Motivating scenario

Let us consider a traffic monitoring and road safety scenario, which monitors the traffic status and sends alerts to the drivers in case of road accidents or traffic congestion.

Figure 4.1 shows the different tasks involved in this application scenario. The IoT devices used in this scenario are: (i) surveillance cameras for capturing video data streams; (ii) traffic sensors (like ultrasonic sensors, radars, and loop detectors) monitor the data and get the number of vehicles; (iii) on-board sensors, speed sensors, and GPS-enabled vehicles calculate the speed and get the location of the vehicles. Surveillance cameras are mostly used to detect road traffic. The data from these devices is collected for processing. Pre-processing of the data, like aggregations, is done on the data to find the cumulative density (no. of vehicles) of a road and

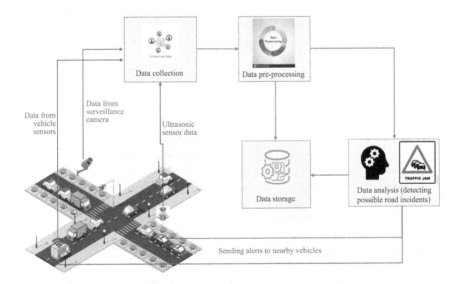

Figure 4.1   Traffic monitoring and road safety in smart cities

Table 4.1   Components and tasks involved in a traffic monitoring scenario

Num	Components	Description
1.	IoT devices	Capturing data from the environment including cameras, ultrasonic sensors, traffic light sensors, etc.
2.	Data collection	The data captured from the IoT devices are collected for further processing
3.	Data pre-processing	(i) Performing aggregation to find the cumulative density of a road; (ii) calculating the avg speed of the vehicles
4.	Data storage	Data from the sensors are stored to support further data analysis
5.	Data analysis	Transforming raw data captured from the sensors to detect possible road incidents and compute peak hours of traffic during different times of the day

calculate the avg speed of the vehicles. Data can either be analyzed in real-time to detect traffic events or stored at a repository for further analysis to detect traffic congestion or predict near misses. For example, traffic lights can be controlled if the number of vehicles exceeds the threshold. For example, the duration of the green signal can be increased. The traffic status (peak traffic hours/statistics of the traffic on the road) can be presented graphically to the users. All these computations are taken care of by IoT middleware. Hence, IoT middleware platforms play a key role in deploying IoT applications. They act as an intermediary and provide data to the IoT applications. The data from these various IoT devices can be sent to IoT middleware platforms using various communication protocols like MQTT, CoAP, AMQP, etc. After the data is received by the middleware, the data can be pre-processed, stored, or analyzed as seen in Figure 4.1. Table 4.1 briefly summarizes the functionality of each component involved in the above scenario. There are different components of a middleware platform that are responsible for all these different computations. We will discuss the different middleware components and their functionalities in detail in Section 4.3.

Considering the above example of the traffic monitoring scenario, where heterogeneous IoT data (e.g., IoT data from surveillance cameras, traffic sensors, onboard vehicle sensors) needs to be analyzed (using ML or complex event processing (CEP)) to predict events (e.g., road congestion or accidents) and send alerts to the users immediately. An IoT middleware platform can provide support to integrate the surveillance cameras, collect the data from them, store the data, provide support to run analysis to process image data, and provide the analyzed data to the IoT application. IoT middleware platforms such as Amazon Web Service [14], Microsoft Azure [15], FIWARE [16], Cumulocity [17], OpenIoT [18], to name a few offer various managed services which take care of the above-mentioned tasks. For example, AWS leverages managed AWS IoT services like IoT Core, IoT Greengrass, IoT Analytics, to collect, store, and analyze data. Similarly, Microsoft Azure provides services like IoT

Edge, IoT Event Hub, Azure Time-series insights for the same tasks. These diverse services offered by various middleware platforms make it a challenging task for IoT application developers to choose the IoT platform that suits the needs of their IoT application. Hence, despite the popularity and widespread use of IoT middleware platforms to host IoT applications, there is no systematic approach to compare the different IoT middleware platforms which can provide a common ground to enable an apple-to-apple comparison.

4.3 Middleware-based architecture of the IoT ecosystem

There exist several definitions of IoT middleware in the literature. The terms IoT middleware, IoT middleware platform, and IoT platform are generally used interchangeably. Razzaque *et al.* [19] have defined the IoT platform as "a software package that integrates devices, networks, and applications." In [20], middleware has been defined as "the software layer between technological and application layers." Bandyopadhyay *et al.* [12] defined IoT middleware as "a software platform providing an abstraction to applications from the things and offering multiple services."

In this section, we discuss the evolution of the middleware-based architecture of the IoT ecosystem and provide an overview of the architecture model considered in this study. The IoT ecosystem is complex, consisting of heterogeneous sources of data, and multiple layers of processing, and follows a layered architecture [21]. During the last decade, various architectures have been proposed by the research community. Figure 1.2 represents some of the most popular IoT architectures, namely (a) Three-layer [22], (b) middleware based [23], (c) SOA based [24], and (d) Five-layer [21] [25].

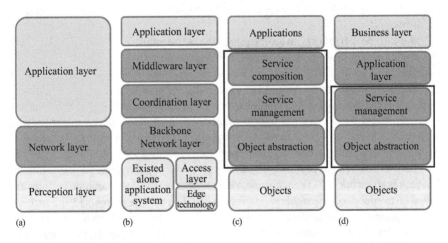

Figure 4.2   IoT architecture. (a) The three-layer IoT architecture. (b) Middleware based. (c) SOA based. (d) Five-layer [24].

The most basic architecture for the IoT ecosystem is a three-layer architecture consisting of a perception layer, a network platform layer, and an application layer (Figure 4.2(a)) [26]. The perception layer [22] is for identifying objects and gathering information. It consists of physical objects and sensor devices. The sensors can be RFID tags, 2D-barcode, cameras, GPS, or Infrared sensor subject to the objects identification method. The collected information from these devices is then passed to the network layer for its secure transmission to the information processing system. The network layer can also be called "Transmission Layer." Its main function is transmitting, and processing information obtained from the perception layer. The transmission medium can be wired, or wireless, and technology can be 3G, UMTS, Wi-Fi, Bluetooth, infrared, ZigBee, etc., depending upon the sensor devices [23]. The application layer includes applications that use IoT technology. The applications of IoT can be smart homes, smart cities, smart health, animal tracking, etc. [27].

The three layered architecture model has been improved in [21,23] with four and five-layered architectures. The middleware layer in Figure 4.2(b) provides functionality like data storage and processing. The IoT devices connect to the middleware and communicate with other devices through different communication protocols like MQTT, HTTP, and ACMP. The middleware receives the information from the IoT devices and the network layer and stores the collected data in the database. It performs data processing and computation on the data [23]. The object abstraction layer in Figure 4.2(c) transfers data produced by the objects layer to the service management layer through secure channels. Data can be transferred through various technologies such as RFID, 3G, GSM, UMTS, Wi-Fi, Bluetooth Low Energy, infrared, and Zig-Bee [24]. The object abstraction, service management, and service composition layer together in Figure 4.2(c) provide all capabilities that a middleware layer typically provides. Similarly, in Figure 4.2(d), the object abstraction, and service management layer can be called a middleware layer since these layers function as a middleware layer. It is shown by a black box in the figure. This layer enables the IoT application programmers to work with heterogeneous objects without consideration of a specific hardware platform.

We can see that there is no uniformity in the architectures described. Furthermore, the problem with most of the proposed IoT architecture is they are domain-specific (vertical IoT silos) [28,29]. Moreover, due to the variety of available IoT architectures, there arise interoperability issues [25], as no standard architecture has been officially adopted. Thus, a mutual understanding is needed to break the IoT Silos so that data can be reused, facilitate interoperability issues, and provide horizontal integration [24]. An architecture that can be used across several application domains is the key to ensuring mutual understanding. Realizing the importance of having a standard architecture for IoT, several IoT-related projects, co-funded by the European Commission under the Seventh Framework (FP7) Programme, were initiated to design a common architecture based on the needs of researchers and the industry. The SENSEI project [30], European Telecommunications Standards Institute (ETSI) [31], IoT-A [32] have been partially successful in defining architectures for different IoT applications. The authors of [33] presents an overview of the work done toward defining such a common architecture. ETSI Machine to machine (M2M) technical committee aimed to define the end-to-end high-level system architecture for M2M. The Internet-of-Things Architecture (IoT-A) project aims to provide a general Architecture Reference Model (ARM) that can be used to derive concrete IoT architectures. While all the efforts are working towards a blueprint architecture, given the evolving nature of IoT, a standard architecture for the IoT ecosystem still exists that has been agreed on universally.

Based on the literature, most IoT applications use a middleware-based architecture. Considering the popularity of middleware and the ease of using them for hosting IoT applications, for this research, we consider a simple three-layer architecture model of the IoT system as recommended by IoT-A [32]. Figure 4.2 shows the layers of the architecture model used by most IoT applications consisting of a device layer, an IoT middleware platform layer, and the IoT application layer. The device layer is responsible for sensing and actuating. It consists of IoT devices that have integrated sensors and actuators. These IoT devices have the capability to register with the cloud securely and have connectivity options for sending and receiving data to and from the cloud. Depending on the type of IoT device, the information can be about location, temperature, orientation, motion, vibration, acceleration, etc. For example, in our traffic monitoring and road safety motivating scenario, the device layer consists of surveillance cameras for capturing video data streams, traffic sensors (like ultrasonic sensors, radars, and loop detectors) to get the number of vehicles crossing a particular road at any point of time, and onboard vehicle speed sensors and GPS to calculate the speed and location of the vehicles. The collected information is then passed to the middleware platform layer for further analysis. The IoT middleware platform layer is an intermediary between IoT devices and IoT applications. It provides functionalities to ease the development and deployment of IoT applications. The middleware platform layer consists of various components to perform different tasks. For example, it provides the ability to collect data from IoT devices and serve it to IoT applications. It can also process and analyze the data collected from IoT devices. The topmost layer, the application layer, is responsible for interacting with the end users, such as providing a response (analyzed data) to the user's query or issuing queries or actuation signals. It is in this layer that users deploy applications. We will analyze existing IoT platforms from the perspective of a middleware-based architecture and discuss the fundamental components of an IoT middleware platform in the next section.

4.3.1 Component and functionalities of IoT middleware platforms

In the previous section, we discussed the different layers in a middleware-based architecture of the IoT ecosystem. In this section, we focus on the fundamental components of the IoT middleware platform layer illustrated in Figure 4.3. The components were identified after analyzing various IoT middleware platforms. Some commonly used IoT middleware platforms have been discussed in Section 4.4.

Device integration and data ingestion: Device integration provides an interface for devices to communicate with the IoT middleware platform. Device integration often involves device registration, device discovery, and device authentication. Device registration makes tracking and monitoring the devices easy, as several devices exist for every IoT deployment. Registering each device to the IoT platform gives a unique

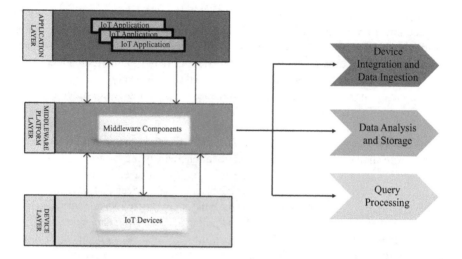

Figure 4.3   Fundamental components of the IoT middleware platform layer

identifier for secure communication with other devices and components of the IoT ecosystem. It also helps with authentication on a network. Device discovery allows users to know the properties and capabilities of IoT devices. Device authentication is required to verify the identity of the devices. After the devices have been registered into the platform, IoT data can be ingested from the devices to the middleware. This can be done using communication protocols like MQTT, CoAP, or AMQP. After the data is ingested, middlewares can transform the data for storage into data stores. One of the most common mechanisms used for data ingestion is Apache Kafka.

Data processing and storage: IoT data can be stored persistently for further analysis, or streaming data can be analyzed in real-time depending on the IoT applications. Applications like the traffic monitoring scenario discussed in Section 4.1 require real-time data analysis to obtain timely insights. This component provides both of these functionalities. Data storage acts as persistent storage for data from IoT devices for further analysis and querying. It stores the processed IoT data streams and historical data that have been cleaned to fit a relational schema. Data can either be stored in relational databases if ACID properties are a priority to speed and scalability, or they can be stored in No-SQL databases like MongoDB, Cassandra, and Hadoop, among others. Amazon S3 and Amazon Relational Database Service (RDS) are examples of data storage mechanisms provided by AWS. Similarly, FIWARE [16] uses a context management generic enabler to store, access, and analyze data. Common mechanisms used for data analysis are ML techniques like classification, clustering, and regression. Data analytics leads naturally to predictive analytics using collected data to predict what might happen. For example, a predictive analysis mechanism like image recognition can be used in the traffic monitoring scenario to predict the possibilities of road congestion. Similarly, in a mobile application for air quality monitoring [34] in a smart city environment, the mobile crowd-sensed data provided in real-time by wearable sensors are used to analyze and infer air quality. The k-means clustering algorithm has been used to understand the correlation between the sensed variables like temperature, humidity, CO, and SO_2 and analyze their contribution to the air quality conditions.

Data retrieval and analysis: Query processing is a crucial factor in data processing for IoT applications, as most IoT applications are data-intensive, and they rely on querying as an elemental mechanism to access and retrieve data. Different types of queries can be issued depending on the IoT application running on the platform. There could be simple or complex queries, or push or pull-based queries. For example, an event-based IoT application will require a push-based query to get a suitable response. A simple push-based query would trigger a rule when any event occurs. For example, a query in such a situation would be "send an alert when there is road congestion, i.e., no_of_cars is greater than 20 on road_x."

4.4   IoT middleware platforms – a summary

With IoT platforms being widely used, various commercial and open-source middleware platforms are being used for hosting IoT applications.

4.4.1   Open source IoT middleware platforms

OpenIoT [18] is an open-source IoT platform that provides an integrated environment for deploying and managing IoT applications. It is licensed under Apache license 2.0. The fundamental concept here is virtual sensors. OpenIoT includes a sensor middleware that eases data acquisition from virtually any sensor. Various components serve different functionalities. OpenIoT uses X-GSN middleware to register the sensors, data acquisition, and sensor deployment. The sensor middleware contains a publish-subscribe middleware responsible for discovering and collecting data from mobile sensors (e.g., wearable sensors, built-in mobile devices). Data storage is enabled by a cloud database, which enables storage of data streams from the sensor middleware. The configuration and monitoring component enables visual management and configuration of functionalities over sensors and services deployed within the OpenIoT platform.

FIWARE [16] is another open-source IoT platform. FIWARE architecture has a set of components called General Enablers (GE). Each GE represents a FIWARE service. This rich suite of generic enablers deals with context management, interfacing with IoT systems, and data processing, analysis, and visualization. The *Orion Context Broker* Generic Enabler is the core and mandatory component of any FIWARE solution. It is a data/context management component. It enables us to manage context information in a highly decentralized and large-scale manner. The data storage mechanism used by this platform is a Context broker service. It uses a connector called *Cygnus* which is responsible for persisting or retrieving from a specific storage. The STH *Comet* Generic Enabler can store a short-term history of context data (typically months) on MongoDB. It can be used to manage the time-series data, e.g., reading the temperature history of a sensor. Orion uses a Publish/Subscribe mechanism to store and retrieve context information. Orion can create context elements, update, and query them. The context elements are represented as JSON key-value pairs following the NGSIV2 standard. FIWARE NGSI v2 API is a Restful API enabling to perform updates, queries, or subscribe to changes on context information. FIWARE also provides several GE to interface with IoT and other systems. The *IDAS* Generic Enabler can connect IoT devices to the platform. IoT sensor enablement is responsible for integrating the sensors into the platform and registering sensor devices. Proton is used to register subscriptions with the context broker and to emit alerts once some unusual pattern in sensor data is detected.

Kaa [35] is an open-source server-based platform developed by CyberVision Corporation. It is suitable for enterprise-grade IoT applications and home-grown IoT projects and experiments. Kaa implements a microservice-based architecture. All Kaa microservices are available as docker images. Most microservices are written in Java, Go, and TypeScript, but users can also implement integrated microservices in Python and Scala. To use multiple services as one integrated platform, they can be deployed in a cluster. In simple terms, Kaa-based IoT solutions would be deployed as a cluster of microservices. One of the key concepts in Kaa is an *endpoint* which represents the things or devices of the IoT ecosystem. Another key concept is a *client*, essentially a gateway. Kaa client can be any software application that recognizes an endpoint and sends and receives data using IoT communication protocols. The communication protocols supported by this platform are HTTP, CoAP, MQTT, and WebSockets. *Endpoint Tokens* are used for identifying any device communicating with the platform. Kaa leverages multiple third-party services to carry out the platform's functionalities. For example, data storage is implemented by Cassandra, Influx, and MongoDB. Similarly, data analysis in Kaa is supported by integrating with Open Distro for ElasticSearch, a third-party open-source data analytics platform. The platform offers data visualization capabilities via the platform component *Web Dashboard Service*. Kaa also provides a pre-configured virtual environment called *Kaa sandbox* for small-scale development and testing. The sandbox can run either in a VirtualBox environment or on AWS EC2. Kaa also integrates business tools like SAP, Salesforce, etc.

ThingSpeak [36] is an open-source cloud-based platform that can be used for applications like smart farming and environment monitoring. Device integration to this platform can be done with MQTT and HTTP. Data processing can be implemented in Ruby, Python, and Node.js. It also provides APIs that support advanced data analysis using MATLAB® scripts. Additionally, it has a web interface that allows users to visualize the data using charts. Widgets can be created in JavaScript/HTML/CSS for a customized dashboard experience.

ThingsBoard [37] supports both cloud and on-premises deployments. ThingsBoard follows a microservice architecture. It supports REST communications with the server. Protocols like MQTT, CoAP, and HTTP can do device integration. The devices can be authenticated using access tokens. The platform leverages Redis, an in-memory data structure for data storage. Furthermore, ThingsBoard uses Zookeeper for coordination on the clusters. For data analysis, the platform uses a Rule Engine, a highly customizable CEP framework for building event-based workflows. ThingsBoard rule engine consists of three main components: (i) *Message*, which is any incoming event. (ii) *Rule Node*, a function executed on an incoming message. (iii) *Rule Chain* are the nodes connected to send outbound messages to the next connected node. ThingsBoard integrates third-party services to operate the platform. For example, ThingsBoard uses Apache Kafka to persist incoming telemetry from HTTP/MQTT/CoAP transports until the rule engine processes it. ThingsBoard also uses Kafka for some API calls between micro-services. The platform also allows us to create customizable IoT dashboards for data visualization.

Node-RED [38] is a Node.js-based middleware platform from IBM. It implements an actor-based architecture. The basic concept of this platform is a *node*, which encapsulates a block of JavaScript codes that performs a specific function. Each node can be called an actor. Node-RED is a lightweight platform built on Node.js and features an event-driven, non-blocking model making it ideal for running on edge devices like Raspberry Pi, Beaglebone Black, and Arduino. The platform supports communication protocols like MQTT and Websockets. The key feature of Node-RED is a visual tool that allows flow-based programming for wiring hardware devices. The tool allows drag-and-drop functionalities to wire up any IoT application. Some other concepts associated with tools are: (i) *Flow*, which is a set of connected nodes. (ii) *Wires* connect the nodes and represent how messages pass through the flow. (iii) *Context*, which is a way to store information between the nodes. (iv) *Message*, which passes between the nodes in a flow.

Agri-IoT [39] is another open-source platform for smart farming applications. The platform has components like a device manager for device authentication and identity, a discovery module for registration and discovery of IoT devices, data aggregation to deal with large volumes of data using time series analysis, and data compression techniques to reduce the size of raw sensory observations, data federation which deals with users' requests. It translates users' requests into RDF Stream Processing (RSP) queries and evaluates them to obtain results. Event detection provides tools for processing annotated and aggregated data streams to obtain farm events, such as the need for irrigation, sick animals, or pest identification in crops. Real-time adaptive reasoning considers the farmer's preferences and dynamic contextual farm-related information (represented by real-time events). To provide optimal decision support in real-time, a dashboard provides immediate and intuitive visual access to the results of processing and analysis of data and events.

Context-as-a-service (CooaS) [29] is a context management platform that manages the interaction and enables applications and services to share context seamlessly without requiring the manual integration of IoT silos. The middleware has various components, namely Security and Communication Manager, Context Query Engine (CQE), Context Storage Management System (CSMS), and Context Reasoning Engine (CRE).

4.4.2 *Commercial IoT platforms*

AWS IoT [14] is a commercial platform that allows communication between Internet-connected devices such as sensors, actuators, smart devices, and the AWS. The device gateway enables communication between publishers and subscribers. It currently supports publishing and subscribing over secure MQTT, WebSockets, and HTTPS. Device software like *AWS IoT Greengrass* also provides local data collection and analysis at the edge, even without internet connectivity. *AWS IoT* Core is a managed service that allows connected devices like cars, lights, smart speakers, cameras, fans, and any other item to interact with cloud applications and other devices quickly and securely. Devices are registered via Device Registry. The Device Shadow feature enables cloud and mobile applications to query data sent from the devices and send commands to devices using a simple REST API. AWS IoT Core rules engine allows filtering, transforming, and acting upon device data on the fly. Amazon IoT uses a variety of durable storage solutions provided by Amazon, like *Amazon RDS*, *Amazon Dynamo Db*, etc. Amazon IoT platform is a highly scalable and can handle a high streaming data rate. AWS uses a managed service called *Amazon Kinesis Firehose* to ingest real-time streaming and bulk data. Amazon Kinesis supports streaming data, enabling us to get timely insights and react quickly to the latest information from IoT devices. Amazon Kinesis integrates directly with the AWS IoT rules engine, creating a seamless way of bridging from a lightweight device protocol of a device using MQTT with the internal IoT applications that use other protocols.

Azure IoT [15] is a commercial cloud-based IoT platform providing scalable Internet of Things (IoT) applications using the Azure IoT managed and platform services. Azure IoT simplifies creating, securing, and managing devices across the entire device lifecycle. *Azure IoT Hub* messaging provides device-to-cloud and cloud-to-device communications. Devices can communicate with the IoT Hub over HTTP, MQTT protocols. The stream processor component in Azure IoT processes large streams of data records and evaluates rules for those streams. Azure uses a data factory or *databricks* for ingesting data. For data storage, Azure IoT integrates warm and cold storage services provided by Microsoft Azure. Azure supports data analysis by the ML subsystem, enabling systems to learn from data and experiences and act without being explicitly programmed. The user management subsystem allows the specification of different capabilities for users and groups to perform actions on devices (e.g., command and control such as upgrading firmware for a device) and capabilities for users in applications.

Cumulocity IoT [17] is another platform in this category, which provides support for IoT device integration, device management, offers streaming and batch analytics, and data visualization capabilities. It has a built-in extensive domain model which stores the domain data. The model can be extended for further uses and is complementary to SSN. Cumulocity also provides API for extending the existing functionality or interfacing Cumulocity IoT with other IT services such as ERP or CRM systems. It is specifically designed to work with Mobile networks. The platform also allows interfacing of IoT devices through software agents. The platform currently supports two main types of agent architecture: *server-side agents* and *device-side agents*. Server-side agents are run in a cloud, hosted on Cumulocity IoT as microservices, whereas device-side agents run on a device in the sensor network. Cumulocity provides a high-level real-time processing language to run IoT business logic. *Apama's Event Processing Language (EPL)* can be used with Cumulocity for real-time processing.

The cockpit application feature provides data visualization functionality. It can be used to manage and monitor IoT data.

ThingWorx is a cloud-based M2M platform by PTC targeted for IIoT solutions. Device integration in this platform is supported by REST API. It provides a tool *AlwaysOn* for communication between edge devices and the platform. Authentication of devices for communicating with ThingWorx is supported by *Applicationkeys*, which are security tokens. Integrates data from various sources like edge devices, and data from sales and ERP systems. SDKs supported by the platform are C, Java, and .NET SDK's. *Edge Microserver (EMS)* allows edge devices and data stored to connect to the platform. The C SDK is the basis for EMS. *Persistence Provider* is a concept in ThingWorx that enables connecting to a data store and performing CRUD operations on the data. The data storage options offered by this platform are H2, PostgreSQL, Microsoft SQL Server, Azure SQL database, and InfluxDB. The persistence provider framework of the ThingWorx platform can be configured to use multiple data stores for a given data provider. This feature can be leveraged to distribute the data ingestion and query processing workload to multiple data stores to overcome the typical RDBMS vertical scalability limitations. It provided data analysis capabilities that allow building predictive models using AI and ML technologies. For data visualization, the platform provides a tool, *mashup widgets*, for creating the functional user interface. Have a dedicated application store called PTC marketplace.

SmartFarmNet [5] is another IoT platform developed for smart framing to increase farm productivity. Currently, crop performance is collected manually under various conditions like soil quality, etc., which is slow. SmartFarmNet has been developed to automate the collection of environmental, soil, fertilization, and irrigation data; automatically correlate such data and filter-out invalid data from the perspective of assessing crop performance; and compute crop forecasts and personalized crop recommendations for any farm.

4.5 Benchmarking IoT middleware platforms

In this section, we introduce benchmarking, terminologies related to benchmarking, and the state-of-the-art in benchmarking IoT middleware platforms.

4.5.1 Introduction to benchmarking

The term benchmarking is defined in the Oxford Dictionary as "Evaluating something by comparison with a standard." Xerox's [40] formal definition of benchmarking is "the continuous process of measuring products, services, and practices against the company's toughest competitors or those companies known as industry leaders." In short, it means "finding and implementing best practices." The practice of benchmarking is now being applied to various other domains. Camp [41] defines benchmarking as creating performance results for a given set of tests. These tests represent the performance of an entire application or a component of the application (also known as Micro Benchmarks). The performance results are used as an indicator of how well the application or application components perform given a specific configuration.

Benchmarking vs. profiling

Benchmarking is often confused with the term profiling. Both benchmarking and profiling are used to measure how a system is performing in varying conditions [41]. However, there is a subtle difference between benchmarking and profiling. While benchmarking answers the question, "How well a system performs?" profiling tells us why a system performs how it performs. The benchmark results are used to compare different systems, whereas the result sets of profiling are used to determine the problematic component of a system. Moreover, in benchmarking, it is essential to define a standard set of datasets and queries to measure the performance of the different systems (e.g., IoT middleware platforms) under consideration fairly. In this research, we consider benchmarking as *"A mechanism by which we can establish benchmarks for different IoT middleware platforms running IoT applications by using a standard set of IoT data and queries."* The benchmarks must be repeatable and can provide the foundations for conducting empirical, experimental comparisons between IoT middleware platforms. By establishing benchmarks, we mean measuring the performance of IoT middleware platforms and comparing them based on certain metrics like query response time, data ingestion rate, security, and accuracy of the analytical mechanism being used by the IoT application.

Benchmarking metrics: For any benchmarking methodology, we need to define metrics or criteria based on which the performance of a system will be evaluated. We call these "benchmarking metrics." These metrics could be performance metrics like throughput, and response time, security metrics like data encryption, and device authentication, or resource usage like CPU, and memory utilization of the underlying resources.Other metrics include scalability, reliability, and availability. Some of the metrics are discussed below:

- *Response time*: average time difference between the time an input arrives and the time a response/outcome is generated.
- *Throughput*: the number of tasks completed per unit of time.
- *Execution time*: time to execute a given task.
- *Data ingestion rate*: time difference between when the data is being generated and when it is being inserted into the platform.
- *Supported query load*: the maximum input a system can process while meeting specific constraints like response time.
- *Scalability*: a system can handle many requests simultaneously.
- *Reliability*: [42] how a system can operate without failure for a given time.
- *Availability*: [42] time for which the system is accessible to the user.

4.5.2 State-of-the-art in benchmarks in IoT

In [43], two middleware platforms FIWARE and M2M have been compared based on a set of qualitative and quantitative metrics. The data used for conducting the benchmarks is a large publish-subscribe dataset from a traffic monitoring scenario that publishes the average traffic speed in each city street on an hourly basis. However, the middleware platforms have been considered a black box without considering the internal implementation. The authors reported that the middleware performance could depend on its different components like the data storage or the underlying communications protocol. However, it only focuses on publish/subscribe middleware platforms. In another work by Medvedev *et al.* [44], OpenIoT has been evaluated based on its data ingestion and storage capability.

Similarly, in another case study by Salhofer *et al.* [45], the FIWARE platform has been thoroughly analyzed and evaluated from an application deployment point of view. However, no performance and load test has been conducted. The web interface falls short on some fundamental functionalities. For example, it is currently not possible to modify, delete, or view existing permissions, which do not make the application fit for real-life use.

Agarwal *et al.* [46] provide a layer-wise comparative analysis of the IoT middleware and define some criteria for the selection of the right IoT middleware platform like availability, deployment type, and pricing model. Cruz *et al.* [47] give a performance evaluation study of a few existing middleware platforms. Qualitative and quantitative metrics have been proposed to evaluate the performance of the IoT Middleware platforms. The proposed metrics were tested with five middleware platforms: InatelPlat, Konker, Linksmart, Orion+STH, and Sitewhere. It has been reported that the different middleware platforms performed differently depending on the metrics. For example, in case of low throughput and packet size, Konker and Linksmart performed better, whereas when error percentage is the priority, Orion +SSH gives the best performance with less than a 1% error rate. Sitewhere operated well with concurrent users.

Some other research efforts towards IoT benchmarks include some benchmarking suites like IoTBench [52], a benchmark suite targeting the IoT edge devices. IoTBench includes seven representative applications from three categories that exhibit diversity in IoT. Shukla *et al.* [51] have proposed RIoTBench, a novel benchmarking suite for evaluating the data ingestion capabilities for IoT Applications. The benchmarking suite comprises of micro- and application-level benchmarks for the evaluation. The conventional processing and analytic tasks that are carried out over real-time IoT data streams have been categorized based on domain requirements. However, the benchmarking suite is limited to DSPS applications that are centrally hosted in the cloud and do not integrate edge or fog. Arlitt *et al.* [50] have introduced IoTABench, a benchmark suite for evaluating data analytics capability. The use case to demonstrate their proposed benchmark is of a smart metering scenario. For the dataset, they have used smart meter data which is generated using a Markov chain-based synthetic data generator. The benchmark consists of synthetic data, and six analytical queries: total readings, total consumption, peak consumption, top consumers, and time of

Table 4.2   Summary of the existing benchmark studies in IoT

Related works	Benchmarking targets	Benchmarking metrics	Capturing application requirements	IoT dataset	IoT queries
BenchIoT [48]	Device layer	Resource usage, performance metrics	NS[b]	NC[c]	NC
TPCx-IoT [49]	Device layer	IoTps[a], throughput	NS	Electric power stations	Real-time analytic queries
IoTAbench [50]	IoT middleware platform layer	NS	NC	Smart meter data	Statistical queries
RIoTBench [51]	IoT middleware platform layer	Latency, throughput, CPU, memory utilization	NS	NC	NC

Source: Text roughly sketched.
[a]Performance metrics.
[b]Not specified.
[c]Not considered.

usage billing. In this benchmark suite, each benchmark represents a distinct use case. However, currently, only one use case has been implemented.

TPC council, which has been successful in creating benchmarks for databases, introduced TPCx-IoT [53], a benchmark for comparing the performance of IoT gateways. They have implemented a use case of power substations of Electric utility providers. They have used a dataset of an electric power substation. The TPCx-IoT workload generator is based on the Yahoo! Cloud Serving Benchmark framework. The TPCx-IoT workloads consist of data ingestion and concurrent queries simulating workloads on typical IoT Gateway systems. The primary metrics used in TPCx-IoT benchmark in the IoTps (performance metric) and $/IoTps (price-performance metric).

After analyzing the existing IoT benchmarks, we have observed that existing research in benchmarking is fragmented, i.e., existing approaches have specific benchmarking targets. By benchmarking targets, we mean the layer of the IoT ecosystem being addressed. For example, in Table 4.2, BenchIoT [48] and TPCx-IoT [49] target the IoT device layer while IoTAbench [50] and RIoTbench [51] focuses on IoT middleware layer. Furthermore, other research in benchmarking for IoT middleware platforms focuses on selected components of middleware platforms. For example, IoTAbench [50] specifically data analysis, whereas RIoT bench is targeted towards data ingestion of the middleware layer. Additionally, some of the benchmarks are application-specific and cannot be applied to more than one use-case [50]. To address these gaps in the literature, we need a comprehensive approach that can be used to benchmark IoT middleware platforms. Hence, a holistic framework that can generate meaningful benchmarks will allow us to compare these different IoT middleware platforms and enable the users to select the appropriate platform for their application deployment. While there has been a lot of work done in related areas like big data, stream processing, etc., there is limited work for IoT. To accelerate the research effort in that direction, we have identified three factors that we think should be considered while developing a methodology for benchmarking IoT middleware platforms. We will discuss them in the next section.

4.6   Towards a holistic framework for benchmarking IoT middleware – challenges and open issues

To develop a holistic framework for benchmarking IoT middleware, we discuss the identified factors and their significance below. We also discuss the challenges and the open issues.

Capturing IoT application requirements: IoT applications are being used in various domains, wherein the requirements of IoT applications vary across these domains. As an example, a real-time application such as the traffic monitoring motivating scenariohas requirements like near-real-time data processing and low latency. Whenever any incident occurs, alerts should be broadcasted to the nearby drivers near an accident location as soon as possible. When deployed in an IoT middleware platform, such applications need to deliver outcomes within certain IoT application requirements. For example, notify the user within "x" milliseconds of any road event occurring, alerts/warnings should be sent, and the nearby drivers should be notified. However, most existing benchmarks do not clearly define the application requirements. While there is some related work that makes the best effort in defining IoT application requirements, this cannot be directly adopted for benchmarking purposes.

Generating IoT dataset: The second criterion is access to an IoT dataset for creating benchmarks. IoT data is different from traditional data. While traditional data is static, IoT data is dynamic, real-time, and changing frequently. In traditional cases, like in the case of database benchmarks, data semantics is unimportant. In the case of IoT applications, we want to know the context of the application, and based on the context, we want to generate datasets that represent the IoT applications. Creating benchmarks for IoT middleware platforms for IoT use cases requires access to large volumes of data generated by IoT devices. However, real data may not always be available to represent events such as earthquakes or road accidents where the velocity of data is far greater. While benchmarks in databases have well-established standard datasets, there is limited literature on IoT benchmarks that focus on generating data for IoT applications. Table 4.2 shows that none of the existing benchmarks takes into consideration the IoT application requirement in being able to generate relevant IoT datasets and IoT queries.

Designing benchmark queries: Queries are another integral part of any benchmarking framework. Limited research efforts exist in designing queries for creating benchmarks in IoT. Groups like TPC that create industry-standard benchmarks have developed such queries for database systems. Similarly, such business queries have been created for the BigBench [54] workload for Bigdata systems. However, we are unaware of such query sets in the IoT domain. The only benchmark by TPC in the IoT domain is TPCx-IoT [49], the first industry-standard benchmark for comparing the performance of IoT gateways. The TPCx-IoT workloads consist of concurrent queries simulating workloads on typical IoT Gateway systems. Other research [50] uses simple statistical queries that are insufficient to represent complex IoT application scenarios. Different IoT applications require queries with different complexities and richness. In a smart parking scenario where a vehicle needs to find a suitable parking spot, if we assume the IoT entity making a query is a car, the query might have attributes like the car's location, which vary. We need to simulate or generate the change of location in the query. Hence, it is evident that traditional database queries will not suffice in creating benchmarks for IoT. We need to generate more high-level queries like context-aware queries (queries with geospatial functions, windowing functions, etc.). Most research in IoT benchmark, do not address this diversity and complexity in query generation. The complexity or richness of queries can impact the performance of benchmarks. This is an open problem [8], and one of the challenges would be generating queries that consider the query richness and diversity.

4.7 Conclusion

Currently, there are several IoT middleware platforms that facilitate connecting to IoT devices, managing the data generated by these devices, and hosting IoT applications. These platforms serve a wide variety of IoT applications with varying requirements. However, there are no standard means to benchmark the IoT middleware platforms. Most research in this area has focused on benchmarking cloud-based services. However, in the current literature, there are limited studies on creating holistic benchmarks for IoT middleware platforms. To develop and deploy IoT applications, choosing from the plethora of existing IoT middleware platforms is a challenge. A holistic and reliable IoT benchmarking framework will allow us to compare these different IoT middleware platforms and enable the users to select the most suitable and optimal IoT middleware platform according to their applications' requirements. We have highlighted in Section 4.6 the gaps in existing research and the challenges. We have also identified some criteria that will address the existing gaps in the literature, including (a) capturing the IoT application requirements; (b) generating IoT data taking into consideration the application's context, e.g., generating event-based data that represents an activity walking; and (c) devise IoT queries that provide a rich characterization of IoT applications.

List of abbreviations

Abbreviations	Meaning
IoT	Internet of Things
ML	Machine learning

AMQP   Advanced message queuing protocol
API   Application programming interface
ARM   Architecture reference model
AWS   Amazon Web Service
CB   Context broker
CEP   Complex event processing
CoAP   Constrained application protocol
CRE   Context reasoning engine
DSPS   Distributed stream processing systems
EPL   Event processing language
ERP   Enterprise resource planning
GIS   Geographic information system
GE   Generic enabler
HTTP   Hypertext transfer protocol
M2M   Machine to machine
MQTT   Message queuing telemetry transport
REST   Representational state transfer
RDF   Resource description framework
RFID   Radio-frequency identification
RSP   RDF stream processing
SOA   Service oriented architecture
TPC   Transaction Processing Performance Council
UMTS   Universal mobile telecommunications system
YCSB   Yahoo Cloud Serving Benchmark

References

[1] Department SR. Internet of Things (IoT) connected devices installed base worldwide from 2015 to 2025; 2016 (accessed September 3, 2020). https://www.statista.com/statistics/471264/iot-number-of-connected-devices-worldwide.

[2] News IB. The IoT in 2030: 24 billion connected things generating 1.5 trillion dollar; 2020 (accessed November 1, 2020). https://iotbusinessnews.com/2020/05/20/03177-the-iot-in-2030-24-billion-connected-things-generating-1-5-trillion.

[3] Ta-Shma P, Akbar A, Gerson-Golan G, *et al.* An ingestion and analytics architecture for iot applied to smart city use cases. *IEEE Internet of Things Journal.* 2017;5(2):765–774.

[4] Ahmed N, De D, and Hussain IJIIoTJ. Internet of Things (IoT) for smart precision agriculture and farming in rural areas. *IEEE Internet of Things Journal.* 2018;5(6):4890–4899.

[5] Jayaraman PP, Yavari A, Georgakopoulos D, *et al.* Internet of things platform for smart farming: Experiences and lessons learnt. *Sensors.* 2016;16(11):1884.

[6]   Forkan ARM, Montori F, Georgakopoulos D, *et al.* An industrial IoT solution for evaluating workers' performance via activity recognition. In: *2019 IEEE 39th International Conference on Distributed Computing Systems (ICDCS)*. IEEE; 2019. p. 1393–1403.

[7]   Analytics I. Top 10 IoT applications in 2020; 2020 (accessed Jan 18, 2020). https://iot-analytics.com/top-10-iot-applications-in-2020/.

[8]   Medvedev A, Hassani A, Zaslavsky A, *et al.* Benchmarking IoT context management platforms: High-level queries matter. In: *2019 Global IoT Summit (GIoTS)*. IEEE. p. 1–6.

[9]   Kamilaris A, Gao F, Prenafeta-Boldu FX, *et al.* Agri-IoT: a semantic framework for Internet of Things-enabled smart farming applications. In: *2016 IEEE 3rd World Forum on Internet of Things (WF-IoT)*. IEEE; 2016. p. 442–447.

[10]   Ngu AH, Gutierrez M, Metsis V, *et al.* IoT middleware: a survey on issues and enabling technologies. *IEEE Internet of Things Journal*. 2016;4(1):1–20.

[11]   Jayaraman PP, Forkan ARM, Morshed A, *et al.* Healthcare 4.0: a review of frontiers in digital health. *Wiley Interdisciplinary Reviews: Data Mining and Knowledge Discovery*. 2020;10(2):e1350.

[12]   Bandyopadhyay S, Sengupta M, Maiti S, *et al.* Role of middleware for internet of things: A study. *International Journal of Computer Science and Engineering Survey*. 2011;2(3):94–105.

[13]   Wire B. Global IoT Middleware Market (2020 to 2025) – Growth, Trends, and Forecasts; 2020 (accessed Jan 18, 2020). https://www.businesswire.com/news/home/20201229005254/en/Global-IoT-Middleware-Market-2020-to-2025—Growth-Trends-and-Forecasts—ResearchAndMarkets.com/.

[14]   Amazon Web Service IoT; (accessed July 31, 2020). https://aws.amazon.com/iot.

[15]   Microsoft Azure IoT; (accessed July 31, 2020). https://azure.microsoft.com/en-au/services/iot-hub.

[16]   Fiware; (accessed July 31, 2020). https://www.fiware.org.

[17]   Cumulocity IoT; (accessed October 15, 2020). https://www.softwareag.cloud/site/product/cumulocity-iot.html.

[18]   Open IoT; (accessed October 15, 2020). http://www.openiot.eu.

[19]   Razzaque MA, Milojevic-Jevric M, Palade A, *et al.* Middleware for Internet of Things: a survey. *IEEE Internet of Things Journal*. 2015;3(1):70–95.

[20]   Fersi G. Middleware for Internet of Things: a study. In: *2015 International Conference on Distributed Computing in Sensor Systems*. IEEE; 2015. p. 230–235.

[21]   Tan L and Wang N. Future Internet: The Internet of Things. In: *2010 3rd International Conference on Advanced Computer Theory and Engineering (ICACTE)*, vol. 5. IEEE; 2010. p. V5-376–V5-380.

[22]   Wu M, Lu TJ, Ling FY, *et al.* Research on the architecture of Internet of Things. In: *2010 3rd International Conference on Advanced Computer Theory and Engineering (ICACTE)*, vol. 5. IEEE; 2010. p. V5–484.

[23]   Khan R, Khan SU, Zaheer R, *et al.* Future Internet: the Internet of Things architecture, possible applications and key challenges. In: *2012 10th*

International Conference on Frontiers of Information Technology. IEEE; 2010. p. 257–260.

[24] Al-Fuqaha A, Guizani M, Mohammadi M, *et al*. Internet of Things: a survey on enabling technologies, protocols, and applications. *IEEE Communications Surveys & Tutorials*. 2015;17(4):2347–2376.

[25] Di Martino B, Rak M, Ficco M, *et al*. Internet of Things reference architectures, security and interoperability: a survey. *Internet of Things*. 2018;1:99–112.

[26] Yang Z, Yue Y, Yang Y, *et al*. Study and application on the architecture and key technologies for IOT. In: *2011 International Conference on Multimedia Technology*. IEEE; 2011. p. 747–751.

[27] Burhan M, Rehman RA, Khan B, *et al*. IoT elements, layered architectures and security issues: a comprehensive survey. *Sensors*. 2018;18(9):2796.

[28] Zaslavsky A and Jayaraman PPJU. Discovery in the Internet of Things: the Internet of Things (ubiquity symposium). *Ubiquity symposium*. 2015; 2015(October):1–10.

[29] Hassani A, Medvedev A, Haghighi PD, *et al*. Context-as-a-service platform: exchange and share context in an IoT ecosystem. In: *2018 IEEE International Conference on Pervasive Computing and Communications Workshops (PerCom Workshops)*. IEEE; 2018. p. 385–390.

[30] Presser M, Barnaghi PM, Eurich M, *et al*. The SENSEI project: integrating the physical world with the digital world of the network of the future. *IEEE Communications Magazine*. 2009;47(4):1–4.

[31] Grieco LA, Alaya MB, Monteil T, *et al*. Architecting information centric ETSI-M2M systems. In: *2014 IEEE International Conference on Pervasive Computing and Communication Workshops (PERCOM WORKSHOPS)*. IEEE; 2014. p. 211–214.

[32] De Loof J, SAP CM, Meissner S, *et al*. Internet of Things—architecture IoT-A deliverable D1. 5–Final Architectural Reference Model for the IoT v3. 0.

[33] Krčo S, Pokrić B, and Carrez F. Designing IoT architecture (s): a European perspective. In: *2014 IEEE World Forum on Internet of Things (WF-IoT)*. *IEEE; 2014. p. 79–84*.

[34] Hromic H, Le Phuoc D, Serrano M, *et al*. Real time analysis of sensor data for the Internet of Things by means of clustering and event processing. In: *2015 IEEE International Conference on Communications (ICC)*. IEEE; 2015. p. 685–691.

[35] Kaa Platform; 2021 (accessed July 3rd, 2021). https://www.kaaiot.com/.

[36] ThingSpeak; 2021 (accessed July 3rd, 2021). https://thingspeak.com/pages/learn_more.

[37] Thingsboard; 2021 (accessed July 3rd, 2021). https://thingsboard.io/.

[38] Node-RED; 2021 (accessed July 3rd, 2021). https://nodered.org/docs/.

[39] Kamilaris A, Gao F, Prenafeta-Boldu FX, *et al*. Agri-IoT: a semantic framework for Internet of Things-enabled smart farming applications. In: *2016 IEEE 3rd World Forum on Internet of Things (WF-IoT)*. IEEE; 2016. p. 442–447.

[40] Camp RC. A bible for benchmarking, by Xerox. *Financial Executive*. 1993; 9(4):23–28.

[41]   Kruckenberg M and Pipes J. Benchmarking and profiling. *Pro MySQL*. 2005. p. 189–234.

[42]   Garg SK, Versteeg S, and Buyya R. Smicloud: a framework for comparing and ranking cloud services. In: *2011 Fourth IEEE International Conference on Utility and Cloud Computing*. IEEE; 2011. p. 210–218.

[43]   Aguiar A and Morla R. Lessons learned and challenges on benchmarking publish-subscribe IoT platforms. In: *Proceedings of the 2nd Workshop on Benchmarking Cyber-Physical Systems and Internet of Things*; 2019. p. 24–29.

[44]   Medvedev A, Hassani A, Zaslavsky A, *et al*. Data ingestion and storage performance of iot platforms: Study of openiot. In: *International Workshop on Interoperability and Open-Source Solutions*. Springer. p. 141–157.

[45]   Salhofer P. Evaluating the FIWARE Platform. In: *Proceedings of the 51st Hawaii International Conference on System Sciences*; 2018.

[46]   Agarwal P and Alam M. Investigating IoT Middleware Platforms for Smart Application Development. In *Smart Cities—Opportunities and Challenges: Select Proceedings of ICSC 2019*, pp. 231–244. Springer Singapore, 2020.

[47]   da Cruz MA, Rodrigues JJ, Sangaiah AK, *et al*. Performance evaluation of IoT middleware. *Journal of Network and Computer Applications*. 2018;109:53–65.

[48]   Almakhdhub NS, Clements AA, Payer M, *et al*. Benchiot: a security benchmark for the Internet of Things. In: *2019 49th Annual IEEE/IFIP International Conference on Dependable Systems and Networks (DSN)*. IEEE; 2019. p. 234–246.

[49]   TPCx-IoT); 2021 (accessed June 1, 2021). http://tpc.org/tpcx-iot/default5.asp.

[50]   Arlitt M, Marwah M, Bellala G, *et al*. Iotabench: an Internet of Things analytics benchmark. In: *Proceedings of the 6th ACM/SPEC International Conference on Performance Engineering*. p. 133–144.

[51]   Shukla A, Chaturvedi S, Simmhan YJC, *et al*. Riotbench: an IoT benchmark for distributed stream processing systems. *Concurrency and Computation: Practice and Experience*. 2017;29(21):e4257.

[52]   Lee CI, Lin MY, Yang CL, *et al*. IoTBench: a benchmark suite for intelligent Internet of Things edge devices. In: *2019 IEEE International Conference on Image Processing (ICIP)*. IEEE; 2019. p. 170–174.

[53]   Poess M, Nambiar R, Kulkarni K, *et al*. Analysis of tpcx-iot: the first industry standard benchmark for IoT gateway systems. In: *2018 IEEE 34th International Conference on Data Engineering (ICDE)*. IEEE; 2018. p. 1519–1530.

[54]   Wang L, Zhan J, Luo C, *et al*. Bigdatabench: a big data benchmark suite from internet services. In: *2014 IEEE 20th International Symposium on High Performance Computer Architecture (HPCA)*. IEEE; 2014. p. 488–499.

Chapter 5

SLA conceptual model for IoT applications

Awatif Alqahtani[1], Ellis Solaiman[2] and Rajiv Ranjan[2]

Since SLAs specify the contractual terms that are formally used between consumers and providers, there is a need to aggregate QoS requirements from the perspectives of Clouds, networks, and devices to deliver the promised IoT functionalities. Therefore, the main objective of this chapter is to provide a conceptual model of SLA for the IoT as well as rich vocabularies to describe the QoS and domain-specific configuration parameters of the IoT on an end-to-end basis. We first propose a conceptual model that identifies the main concepts that play a role in specifying end-to-end SLAs. Then, we identify some of the most common QoS metrics and configuration parameters related to each concept. We evaluated the proposed conceptual model using a goal-oriented approach, and the participants in the study reported a high level of satisfaction regarding the proposed conceptual model and its ability to capture main concepts in a general way.

5.1   Introduction

IoT applications are mostly time-sensitive applications. Thus, it is important to consider when data need to be collected, what the next processing step is, and where to process each step. Furthermore, the associated QoS requirements for each step should be specified in an unambiguous way. Therefore, there is a need to aggregate QoS requirements from the perspectives of Clouds, networks, and IoT devices layers to deliver the promised IoT functionalities at the required quality level, as agreed upon within the SLA.

Consumers of IoT-based services have certain levels of expectations with respect to the quality of service provision. Therefore, it is important for an SLA to specify consumer requirements in relation to provider capabilities. The SLA provides a guarantee procedure that consumers' requirements will be met. However, IoT applications are mostly time sensitive. For example, in IoT-based emergency response

[1]Computer Science and Engineering, College of Applied Studies and Community Service, King Saud University, Saudi Arabia
[2]Computing School, Newcastle University, UK

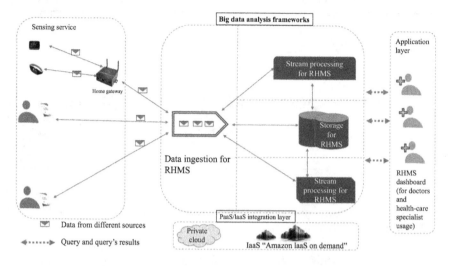

Figure 5.1   Cooperated layers to deliver RHMS

(ER) applications, data from deployed sensors must be received and analyzed immediately and accurately. Any delay in data transfer is unacceptable. Other examples are
the prompt response required for natural disasters such as earthquakes, floods, and
tsunamis [278]. Therefore, for such applications and others, ensuring that consumer
requirements are accurately and unambiguously specified within SLAs is crucial.
Accurately specified SLAs are contracts that can form the basis of a strategy to reg-
ulate and automatize transactions and activities between interacting parties (service
providers and consumers).

For further illustration, let us consider a remote health-monitoring service
(RHMS), in which patient data are collected from different sources (e.g., heartbeat
sensors, smart cameras and mobile accelerometers) (Figure 5.1). The filtered data are
then transferred to a data-processing platform within the Edge/Cloud (depending on
the required level of processing capabilities and/or storage capacity) layer for further
analysis. However, since the time factor is very important for this type of application,
any unpredicted delay in one or more of the data flow stages (e.g., collecting, transferring, ingesting, analyzing) will affect the accuracy and suitability of the actions
taken. Therefore, the performance of an RHMS relies not only on the correctness of
the provided functionalities but also on the quality of the offered services across the
Edge and/or Cloud computing environments. Therefore, SLAs undoubtedly need to
consider requirements across all layers of the Edge and/or Cloud environment, for
example, at what rate data should be collected, transferred, and ingested and how fast
and accurate the analysis should be.

Traditional SLAs that focus on availability and reliability are not enough for IoT
applications due to the need for strict SLA guarantees (of functions such as accuracy
and speed of event of interest (EoI) detection) [1]. Furthermore, having an individual

SLA management mechanism for each layer of the IoT is inadequate because of the huge dependency across layers [2]. Thus, within an end-to-end SLA, there is a need to express constraints/policies that determine which data can be processed within the Edge data centres as well as which data need to be exported to be processed/analyzed in Cloud data centres under certain constraints. Therefore, specifying the contractual terms of an SLA on an end-to-end basis is important not only to specify the end-to-end QoS requirements but also to assure consumers that their QoS requirements will be observed across computing environments to deliver services that match their expectations. This will aid service providers in operating their services at an adequate level, which will then increase consumers' trust, as it protects their rights if they encounter any damage during the contract period [3,4].

When specifying SLA terms on an end-to-end basis within a formal syntax language, standardizing the vocabularies used to describe the offered/requested services is crucial. With the multi-layered nature of IoT applications, there is a possibility of having more than one provider. Having multiple providers is a serious issue that leads to the need to standardize the terminologies used within the SLA to avoid ambiguity. For example, within the Cloud environment, there is a lack of standardized vocabularies in expressing SLAs. For example, availability is expressed differently by well-known Cloud providers: Amazon EC2 offers availability as a monthly uptime percentage of 99.95%, Azure offers availability as a monthly connectivity uptime service level of 99.95%, and GoGrid offers a server uptime of 100% and an uptime of the internal network of 100% [5]. Furthermore, within the Edge environment, sampling rate [6] and sampling frequency [7] are used interchangeably to describe the rate at which a sensor sends data. Indeed, unifying metrics and terminologies as well as proposing a taxonomy will lead to a well-designed SLA, which in turn will provide a successful interaction between consumers and providers. Therefore, standardizing the vocabularies used to describe the offered services and the requested services may play a significant role in minimizing the ambiguity between cooperating parties.

A consumer who wishes to start an SLA must first select a service provider/s. Selecting service provider/s can be a challenging process, especially when considering the multi-layered nature of the IoT. To illustrate, consider the RHMS scenario, in which the IoT application administrators would aim to find the best set of providers that match their requirements. Since IoT applications have a multi-layered architecture, IoT administrators need to consider different categories of providers (e.g., network provider, Cloud provider) and find the best candidate for each category. Most popular Cloud providers (e.g., AWS, MS Azure, Oracle) currently provide descriptive take-it-or-leave-it SLAs for their services. When consumers need to compare such SLAs from different providers to select the most suitable, they must evaluate them manually [8]. IoT applications can potentially be much more complex than Cloud applications, and such a comparison, therefore, becomes more difficult. Therefore, standardizing the vocabularies used to describe the QoS of the offered services and the requested services can be a first step towards enhancing the process of selecting service providers using certain search criteria.

As a result, we attempt to contribute to the SLA of the IoT by proposing a conceptual model that captures the knowledge base of IoT-specific SLAs.

This chapter contributes to the SLA for the IoT by:

- Proposing an SLA conceptual model.
- Introducing key concepts of SLA for IoT and the related vocabulary terms that can be used for specifying QoS and configuration parameters.
- Evaluating the proposed conceptual model using a questionnaire-oriented approach from the domain experts' point of view.

In the following text, Section 5.2 introduces the proposed conceptual model for IoT applications. Then, Section 5.3 presents the vocabulary terms that can be part of an SLA to reflect the QoS and configuration requirements. We evaluate the proposed conceptual model in Section 5.4.

5.2   An end-to-end SLA conceptual model for IoT applications

An end-to-end IoT ecosystem includes components through which application data flows. Components can include services (e.g., a sensing service or real-time analysis service), infrastructure resources (e.g., IoT devices, Edge resources, and Cloud resources) and/or humans. In end-to-end SLA, it is important to consider the requirements for all of the services and infrastructure resources involved to deliver the IoT application. Considering an SLA on an end-to-end basis is essential because establishing the SLOs of both services and infrastructure resources has an impact on establishing SLOs at the application level. For example, in an RHMS, an SLO (SLO_{app1}) for urgent case detection, which requires a response within less than Y time units, is an SLO at the application level, and it involves many activities, such as analyzing real-time data. Analyzing real-time data requires a stream-processing service at an acceptable level of latency, and if the stream-processing service exceeds this level, then SLO_{app1} might be violated.

As a result, we propose a conceptual model that captures the knowledge base of IoT-specific SLAs. The conceptual model expresses the key entities of the IoT ecosystem and the relationships among those entities within the SLA context. Due to the lack of a standard IoT architecture, we refer to our reference IoT architecture as presented in [9] to identify the main concepts and the relationships among them.

Figure 5.2 presents our conceptual model. In the following section, we describe the concepts covered in the conceptual model and give a brief discussion of the relationships associated with these concepts.

The conceptual model is composed of the following entities:

1. SLA: The SLA includes basic data, such as the title of the SLA, the corresponding ID, the type of application (i.e., smart home, smart health, etc.), and the start and end dates.
2. Party: The part describes an individual or group involved in the SLA and usually includes a named company or a judicial entity [10]. For example, in an RHMS, the parties could be the hospital management group, patient, network provider, and Cloud resource providers.

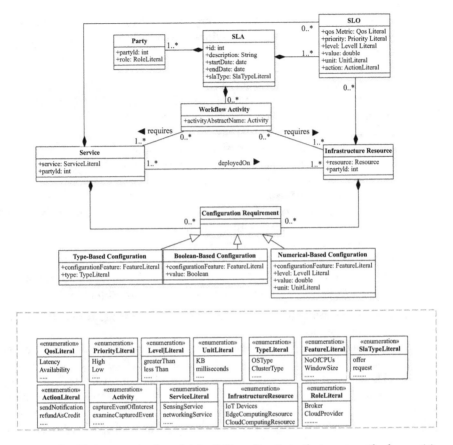

Figure 5.2 SLA conceptual model for IoT applications that capture the key entities of an SLA and the corresponding relationships [9]

3. SLO: The SLO provides the quantitative means to define the level of a service that a consumer can expect from a provider. It expresses the objective(s) of an agreement for both the application and any involved services and infrastructure resources. The SLO quantifies the required value of a QoS metric. For example, an SLO (at the application level) of an RHMS could be the response to urgent cases within Y time units. The QoS metric in this example is `response time`, and the constraint is less than Y time units. Furthermore, SLO parameters can be used to specify an SLO for low-level services; for example, for a data-ingestion service, an SLO can be: *ingest data with latency less than Z time units*. For an infrastructure resource such as the CPU of a VM, an SLO can be: *CPU utilization is greater than 80%.*

4. Workflow activity: IoT applications have certain activities that must be considered as part of the application requirements to function correctly. For example, in an RHMS, the possible workflow activities include capturing interesting data,

analyzing real-time data, and storing interesting results in a database (e.g., SQL or NoSQL). In general, workflow activities mostly include:

- Capturing events of interest.
- Examining the captured events of interest on the fly.
- Filtering the captured events of interest.
- Aggregating the captured events of interest.
- Ingesting data from one or more data resources.
- Small-scale real-time data analysis.
- Large-scale real-time data analysis.
- Large-scale historical data analysis.
- Storing structured data.
- Storing unstructured data.

5. Service: This concept covers the main services that can be run/deploy to perform certain functionality. To achieve SLOs at the application level, it is important to establish adequate cooperation between particular services under the SLO constraints. For example, in an RHMS, to detect urgent cases within Y time units, it is necessary to transfer data from sensors to the ingestion service using networking service and to process data on the fly using stream-processing service.

Here, we list the most common services that can cooperate to deliver the SLOs of an IoT application.

(a) Sensing service: This service collects data using IoT devices and sends the collected data through a communication protocol to a higher layer. The sensing service specifies the type of data and when to collect the data. For example, in an RHMS, a heartbeat sensor attached to the chest and an accelerometer as a hand-wrist device reflect a patient's health state continuously or periodically based on what has been specified within the SLA for the service.

(b) Networking service: This service transfers the collected data from one layer to another. For example, in an RHMS, a home gateway uses the network to deliver collected data to the Cloud for further analysis under certain bandwidth requirements.

(c) Ingestion service: This service ingests data from many data producers and then forwards the data to subscribed/interested destinations such as storage and analysis services under certain requirements, such as throughput limits.

(d) Batch processing service: A batch-processing service receives data from resources such as ingestion layers, appends them to a master data set, and then provides batch jobs. For example, in an RHMS, to identify urgent cases, it is important to run machine-learning algorithms on historical patient records to recognize patterns regarding certain health issues and establish a predictive model. The predictive model can be used later with the real-time data of current patients to detect particular health issues. Batch views can be computed/queried within response time constraints, as specified by consumers/subscribers.

(e) Stream-processing service: This service processes incoming data from data resources such as an ingestion service to complete real-time tasks. For example, collected data are processed on the fly, and if the analysis shows an abnormality such as a high heart rate, then appropriate action is required, such as sending an ambulance. However, to exploit real-time data to the greatest extent possible, consumers/subscribers can specify certain requirements such as the maximum acceptable latency for computing/querying real-time views.

(f) Machine-learning service: This is a service that applies different machine-learning algorithms for different purposes, such as providing predictions and extracting different dimensions of knowledge from collected data. For example, the service may apply a machine-learning algorithm to historical data collected from previous flood incidents as training data to create a model for predicting a flood based on incoming real-time data; this approach may prevent disasters from happening or at least reduce damage by warning people in advance.

(g) Database service (SQL and NoSQL databases): This service is used by ingestion, batch and stream-processing services to store or retrieve data, batch views and real-time views as intermediate or final data sets. Consumers can provide their requirements, such as setting a query response time, and specify whether data encryption is required.

6. Infrastructure resource: This concept covers the required hardware for computations, storage, and networking, which is essential for deploying/running the above-mentioned services. The infrastructure resources can be IoT devices, Edge resources, and Cloud resources.

(a) IoT devices: These devices include intelligent devices/objects with the ability to execute actions and reflect the physical world.

(b) Edge resources: These resources allow data processing to take place at the Edge of a network and include various types of resources, such as border routers, set-top boxes, bridges, base stations, wireless access points, and Edge servers [11]. These examples of Edge resources can be used to support Edge computations with specialized capabilities [11].

(c) Cloud resources: These resources provide infrastructure as a service (IaaS) and are mostly located geographically far from the source (e.g., IoT device) [11].

The relationships among the above entities, which are depicted in the conceptual model (Figure 5.2), are as follows. There is a one-to-many relationship between the SLO and the SLA entities to express the SLO constraints at the application level. Therefore, each SLA entity has a composite relationship with an SLO entity. An example of SLO at the application level could be the *end-to-end response time of an application should be less than Y time units*. Furthermore, an SLA has a composite relationship with parties since parties are responsible for providing a service, using a service and/or playing third-party roles (e.g., to monitor a service).

Additionally, an IoT application has a set of workflow activities (e.g., capture an EoI or analyze real-time data) that cooperate to deliver the application. Therefore, there is a composite relationship between the SLA and WorkflowActivity entities. Each workflow activity requires a service (e.g., a sensing service, networking service, or stream processing service). Each service is deployed on one of the infrastructure resources (e.g., an IoT device, an Edge resource, or a Cloud resource). Furthermore, each one of the services (e.g., sensing is a service) and infrastructure resources (e.g., VM is an infrastructure resource) can have an SLO/SLOs. For example, maximizing the level of data freshness could be an SLO for sensing services, and maximizing CPU utilization could be an SLO for a VM). Furthermore, each one of the services and infrastructure resources can have zero or more configuration parameters (e.g., the sample rate of the sensing service and number of CPUs per VM of an infrastructure resource). Therefore, there is an association relationship between `InfrastructurResource` and `Service` and composite relationship between `InfrastructurResource`, `Service`, `SLO` and `ConfigurationRequirement` entities. The dashed rectangle has a set of predefined data types which are defined as enumeration.

5.3 Vocabulary terms of the configuration parameters and QoS metrics

In this section, we cover the "service" and "infrastructure resource" concepts of the considered services and infrastructure resources, with their sub-classes depicted in Figure 5.2, in depth. We describe the "service" and "infrastructure resource" concepts bellow with some of the related QoS metrics and configuration parameters.

We search the literature to collect vocabulary terms that are related to the QoS metrics and configuration parameters. The reason behind considering the terms related to configuration parameters is the strong correlation between the QoS and configuration parameters; for example, the data publishing rate, as a configuration parameter, affects the data freshness as a QoS metric. This step comes after specifying the main components of the IoT reference architecture; then, the vocabulary terms that can be used to express consumer requirements are identified for each component. We believe that identifying domain-specific terms is the first step in providing unified/standardized vocabularies to mitigate the risk that can be caused by the ambiguity between the different providers who cooperate to deliver an IoT application (Sections 5.3.2 and 5.3.1).

5.3.1 Infrastructure resources

Infrastructure resources include the name of the infrastructure resource used to deploy/host a service. An infrastructure resource includes the following components.

5.3.1.1 IoT devices

IoT devices consist of heterogeneous sets of devices such as sensors that capture information about the physical world by sensing some physical parameters of interest or detecting other smart objects [12]. There are several QoS metrics related to perception layers, such as the optimum number of active sensors, sensor quality, energy consumption, data volume, trustworthiness, coverage, and mobility [6,7,13].

However, some of these identified metrics may be inconsiderable for a single IoT device [7], and these metrics are not trivial when considering the number of deployed devices that cooperate to deliver a service. For example, a sensor with a power consumption value equal to 0.9 Watt-seconds seems fine, but when a network of hundreds of sensors is deployed, the cumulative value of the power consumption makes a difference [7].

IoT communication protocols can be varied in their communication range, bandwidth and power consumption. Thus, it is important to consider support for different types of protocols, and the most appropriate type that satisfies the application requirements should be selected. For example, if the power consumption is the most important key requirement, then ZigBee, as a communication protocol that can be characterized as a low power consumption protocol [14], should be used; alternatively, WiMax is a protocol that provides a high communication bandwidth. Therefore, it is essential to select devices that support the preferred communication protocol. Some of the available communication protocols are Bluetooth, Wi-Fi, ZigBee, 6LowPAN, Cellular, ANT, Z-Wave, Thread, WiMax, and NFC.* Table 5.1 lists a number of vocabulary terms that can be used to express the requirements related to IoT devices.

5.3.1.2 Edge resources

In an Edge layer, intelligent computation abilities are allocated to Edge resources (a gateway, server, etc.) to improve performance and reduce unnecessary data transfers to Cloud data centres. Edge resources contain sensitive personal and social data, and data management and control tasks are moved to the Edge to be managed in a secure and private manner [16]. Edge resources mostly include border routers, set-top boxes, bridges, base stations, wireless access points, Edge servers, etc. These examples of Edge resources can be equipped to support Edge computations with specialized capabilities [11]. A gateway typically links devices with the Cloud layer where data can be processed, stored, and analyzed. The IoT devices (e.g., sensors) can work without a gateway if the sensors have the ability to communicate directly with the Internet. In this case, sensors might have lightweight functionality [17]. Furthermore, for a more cost-effective approach with typical sensors that do not have gateway capability, it is possible to use many-to-one mapping, where many sensors can be connected to one gateway, which then increases the data transfer capability [17].

Smart gateways can handle resource constraints on the processing power, power consumption, and bandwidth of connected devices by allowing constrained devices to outsource some functionalities to the gateway. These gateways can be provided with local databases for temporarily storing sensed data, as well as enhancing data fusion, aggregation, and internal device communication [18]. When specifying the QoS for an application, it is necessary to decide whether to deploy typical sensors and

---

*See [15] for further details and a comparison of communication protocols.

Table 5.1   Terminology/vocabulary definitions related to IoT devices

Terminology	Definition/description/example
Device accuracy	Description of how well the device reflects an interesting event.
Device precision	Description of how precisely the device reads an interesting event in a stable manner.
Type of device	For example, sensors and RFID tags.
Number of devices	The number of devices.
Mobility of devices	Specification of whether the device is fixed or mobile (this feature affects network coverage).
Communication mechanism	The mechanism of pushing/pulling data to/from the next layer. This mechanism can be a built-in hardware feature, a software feature or both.
Communication technology	The communication protocol with other devices that are supported, such as by Wi-Fi and Bluetooth. This technology can be a built-in hardware feature, a software feature or both.
Battery life	Battery life is a measure of battery performance and longevity, which can be quantified in several ways: as the run time on a full charge, as the milliampere hours estimated by a manufacturer, or as the number of charge cycles until the end of useful life.
Warranty period	The time period in which a purchased device may be returned or exchanged.
Storage size	The storage size of an IoT device that can be used to store data.
Memory capacity	The maximum or minimum amount of memory an IoT device has.
CPU capacity	The capability and speed of a processor which reflects how many operations it can perform within a given amount of time.

a gateway or a smart sensor. For example, using smart sensors (a smart sensor (with some processing capabilities) can behave as an IoT or an Edge resource) reduces the delay that is required for transferring data to the Cloud layer, which might be located at a distance position, and the data can be processed within Edge resources instead of forwarding them to the next layer.

Some configuration parameters can affect the overall QoS of an IoT application. For example, the data publishing rate at the gateway is a concern because an increase in this rate might cause the broker network to be "overloaded," which then causes messages to be dropped [19]. Another configuration parameter is the buffer size, which plays a significant role in the performance of an IoT gateway. For instance, the authors of [20] proposed a multi-threaded gateway and considered different values for different parameters, including different buffer sizes to enhance gateway performance when evaluating the proposed model. Table 5.2 lists a number of vocabulary terms that can be used to express the requirements related to Edge resources.

5.3.1.3   Cloud resources

Most Cloud data centers are distributed internally across several physical data centers. As a result, many Cloud providers not only provide fault tolerance for a single machine

Table 5.2   Terminology/vocabulary definitions related to Edge infrastructure resources

Terminology	Definition/description/example
Availability	The ratio of the time that the resource is functioning as expected and ready for use divided by the total run time.
Type of device	For example, a mobile, raspberry pi, or server devices.
Gateway throughput	The amount of data transferred through the gateway per second.
Gateway delay	The delay in data collection from nodes.
Publishing rate	Specifies when data need to be sent.
Number of devices	Total number of devices within the Edge infrastructure.
Mobility of devices	Specification of whether a device is fixed or mobile (this feature affects network coverage).
Communication mechanism	The mechanism of pushing data to the next layer or pulling data from the next layer; it can be a built-in hardware feature, a software feature or both.
Communication technology	The communication protocols with other devices, such as the communication protocols based on Wi-Fi and Bluetooth. Such protocols can be a built-in hardware feature, a software feature or both.
Storage/buffer size	The buffer/storage size that can be used to buffer/store data due to limited throughput for incoming data or to buffer/store data until delivery confirmation is received.
Memory capacity	The maximum or minimum amount of memory an Edge resource is capable of having.
CPU capacity	The capability and speed of a processor which reflects how many operations it can perform within a given amount of time.

or single rack but also provide resilience for full data center failures, which yields a high level of reliability. Cloud providers supply computer resources on an on-demand basis. This approach quickly enables (typically in minutes) an arbitrarily large number of computing nodes to be accessed with scale-up and scale-down possibility [21].

Cloud resources can have one or more than one SLO; for example, an SLO can be "CPU utilization should be more than 80%." Furthermore, a Cloud resource can have a configuration parameter, such as a number of vCPUs. Most Cloud systems provide a variety of storage system functions, such as those for the storage bandwidth, size, cost, latency, and access control for different storage types, including local instance storage, distributed block storage, distributed file systems and object (blob) storage. These various services can lead to very different choices regarding software design depending on the system or application requirements [21]. Table 5.3 lists a number of QoS and configuration parameters for Cloud resources. There are different types of instances, e.g., instances with more RAM versus more storage, or with specific hardware components, such as GPUs or FPGAs [21].

5.3.2 Service concept

To achieve SLOs at the application level, it is important to rely on adequate coopera-tion among some services under the SLO constraints. Therefore, we use the service

Table 5.3   Terminology/vocabulary definitions related to Cloud infrastructure resources

Terminology	Definition/description/example
Availability	The ratio of the time that the resource is functioning as expected and ready for use divided by the total run time.
CPU utilization	Percentage representing how the CPU is being utilized.
Outage length	The length that the resource is not available.
Throughput	The data transfer rate to and from a Cloud resource per second.
Storage size	Available disc space for data storage purposes.
Storage bandwidth	Measure of the capacity to transfer data between a service and storage.
Storage type	Type of storage for a service (e.g., local SSD or local HDD).
Input/output storage operations	The specified number of input/output operations for storage.
Access protocols	Cloud access protocols.
Memory capacity	The memory capacity is the maximum or minimum amount of memory a computer or hardware device is capable of having or the amount of memory required for a program to run.
Network bandwidth	Network speed among the internal service nodes involved (e.g., 100BASE-T, 100BASE-SX).
vCPU capacity	The capacity of each virtual central processing unit (vCPU) which reflects how many operations a vCPU can perform within a given amount of time.
No. of vCPUs	The number of vCPUs per VM.
No. of cores per VM	The number of cores per VM.
Vertical scale-down limit	The minimum number of CPUs if scaling is not automatic.
Vertical scale-up limit	The maximum number of CPUs if scaling is not automatic
Horizontal scale-up limit	The maximum number of VMs if scaling is not automatic.
Horizontal scale-down limit	The minimum number of VMs if scaling is not automatic.
Replication factor	The number of copies of data that one wants the cluster to maintain.

concept to capture the name of the required services. A service has one or more SLO constraints and configuration requirements, including but not limited to those for sensing, networking, stream processing, batch processing, database management, and machine-learning algorithm services. Each one of the previously mentioned services can have one SLO or more; for example, an SLO for stream processing services can be "minimizing latency to be less than 5 time units." Furthermore, each of the previously mentioned services can have configuration requirements; therefore, there is a relationship between the service and configuration requirement concepts. For example, a service such as stream processing can specify a requirement related to the "window size" (the window size is a configuration parameter). In the following section, we list the most common services that can cooperate to deliver an IoT application.

5.3.2.1 Sensing services

A sensing service is responsible for collecting data from IoT devices and sending the collected data through a communication protocol to another layer. The sensing service specifies the number of sensors, type of sensors, and sampling rate. In an RHMS, for example, to provide a sensing service, we need to specify the type of sensors associated with a patient, such as a heartbeat sensor attached to the chest and an accelerometer on the hand/wrist to reflect the patients' activities. A sensing service is associated with different parameters that play a significant role in the overall QoS of an IoT application.

For example, different applications require varying sampling rates depending on their criticality. The sampling rate determines the frequency at which an observed phenomenon is measured by a sensor (e.g., 5 Hz) [6]. Moreover, gaps in historical data can cause IoT applications to behave unexpectedly, which affects the final outcome and can lead to a bad user experience. Therefore, the IoT platform must attempt to maximize data freshness [22]. The importance of the freshness parameter from the perspectives of both producers and consumers has been recently discussed in [23]. The authors argued that for transient IoTs, both data of interest and data packets should have a certain freshness to perform accurate caching and retrieval operations. Additionally, old content is automatically discarded from data storage as a consequence of the freshness requirement [24]. Moreover, data freshness is one of the security requirements in the IoT because if an attacker first captured data and resent them, the data will become old [25,26].

Another metric is data quality, which is a complicated metric since it relies on other metrics, such as data accuracy [27]. Data accuracy, itself, is affected by data freshness and precision [28], reflecting the high dependence among metrics. Furthermore, application objectives such as reducing energy consumption and nonfunctional properties are interdependent. For example, increasing the sampling rate plays a significant role in enhancing data freshness, which in turn improves the information quality; however, this change decreases battery life (i.e., increases energy consumption). Table 5.4 lists some of the vocabulary terms that can be used to express the QoS constraints and configuration parameters relevant to sensing services.

5.3.2.2 Networking services

Networking services are used for passing the collected data from one layer to another and provide a bidirectional connection for cases in which an instruction needs to be sent to one or more devices. For example, in an RHMS, gateways use the network to deliver collected data to the Cloud for further analysis. A networking service is also used when a command is sent back to a sensor, for example, to reconfigure the sampling rate, collect more data, or check a patient's status. Thus, a network service is responsible for transferring data between an IoT and an Edge resource [29]. Furthermore, in some cases, an IoT device has the ability to communicate without needing a gateway; in such a case, the networking service is used to immediately

Table 5.4   Terminology/vocabulary definitions related to sensing services

Terminology	Definition/description/example
Availability	The ratio of the time that the service is functioning as expected divided by the total run time.
Data freshness	The age of sensor data because data cannot always be transmitted in real time/near-real time.
Sampling rate	The rate at which a sensor measures an observed phenomenon (e.g., 5 Hz). Different applications require different sampling rates based on their criticality.
Data accuracy	The error rate of data. It is possible to specify the average number of errors over a given time period.
Data integrity	Data integrity reflects the degree to which data have been maintained or altered.
Data type	e.g., Capturing weather temperature or humidity.

connect the device to Cloud services (e.g., ingestion service and/or stream processing service). The quality of the network plays a significant role in delivering the data within the acceptable time limit before data lose value. Therefore, considering the QoS requirements of the network layer is crucial.

QoSs have been extensively researched in the field of network communications and have well-defined and measurable characteristics, such as throughput, jitter or packet loss [28], which impact the network delay [30–34]. Table 5.5 lists some of the vocabulary terms that can be used to express QoS constraints and configuration parameters that are relevant to networking services.

5.3.2.3   Ingestion services

An ingestion service describes how data can be ingested from many data producers [35] and then forwarded to subscribed/interested destinations, such as a storage service, analysis service, and/or application. An ingestion service can be associated with different parameters, such as configuration requirements (e.g., the number of servers/nodes and compression/decompression support) and some SLO constraints (e.g., maximizing throughput and minimizing latency).

In ingestion service, data often come from a variety of sources, including web logs, databases, various kinds of applications, etc., making it hard to understand what sort of data the system will ingest. One alternative is to use big data (BD) software, which can collect and aggregate data from various sources. Projects such as Flume[†] and Scribe[‡] enable the collection, aggregation, and transfer of large quantities of log information from many distinct sources to a centralized data storage center [36].

[†]http://flume.apache.org/
[‡]https://github.com/facebookarchive/scribe/wiki

Table 5.5   Terminology/vocabulary definitions related to networking services

Terminology	Definition/description/example
Availability	The ratio of the time that a network is fully operational as expected and ready for use divided by the period of time.
Link bandwidth	The maximum amount of data that can be transferred through a link per second.
Network delay	The delay in data transmission.
Data-in rate	The amount of incoming data per time unit.
Data-out rate	The amount of outgoing data per time unit.
Jitter	The time delay variance between data packets over a network in milliseconds (ms).
Packet loss rate	The ratio of the number of packets lost to the total number of packets sent. Each packet has a deadline for execution, and if meeting this deadline is not possible, the scheduler tries to minimize the number of packets lost due to deadline issues.
Data integrity	Data integrity reflects the degree to which data have been maintained or altered.

Data retention is one of the parameters that service consumers need to specify to indicate how long data can be stored before they are deleted. Therefore, the data rate and data retention time are interdependent since they represent key factors related to resource storage. For example, in Kafka,[§] the data rate of a partition is the rate at which it generates information; in other words, it is the average size of the message multiplied by the amount of messages per second. The data rate indicates how much retention space is needed in bytes for a given amount of time to ensure retention. If there is a lack in knowledge regarding the data rate, the retention space needed to meet a time-based retention goal cannot be calculated properly [37].

Messaging systems provide some replication-related functionality to improve various factors, including reliability, fault tolerance, and accessibility for replicating data/messages on different servers. For example, replication is used by default in Kafka; even unreplicated topics are implemented as replicated topics [38]. Data encryption, data compression, and a delivery guarantee mechanism are application dependent, so if providing a low-latency solution is important, then the data encryption delivery guarantee mechanism will cause delays. Furthermore, if reliability is important, then providing a delivery guarantee mechanism that ensures that messages/data/requests are delivered using the ingestion service is crucial. In other cases, when throughput is highly prioritized over latency, data compression is a key concern. The available messaging systems provide compression, encryption and delivery guarantee mechanisms; as an example, Amazon Kinesis Data Firehose[||] enables the

[§]https://kafka.apache.org/
[||]https://docs.aws.amazon.com/firehose/latest/dev/what-is-this-service.html

Table 5.6   Terminology/vocabulary definitions related to ingestion services

Terminology	Definition/description/example
Availability	The ratio of the time that the ingestion service is functioning as expected divided by the period of time.
Throughput	The amount of data transferred through the messaging platform per second.
Latency	The time required to process a single input/output transaction before forwarding it to its destination within the ingestion service framework.
Data-in rate	The amount of incoming data per time unit.
Data-out rate	The amount of data output per time unit.
Data retention time limit	The limit of how long data can be saved in the ingestion layer.
Publishing rate	Rate at which data is sent to a message broker.
Storage size	The amount of storage that can be used to store data due to limited throughput constraints considering the amount of incoming data, to store data until delivery confirmation, or to store data during the specified retention time.
Replication factor	How many replicas can be stored.
Data compression support	A Boolean value that expresses whether data can be compressed/decompressed depending on the requirements.
Data encryption support	A Boolean value that expresses whether data can be encrypted/decrypted depending on the requirements.
Delivery guarantee mechanism	It reflects if data have been delivered to the destination. It affects the workload if the type of delivery guarantee mechanism requires sending an acknowledgment back to the data producer.
Data integrity	Data integrity reflects the degree to which data have been maintained or altered.
Name of ingestion framework	e.g., RabbitMQ, Amazon Kinesis Data Firehose, Flume, Scribe.

compression of information before it is delivered, and it supports the GZIP, ZIP, and SNAPPY compression formats [39]. Amazon Kinesis Data Firehose, also, allows for data encryption using the AWS Key Management Service [39]. RabbitMQ[¶] and Kafka both offer long-lasting messaging guarantees. Both offer at-most-once and at-least-once guarantees, but in very restricted situations, Kafka provides precisely once guarantees [40]. Table 5.6 lists some of the vocabulary terms that can be used to express some of the QoS constraints and configuration parameters that are relevant to ingestion services.

5.3.2.4   Stream processing services

A stream processing service refers to processing incoming data from different data sources and/or ingestion services to compute real-time views. Furthermore, real-time

---

[¶]https://www.rabbitmq.com/

views can be combined with saved computed batch views using a database framework (such as Cassandra**) to answer some questions that rely on both real-time views and batch views. In an RHMS, data can be collected using different sensors, such as wearable accelerometers, that can be augmented by distributed-motion sensors for activity recognition purposes [41]. If the collected data show abnormality for a given activity, such as an elderly person falling down, then an appropriate action, such as sending an ambulance, is required. However, applications such as RHMSs rely on real-time data; therefore, any delay in data processing could cause the data to lose their value.

High throughput and low latency are very important QoS requirements in stream processing. If incoming data are not analyzed in real or near-real time, then the action taken may not be appropriate since actions are based on data that are no longer considered real-time/near-real-time data due to the delay. Another important metric is data completeness, which "measures the percentage of incoming stream data that are used to compute the query results." [42]. To illustrate the concept of data completeness, consider a data stream with a number of incoming tuples. In the ideal case, the query should be performed using a large sliding window, e.g., containing 30 tuples; however, due to resource constraints, 15 tuples are sampled and used to execute the query, which represent 50% of the 30-tuple window size. The sampling method decreases the query data completeness to 50% [42]. Furthermore, another QoS metric is the miss ratio, which "evaluates the number of queries that are not completed within the given time constraints" [42].

In addition, the single-point resource estimation is insufficient to handle stream processing workloads in which information flows endlessly through the operator graph and yields changes in performance and resource demands. Therefore, to illustrate the effects of certain configuration parameters on performance and resource usage, consider the work in [43] as an example. Khoshkbarforoushha *et al.* [43] presented a novel method using mixed density networks, a mixed structure of neural networks and mixed models to estimate the resource usage of data stream processing workloads in the Cloud. To train the proposed model, a set of features was used as the model input; the set included the size of windows that can be expressed in time units (second) or tuple units (number), the sliding value of the window type, the average arrival rate of tuples (tuple/second) to query, the total number of nested sub-queries and the operator type. The set of features was customized based on the prediction goal because the impact varied with respect to the CPU and memory. A feature that is correlated with memory consumption may not be correlated with CPU usage. For example, the selection results for features suggest that the size of the window has an insignificant effect on the prediction of CPU use but a notable influence on the prediction of memory use [43].

Furthermore, the QoS requirements of stream processing are affected by other configuration parameters, such as the window size and query size; in addition, the choice of a stream processing framework affects the QoS. For instance, selecting a

---

**http://cassandra.apache.org/

framework (such as Spark streaming)[††] that stores data before processing affects the latency level; Apache storm[‡‡] can process data immediately with no need to store them first [44]. Table 5.7 lists key terms/definitions related to stream processing services to express requirements for both QoS metrics and configuration parameters.

5.3.2.5   Batch processing services

A batch processing service refers to receiving data from ingestion layers and/or other data sources, appending the data to the master dataset and then obtaining batch views; moreover, the computed batch views can be stored for inquiry purposes. Batch processing can be based on incremental algorithms or recomputation algorithms [45] considering the type of job that needs to be accomplished. For example, in an RHMS, if hospital management is interested in recording some statistics regarding the detected urgent cases, one interesting statistic might be the total number of urgent cases that have been detected. The count function can then be applied using an incremental algorithm or recomputation algorithm. However, since new detected cases can quickly reach the previous total number of detected cases, an incremental algorithm could be more suitable. The reason for choosing an incremental algorithm in this case is that the total number can be calculated without considering the entire dataset; this process avoids the need for additional computational resources since it only requires an increment establishment step.

However, if the query must consider the whole dataset, such as for a query regarding the average age of people who have a certain health issue, then whenever new cases arrive, there is a need to recompute the average considering all of the recorded ages, which requires a recomputation algorithm. Selecting the appropriate algorithm is important. Recomputation algorithms require computational efforts/resources to handle the master dataset, while less computational resources are required for incremental algorithms. However, a recomputation algorithm is more robust since it is human–fault tolerant because batch views are continuously recomputed [45].

In batch processing services, the throughput and query response time are key QoS requirements in which users are interested. The related terminology/vocabulary definitions are used to express configuration requirements (such as the number of map and reduce tasks and the batch size). Furthermore, the choice of which batch processing framework to select affects the QoS. For instance, Hadoop[§§] is a powerful batch processing framework; however, it is not the appropriate choice when there is a need to apply machine learning algorithms because it requires data to be reloaded from the disc, which increases the latency; therefore, Apache Spark could be the ideal choice [44].

Furthermore, the authors of [46] presented a mathematical model for the optimum number of map tasks in MapReduce resource provisioning to estimate the optimum number of mappers based on the resource specifications and data set size. The MapReduce library divides input data into several input splits. A map task reads an input split

[††]https://spark.apache.org/streaming/
[‡‡]https://storm.apache.org/
[§§]https://hadoop.apache.org/

Table 5.7   Terminology/vocabulary definitions related to stream processing services

Terminology	Definition/description/example
Throughput	The stream size processed per second.
Latency	The time required to process a single input/output transaction for a stream processing service.
Data completeness	Measurement of "the percentage of incoming stream data that are used to compute the query results" [42].
Miss ratio	"Miss ratios measure the percentage of queries that are not finished within the given deadlines" [42].
Time-based window size	The size of the window with respect to the time required to process data that occur within the window. The window size can be over time or based on a number of records/messages.
Event-based window size	The size of the window based on a number of events/records/messages within a given window.
Sliding window	Determines the length of the window and the portion of the range that is retrieved when the window moves forward; the intervals can overlap. This value can be time based, count based, or based on a hybrid scheme.
Tumbling window	A series of fixed-sized, non-overlapping, and contiguous time intervals.
Micro batch size	Specification of the size of data that need to be buffered first before being processed; however, in stream processing, data are not required to be stored first. It is better if data are processed in active mode, which means that data are processed as they arrive and not when they are pulled.
Data arrival rate	Specification of how many data points are expected to be received per second.
Write capacity	Specification of the capacity of writing in one go.
Read capacity	Specification of the capacity of reading in one go.
Replication factor	Expression of how many replicates can be stored.
Total number of queries	Specification of how many queries should be considered.
Data Compression support	A Boolean value that expresses whether data can be compressed/decompressed depending on the requirements.
Data Encryption Support	A Boolean value that expresses whether data can be encrypted/decrypted depending on the requirement.
Data Integrity	Data integrity reflects the degree to which data have been maintained or altered.
Name of stream processing framework	e.g., Spark streaming, Apache storm

and processes the input split using the user-defined map function. The map function takes input key/value pairs and creates a set of pairs for an intermediate key/value. The mapper memory buffers the intermediate key/value pairs. If the size of the data set reaches the memory buffer threshold, intermediate key/value pairs are stored on the local disc and partitioned to reduce the task requirements using the hash function. The reduce tasks involve reading and sorting steps for the intermediate data and group data with the same key. Then, the key and intermediate value sets are sent as inputs to the reducer to be written to the reducer's memory, and the reduction function is invoked [47]. The output of the reduction function is concatenated and then written to the output file [46]. The MapReduce model and Hadoop Open Source Implementation have proven effective for large data processing tasks and were inherently built for batch and processing jobs with high throughput requirements [48]. Throughput, as a QoS metric, indicates the number of MapReduce jobs completed per time unit (e.g., minutes) [49]. Furthermore, it should be noted that the number of map tasks can be used as a cost estimator, as applied in [49]. Table 5.8 lists the terminology/vocabulary definitions related to expressing the QoS metrics and configuration parameters of batch processing services.

5.3.2.6　Machine-learning services

A machine-learning service refers to a service that permits the use of various machine-learning algorithms to predict the purposes and different dimensions of knowledge from the information collected. For instance, a machine algorithm can be applied to historical data collected from patients with heart attack incidents to obtain training

Table 5.8　Terminology/vocabulary definitions related to batch processing services

Terminology	Definition/description/example
Throughput	The number of batches that can be processed per second.
Response time	The time required to process a submitted job and receive a response.
Batch size	The limit on the size of each batch that is submitted to be processed.
No. of batch jobs	The number of submitted batch jobs.
Process running frequency	Specification of how frequently the process needs to be run, e.g., twice per hour.
Max. memory of the map task	Amount of memory assigned to the map task.
Max. memory of the reduce task	Amount of memory assigned to the reduce task.
No. of mappers	The number of mappers.
No. of reducers	The number of reducers.
Write capacity	The capacity of writing in one step.
Read capacity	The capacity of reading in one step.
Replication factor	Expression of how many replicas can be stored.
Total number of queries	Expression of how many queries should be considered.
Data compression support	A Boolean value that expresses whether data can be compressed/decompressed depending on the requirements.
Data encryption support	A Boolean value that expresses whether data can be encrypted/decrypted depending on the requirements.
Data integrity	Data integrity reflects the degree to which data have been maintained or altered.
Name of batch processing framework	e.g., Hadoop

*Table 5.9   Terminology/vocabulary definitions related to machine-learning
          algorithm services*

Terminology	Definition/description/example
Accuracy	The accuracy of the analysis.
Class of ML	The name of the class in which an algorithm is classified. For example, the supervised learning involves classification and regression algorithms, and the unsupervised learning class includes clustering and association algorithms.
Name of ML algorithm	Specifies the name of the algorithm required, such as logistic regression, decision forest, decision jungle, neural network, support vector machine, principal component analysis (PCA)-based anomaly detection, K-means, or naive Bayes.
Way to run the ML algorithm	Examples of this process are sequential and MapReduce.
Data integrity	Data integrity reflects the degree to which data have been maintained or altered.

data. Then, the training data can be used to create a model to predict heart attack cases based on incoming real-time data, which can prevent emergencies from happening or at least reduce patient damage by warning patients in advance.

In terms of practical needs, there are different QoS metrics, including speed, accuracy, price, etc., as in most topic detection and tracking (TDT) applications. Furthermore, different types of algorithms for machine learning affect accuracy and speed differently. The algorithm class reflects the type of algorithm, including classification, clustering, etc., whereas the algorithm name refers to the specific algorithm used, such as K-means, linear discriminant analysis (LDA) and naive Bayes.[III] Different algorithms, even if they are from the same class, can have different impacts on the performance of a system. For example, some clustering algorithms, such as the K-means and Canopy algorithms, differ substantially in the speed of execution; specifically, K-means has more than one iteration, while Canopy has only one iteration [51]. Table 5.9 shows a list of the main QoS metrics and configuration parameters that are related to machine learning services.

5.3.2.7   Database services

A database service can be used for data retrieval with different services, such as ingestion, batch, and streaming services. The database service stores incoming data as an intermediate or final dataset, a set of computed batch views or set of computed real-time views. For instance, the incoming data can be initially stored, such as with HDFS in Hadoop, before any further processing. Then, the data can be retrieved for

---

[III] Refer to [50] for further details about machine learning algorithms

Table 5.10   Terminology/vocabulary definitions related to database services

Terminology	Definition/description/example
Throughput	The queries that can be processed per second.
Response time	The time from when a user sends a request to when they receive a response.
Type of database	For example, SQL or NoSQL.
Type of NoSQL	For example, a key-value, document-based, graph-based, or column-based NoSQL.
Read error rate	The number of errors associated with reading attempts per time unit (seconds).
Cache hit ratio	The ratio of cache hits to misses, expressed as a percentage. A cache hit is when the data requested for processing are found in the cache memory. A cache miss is when the data requested for processing are not found in the cache memory.
Write error rate	Rate of errors associated with writing attempts per time unit (seconds).
Write capacity	The capacity of writing in one step.
Read capacity	The capacity of reading in one step
Replication factor	Expression of how many replicas can be stored.
Compression support	A Boolean value that expresses whether data can be compressed/decompressed depending on the requirements.
Data encryption support	A Boolean value that expresses whether data can be encrypted/decrypted depending on the requirements.
Data Integrity	Data integrity reflects the degree to which data have been maintained or altered.

analysis or can be processed on the fly, and the derived results are stored in a database such as Cassandra.

There are different types of databases that are selected based on the purpose of the application and the required QoS. For example, in stream processing, data can be stored in databases that support low-latency read and write operations, whereas cases that require immutable data can use durable object storage platforms such as Amazon S3,¶ which is preferable to other methods. Furthermore, to handle large amounts of data, a distributed storage platform is employed, such as the available open-source distributed database Druid,*** which supports data ingestion as well as queries with low latency, and Apache HBase,††† which supports the random and real-time reading/writing of large volumes of data. However, the selection of the appropriate platform to use is affected by some factors, such as the query response time [44]. Table 5.10 lists some of the most common QoS metrics and configuration parameters of database services.

¶https://aws.amazon.com/s3/
***http://druid.io/
†††http://hbase.apache.org/

5.4 Evaluation

In this section, we present our evaluation approach to assess the proposed conceptual model. We have applied a goal-oriented questionnaire approach, and further details of the evaluation procedure and results are presented in the following sections.

5.4.1 Experiment

The main purpose of the conducted experiment is to evaluate the proposed conceptual model and to determine if it meets the relevant predefined goals: generality, based on the coverage of general concepts that are common in IoT applications; coverability, or the extent to which IoT application requirements are covered considering the main concepts that can be used within an SLA to express QoS constraints and configuration requirements; and accuracy, which reflects the extent to which the conceptual model is accurate and the overall satisfaction level.

5.4.2 Participants

The potential users of our proposed work are IoT administrators. Therefore, we performed an experiment in which the research interests/topics of participants were mainly related to IoT. The study was conducted with 15 participants; most of them were Ph.D. students who were working on topics related to IoT, such as remote health and smart city applications. Their research interests include Cloud computing, Edge computing, and networking.

5.4.3 Procedure

The experiment was carried out following a well-defined procedure. First, one-on-one discussions were conducted in which each participant received an introduction to the SLA and the reference architecture of the IoT, and a presentation was given

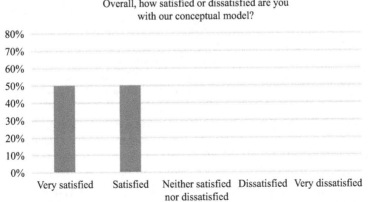

Figure 5.3   Results of the evaluation: satisfaction

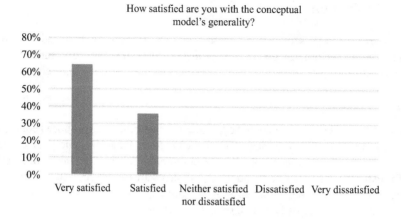

Figure 5.4   Results of the evaluation: generality

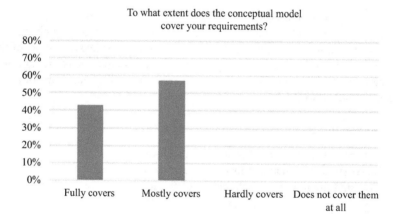

Figure 5.5   Results of the evaluation: coverability

on the conceptual model. The participants were allowed to discuss and comment on the conceptual model. A use case was employed for scenario clarification purposes (an RHMS). At the end of this period, the participant was asked to submit a written version of the questionnaire in which there were four questions related to the conceptual model. Furthermore, there was a comment textbox to allow the participants to comment and make suggestions, provide criticisms, or give other feedback. The three questions related to the conceptual model were as follows:

- Overall, how satisfied or dissatisfied are you with our conceptual model?
- To what extent does the conceptual model cover your requirements?
- How satisfied are you with the conceptual model's generality?

5.4.4 Experimental results

Figures 5.3–5.5 show the results based on participants' answers in regard to the proposed conceptual model. Fifty percent of participants described their overall satisfaction level as satisfactory, while the other 50% were very satisfied. Regarding the coverability (capturing the main-related concepts) of the conceptual model, more than 40% of participants answered that the model provided full coverage, and the rest of the participants answered "mostly covered." Regarding the generality of the conceptual model, more than 60% of participants were very satisfied, and the rest were satisfied. There were a few comments regarding concept names that describe resources, and it was suggested to change "resources" to "infrastructure resources." Furthermore, there was a comment regarding the presentation of the conceptual model as follows: "it would be better if it (the conceptual model) was represented in hierarchical view."

5.5 Conclusion and future work

In this chapter, we tried to overcome one of the end-to-end SLA specification challenges related to the heterogeneity of key QoS metrics across the computing environment. We proposed a conceptual model for IoT-specific SLA. Then, we identified domain-specific vocabulary terms that can be used as a starting point for an SLA specification considering both the QoS constraints and configuration parameters across layers. However, there is a limitation in the presented work related to the sample size of participants that evaluated the SLA conceptual model. However, the reason for the small size is that we sought participants with domain-specific knowledge, especially that we, mainly, were looking to review our conceptual model with experts. In future work, we will try to extend the identified services and infrastructure resources and identify a list of vocabulary terms related to QoS metrics and possible configuration parameters. Furthermore, we will try to evaluate the proposed model with a larger sample size.

References

[1] Wang M, Ranjan R, Jayaraman PP, *et al.* A case for understanding end-to-end performance of topic detection and tracking based big data applications in the cloud. In: *International Internet of Things Summit.* Springer; 2015. p. 315–325.

[2] Alqahtani A, Solaiman E, Buyya R, *et al.* End-to-end QoS specification and monitoring in the Internet of Things. *Newsletter, IEEE Technical Committee on Cybernetics for Cyber-Physical Systems.* 2016;1(2):9–13.

[3] Skene PJ. Language support for service-level agreements for application-service provision. Doctoral thesis, University of London. 2007.

[4] Kritikos K, Pernici B, Plebani P, *et al.* A survey on service quality description. *ACM Computing Surveys (CSUR).* 2013;46(1):1.

[5]　Alkandari F and Paige RF. Modelling and comparing cloud computing service level agreements. In: *Proceedings of the 1st International Workshop on Model-Driven Engineering for High Performance and CLoud Computing. MDHPCL'12*. New York, NY: ACM; 2012. p. 3:1–3:6. Available from: http://doi.acm.org/10.1145/2446224.2446227.

[6]　Jayaraman PP, Mitra K, Saguna S, *et al.* Orchestrating quality of service in the cloud of things ecosystem. In: *2015 IEEE International Symposium on Nanoelectronic and Information Systems*. 2015; p. 185–190.

[7]　Liu X, Wang Q, Sha L, *et al.* Optimal QoS sampling frequency assignment for real-time wireless sensor networks. In: *In RTSS*. 2003.

[8]　Wu L and Buyya R. Service level agreement (SLA) in utility computing systems. In: *Performance and Dependability in Service Computing: Concepts, Techniques and Research Directions*. Hershey, PA: IGI Global; 2012. p. 1–25.

[9]　Alqahtani A, Li Y, Patel P, *et al.* End-to-end service level agreement specification for IoT applications. In: *2018 International Conference on High Performance Computing Simulation (HPCS)*; 2018. p. 926–935.

[10]　Galati A, Djemame K, Fletcher M, *et al.* A WS-agreement based SLA implementation for the CMAC platform. In: Altmann J, Vanmechelen K, Rana OF, editors, *Economics of Grids, Clouds, Systems, and Services*. Cham: Springer International Publishing; 2014. p. 159–171.

[11]　Mahmud R and Buyya R. Fog computing: a taxonomy, survey and future directions. *CoRR*. 2016;abs/1611.05539.

[12]　Dingle NJ, Knottenbelt WJ, and Wang L. Service level agreement specification, compliance prediction and monitoring with performance trees. In: *22nd Annual European Simulation and Modelling Conference (ESM 2008)*; 2008. p. 137–14.

[13]　Bianco P, Lewis G, and Merson PP. Service level agreements in service-oriented architecture environments. *Technical Report CMU/SEI-2008-TN-021*, Carnegie Mellon; 2008.

[14]　Dementyev A, Hodges S, Taylor S, *et al.* Power consumption analysis of Bluetooth Low Energy, ZigBee and ANT sensor nodes in a cyclic sleep scenario. In: *2013 IEEE International Wireless Symposium (IWS)*; 2013. p. 1–4.

[15]　Elhadi S, Marzak A, Sael N, *et al.* Comparative study of IoT protocols. In: *Smart Application and Data Analysis for Smart Cities (SADASC'18)*; 2018.

[16]　Garcia Lopez P, Montresor A, Epema D, *et al.* Edge-centric computing: vision and challenges. *SIGCOMM Computer Communication Review*. 2015;45(5):37–42. Available from: http://doi.acm.org/10.1145/2831347.2831354.

[17]　Buyya R and Dastjerdi AV. *Internet of Things: Principles and Paradigms*. Amsterdam: Elsevier; 2016.

[18]　Rahmani A, Thanigaivelan N, Gia T, *et al.* Smart e-health gateway: bringing intelligence to Internet-of-Things based ubiquitous healthcare systems. In: *2015 12th Annual IEEE Consumer Communications and Networking Conference (CCNC)*; 2015.

[19]   Banavar G, Chandra T, Mukherjee B, *et al.* An efficient multicast protocol for content-based publish-subscribe systems. In: *Proceedings. 19th IEEE International Conference on Distributed Computing Systems (Cat. No. 99CB37003).* Piscataway, NJ: IEEE; 1999. p. 262–272.

[20]   Banaie F, Misic J, Misic VB, *et al.* Performance analysis of multithreaded IoT gateway. *IEEE Internet of Things Journal.* 2018;34:9541–9563.

[21]   Zukowski M. Cloud-based SQL Solutions for Big Data. In: *Encyclopedia of Big Data Technologies.* Cham: Springer; 2018. p. 1–7.

[22]   Vasisht D, Kapetanovic Z, Won J, *et al.* Farmbeats: an IoT platform for data-driven agriculture. In: *14th {USENIX} Symposium on Networked Systems Design and Implementation ({NSDI} 17);* 2017. p. 515–529.

[23]   Quevedo J, Corujo D, and Aguiar R. Consumer driven information freshness approach for content centric networking. In: *2014 IEEE Conference on Computer Communications Workshops (INFOCOM WKSHPS).* Piscataway, NJ: IEEE; 2014. p. 482–487.

[24]   Hail MAM, Amadeo M, Molinaro A, *et al.* On the performance of caching and forwarding in information-centric networking for the IoT. In: *International Conference on Wired/Wireless Internet Communication.* Berlin: Springer; 2015. p. 313–326.

[25]   Pirbhulal S, Zhang H, E Alahi M, *et al.* A novel secure IoT-based smart home automation system using a wireless sensor network. *Sensors.* 2017;17(1):69.

[26]   Gope P and Hwang T. BSN-Care: a secure IoT-based modern healthcare system using body sensor network. *IEEE Sensors Journal.* 2015;16(5):1368–1376.

[27]   Martinho R and Domingos D. Quality of information and access cost of IoT resources in BPMN processes. *Procedia Technology.* 2014;16:737–744.

[28]   Kolozali S, Bermudez-Edo M, Puschmann D, *et al.* A knowledge-based approach for real-time IoT data stream annotation and processing. In: *2014 IEEE International Conference on Internet of Things (iThings), and IEEE Green Computing and Communications (GreenCom) and IEEE Cyber, Physical and Social Computing (CPSCom);* 2014. p. 215–222.

[29]   Calbimonte JP, Riahi M, Kefalakis N, *et al.* Utility Metrics Specifications. OpenIoT Deliverable D422. Infoscience, the École Polytechnique Fédérale de Lausanne (EPFL); 2014.

[30]   Li B and Yu J. Research and application on the smart home based on component technologies and Internet of Things. *Procedia Engineering.* 2011;15(Supplement C):2087–2092. CEIS 2011. Available from: http://www.sciencedirect.com/science/article/pii/S1877705811018911.

[31]   Council CSC. Practical Guide to Cloud Service Agreements Version 2.0. The Object Management Group (OMG); 2011. Supplement C. Available from: http://www.cloud-council.org/deliverables/CSCC-Practical-Guide-to-Cloud-Service-Agreements.pdf.

[32]   Kim EC, Song JG, and Hong CS. An integrated CNM architecture for multi-layer networks with simple SLA monitoring and reporting mechanism. In: *Network Operations and Management Symposium, 2000. NOMS 2000. 2000 IEEE/IFIP;* 2000. p. 993–994.

[33] Bhuyan B, Sarma HKD, Sarma N, *et al.* Quality of service (QoS) provisions in wireless sensor networks and related challenges. *Wireless Sensor Network*. 2010;2(11):861.

[34] Duan R, Chen X, and Xing T. A QoS architecture for IoT. In: *2011 International Conference on Internet of Things and 4th International Conference on Cyber, Physical and Social Computing*; 2011. p. 717–720.

[35] Ranjan R. Streaming big data processing in datacenter clouds. *IEEE Cloud Computing*. 2014;1(1):78–83.

[36] Villalpando LEB, April A, and Abran A. Cloud measure: a platform for performance analysis of cloud computing systems. In: *2016 IEEE 9th International Conference on Cloud Computing (CLOUD)*. IEEE; 2016. p. 975–979.

[37] Mancill T. Best Practices for Apache Kafka; 2018 (Accessed on 07/03/2019). https://blog.newrelic.com/engineering/kafka-best-practices/.

[38] Kafka A. Apache Kafka; 2017 (Accessed on 07/03/2019). https://kafka.apache.org/documentation/#gettingStarted.

[39] AWS AWS. Amazon Kinesis Data Firehose FAQs; 2019 (Accessed on 07/03/2019). https://aws.amazon.com/kinesis/data-firehose/faqs/.

[40] Vanlightly J. RabbitMQ vs Kafka Part 4 – Message Delivery Semantics and Guarantees – Jack Vanlightly; 2017 (Accessed on 07/04/2019). https://jack-vanlightly.com/blog/2017/12/15/rabbitmq-vs-kafka-part-4-message-delivery-semantics-and-guarantees.

[41] Patel S, Park H, Bonato P, *et al.* A review of wearable sensors and systems with application in rehabilitation. *Journal of NeuroEngineering and Rehabilitation*. 2012;9(1):21. Available from: http://dx.doi.org/10.1186/1743-0003-9-21.

[42] Yuan Wei, Son SH, and Stankovic JA. RTSTREAM: real-time query processing for data streams. In: *Ninth IEEE International Symposium on Object and Component-Oriented Real-Time Distributed Computing (ISORC'06)*; 2006. p. 10.

[43] Khoshkbarforoushha A, Ranjan R, Gaire R, *et al.* Resource Usage Estimation of Data Stream Processing Workloads in Datacenter Clouds. ArXiv. 2015;abs/1501.07020.

[44] Díaz M, Martín C, and Rubio B. State-of-the-art, challenges, and open issues in the integration of Internet of Things and cloud computing. *Journal of Network and Computer Applications*. 2016;67:99–117.

[45] Marz N and Warren J. Big data: principles and best practices of scalable realtime data systems, 1st ed. Greenwich, CT, USA: Manning Publications Co.; 2015.

[46] Hlaing HH, Kanemitsu H, Nakajima T, *et al.* On the optimal number of computational resources in MapReduce. In: *International Conference on Cloud Computing*. Berlin: Springer; 2019. p. 240–252.

[47] Verma A, Mansuri AH, and Jain N. Big data management processing with Hadoop MapReduce and spark technology: a comparison. In: *2016 Symposium on Colossal Data Analysis and Networking (CDAN)*. Piscataway, NJ: IEEE; 2016. p. 1–4.

[48] Shahrivari S. Beyond batch processing: towards real-time and streaming big data. *Computers*. 2014;3(4):117–129. Available from: https://www.mdpi.com/2073-431X/3/4/117.

[49]   Eldawy A and Mokbel MF. Spatialhadoop: a mapreduce framework for spatial data. In: *2015 IEEE 31st International Conference on Data Engineering*. Piscataway, NJ: IEEE; 2015. p. 1352–1363.

[50]   Das K and Behera RN. A survey on machine learning: concept, algorithms and applications. *International Journal of Innovative Research in Computer and Communication Engineering*. 2017;5(2):1301–1309.

[51]   Wang M, Jayaraman PP, Solaiman E, *et al.* A multi-layered performance analysis for cloud-based topic detection and tracking in Big Data applications. *Future Generation Computer Systems*. 2018;87:580–590.

Chapter 6

SLA representation and awareness within blockchain in the context of IoT

Ali Alzubaidi[1], Karan Mitra[2] and Ellis Solaiman[3]

Recently, there has been an interest in employing blockchain for the service level agreement (SLA) management lifecycle, which includes, but is not limited to, negotiation, monitoring, compliance assessment, billing, enforcement, and termination. Hence, representing SLA content within a blockchain is essential for providing smart contracts with the necessary awareness for conducting related tasks. This study categorises existing SLA representation methods in the literature and highlights their issues. Therefore, it suggests a set of principles, abbreviated as IRAFUTAL, that aims to realise a robust SLA representation approach that can serve various tasks related to blockchain-based SLA management. This study employs Hyperledger Fabric for implementing an SLA data manager that adheres to these principles. Then, it demonstrates the usage of the proposed SLA representation approach for SLA definition and negotiation over a blockchain network.

6.1 Introduction

Following the proliferation of blockchain technology, there has been an interest in employing it for SLA management purposes [1]. The application of blockchain-based SLA solution can be found in different domains such as cloud, telecommunication, and more recently IoT; which is the domain of application chosen for this study. Regardless of the SLA domain, the concept of smart contracts can be leveraged to shift untrusted processes related to SLA management such as compliance assessment, penalty enforcement, and billing. However, smart contracts need to maintain appropriate SLA awareness level in order to facilitate the automation such tasks. To appreciate the significance of SLA representation within blockchain, consider a set of decentralised smart contracts that assess a service provider's compliance with an established SLA. To do so, these smart contracts should be aware of relevant SLA content (i.e. quality requirements promised by the service provider). If the SLA is

[1]College of Engineering and Computers, Umm Al Qura University, Saudi Arabia
[2]Department of Computer Science, Electrical and Space Engineering, Luleå University of Technology, Sweden
[3]School of Computing Science, Newcastle University, Newcastle Upon Tyne, United Kingdom

externally stored on a centralised server, then we argue this practice can negatively impact the effectiveness of a decentralised compliance assessment in two main ways. First, one can question the degree of trust that should be given to the external host considering that it can be susceptible to a single point of failure such as a malicious act or unavailability [2,3]. Second, SLA is customarily expected to evolve due many reasons such as a renegotiation, error rectification. Given the replication of smart contract execution by multiple blockchain validators, there is a probability that SLA modifications will cause validators to obtain inconsistent versions of the SLA [4]. For instance, consider a case where a few of the validators receive the most recent SLA version while the rest of them happen to receive a cached version of the previous SLA content. Although the blockchain validators execute the same smart contract, they may produce various outputs due the distinctive SLA versions they receive; eventually preventing them from reaching a proper consensus on transactions validity.

As a result, SLA representation should be represented within blockchain rather external hosts, which does only resolve such issues, but also promises several advantages such as:

- SLA immunity from malicious behaviour or unavailability.
- Smart contracts can maintain the necessary awareness of the SLA structure and content.
- Smart contracts are relieved from obtaining SLA content from external hosts.
- Validators can execute smart contracts in a deterministic manner [5]; meaning that the same input to the smart contract must always produce the same output.
- Validators can reach a consensus on the validity and finality of smart contract execution [6].

By examining related works, in Section 6.2.2, we find that most of them conveniently encode SLA structure and content directly into the logic of the smart contract. Given the tight coupling of SLA content with the smart contract, the SLA inherits the immutability of the smart contract. While SLA immutability resolves trust issues related to externally trusted hosts, it does not align well with SLA evolution. That is, SLA can be normally expected to mutate from its origin for a variety of reasons such SLA definition, error-rectification, renegotiation, and general maintenance [7]. Additionally, the process of encoding SLA as a smart contract and deploying it to compatible blockchain platforms are not easy tasks for ordinary end-users. Such tasks there will require subject–matter experts (i.e. developers, operators, security auditing, etc.) [8]. For that, this study proposes a blockchain-based SLA representation and awareness approach that avoids issues found in relevant studies while maintaining elasticity and ease of use needed for SLA definition, renegotiation, and error rectification.

Chapter organisation: This chapter delves into this matter and organises its sections as follows: first, Section 6.1.1 overviews the definition of SLA key elements and sheds light on SLA negotiation. Section 6.2 overviews and categorises SLA representation methods in related works. Then, Section 6.3 suggests a set of principles, abbreviated as IRAFUTAL, that aims to address issues found in existing blockchain-based SLA solutions. Section 6.4 takes advantage of a formal IoT-based SLA specification tool to model SLA at the blockchain's state storage level. Section 6.5 demonstrates the advantage of the proposed SLA representation approach by implementing an SLA manager in the form of a smart contract that elastically operates SLA within the blockchain. Finally, Section 6.6 evaluates the proposed SLA representation approach by extending the SLA manager to serve the purposes of SLA definition and negotiation. It aims to demonstrate how the proposed SLA approach can mitigate the drawbacks of the existing SLA representation approach and what potentials it can promise for the practice of blockchain-based SLA.

6.1.1 Overview on SLA definition and negotiation

Service level agreement (SLA) is a contractual method that regulates and governs the relationship between service providers and consumers [9,10]. There have been in practice several well-established organisations that contribute their effort in standardising the SLA practice ISO [11], C-SIG-SLA [12], Vlacheas *et al.* [13], TMForum [14], OMG Cloud Working Group [15], and others. They agree that the minimal form of an SLA should define the following:

- *SLA participants*: involved parties and their roles (i.e. service provider, consumers, and probably a third party such as auditors and assessors).
- *Service level objectives (SLOs)*: a set of obligations and responsibilities carried out by the service provider. This chapter maps an SLO to a measurable service quality requirement such as availability, throughput, latency, jitter, and packet loss rate [16]. For instance, the availability must not be less than 99.9% all the time.
- *Violation consequences*: a set of measures that follow a failure in meeting the SLOs such as imposing a penalty (e.g. financial service credit).
- Dates of SLA establishment and termination, and what conditions that trigger them.

Girs *et al.* [17] conducts an extensive survey on SLA definition and modelling in the context of Cloud-based IoT services. To date, the most mature SLA definition and specification framework we can find in the context of IoT is the one proposed by [18], which covers the requirements of an end-to-end IoT ecosystem. This study adopts their proposed SLA framework in composing and defining a simplified SLA example between an IoT service provider and a consumer, an example of which is presented in Figure 6.1.

The agreement comprises three main sections: SLA parties, SLOs, and violation consequences. The SLA parties section (lines 1–13) consists of the details of both the service provider and a consumer. The SLOs section dictates a set of quality requirements promised by the service provider. Whereas the first SLO (lines 15–22) stipulates a quality requirement, *Availability* $\geq$ 99%, the second SLO (lines 23–30) states a quality requirement, *Latency* $<$ 3 *seconds(s)*. The last section lists a set of example violation consequences (lines 32–46) in the form of penalties applied on the obligated party (the service provider), shall it fail to scale to the exceptions of the consumer. For instance, a failure to meet the availability requirement *QoS0001* incurs a financial credit of 25% of the agreed cost. The latency requirement *QoS0001* incurs a financial credit of 50% for every 1,000 breaches.

Figure 6.1   SLA example between a service provider and consumers

As with any contractual method, SLA can be negotiated either before or after the SLA establishment [19]. For that, the ISO/IEC 19086-1 standard [20] recommends accounting for changes to the SLA. That is, some service providers may customise a predefined SLA, such as the one presented in Figure 6.1, to match some consumers' specific requirements [21]. For example, a consumer may suggest an amendment to the SLA before engagement in the contractual relationship. On the other hand, a renegotiation may also occur after SLA establishment [22], which can be triggered due to a constant failure by the service provider in satisfying the promised quality requirements. Subsequently, the SLA participants may consider adapting the SLA version to match a realistic performance [13].

Moreover, consider the possibility of a new owner acquiring a service provider or merging with another organisation. Therefore, the SLA may also change accordingly to reflect the new service provider and any updates on SLA terms. There are also cases where constant SLA violations lead to termination. Service providers and consumers may renegotiate the SLA instead of termination [9,23].

6.2   SLA representation in related works

The awareness of SLA content is critical for any automated task such as monitoring, compliance assessment, penalty enforcement, billing, and other related SLA management [24,25]. The quest of this section is to investigate how existing blockchain-based SLA solutions represent SLA and to what level of SLA awareness smart contracts may achieve in their approaches. By investigating the related studies, we can categorise different SLA representation approaches found in related works as follows.

6.2.1   SLA-agnostic approaches

This category describes a blockchain-based solution as an SLA-agnostic when it may resolve some trust issues related to the SLA practice but omits to represent fundamental SLA properties within blockchain such as involved parties, quality requirements, violation consequences, and so forth. As a result, it can be difficult or impractical to attain the SLA awareness level needed for conducting SLA-related tasks [9]. Consequently, smart contracts cannot automate and conduct tasks such as SLA establishment, monitoring, compliance assessment, and penalty enforcement. This section diverges this class of approaches further into two sub-categories which are the following.

6.2.1.1 Zero representation within blockchain

As in Figure 6.2(a), smart contracts may serve some SLA purposes but do not represent SLA structure or content. For instance, Wonjiga *et al.* [26] assume an SLA where a cloud provider guarantees the integrity of consumer data. While they use blockchain to achieve this SLA objective, their work does not seem to represent SLA structure or content within the blockchain. Similarly, Singi *et al.* [27] use blockchain to enforce SLA compliance regarding software-related licences and security policies. However, their work only represents the subject of the SLA, which are the licences and politicises, whereas the SLA itself does not seem to take place within the blockchain.

6.2.1.2 Implicit SLA representation

As in Figure 6.2(b), SLA can have an implicit form of presence within the blockchain environment. Albeit, smart contracts still cannot fully reason about SLA structure or content. For instance, Nakashima and Aoyama [28] use blockchain for SLA integrity verification purposes. For that, their work composes SLAs in the form of an RDF-formatted document (resource description framework) and then generates a hash of it to be deposited by a smart contract into the blockchain. This approach can help reveal and invalidate any unauthorised modification, which can be realised by comparing the immutable hash of the SLA stored in the blockchain with the actual SLA residing in the external world [3]. Nevertheless, smart contracts cannot use the locally stored hash to reason the SLA content. However, smart contracts can be used to verify the integrity of the externally stored SLA.

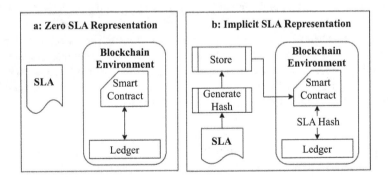

Figure 6.2   Examples of SLA-agnostic approaches

6.2.2 SLA-aware approaches

This category deems blockchain-based solutions to be SLA-aware when smart contracts serve SLA purposes while maintaining sufficient awareness of SLA structure and content. As a result, smart contracts can conduct and automate SLA-related tasks in a truly decentralised manner, examples of which include, but are not limited to, SLA negotiation, compliance assessment, enforcement, billing, termination and so forth. Most of the existing blockchain-based SLA studies explicitly encode SLA structure and content (parties, quality requirements, penalties, etc.) in the smart contract. Following are commonly used methods for stating SLA in smart contracts.

6.2.2.1 Deployment to compatible decentralised storage

As in Figure 6.3(a), some blockchain-based SLA approaches take advantage of compatible decentralised storage systems to resolve some issues related to SLA central hosting, such as unavailability of the hosting server or misconduct by a central authority. Therefore, enabling smart contracts to make use of externally hosted SLA while maintaining immutability and consistency. For instance, Kapsoulis [29] propose a tool that adopts that ISO 19086-2 SLA standard for producing a JSON-formatted SLA. Then, the generated SLA document can be deployable into decentralised storage, namely, InterPlanetery File System (IPFS) [30], which can be accessed by smart contracts and monitoring tools. While hosting SLA externally in decentralised storage systems is appealing in terms of immutability, consistency, and availability, such scheme introduces unnecessary architecture complexity in terms of infrastructure, networking, cost, execution fees, and maintenance. Additionally, the stored SLA cannot be modified, which is a feature necessary for SLA renegotiation and error-rectification. Moreover, if smart contracts sought SLA awareness by calling an externally hosted SLA that would violate the transaction flow in most blockchain platforms [31].

6.2.2.2 Manual smart contract development

SLA representation within the blockchain network can present an alternative approach for mitigating the complexity of external decentralised storage systems. As Figure 6.3(b) illustrates, some existing approaches leverage smart contracts for expressing SLA structure and content (i.e. a quality requirement *latency* $\leq$ 3 milliseconds (ms)). Consequently, smart contracts can maintain the necessary SLA awareness without needing to query the external world, either centralised or decentralised storage systems. Therefore, smart contracts can use SLA awareness to conduct and automate actionable procedures related to the expressed SLA. For instance, when a smart contract receives a breach of the stated quality requirement, it can have the necessary awareness of relevant consequences (i.e. penalties) to be enforced on the service provider. For instance, the authors of [32] encode SLA terms directly into the logic of the smart contract, which enables conducting SLA management tasks related to penalty enforcement and SLA termination. This approach benefits from blockchain features such as immutability, consistency, decentralisation, and high availability. However, the process of representing SLA content in the form of a smart contract

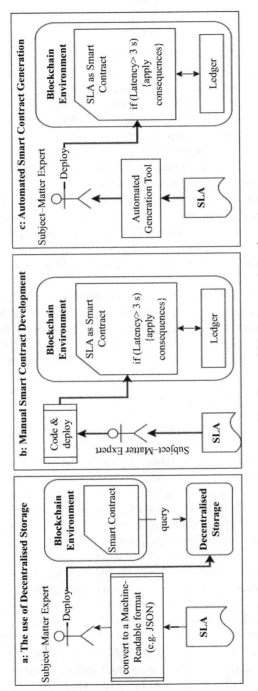

Figure 6.3   Types of SLA-aware approaches

requires a subject–matter expert in terms of smart contract development or deployment to the Blockchain.

6.2.2.3   Automated smart contract generation

Expressing an SLA in the form of a smart contract is difficult for non-expert users. There have been some efforts to realise an automated smart contract generation mechanism. For instance, the authors of [33] devise a translator tool that accepts agreements in the form of a Business Process Model and Notation (BPMN). It can recognise some critical properties of a BPMN document expressed in an Extensible Markup Language (XML) format. The translator tool transforms the file into an actionable smart contract written in Solidity programming language and deployable to the Ethereum network. Reference [5] uses an off-chain framework translator tool called SLA2C, proposed in their previous work [4], which transforms SLA into a solidity smart contract. However, the SLA2C framework can only recognise their formal language called 'SLAC', previously proposed in [34]. The work in [35] provides a graphical user interface (GUI) to enable defining quality requirements. Accordingly, it generates a solidity smart contract populated with user inputs and deploys it to Ethereum virtual machine (EVM)-compatible blockchain networks.

As seen in these example studies [5,33], their translation tools require a machine-readable format to generate Solidity smart contracts deployable to the Ethereum network. The most user-friendly translation tool is the one proposed by [35], which provide a GUI for the end-user. Nevertheless, as presented in Figure 6.3(c), generated smart contracts still need subject–expert matters for executing the deployment stage.

6.2.3   SLA negotiation in related works

As discussed earlier, conventional SLA representation tends to encode SLA structure and content directly into the smart contract to achieve SLA awareness needed by relevant tasks such as monitoring, enforcement, and billing. Consider the fact that smart contracts are immutable and cannot be amended [36], which hinders on-chain SLA negotiation either before or after SLA establishment. Figure 6.4(a) illustrates a typical lifecycle for SLA negotiation in conventional approaches, where SLA content and structure are encoded directly in the smart contract. Therefore, SLA negotiation can only be manually conducted off-chain. Thus, there is always the need for the development and deployment of a new smart contract that accommodates new changes. This is evident in many existing blockchain-based SLA approaches. For instance, Reference [32] states in its conclusion that their approach cannot address SLA negotiation because it needs human intervention, particularly in terms of smart contract development and deployment; thus, leaving it to future work. Reference [5] also recognises the need for conducting SLA negotiation off-chain before encoding SLA in the form of a smart contract and deploying it to the blockchain side. Reference [37] also has a similar approach in terms of manual SLA negotiation and deployment in the form of a smart contract to the blockchain side. To the best of our knowledge, there has not been to date any relevant work that addresses SLA negotiation within the blockchain. A

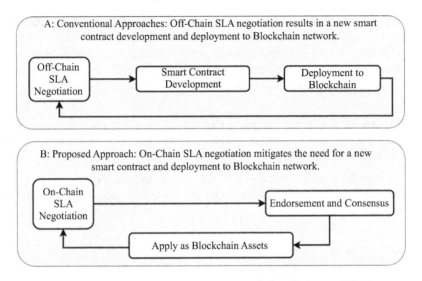

Figure 6.4   SLA negotiation lifecycle in conventional and proposed SLA representation approaches

better alternative is as shown in Figure 6.4(b), where this process does not require off-chain negotiation and subject–matter experts for blockchain-related matters such as smart contract development and deployment, which is demonstrated in Section 6.6.3.

6.3   IRAFUTAL: proposed principles for SLA representation

By examining the advantages and disadvantages of existing approaches for SLA representation within blockchain, this section formulates a set of principles to be followed by a proposed SLA representation approach developed based on these principles. This chapter collectively refers to them as *IRAFUTAL*, an abbreviation that combines the first letter of each principle. The set of IRAFUTAL principles are as follows:

Identifiable and reusable
The SLA representation should enable SLA composition based on independent, unique, and identifiable SLA components including, but not limited to, involved SLA participants, quality requirements, violation consequences. These components can be reusable in different SLAs for various purposes. For instance, the same SLA participant can be reused or referred to in multiple SLAs or smart contracts. Moreover, The same applies to other SLA components. This practice encourages linkability which facilitates fact gathering about each SLA property. For instance, consider various agreements associated with a service provider. Therefore, one can query what existing SLAs this particular provider engages with or what quality requirements are under its responsibility. Such a practice also mitigates redundancy caused by restating SLA components in various places, either in the same SLA or elsewhere. This

practice also reduces the complexity of smart contract development and facilitates the maintenance of the overall blockchain-based SLA solutions. For instance, it would be less prone to human error and easier to identify the root cause of a problem if SLA components are defined once and reused multiple times. Therefore, rectifying an error or applying a remedy on one component would also apply elsewhere by default.

Accessible by smart contracts

Smart contracts, which represent SLA-related tasks, must have the ability to internally access SLA properties within a blockchain environment. This is to provide a smart contract with necessary SLA awareness while mitigating the following:

- The need for trusting central or third party for hosting the SLA.
- Unnecessary complex architecture due to SLA hosting in external decentralised storage.

Flexible

No one SLA template fits all SLA-related scenarios. Moreover, SLA templates can impose boundaries that can arbitrarily constrain blockchain-based SLA solutions, thus limiting solution creativity and viability of blockchain as an underlying solution. Therefore, the SLA representation within blockchain should refrain from imposing a specific SLA template. Alternatively, SLA representation should encourage a modular specification of SLA structure and properties. Otherwise, a set of straightforward implications could materialise as in the following:

- Null values because of some irrelevant template properties.
- The need to circumvent imposed SLA properties which could complicate smart contract development.
- Waste of computation or storage capacity.

User-friendly

As can be seen in Figure 6.3, most existing solutions require subject–matter experts to represent SLA in the form of smart contracts. However, this can hinder smooth SLA definition and negotiation, which does not align well with a typical SLA lifecycle. Therefore, SLA representation within blockchain should consider mitigating the need for subject–matter experts, where end-users can define SLA content independently (i.e. via a GUI).

Tamper-proof

SLA acts as a source of truth for relevant affairs such as monitoring, compliance, penalty enforcement, and dispute resolution. Therefore, SLA must be immune from unintended modification and malicious acts. Otherwise, the outcomes of related tasks are useless, even if they operate in a smart contract running on a blockchain environment. SLA can benefit from several blockchain features such as immutability, auditability, decentralisation, consensus mechanism, and resistance to the single point of failure.

Amendable

The SLA representation approach should anticipate modification that normally occurs within a typical SLA lifecycle. For example, consider an established SLA which states

Latency < 3 *s*. For any reason, such as renegotiation or error rectification, this SLA clause may have to be changed or deprecated. Assume this clause is explicitly stated within a smart contract, as shown in Figure 6.3. Given the immutability of smart contracts, such an amendment is impossible [31,36]. Alternatively, there would be the need for creating a new smart contract or applying workarounds, examples of which are covered in [38] as well as [39] which are applicable to Ethereum. Even in the case of Hyperledger Fabric, such a change to the smart contract requires a Chaincode upgrade, which is a constrained and governed process that does not only call for endorsement by validator nodes but also is conducted by developers and network operators [40]. Therefore, the challenge is to enable SLA modification during smart contract runtime in a decentralised manner.

Loosely coupled

SLA awareness is central for SLA management tasks (compliance assessment, penalty enforcement, and billing). However, when modelling such tasks in the form of smart contracts, it is important to achieve a minimum degree of dependency as possible between them and the SLA itself. To clarify, consider the example smart contract snippet presented in Figure 6.3(b), and note that violating the quality requirement *Latency* < 3 *s* must incur the service provider's liability of consequences (i.e. penalty). If the enforcement logic is tightly coupled with a fixed SLA content, any introduced change to either of them would highly likely require revising all dependent SLA-related content or tasks. Therefore, the SLA representation approach should enable separation of concern, where SLA content is segregated from the logic of any SLA-related tasks such as penalty enforcement, compliance assessment, and so forth.

6.4 Proposed SLA representation approach

By considering the IRAFUTAL principles, discussed in Section 6.3, this chapter proposes an SLA representation approach that leverages the state storage capability employed by most blockchain platforms such as Ethereum and Hyperledger Fabric.

6.4.1 Overview of the state storage capability

Most existing blockchain platforms complement smart contracts with state storage that organises data in the form of (*key, value*) [41]. This study focuses on the usage of Hyperledger Fabric as an underlying blockchain platform. Therefore, the outcomes of this study are highly influenced the Hyperledger Fabric's adopted implementation philosophy of blockchain technology. However, generalisation can be extended to other blockchain platforms wherever intersections and commonality are found. In Hyperledger Fabric, every endorsing node (validator) maintains a smart contract and copy of the shared ledger, where the latter comprises both the state storage and a chain of blocks. The primary benefit of the state storage capability is that it provides fast access to the state of stored assets. Hence, it mitigates the need for traversing the blockchain [42]. It is worth noting that the state storage persists the latest state of a blockchain asset in records, formatted as (*key, value, version*), where *key* identifies an asset, *value* reflects the latest state of the asset, and *version* is a track of changes on this particular asset.

A key benefit of the state storage capability is that it enables data mutation on the latest state (*value*) of stored assets. However, no state change is accepted unless supported with immutable transactions that are included in the shared ledger in append-only fashion [43]. Every smart contract has direct access to its state storage and can invoke other smart contracts to access theirs as well [44]. The modifiability of the state storage enables smart contracts to execute typical CRUD operations (Create, Read, Update, and Delete) on assets stored in their state storage [45]. Nevertheless, smart contracts do not execute any functionality unless triggered with a valid transaction that undergoes a consensus mechanism and passes all validation checks and complies with the endorsement policy in place [46,47]. That is, a transaction must be committed successfully into the ledger before being reflected on the state storage [40]. Accordingly, one can think that state storage is about data representing the state of stored assets, while the underlying blockchain is about a chain of transaction logs that support the legitimacy of the latest state of stored assets.

6.4.2   SLA as blockchain assets

Persisting SLA within blockchain mitigates trust issues related to central authorities and third parties and resists malicious acts such as forgery [5]. The proposed approach takes advantage of the state storage capability for realising SLA in the form of blockchain assets, which complies with IRAFUTAL principles, discussed in Section 6.3. In essence, the proposed approach discourages stipulating SLA content explicitly in the smart contract. Rather, it uses state storage for decoupling SLA content from the business logic defined in the smart contract. Figure 6.5 illustrates the primary difference between the proposed approach and conventional SLA representation approaches (see Section 6.2.2). To elaborate key difference points, most surveyed

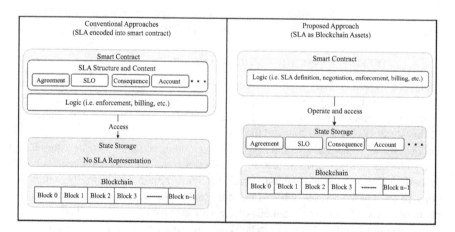

Figure 6.5   Conventional SLA representation approaches vs. the proposed approach

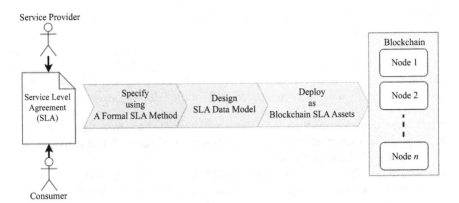

Figure 6.6   Overview to the process of SLA modelling as blockchain assets

blockchain-based SLA solutions tend to fully, or to a great extent, encode SLA content directly into the smart contract. In contrast, the proposed approach refrains from directly encoding the actual SLA content in a smart contract. Instead, it designates the state to storage for storing in the state storage in the form of blockchain-based SLA assets. Therefore, smart contracts can maintain SLA awareness while independent of the SLA content. Moreover, smart contracts can serve various supported SLA agreements since they are no longer attached to a specific one. Vice versa, SLA content is liberated from the immutability and lifecycle of a particular smart contract. For instance, an SLA agreement stored may not concern a change to a smart contract serving an enforcement task or introducing a new smart contract. This is in contrast to conventional approaches, where an adaptation of the smart contract severely impacts the lifecycle of the stored data [38,39].

Figure 6.6 overviews the process of modelling SLA in the form of blockchain assets. Essentially, it utilises an SLA specification tool to generate a formal SLA document. Then, it decomposes the generated SLA document into a logical collection of independent components. It also considers and constrains the association between these components. The outcome is an SLA data model deployable in blockchain assets and stored at the state storage. Following, this study elaborates this process with an example SLA model.

6.4.3   Formal SLA specification

Formal SLA specification is a pivotal step for accomplishing a well-structured SLA document as well as for resolving issues associated with ordinary SLA documents (textual-based or semi-structured), such as ambiguity, incompleteness, and lack of interoperability [17]. Furthermore, the absence of a formally specified SLA hinders effective maintainability and automation of SLA-related tasks such as service discovery, provisioning, incident management, monitoring, and enforcement

[18,48]. Therefore, this study suggests modelling SLA data by utilising formal SLA specification methods.

There are in the literature a set of frameworks and tools dedicated for formal SLA specification; examples of which are surveyed in [13,17]. While any proper formal SLA specification frameworks and tools can be nominated, this study selects a specification framework contributed in [18] for the following reasons:

- It is IoT-domain specific, which aligns well with the purposes of this study.
- It provides an open-source toolkit that helps specify an SLA that complies with their proposed formal method.
- It generates the SLA in a machine-readable format (namely, JSON).
- To the best of our knowledge, there is no other alternative dedicated to IoT-based SLA purposes.

The selected framework is used for specifying and generating an example JSON-formatted SLA, as presented in Figure 6.1 and elaborated in Section 6.1.1. For demonstration purposes, the generated example SLA is deliberately generic for the sake of demonstrating SLA modelling and representation within the blockchain.

6.4.4 Designing an SLA data model

This stage seeks the realisation of an IRAFUTAL-compliant SLA data model that acts as a blueprint that governs SLA assets, their properties, content, and association with each other. In essence, the modelling process utilises the formally specified SLA document (generated in the previous step) to capture the overall SLA structure and its key properties. Figure 6.7 depicts an example SLA data model which is influenced, to a great extent, by the grammar and framework of the selected SLA specification tool. It highlights the association between independent components of the SLA model. It also adapts the formally specified SLA document, in Figure 6.1, to accommodate additional SLA components and properties (specifically, monitoring and escrow account), which are not captured by the selected SLA framework.

6.4.4.1 Highlights on the example SLA model

According to the example SLA model, there are a collection of SLA components, which are SLA agreement SA, SLA participant SP, quality requirement Q, violation consequence VC, and escrow account EA. There can be a set of independent and uniquely identified instances created from any of these SLA components $s_i \in \{SA, SP, Q, VC, EA\}$. These instances will be eventually stored in the form of blockchain assets at the state storage level. The SLA model intentionally decouples these components from each other to enable separation of concern and reusability. Albeit, the agreement component SA maintains a relationship with other components by leveraging the concept of association. See Figure 6.8 which visualises the relationship between them such that agreement acts as a tree root, while others act as tree leaves. Every SLA agreement is considered enforceable within a specified duration and has a flag property that indicates whether it is active or terminated. It is important

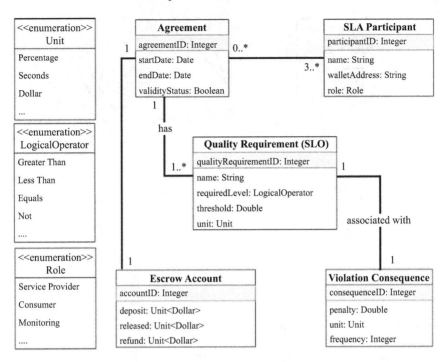

Figure 6.7 Example of IRAFUTAL-compliant SLA model based on formally specified SLA document

to note that an SLA agreement $sa_i \in SA$ cannot exist without its dependencies. Furthermore, the SLA agreement component SA extends its properties to all dependent components.

The SLA model in Figure 6.7 declares that each agreement must be associated with at least three participants $sp_i \in SP$, at least a quality requirement $q_i \in Q$, and exactly an escrow account $ea_i \in EA$. Regarding the participants, they can take the role of service provider, consumer, or monitoring. To simplify the expression of quality requirements, the example SLA model only supports quantifiable and measured quality requirements in the form of $<$ *qualityname* $><$ *logicaloperator* $><$ *value* $><$ *unit* $>$ (i.e. *Availability* > 99%), which is sufficient for this study. The quality requirement definition can serve monitoring, compliance assessment, and proactive enforcement (i.e. corrective actions). A quality requirement shall not exist without being associated with a violation consequence $vc \in VC$ for the purposes of reactive enforcement (i.e. imposing penalty) and billing purposes. The SLA model supports providing instruction on what penalty to impose on the service provider. The SLA model supports defining the financial penalty as violation consequence in the form of $<$ *value* $><$ *unit* $>$ (i.e. 25%). The violation consequence must indicate the frequency of applying the penalty per month. For example, one can define a penalty of 5% for every 1,000 violation indecent to the latency requirement (see Figure 6.1).

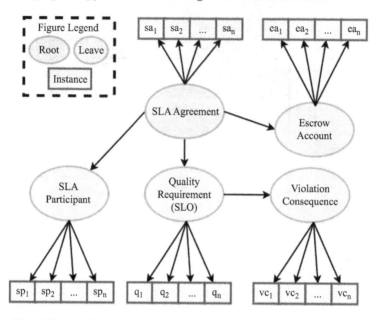

Figure 6.8   Relationship between agreement component and other SLA components

Smart contracts can apply penalties on escrow accounts associated with the agreement. The escrow account assumes a prepaid payment method. However, postpaid payment methods can be supported as well in a similar manner. For simplicity, the escrow account assumes two parties: the service provider and the consumer. The consumer deposits an agreed amount in advance, held by the smart contract and then realised by the end of the agreement.

6.4.4.2   Deployment to blockchain

The SLA model acts as a blueprint that governs and constrains SLA representation, structure, and operation. This study uses Hyperledger Fabric (HLF) to deploy the SLA model into the blockchain network. The HLF platform employs Chaincode capability to implement two main components. The first component is the state storage, which this study utilises to implement the SLA data model in Figure 6.7. Therefore, the state storage can store instances of the SLA components $s_i \in \{SA, SP, Q, VC, EA\}$ in the form of a blockchain asset that complies with the deployed SLA data model. The second component is the smart contract that has the privilege to access and operate stored SLA assets. The smart contract can encode the logic of any SLA-related task such as SLA definition, negotiation, compliance assessment, penalty enforcement, and billing.

Figure 6.9 uses an example of a possible blockchain-based architecture which can be conceivable due to the concept of decoupling the logic of SLA-related tasks from SLA content. Since SLA is being represented as blockchain assets, every SLA-related

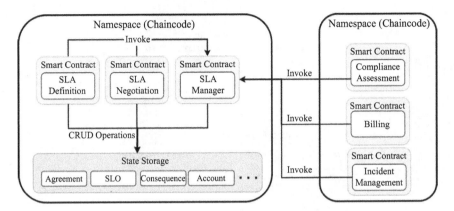

Figure 6.9   SLA model at the state storage and possible applications as smart contracts

task can reuse stored SLA assets for its purposes. The architecture also suggests that every smart contract can maintain awareness of and access to SLA assets, whether it shares the same namespace of the state storage or not.* If a smart contract shares the same namespaces as the state storage, then it can directly access SLA assets persisted in the state storage. Otherwise, internal smart contracts can provide external counterparts with a proper access privilege to their state storage. For instance, the compliance assessment smart contract can invoke the SLA manager smart contract, as per in Figure 6.9.

Based on the example SLA data model, this chapter implements an SLA manager in the form of smart contract. Figure 6.10 depicts the SLA manager, which assumes the role of a smart contract that interfaces between the blockchain-based state storage and authorised invokers (i.e. end-users, external applications, other smart contracts), it is assigned with two primary tasks, as follows:

- Enforcing the example SLA data model at the state storage.
- Serving basic CRUD operations (Create, Read, Update, Delete) for authorised invokers.

6.5   Implementation of the SLA data model

The main objective of an SLA data model is to enforce a set of rules and association constraints when representing SLA-related data within blockchain, particularly at the level of state storage. The example SLA data model S, in Figure 6.7, consists of a set of SLA components; namely, SLA agreement (SA), SLA participant (SP), escrow

---

*https://hyperledger-fabric.readthedocs.io/en/release-2.2/developapps/chaincodenamespace.html

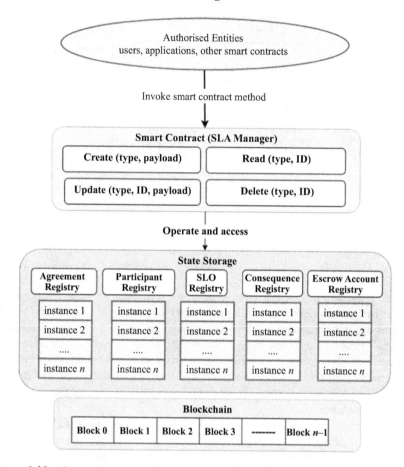

Figure 6.10   A smart contract that controls and interfaces with the deployed SLA data model

account (*EA*), quality requirement (*Q*), and violation consequences (*VC*). Hereafter, this chapter uses the convention $S = \{SA, SP, EA, Q, VC\}$ to denote components of the SLA data model. This study leverages the state storage to persist any instance of these SLA components $s \in S$ (see Figure 6.8) to achieve the IRAFUTAL principles (refer to Section 6.3).

HLF adopts a schema-less style for data representation at the state storage. It mainly organises data in the form of (k, v, ver), where k denotes asset key, v denotes asset value, and *ver* denotes the asset version. Every $\{k_i \in K\}$ is unique, which assist identification of, and access to stored SLA assets. Because the state storage is schema-free, every $\{v_i \in V\}$ can represent any component of the SLA data model $s \in S$; therefore, v_i can be different in size compared to another v_j. Altogether is ideal for implementing the example SLA data model due to the variation in the properties of each SLA component. Accordingly, we can state that $v_i \in S$, where $S = \{SA, SP, EA, Q, VC\}$

which means that the value v_i can hold any SLA component in S. For instance, assume a quality requirement q_i to be a blockchain asset complying with the SLA data model. Therefore, it would exist in the state storage as (k, q, ver). This also applicable to other components of the SLA data model where we can have (k, sp_i, ver) for SLA participants, (k, vc_i, ver) for violation consequences, (k, ea, ver) for escrow accounts, and (k, sa_i, ver) for SLA agreements. The last element ver indicates the current version of the SLA asset, such that $ver + 1$ implies a change to the state of the SLA asset.

6.5.1   The logic of SLA asset manager

Having represented and implemented SLA assets at the state storage, this study proceeds to illustrate the logic of a smart contract that interfaces between authorised invokers and the SLA assets; hereafter, referred to as *SLA manager*. In essence, smart contracts act as a gateway to state storage; and thus, they play a vital role in ensuring compliance with the SLA data model. The importance of the smart contract lies in the fact that they are autonomous; hence, they are not subject to the influence of any single authority. Figure 6.10 depicts the SLA manager as a smart contract that serves CRUD operations (Create, Read, Update, and Delete). Authorised entities can invoke the provided methods to access and operate SLA assets $S = \{SA, SP, EA, Q, VC\}$. For each smart contract invocation, and no matter which method invoked, the SLA manager ensures adherence with the example SLA data model, see Figure 6.7.

   To invoke a smart contract method, authorised entities must submit a transaction $T(J)$, where T indicates the transaction and J denotes a payload transported by the transaction. Consider that the state storage organises and stores SLA assets in the form of records structured as (k, v, ver). Accordingly, creating a record for an SLA asset requires the payload J to contain the definition of the SLA asset. For example, assume J that defines a quality requirement as $\{q_i \in Q \mid q \leftarrow Latency \leq 3\ s\}$. Therefore, J can be used to construct an SLA asset $s \in S$ in the form of (k, v, ver). When updating an existing SLA asset $s_i \in S$, the payload J would state (k, v), where k identifies an existing SLA asset $s \in S$, and v implies the updated definition of the SLA asset. Reading existing SLA assets is important for query purposes to benefit smart contracts assigned with SLA-related tasks. For that, authorised entities can invoke read functionality with $T(J)$, where J holds the key k of an existing SLA asset. For example, but not limited to, quality requirements $q_k \in Q$ are pivotal for monitoring and compliance assessment. Another example is escrow accounts $ea_k \in EA$ and SLA participants $sp_k \in SP$ serve billing and accountability purposes, respectively. Deleting an SLA asset also requires J to the key k of the intended asset. Noteworthy that while CRUD operations are possible within blockchain at the state storage, they are subject to the logic defined at the smart contract and rigorous validation and a consensus mechanism imposed by the underlying blockchain platform. Additionally, any operation does not execute unless supported by a transaction immutably committed at the blockchain ledger.

6.5.1.1   Naive SLA manager approach

As being discussed in Section 6.5, SLA assets $s \in S$ can vary in terms of their structure and properties. This variation can pose a challenge to design CRUD methods that

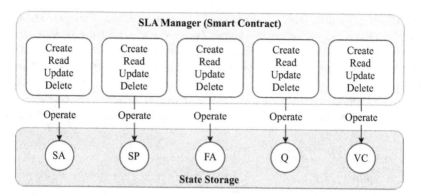

Figure 6.11   Naive SLA manager approach for managing SLA assets

situate all SLA assets $s_i \in S$. A naive approach would handle this variation by dedicating CRUD methods tailored specifically for every SLA asset, an example of which is in Figure 6.11. The naive approach leads to unnecessary repetition of CRUD functionalities for every SLA asset, which complicates communication between authorised entities and the smart contract and poses difficulties for the maintenance of the smart contract itself. The aftermath is particularly eminent when there is a large quantity of SLA components.

6.5.1.2   Enhanced SLA manager approach

Figure 6.10 presents an enhanced alternative, which addresses the variation of SLA assets with a rule-based mechanism that enables generalising each of the CRUD methods for any supported SLA components. This approach enables authorised entities to communicate with generalised CRUD methods that process and operate SLA assets. To elaborate, assume a transaction $T(J)$, where J can be a JSON-formatted payload. Authorised entities must explicitly indicate in the payload J which SLA asset is concerned. Therefore, the SLA manager will have the ability to reason about the intent of the transaction and determine which component of the SLA data model to impose on received transactions. Ideally, any CRUD operation should occur due to mutual understanding between involved participants, for example, by providing multi-signature with the deletion transaction, which proves the authenticity of intent by all concerned parties. HLF employs the concept of endorsement policy which enables specifying which entities to be involved in the transaction approval [40]. This section delves further into each CRUD operations and illustrates how they can handle various components of the SLA data model $s_i \in S$.

Creation of SLA assets

This section demonstrates the creation of any number of SLA assets, whether agreements, participants, quality requirements, violation consequences, and an escrow account. The SLA manager serves as a generalised creation method for any supported

```
1 ▾ {
2 ▾   "args": [
3         "SLA component type",
4         "SLA asset definition ...",
5 ▾       [
6             "Association with existing SLA assets ..."
7         ]
8     ]
9 }
```

Figure 6.12   Generic JSON-formatted schema for defining various SLA assets

SLA asset. As per Algorithm 1, the creation method consumes JSON-formatted pay-load J submitted as transaction $T(J)$ by authorised entities. For every received $T(J)$, the creation method runs a rule-based mechanism to examine which component of the SLA data model to impose on the received JSON-formatted payload J.

Figure 6.12 depicts a set of example JSON-formatted payloads for defining various SLA assets, which are compatible with the SLA data model. The definition of any SLA asset requires the JSON payload to specify the following:

1. An SLA component type, which can be any supported element of the SLA data model $\{SA, SP, EA, Q, VC\}$.
2. The definition of the SLA component as per the SLA data model.
3. If required, identifiers of dependencies (existing SLA assets to be associated with), as per the SLA data model.

Figure 6.13 shows the compatible definition of various assets as well as an accept-able order for creating them. The association constraints imposed by the SLA data model influences the order in which the SLA component should be defined. The order means that no SLA component associates with others unless they exist and are committed to the ledger beforehand. For example, no SLA agreement $(sa_i \in SA)$ can be defined unless associated with other existing assets per the SLA data model as follows:

- Exactly one escrow account $\{ea_i \in EA\}$.
- At least one quality requirement $\{q_1, q_2, \ldots, q_n \in Q\}$.
  - Every quality requirement $\{q_i \in Q\}$ depends on exactly one existing violation consequence $\{vc_i \in VC\}$.
- At least, three participants $\{sp_1, sp_2, \ldots, sp_n \in SP\}$. One of the them assumes the role of a service provider, the second participant assumes the role a consumer, while the third can assume a compliance role such as a monitoring tool or an auditor and so-forth.

Algorithm 1 illustrates the logic of processing received transactions $T(J)$, which results in the creation of SLA assets, where J is a JSON-formatted payload. The creation method deserialises the JSON payload and runs a rule-based mechanism to reason about which component of the SLA data model to impose on the received

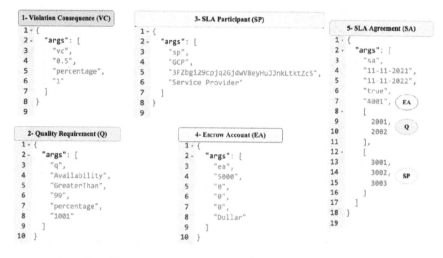

1- Violation Consequence (VC)
```
1 {
2    "args": [
3        "vc",
4        "0.5",
5        "percentage",
6        "1"
7    ]
8 }
9
```

3- SLA Participant (SP)
```
1 {
2    "args": [
3        "sp",
4        "GCP",
5        "3FZbg129cpjq2GjdwV8eyHuJJnkLtktZc5",
6        "Service Provider"
7    ]
8 }
9
```

5- SLA Agreement (SA)
```
1 {
2    "args": [
3        "sa",
4        "11-11-2021",
5        "11-11-2022",
6        "true",
7        "4001",          EA
8        [
9            2001,
10           2002           Q
11       ],
12       [
13           3001,
14           3002,          SP
15           3003
16       ]
17   ]
18 }
19
```

2- Quality Requirement (Q)
```
1 {
2    "args": [
3        "q",
4        "Availability",
5        "GreaterThan",
6        "99",
7        "percentage",
8        "1001"
9    ]
10 }
```

4- Escrow Account (EA)
```
1 {
2    "args": [
3        "ea",
4        "5000",
5        "0",
6        "0",
7        "0",
8        "Dollar"
9    ]
10 }
```

Figure 6.13   Examples of compatible JSON-formatted payloads for defining various SLA assets

payload. If the stated SLA component is supported, the SLA manager then validates the JSON payload accordingly. It also checks whether the payload attempts to associate with non-existing assets. Afterwards, the SLA manager composes the SLA asset and persists in the state storage in the form of (k, v, ver) by extracting and using relevant properties of the JSON payload.

Creating the overall SLA agreement (SA) is done similarly to quality requirements Q in terms of association. However, the SLA agreement is more complex because it associates with multiple and various SLA components. Consider the example JSON payload for creating an SLA agreement in Figure 6.13, (the 5th JSON payload), which states main agreement properties and links to the following:

- One escrow account identified with $ea_1 = 4001$.
- Two quality requirements, identified as $q_1 = 2001$ and $q_2 = 2002$, respectively.
- Three SLA participants, identified as $sp_1 = 3001$, $sp_2 = 3002$ and $sp_3 = 3003$, respectively.

As per the SLA data model, the SLA manager validates whether the payload is associated with minimum SLA assets. Yet, the SLA agreement $sa_i \in SA$ does not explicitly state any violation consequences since it is sufficient to only specify their respective quality requirements. For the rest of the SLA components, the smart contract does not have prior knowledge of how many SLA assets are to be associated with this agreement. Therefore, the smart contact undertakes extra measures by traversing through every defined instance of escrow accounts EA, quality requirements Q and participants SP.

First, line 1 in Algorithm 2 declares an array of three elements which are $|EA|$, $|Q|$, and $|SP|$. Each one of them defines the minimum instances of each cosponsoring

---

Algorithm 1: Creation of SLA asset in accordance with the SLA data model

---

Require: J ▷ JSON-formatted SLA components from 1 to 4 in Figure 6.13
Ensure: Adherence to SLA model
1:   $S = \{VC, Q, SP, EA, SA\}$ ▷ supported types of SLA component
2:   **if** $J[0] \in S$ **then**   ▷ is it a recognised SLA type?
3:    **if** $J[0] \leftarrow VC$ **then**   ▷ Is it a violation consequence component?
4:     **if** J complies with VC **then**
5:      $vc_{penalty} \leftarrow J[1]$ ▷ assign penalty
6:      $vc_{unit} \leftarrow J[2]$ ▷ assign component type
7:      $vc_{frequency} \leftarrow J[3]$ ▷ assign violation frequency
8:      vc_{k++} ▷ assign a unique key
9:      $vc_k \in VC$ ▷ add *vc* instance to Violation Consequence registry
10:     **else**
11:      reject J
12:     **end if**
13:    **else if** $J[0] \leftarrow Q$ **then**   ▷ Is it a quality requirement unit?
14:     **if** J complies with Q **then**
15:      $q_{name} \leftarrow J[1]$ ▷ assign name for the quality requirement
16:      **if** $J[2] \in Operators$ **then**   ▷ Is the logical operator recognised? e.g. Greater Than
17:       $q_{level} \leftarrow J[2]$ ▷ assign required level
18:      **else**
19:       abort
20:      **end if**
21:      $q_{threshold} \leftarrow J[3]$ ▷ assign threshold
22:      **if** $J[3] \in VC$ **then**   ▷ query whether there exists the instance of violation consequence
23:       $q_{vc} \leftarrow J[4]$ ▷ associate with the violation consequence
24:      **else**
25:       abort
26:      **end if**
27:      q_{k++} ▷ assign a unique key
28:      $q_k \in Q$ ▷ add *q* instance to Quality Requirements registry
29:     **else**
30:      reject J
31:     **end if**
32:    **else if** $J[0] \leftarrow SP \vee EA \vee SA$ **then**   ▷ or other types of SLA components
33:     Instantiation is done in a similar manner to the above ...
34:    **end if**
35: **else**
36:   Reject
37: **end if**

SLA component as per the SLA data model (see Figure 6.7). For example, $|EA| = 1$, $|Q| = 1$, and $|SP| = 3$. Figure 6.14 depicts seven main elements of the JSON payload representing the complete SLA agreement. Line 7 loops through JSON payload starting from $|J| - 3$, which is the fourth element, until $|J| - 1$, which is the last element. Note that $|J| - 3$ points to an existing escrow account, $|J| - 2$ points to a collection of quality requirements, and lastly $|J| - 1$ points to a collection of participants.

Algorithm 2: Agreement composition

Require: J ▷ JSON-formatted SLA Agreement (the 5th component in Figure 6.13)
Ensure: Adherence to SLA Model
 1: $sdm \leftarrow [|EA|, |Q|, |SP|]$ ▷ an array of minimum instances of each SLA component as per Figure 6.7
 2: **if** $J[0] \leftarrow SA$ **then**   ▷ SLA Agreement
 3:     **if** J complies with SA **then**
 4:        $sa_{startDate} \leftarrow J[1]$ ▷ assign start date
 5:        $sa_{endDate} \leftarrow J[2]$ ▷ assign end date
 6:        $sa_{validityStatus} \leftarrow J[3]$ ▷ assign validity Status
 7:        $from \leftarrow |J| - 3$ ▷ Loop beginning. $|J|$ denotes the JSON (array) size
 8:        $to \leftarrow |J| - 1$ ▷ Loop beginning
 9:        **for** $(x = from, x <= to, x++)$ **do**   ▷ examine correct association
10:            $size \leftarrow |J[x]|$ ▷ denotes the size of the current JSON element
11:            **if** $size \neq sdm[x - 4]$ **then**   ▷ validate minimum elements against the SLA model
12:                Abort
13:            **end if**
14:            **for** $(i = 0, i <= size - 1, i++)$ **do**   ▷ Loop through the current JSON element
15:                **if** $J[x][i]$ non-Exist **then**
16:                    Abort
17:                **end if**
18:            **end for**
19:        **end for**
20:        sa_{k++} ▷ assign a unique key
21:        $sa_k \in SA$ ▷ add sa instance to agreements registry
22:     **else**
23:        reject J
24:     **end if**
25: **end if**
26: **Example Output: See Figure 6.15**

Second, the inner iteration in Figure 6.14 validates that each specified component from $|J| - 3$ to $|J| - 1$ adheres to the minimum required instance as per enforced by the SLA data model. Finally, upon the success of SLA agreement creation, the SLA manager informs all concerned participants about this event and supplies them with the complete agreement in a JSON-formatted document, as per in Figure 6.13.

Reading SLA assets

Any SLA-related tasks (i.e. monitoring, enforcement, billing, etc.) can maintain SLA awareness by accessing existing SLA assets at the state storage. For instance, monitoring tools residing in the external world need to maintain awareness of quality requirements, which enables setting thresholds of when to consider the service provider is in violation [49]. Other SLA tasks can be encoded in the form of smart contracts such as compliance assessment [3] and enforcement of violation consequences [35,50]. The SLA manager smart contract exposes a read method that enables authorised entities to query existing SLA assets. The read method requires invokers to supply both the *id* and *type* of the asset, which enables the SLA manager to query

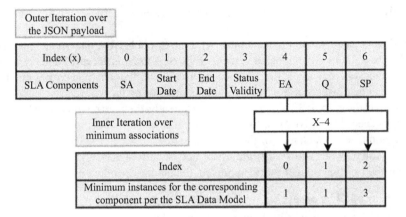

Outer Iteration over the JSON payload							
Index (x)	0	1	2	3	4	5	6
SLA Components	SA	Start Date	End Date	Status Validity	EA	Q	SP

Inner Iteration over minimum associations	X–4		
Index	0	1	2
Minimum instances for the corresponding component per the SLA Data Model	1	1	3

Figure 6.14   Validating minimum instances of each component in the JSON payload against the SLA data model

the state storage. If the asset exists, the SLA manager retrieves it and responds to the invoker with a JSON-formatted document as per in Figure 6.13.

Updating SLA assets

Authorised entities can invoke the SLA manager to update existing SLA assets. During an SLA lifecycle, an amendment can be introduced for several reasons [7] such as:

- Customising a default SLA agreement during the negotiation stage.
- Adjusting an SLA due to renegotiation or recent performance report.
- Reflecting the service provider's performance on related assets such as escrow accounts.
- Rectification an error in the SLA agreement.
- SLA termination.

As per the IRAFUTAL principles discussed in Section 6.3, such a process should be user-friendly and avoid the need for subject–matter experts such as smart contract developers or blockchain operators. Furthermore, the proposed approach encourages amendable, independent, reusable, and identifiable SLA assets by representing them at the state storage. Accordingly, a GUI or an automated tool (external applications or other smart contracts) can interface with the SLA manager to update existing SLA assets with proper authorisation and authentication. Some uses of the update functionality include modifying properties' values of existing SLA assets as well as adding or removing the association with others.

Figure 6.10 illustrates a generic update functionality served by the SLA manager, which can adjust any existing SLA asset. The process of updating an SLA asset executes similarly to the creation method, presented in Algorithms 1 and 2. The only difference between SLA creation and update methods is that authorised invokers must supply a key $s_k \in S$, identifying an existing SLA asset. Otherwise, the SLA manager must reject the transaction.

The updated version must comply with the example SLA data model presented in Figure 6.7. Once the updated version of the SLA asset is accepted and committed to the blockchain records, the SLA manager informs all concerned parties about the change to readjust accordingly. For example, monitoring tools need awareness of any changes in the current SLA agreement. Consequently, they can readjust thresholds and triggers accordingly. Noteworthy mentioning is that the successfulness of an update operation leads to a change of the asset version $(k, v, ver + +)$. The version change is concerned by the Multi-Version Concurrency Control (MVCC) [51]; a mechanism employed by Hyperledger fabric to prevent the double-spending problem [52].

Deletion of SLA assets

While this study generally discourages assets deletion, it discusses it to refute misconceptions about asset deletion and elaborate on the difference between state storage and blockchain. First of all, the state storage maintains the last state of the SLA assets, while the ledger's blockchain maintains all transactions about stored assets. While the state storage is amendable such that it accepts typical CRUD operations, no amendment is applied unless supported with a valid transaction that passes all validation checks, endorsement policies, and consensus mechanism imposed by the underlying blockchain platform, namely, HLF [42,52]. Therefore, deleting an asset from the state storage does not necessarily mean deleting the log of transactions from the ledger's blockchain.

Asset deletion may be desired when there is an orphan asset that is of no use any longer. For instance, consider an agreement associated with three quality requirements. For any reason, the agreement has been updated to be associated with only two quality requirements. This is where an SLA asset can be left abandoned and not used. While it is possible to delete any existing asset from the state storage, this study discourages the deletion of any SLA asset with consideration of the following:

- When deleting an asset (i.e. SA or Q) may leave dependencies orphan and unused.
- The SLA data model encourages the usability of SLA components. For example, the same quality requirement may be associated with different agreements. Therefore, deleting an agreement and all its dependencies will harm other agreements that share in common these dependencies.

6.6 Evaluation and observation

6.6.1 Failure test units

Unlike traditional deployment practice, it is difficult to rectify an error or conduct maintenance on smart contracts after their deployment to the blockchain network [36,38]. For that, the smart contract must undergo careful testing coverage to ensure its compliance with the SLA data model and meeting expected behaviour. Table 6.1 shows a set of basic failure test units conducted on the smart contract before deployment

Table 6.1   *Failure tests conducted on the SLA manager smart contract*

Expectation	Test	Methods
Reject unrecognised asset type	SLA component with the correct structure according to the SLA data model. However, stating a type other than {VC, Q, SP, EA, SA}	Create Update
Reject unrecognised asset structure	SLA component with a recognised SLA asset type {VC, Q, SP, EA, SA}. However, the structure violates the SLA data model	Create Update
Reject incorrect value type	– Define unrecognised currency for an escrow account – Define unrecognised logical operators (i.e. XOR) – Define a string value where it should be integer	Create Update
Association with only existing SLA asset	Attempt creating SLA assets without creating their dependencies beforehand	Create Update
Reject unrecognised ID	Use non-existing ID	Update Read Delete

to the blockchain side. While this test coverage does not claim to be exhaustive, it demonstrates how to mitigate and account for failure threats to the smart contract (SLA manager). The table presents a set of testing units on the SLA manager. For each of them, there is the following:

- **Expectation:** a description of normal behaviour.
- **Test:** a failure deliberately crafted to push issues on the surface.
- **Methods:** CRUD methods are subject to the test unit and must meet the expectations.

The Smart contract underwent multiple development iterations until it reached a sufficient level of maturity suitable for this study. This study does not approve any development iteration unless it passes at least the listed test units in Table 6.1. The testing implementation is available in the public GitHub Repository (see footnote †). Further experiments in this chapter and the following chapters build on top of these testing units.

6.6.2   Use case 1: SLA definition

The section evaluates a basic application that demonstrates the use of the SLA manager for composing a set of reusable SLA assets at the state storage. Figure 6.15 illustrates and demonstrates a graph of SLA assets created via the SLA manager, which satisfies the IRAFUTAL principles, discussed in Section 6.3. Every SLA asset of the graph is instantiated from SLA components supported by the example SLA data model

---

†https://github.com/aakzubaidi/slaController

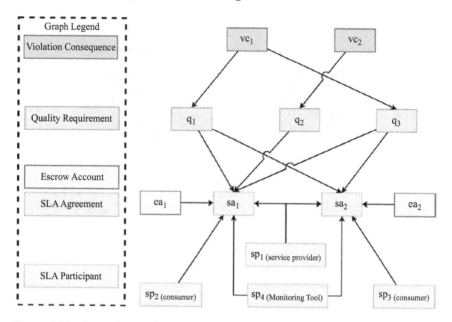

Figure 6.15   Example graph of reusable instances SLA units persisted at state storage

$\{VC, Q, SP, EA, SA\}$. The presented graph is achievable thanks to the association constraints imposed by the SLA data model. It consists of a service provider sp_1 that is engaged in two SLA agreements $\{sa_1, sa_2\}$. There is also a monitoring tool sp_4, which participates in the two SLA agreements. Each SLA agreement is associated with a separate escrow accounts $\{ea_1, ea_2\}$ and two different SLA consumers $\{sp_2, sp_3\}$. There are two violation consequence assets $\{vc_1, vc_2\}$ and three quality requirements $\{q_1, q_2, q_3\}$. Both of the quality requirements $\{q_1, q_3\}$ make use of the same violation consequence vc_1. It is also possible to use a different violation consequence as in the case with q_2 and vc_2, respectively. Finally, the SLA agreement sa_1 states all existing quality requirements $\{q_1, q_2, q_3\}$. On the other hand, the other SLA agreement sa_2 shares in common the quality requirements $\{q_1, q_3\}$.

6.6.3   Use case 2: SLA negotiation

Conventional SLA representation approaches hinder smooth and effective SLA negotiation (Section 6.2.3 provides further detail). On the other hand, the proposed approach enables instant and user-friendly SLA negotiation within a blockchain environment. Consequently, eliminating, to the minimum possible, the need for blockchain experts such as smart contract developers and operators (refer to Figure 6.4(b)). Assuming a proper GUI is in place, SLA negotiation can benefit from the

SLA manager, as shown in Figure 6.9. Noteworthy is that the SLA manager materialises the proposed SLA representation approach and complies with the IRAFUTAL principles. While modelling a robust SLA negotiation protocol is not the ultimate goal of this study, a basic negotiation protocol is built on top of the SLA manager to demonstrate the usefulness of the proposed approach in resolving issues related to conventional approaches. Moreover, this section highlights some considerations regarding this matter, which can be useful for future work and of interest to researchers in the domain.

Regarding the use case of SLA negotiation, consider that the SLA manager serves basic CRUD operations for SLA assets. Note that the SLA manager enforces the example SLA data model on any operation on SLA assets. Therefore, a supplementary smart contract for SLA negotiation acts as a second layer on top of the SLA manager. The smart contract mediates between service providers and consumers $\{sp \in SP\}$, with the purpose to aid them to reach an SLA agreement over the blockchain. Assuming a GUI is in place, SLA participants can partake in a contractual session to propose, approve, or reject any action supported by the SLA manager on SLA components, given that they comply with the example SLA data model. Figure 6.16 overviews the concept of SLA negotiation over blockchain and illustrates primary components typically involved in the process. First, there is a smart contract dedicated to basic SLA negotiation functionalities, which enables proposing, approving or rejecting actions on SLA components. The smart negotiation contract leverages CRUD operations provided by the SLA manager for conducting the negotiation functionalities. HLF provides endorsement and consensus mechanisms, exploited to facilitate consensus and endorsement on these functionalities. The GUI interfaces with the SLA negotiation smart contract and exposes the negotiation functionalities in a user-friendly manner for SLA participants.

Figure 6.16 presents a basic SLA negotiation protocol designed and implemented to demonstrate the advantages of the proposed SLA representation. The implementation of the basic SLA negotiation protocol is publicly available as an open-source project on GitHub.[‡] As per the basic protocol, the SLA negotiation smart contract mediates between the involved parties and enable them to propose a new or customised SLA agreement compatible with the example SLA data model. The GUI enables composing all dependencies $\{VC, Q, SP, EA\}$ of an SLA agreement $sa_i \in SA$. The GUI produces a JSON payload for each SLA component, similar to the examples presented in Figure 6.13. The GUI interfaces with the SLA manager and automatically submits a series of transactions to create an SLA asset for each JSON payload. For a successful creation, the order of these transactions and the format of their attached payloads must comply with the SLA data model as discussed in Section 6.5.1.2.

Following the creation of all agreement dependencies, the service provider proposes a complete SLA agreement SA, which associates with all desired dependencies in $\{VC, Q, SP, EA\}$, an example of which is in Figure 6.13. The GUI interfaces with the negotiation smart contract, and invokes the *propose* to start the negotiation process as

[‡]https://github.com/aakzubaidi/slaController

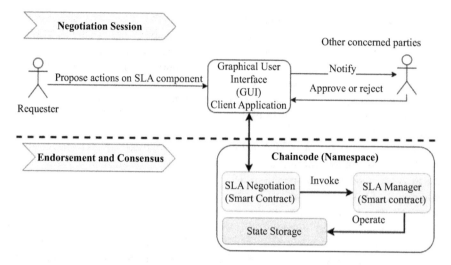

Figure 6.16   Overview on SLA negotiation session over blockchain

illustrated in the basic negotiation protocol (see Figure 6.17). The negotiation smart contract notifies all involved participants of created SLA proposal and provides them with the key of the newly created SLA agreement key sa_k.

For negotiation purposes, the validity status of the SLA agreement component is by default set to *false* to indicate that this agreement is not yet established and enforced (refer to the SLA data model in Figure 6.7). The validity status of the SLA agreement does not change to *true* unless all involved participants approve the proposed SLA agreement. In addition, the agreement component *SA* is adjusted to include two properties for each involved participant: vote (Boolean) and signature (String), which are set to null by default. These properties reflect the vote integrity of each SLA participant whether they approve or reject the proposed SLA agreement. The signature property holds the participant's signature for vote integrity purposes.

The service provider may attempt to establish the SLA at any point in time by invoking the negotiation smart contract; outcomes of which can be one of the following:

- The proposed SLA agreement meets an endorsement policy (i.e. all parties must approve). Accordingly, the validity status becomes *true*, declaring the confirmation and enforcement of the proposed SLA agreement. In practice, this event could trigger further actions as well, such as service provisioning, monitoring, billing, and payment [5,53].
- All or some of the concerned parties have not engaged in the voting process. Therefore, the negotiation smart contract notifies parties who neglected to vote. In this case, the service provider may try again to establish the SLA.
- All have voted; however, the proposed SLA agreement does meet the endorsement policy in place. In this case, the service provider may abandon this agreement or

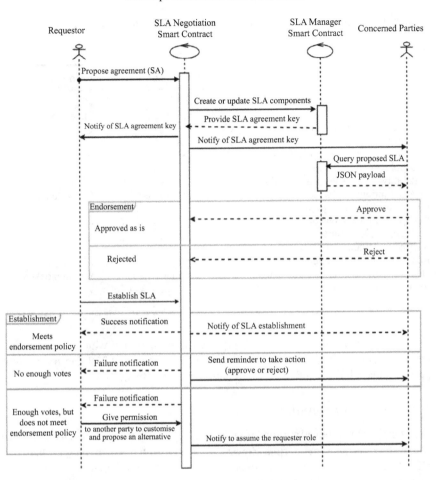

Figure 6.17 Basic SLA negotiation protocol: a use case

offer a concerned party the opportunity to propose an updated version of the SLA agreement. In this case, the SLA negotiation smart contract resets all properties of SLA agreements related to the voting process (validity status = false) and (vote = false, signature = false) for every involved participant. Subsequently, the selected party (i.e. consumer) may attempt to reiterate the negotiation process, as illustrated in the basic negotiation protocol (see Figure 6.17). Unlike the service provider, involved parties can only update existing SLA sa_k, assigned by the service provider.

To sum up, while the example basic negotiation protocol does not claim to be exhaustive, it demonstrates how the proposed SLA representation approach can facilitate negotiation within blockchain in a user-friendly and timely manner without the need for blockchain experts or the need to migrate from existing smart contracts.

Table 6.2   Comparison table between conventional and proposed SLA representation approaches

Facet	Conventional Approaches	Proposed Approach
Representation with blockchain	✓	✓
Represented at:	Smart contract	State Storage
Immutable ledger records	✓	✓
Deterministic execution	✓	✓
SLA Awareness within blockchain	✓	✓
Decoupling logic from SLA	✗	✓
Suitability for SLA tasks automation	✓	✓
SLA definition:	Blockchain Experts	User-friendly
Modifiable SLA definition	✗	✓
Resistance to malicious modification	✓	✓
Verifiable SLA integrity	✓	✓
SLA host availability	✓	✓
Reusability of SLA content	✗	✓
Negotiation before SLA establishment	External to blockchain	Within blockchain
Renegotiation after SLA establishment	✗	✓
Error-rectifiability	✗	✓

This chapter presented an SLA representation approach which counters limitations of conventional approaches, discussed in Section 6.2.2. Table 6.2 presents prominent similarities and differences between both of them.

6.6.4   Threats to validity

In principle, the proposed approach can be also applicable to any blockchain platform where state storage is supported. However, this approach has been only evaluated on HLF. It would be also interesting to conduct this study on Ethereum, where the programming language for smart contract is constrained and transaction are executed at cost. While HLF by default supports data modelling, Ethereum seems to only enable this approach by applying the data segregation patterns which separates between the business logic and data model [39]. A limitation of the proposed approach is that it only considers quantifiable quality requirements for the sake of demonstration. Notwithstanding, there remains the challenge of representing non-quantifiable requirements, a practice that while exist, but is generally discouraged by most contemporary SLA frameworks and guidelines. While the proposed approach demonstrates the advantages of SLA representation at the state storage, a future work needs to consider more complex SLA structure such as conditional statement and exception.

6.7   Conclusion

This chapter presented an SLA representation approach that addresses the limitations of conventional approaches, discussed in Section 6.2.2. Table 6.2 presents prominent similarities and differences between both of them. In terms of resemblances, both represent SLA within blockchain which provides smart contracts with the necessary awareness and preserves important properties such as deterministic execution, integrity, high availability, ease of access, and immunity from malicious behaviour. On the other hand, they differ mainly regarding the mechanism of SLA representation within the blockchain. Whereas conventional approaches represent SLA in the form of a smart contract, the proposed approach primarily decouples SLA from the smart contract's logic and represents it at the state storage level. While the presented approach attains key benefits of conventional approaches, it mitigates its limitations in several ways by satisfying the IRAFUTAL principles, discussed in Section 6.3. Moreover, it aligns well with a typical SLA lifecycle which normally expects SLA modification due to either negotiation before SLA establishment or renegotiation afterwards. It also enables SLA definition and error rectification in a user-friendly and timely manner while mitigating the need for blockchain experts to the minimum possible. The next chapters experiment and evaluate the proposed SLA representation approach for other key stages of a typical SLA lifecycle: SLA monitoring, compliance assessment, and penalty enforcement in the context of IoT.

References

[1] N. Hamdi, C. El Hog, R. Ben Djemaa, and L. Sliman. "A survey on SLA management using blockchain based smart contracts." In *International Conference on Intelligent Systems Design and Applications*, pp. 1425–1433. Cham: Springer International Publishing, 2021.

[2] E. D. Pascale, H. Ahmadi, L. Doyle, and I. Macaluso, "Toward scalable user-deployed ultra-dense networks: blockchain-enabled small cells as a service," *IEEE Communications Magazine*, vol. 58, no. 8, pp. 82–88, 2020.

[3] M. S. Rahman, I. Khalil, and M. Atiquzzaman, "Blockchain-enabled SLA compliance for crowdsourced edge-based network function virtualization," *IEEE Network*, vol. 35, no. 5, pp. 58–65, 2021.

[4] R. B. Uriarte, R. de Nicola, and K. Kritikos, "Towards distributed SLA management with smart contracts and blockchain," in *2018 IEEE International Conference on Cloud Computing Technology and Science (CloudCom)*. Piscataway, NJ: IEEE, Dec 2018, pp. 266–271. Available: https://ieeexplore.ieee.org/document/8591028/.

[5] R. B. Uriarte, H. Zhou, K. Kritikos, Z. Shi, Z. Zhao, and R. De Nicola, "Distributed service-level agreement management with smart contracts and blockchain," in *Concurrency and Computation: Practice and Experience*, Apr 2020. Available: https://onlinelibrary.wiley.com/doi/abs/10.1002/cpe.5800.

[6] K. Christidis and M. Devetsikiotis, "Blockchains and smart contracts for the Internet of Things," *IEEE Access*, vol. 4, pp. 2292–2303, 2016. Available: http://ieeexplore.ieee.org/document/7467408/.

[7] S. Mubeen, S. A. Asadollah, A. V. Papadopoulos, M. Ashjaei, H. Pei-Breivold, and M. Behnam, "Management of service level agreements for cloud services in IoT: a systematic mapping study," *IEEE Access*, vol. 6, pp. 30184–30207, 2018. Available: https://ieeexplore.ieee.org/document/8016558/.

[8] W. Cai, Z. Wang, J. B. Ernst, Z. Hong, C. Feng, and V. C. Leung, "Decentralized applications: the blockchain-empowered software system," *IEEE Access*, vol. 6, pp. 53019–53033, 2018.

[9] O. F. Rana, M. Warnier, T. B. Quillinan, F. Brazier, and D. Cojocarasu, "Managing violations in service level agreements," in *Grid Middleware and Services*. Boston, MA: Springer US, 2008, pp. 349–358. Available: http://link.springer.com/10.1007/978-0-387-78446-5_23.

[10] K. T. Kearney and F. Torelli, "The SLA model," in *Service Level Agreements for Cloud Computing*. New York, NY: Springer New York, 2011, pp. 43–67. Available: http://link.springer.com/10.1007/978-1-4614-1614-2_4.

[11] ISO, ISO/IEC 19086-2:2018 – Cloud Computing – Service Level Agreement (SLA) Framework – Part 2: Metric Model. Available: https://www.iso.org/standard/67546.html.

[12] C-SIG-SLA, Cloud Service Level Agreement Standardisation Guidelines | Shaping Europe's Digital Future, 2014. Available: https://ec.europa.eu/digital-single-market/en/news/cloud-service-level-agreement-standardisation-guidelines.

[13] N. B. Vlacheas, D. Kyriazis, E. Protonotarios, *et al.*, *SLA specification and Reference Model-a D3.2 Status Final for Submission (updated after final review)*, 2016. Available: http://slalom-project.eu/sites/default/files/slalom/public/content-files/article/SLALOMD3.2_v1.1_UPDATED.pdf.

[14] TMForum, "Enabling End-to-End Cloud SLA Management," TMForum, Tech. Rep., 2014. Available: https://www.tmforum.org/resources/technical-report-best-practice/tr178-enabling-end-to-end-cloud-sla-management-v2-0-2/.

[15] OMG Cloud Working Group, "Practical Guide to Cloud Service Agreements Version 3.0," Object Management Group, Tech. Rep., 2019. Available: https://www.omg.org/cloud/deliverables/Practical-Guide-to-Cloud-Service-Agreements.pdf.

[16] S. K. Garg, S. Versteeg, and R. Buyya, "A framework for ranking of cloud computing services," *Future Generation Computer Systems*, vol. 29, no. 4, pp. 1012–1023, 2013.

[17] S. Girs, S. Sentilles, S. A. Asadollah, M. Ashjaei, and S. Mubeen. "A systematic literature study on definition and modeling of service-level agreements for cloud services in IoT." *IEEE Access* 8 (2020): 134498–134513.

[18] A. Alqahtani, E. Solaiman, P. Patel, S. Dustdar, and R. Ranjan, "Service level agreement specification for end-to-end IoT application ecosystems," *Software: Practice and Experience*, vol. 49, no. 12, pp. 1689–1711, 2019. Available: https://onlinelibrary.wiley.com/doi/abs/10.1002/spe.2747.

[19] E. Yaqub, P. Wieder, C. Kotsokalis, *et al.*, "A generic platform for conducting SLA negotiations," in *Service Level Agreements for Cloud Computing*, pp. 187–206, 2011. Available: https://link.springer.com/chapter/10.1007/978-1-4614-1614-2_12.

[20] ISO/IEC 19086-1:2016 – Information Technology – Cloud Computing – Service Level Agreement (SLA) Framework – Part 1: Overview and Concepts. Available: https://www.iso.org/standard/67545.html.

[21]   A. Keller and H. Ludwig, "The WSLA framework: specifying and monitoring service level agreements for web services," *Journal of Network and Systems Management*, vol. 11, no. 1, pp. 57–81, 2003. Available: http://link.springer.com/10.1023/A:1022445108617.

[22]   T. Labidi, A. Mtibaa, W. Gaaloul, and F. Gargouri, "Ontology-based SLA negotiation and re-negotiation for cloud computing," in *Proceedings – 2017 IEEE 26th International Conference on Enabling Technologies: Infrastructure for Collaborative Enterprises, WETICE 2017*, pp. 36–41, Aug 2017.

[23]   L. Wu and R. Buyya, "Service level agreement (SLA) in utility computing systems," *Grid and Cloud Computing*, pp. 286–310, 2010. Available: https://arxiv.org/abs/1010.2881v1.

[24]   L. De Marco, F. Ferrucci, and M.-T. Kechadi, "SLAFM – a service level agreement formal model for cloud computing," in *Proceedings of the 5th International Conference on Cloud Computing and Services Science*. SCITEPRESS – Science and Technology Publications, 2015, pp. 521–528. Available: http://www.scitepress.org/DigitalLibrary/Link.aspx?doi=10.5220/000545180 5210528.

[25]   S. Tata, M. Mohamed, T. Sakairi, N. Mandagere, O. Anya, and H. Ludwig, "rSLA: a service level agreement language for cloud services," in *2016 IEEE 9th International Conference on Cloud Computing (CLOUD)*. Piscataway, NJ: IEEE, Jun 2016, pp. 415–422. Available: http://ieeexplore.ieee.org/document/7820299/.

[26]   A. T. Wonjiga, S. Peisert, L. Rilling, and C. Morin, "Blockchain as a trusted component in cloud SLA verification," in *Proceedings of the 12th IEEE/ACM International Conference on Utility and Cloud Computing Companion – UCC '19 Companion*. New York, NY: ACM Press, 2019. Available: https://doi.org/10.1145/3368235.3368872.

[27]   K. Singi, V. Kaulgud, R. P. Jagadeesh Chandra Bose, and S. Podder, "CAG: Compliance adherence and governance in software delivery using blockchain," in *Proceedings – 2019 IEEE/ACM 2nd International Workshop on Emerging Trends in Software Engineering for Blockchain, WETSEB 2019*. Institute of Electrical and Electronics Engineers Inc., May 2019, pp. 32–39.

[28]   H. Nakashima and M. Aoyama, "An automation method of SLA contract of Web APIs and its platform based on blockchain concept," *Proceedings – 2017 IEEE 1st International Conference on Cognitive Computing, ICCC 2017*, pp. 32–39, Jun 2017. Available: http://ieeexplore.ieee.org/document/8029220/.

[29]   N. Kapsoulis, A. Psychas, A. Litke, and T. Varvarigou, "Reinforcing SLA consensus on blockchain," *Computers*, vol. 10, no. 12, p. 159, 2021. Available: https://www.mdpi.com/2073-431X/10/12/159/htm https://www.mdpi.com/2073-431X/10/12/159.

[30]   J. Benet, *IPFS – Content Addressed, Versioned, P2P File System*, Jul 2014. Available: https://arxiv.org/abs/1407.3561 http://arxiv.org/abs/1407.3561.

[31]   S. Wang, L. Ouyang, Y. Yuan, X. Ni, X. Han, and F.-Y. Wang, "Blockchain-enabled smart contracts: architecture, applications, and future trends," *IEEE Transactions on Systems, Man, and Cybernetics: Systems*, pp. 1–12, 2019. Available: https://ieeexplore.ieee.org/document/8643084/.

[32] E. J. Scheid, B. B. Rodrigues, L. Z. Granville, and B. Stiller, "Enabling dynamic SLA compensation using blockchain-based smart contracts," in *2019 IFIP/IEEE Symposium on Integrated Network and Service Management, IM 2019*, 2019, pp. 53–61.

[33] I. Weber, X. Xu, R. Riveret, G. Governatori, A. Ponomarev, and J. Mendling, "Untrusted business process monitoring and execution using blockchain," in *Lecture Notes in Computer Science (including subseries Lecture Notes in Artificial Intelligence and Lecture Notes in Bioinformatics)*. Cham: Springer, Sep 2016, vol. 9850 LNCS, pp. 329–347.

[34] R. B. Uriarte, F. Tiezzi, and R. D. Nicola, "SLAC: a formal service-level-agreement language for cloud computing," in *2014 IEEE/ACM 7th International Conference on Utility and Cloud Computing*. Piscataway, NJ: IEEE, Dec 2014, pp. 419–426. Available: http://ieeexplore.ieee.org/document/7027520/.

[35] P. Kochovski, V. Stankovski, S. Gec, F. Faticanti, M. Savi, D. Siracusa, and S. Kum, "Smart contracts for service-level agreements in edge-to-cloud computing," *Journal of Grid Computing*, vol. 18, no. 4, pp. 673–690, Dec 2020. Available: https://doi.org/10.1007/s10723-020-09534-y.

[36] W. Zou, D. Lo, P. S. Kochhar, X.-B. D. Le, *et al.*, "Smart contract development: challenges and opportunities," *IEEE Transactions on Software Engineering*, vol. 47, pp. 1–1, 2019.

[37] H. Zhou, C. de Laat, and Z. Zhao, "Trustworthy cloud service level agreement enforcement with blockchain based smart contract," in *2018 IEEE International Conference on Cloud Computing Technology and Science (CloudCom)*. Piscataway, NJ: IEEE, Dec 2018, pp. 255–260. Available: https://ieeexplore.ieee.org/document/8591026/.

[38] B. Marino and A. Juels, "Setting standards for altering and undoing smart contracts," in *Lecture Notes in Computer Science (including subseries Lecture Notes in Artificial Intelligence and Lecture Notes in Bioinformatics)*, vol. 9718. Cham: Springer, 2016, pp. 151–166.

[39] M. Wöhrer and U. Zdun, "Design patterns for smart contracts in the Ethereum ecosystem," in *2018 IEEE International Conference on Internet of Things (iThings) and IEEE Green Computing and Communications (GreenCom) and IEEE Cyber, Physical and Social Computing (CPSCom) and IEEE Smart Data (SmartData)*, 2018, pp. 1513–1520.

[40] E. Androulaki, A. De Caro, M. Neugschwandtner, and A. Sorniotti, "Endorsement in hyperledger fabric," in *Proceedings – 2019 2nd IEEE International Conference on Blockchain, Blockchain 2019*, pp. 510–519, Jul 2019.

[41] T. T. A. Dinh, R. Liu, M. Zhang, G. Chen, B. C. Ooi, and J. Wang, "Untangling blockchain: a data processing view of blockchain systems," *IEEE Transactions on Knowledge and Data Engineering*, vol. 30, no. 7, pp. 1366–1385, 2018.

[42] E. Androulaki, A. Barger, V. Bortnikov, *et al.*, *Hyperledger Fabric: A Distributed Operating System for Permissioned Blockchains*, 2018. Available: http://arxiv.org/abs/1801.10228 http://dx.doi.org/10.1145/3190508.3190538.

[43] D. Yaga, P. Mell, N. Roby, and K. Scarfone, "Blockchain Technology Overview," National Institute of Standards and Technology, Gaithersburg,

MD, Tech. Rep., Oct 2019. Available: http://arxiv.org/abs/1906.11078%0Ahttp://dx.doi.org/10.6028/NIST.IR.8202.

[44]   K. S. S. Wai, E. C. Htoon, and N. N. M. Thein, "Storage structure of student record based on hyperledger fabric blockchain," in *2019 International Conference on Advanced Information Technologies, ICAIT 2019*, pp. 108–113, Nov 2019.

[45]   G. Chung, L. Desrosiers, M. Gupta, *et al.*, *Performance Tuning and Scaling Enterprise Blockchain Applications*, 2019. Available: http://arxiv.org/abs/1912.11456.

[46]   C. Cachin, "Architecture of the hyperledger blockchain fabric," in *Workshop on Distributed Cryptocurrencies and Consensus Ledgers*, vol. Jul, 2016. Available: https://www.zurich.ibm.com/dccl/papers/cachin_dccl.pdf.

[47]   J. Dreyer, M. Fischer, and R. Tönjes, "Performance analysis of hyperledger fabric 2.0 blockchain platform," in *CCIoT 2020 – Proceedings of the 2020 Cloud Continuum Services for Smart IoT Systems, Part of SenSys 2020*. New York, NY: Association for Computing Machinery, Inc, Nov 2020, pp. 32–38. Available: https://dl.acm.org/doi/10.1145/3417310.3431398.

[48]   A. Paschke and M. Bichler, "SLA representation, management and enforcement," in *Proceedings – 2005 IEEE International Conference on e-Technology, e-Commerce and e-Service, EEE-05*, 2005, pp. 158–163.

[49]   K. M. Khan, J. Arshad, W. Iqbal, S. Abdullah, and H. Zaib, "Blockchain enabled real-time SLA monitoring for cloud-hosted services," *Cluster Computing*, vol. 25, pp. 537–559, 2022. Available: https://link.springer.com/article/10.1007/s10586-021-03416-y.

[50]   P. Patel, A. H. Ranabahu, and A. P. Sheth, *Service Level Agreement in Cloud Computing*, Kno.e.sis Publications, 2009. Available: https://corescholar.libraries.wright.edu/knoesis/78.

[51]   P. A. Bernstein and N. Goodman, "Multiversion concurrency control—theory and algorithms," *ACM Transactions on Database Systems (TODS)*, vol. 8, no. 4, pp. 465–483, 1983. Available: http://dl.acm.org/doi/10.1145/319996.319998.

[52]   H. Meir, A. Barger, Y. Manevich, and Y. Tock, *Lockless Transaction Isolation in Hyperledger Fabric*. Piscataway, NJ: IEEE, 2020, pp. 59–66.

[53]   M. Taghavi, J. Bentahar, H. Otrok, and K. Bakhtiyari, "A blockchain-based model for cloud service quality monitoring," *IEEE Transactions on Services Computing*, vol. 13, no. 2, pp. 276–288, 2020.

Chapter 7

IoT monitoring with blockchain: generating smart contracts from service level agreements

Adam Booth[1], Awatif Alqahtani[2] and Ellis Solaiman[1]

A service level agreement (SLA) is a commitment between a client and a provider that assures the quality of service (QoS) a client can expect to receive when purchasing a service. However, evidence of SLA violations in Internet of Things (IoT) service monitoring data can be manipulated by the provider or consumer, resulting in an issue of trust between contracted parties. The following research aims to explore the use of blockchain technology in monitoring IoT systems using smart contracts so that SLA violations captured are irrefutable amongst service providers and clients. The research focusses on the development of a Java library that is capable of generating a smart contract from a given SLA. A smart contract generated by this library is validated through a mock scenario presented in the form of a remote patient monitoring IoT system. In this scenario, the findings demonstrate a 100% success rate in capturing all emulated violations.

7.1 Introduction

In recent years, there has been an uprise in Internet-of-Things (IoT) systems that are now being employed to manage services such as smart energy, smart healthcare, and smart living. A part of this uprise can be attributed to the ease and cost-effectiveness of acquiring systems and services that can be used to develop IoT systems from the cloud platform providers [1].

When acquiring a service from a third party, a service level agreement (SLA) is agreed upon between the service provider and the consumer which details the quality of service (QoS) one can expect to receive. One example could be a cloud-based database service with a QoS rule stating that the service provides a minimum of 1,000 read queries a second. While a service provider will strive to achieve the QoS detailed in the SLA, however, at times, the service provider may fail to meet

[1]Computing School, Newcastle University, UK
[2]Computer Science and Engineering, College of Applied Studies and Community Service, King Saud University, Saudi Arabia

the demands of the SLA which results in an SLA violation. An SLA violation often results in the service provider being penalised in the form of a refund in-service credit.

Detecting SLA violations can be achieved by monitoring the performance of a service against the QoS requirements of the SLA. It is argued that a single party should not be responsible for this monitoring [2], yet challenges and trust issues arise when multiple parties are monitoring a system due to the possibility of foul play. This issue of trust arises from the possibility of a party being able to tamper with the monitoring data they have captured to give a false account of the services performance. For example, if the service provider is monitoring the service and the captured data shows they have committed a violation, they could alter these logs and deny the occurrence. Alternatively, the service consumer may tamper with the monitoring data they have captured to falsely accuse the service provider of committing an SLA violation. With parties being able to tamper with the monitoring data they have captured, it is therefore difficult to achieve trust between parties and to determine what has actually occurred. One solution to solve this issue is to recruit a trusted third party (TTP) to monitor the service on behalf of both the service provider and the consumer. However, as mentioned by Aniello *et al.*, this solution results in added cost to the system along with a potential single point of failure [3]. Therefore, rather than using a TTP a better solution may be to use blockchain technology and smart contracts to monitor services to detect SLA violations.

Blockchain technology provides a distributed, immutable data store such that once data has been recorded onto the blockchain, it is extremely difficult to alter it. Along with this data immutability, blockchain removes the possibility of a single point of failure due to the distributed nature of the technology. This aspect of distribution and immutability could remove issues of trust among parties as they would not be able to tamper with the data recorded and can take part in maintaining the blockchain. However, blockchain alone is not enough as logic is still required to evaluate the performance of a service to determine if an SLA violation has occurred. Some blockchain platforms such as Ethereum and Hyperledger Fabric provide a runtime environment for smart contracts, allowing for applications to be executed on top of the blockchain. Therefore, a smart contract could be developed for a specific SLA and deployed to a blockchain platform to monitor a service autonomously. This would result in a solution to monitoring services for SLA violations in a trustworthy and irrefutable fashion.

While a person could manually develop a smart contract to monitor a service for a given SLA, a better alternative may be to develop software that can interpret an SLA and automatically generate a monitoring smart contract. Research such as [2,4] have provided formal tools and languages that can define SLAs in a non-ambiguous format allowing for software to interpret these SLAs and extract various requirements from them. Alqahtani *et al.* have developed an end-to-end IoT SLA generation tool such that a person can define an SLA for an entire IoT system [4]. SLAs produced by this tool could be interpreted by a piece of software to automatically generate a smart contract capable of monitoring the entire IoT system. The aim of this research is to develop software that can achieve this goal of generating a smart contract for monitoring an entire IoT system from an SLA produced by the end-to-end IoT SLA generation tool [4].

The software produced in this research is a Java programming library that can interpret an SLA and produce a smart contract for monitoring an entire IoT system. The smart contracts generated by this library target the Hyperledger Fabric blockchain platform as this platform provides the ability to deploy a consortium blockchain network which removes unwanted side effects such as publicly available data and transaction costs that are not as easily achieved when using a public blockchain. We aim to reflect the effectiveness of deploying a smart contract on blockchain in automating SLA monitoring in a more trustworthy fashion. Thus, we develop a Java library that can extend our work by converting the generated SLAs to a smart contract that is deployable to a blockchain platform and is capable of monitoring an entire IoT system for SLA violations.

Contribution

- Develop a Java library such that it can generate smart contracts capable of monitoring an IoT system for SLA violations.
- Evaluate the correctness of the smart contracts generated by comparing the smart contracts against the original SLAs.
- Deploy the generated smart contract onto a Hyperledger Fabric blockchain network.
- Evaluate the performance of the smart contract to reflect its effectiveness in capturing SLA violation in autonomously.

7.2 Background

7.2.1 IoT

IoT systems are growing in popularity with the expected number of IoT devices to exceed 50 billion by the year 2025 [5]. As research and developments increase in IoT, more services and devices are being deployed that are used in everyday life such as transport, healthcare, and smart living. As reliance and responsibility is placed on these systems developed, it is important to ensure that these IoT systems function correctly and do not fail or degrade.

An IoT system typically consists of multiple layers, with each layer providing some sort of service and functionality to the system. These layers often take advantage of services that are either provided by the third-party vendors or developed by the organisation that is creating the system. For example, if an organisation were to develop a smart patient monitoring system, the organisation may develop their own devices that perform the physical monitoring of the patient while acquiring a cloud-based data analytics service from a third party to analyse the data collected.

Figure 7.1 shows a simple IoT system illustrating the various layers. The first layer is the sensor layer, which in this case is responsible for sensing the environment for the temperature and location. The second layer is the edge layer, which is responsible for collecting data from these sensors and performing some operations on the data such as compression. This compressed data is then provided to a data analytics service

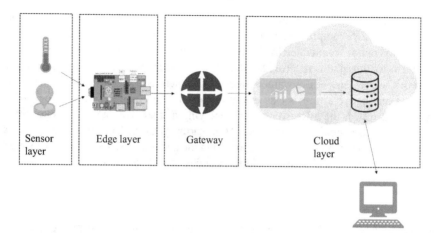

Figure 7.1   Simple IoT system

(cloud layer) via networking services (gateway layer). Once the data has been received and analysed by the data analytics service, the results are stored in a database on the cloud. A user is then able to query this database for statistics and data analytics.

Due to the structure of a typical IoT system, each layer is often relying on some other layer in the system in order to achieve the overall goal. This nature of relying on other layers and services within an IoT system in turn requires monitoring for each service used to ensure that all services are running optimally. This is required as if a layer or service fails or severely degrades in performance, it may have an impact on the overall system. For example, if all gateway services that are responsible for routing data to a data analytics service fail, then this collected data will not be received and the data may be lost. There has been much research into monitoring cloud-based services and IoT systems such as [6–8] with many tools being developed to monitor specific aspects of a system.

7.2.2   SLAs

A SLA is an agreement made between a service provider and a service consumer that expresses the various QoS properties of the service to be provided. For example, a cloud-based database service may include rules in the SLA such as 'the availability will always be above 99.999 per cent' and 'the database is able to achieve a minimum of 1000 database queries per second'. The SLA therefore allows a service consumer to determine if the service is capable of achieving the various performance requirements that their IoT system requires.

While service providers who have agreed to an SLA will strive to meet at least the minimum requirements of the agreement, sometimes the provider may fail to achieve them. This failure is known as an SLA violation. When an SLA violation occurs, often the service provider will be penalised for not meeting the service requirements. This penalty is often defined with the SLA, outlining the process of filing a report of a violation and what the penalty will be based on the situation. A service provider will often provide some form of refund as a penalty when an SLA violation has occurred.

7.2.3 Blockchain

Blockchain is effectively an indelible, distributed ledger such that once a piece of data or a transaction has been written to the ledger, it cannot be edited or removed. The first widely used blockchain platform was the cryptocurrency Bitcoin, developed under the pseudonym of Satoshi Nakamoto [9]. Two other classifications of blockchain exist which are private and consortium blockchains. A private blockchain is typically owned and utilised by a single organisation and only members of that organisation may read/write to the blockchain. Private blockchains are the most restrictive in terms of access and is often internal to a single organisation [10].

A consortium blockchain is often owned and utilised by two or more organisations and members of the consortium take part in administrating the blockchain along with taking part in validation and consensus. Members are able to access the ledger whilst preventing the general public from being able to access the blockchain through various security measures and access policies. Therefore, consortium blockchains are particularly useful when multiple organisations wish to have a private blockchain that all members of a consortium can access [10]. The most important aspects of a blockchain network is its validation process and consensus algorithm. Validation is the process of validating submitted transactions to ensure that the transaction is non-malicious and prevents issues such as double spending [11]. Valid transactions are grouped together to form a block which is then appended to the blockchain via a consensus protocol.

While different blockchain platforms may utilise different consensus algorithms and may restrict read/write access, the formation of a blockchain is typically the same. A block is generated from a group of transactions that is validated by members of the blockchain. Once a block is validated, it is then added to the blockchain by following the consensus protocol in use. A block is appended to a blockchain by including the hash value of the previous block, which is derived by using some form of hashing algorithm such as SHA256. A hashing algorithm computes a fixed length value based on a block of data such that if a single bit were to be changed in the block of data, a different hash value would be generated. By including the hash value of the previously generated block in the newly generated block, this forms a chain linking each block to its predecessor [9]. This process of including the hash value of the previous block in turn provides immutability to the blockchain. Figure 7.2 illustrates this linkage between blocks in a blockchain.

7.2.4 Smart contracts

Smart contracts are computer programs that are implementations of formal contracts agreed to by two or more parties [12]. A smart contract is responsible for detecting events and deviations of a contract and automatically carrying out actions based on those events captured [13]. For example, if a person who has agreed to a contract and a clause of that contract states the person must provide some service by a certain date

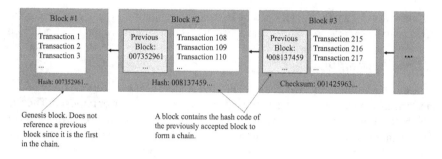

Figure 7.2   Blockchain structure

and fails to do so, the smart contract would detect this violation of the contract and issue some form of fine defined in the contract autonomously.

While smart contracts may provide an efficient and convenient way of mediating a contract, however, some issues exist in gaining the trust of the smart contract between parties. First, if a smart contract is running on a single machine, this results in a single point of failure such that if the computer fails, the smart contract will not capture any events and will therefore not carry out the various required actions, thus failing to meet the contract requirements. Another issue is trusting that the smart contract will not be tampered with. For example, if a party member owns the machine that is running the smart contract or has some other form of access to it, they may be able to modify the code of the smart contract to benefit in some way.

The above issues of smart contracts, however, can be avoided using blockchain technology. Some blockchain platforms such as Ethereum and Hyperledger Fabric provide the ability to deploy a smart contract to the blockchain, such that all members taking part in the validation and consensus protocol execute the contract and record the results. Since the smart contract is distributed on the blockchain, there is no single point of failure and it can be trusted that the smart contract will be executed. In addition, due to the immutable nature of blockchain technology once a smart contract has been deployed to the blockchain, the code of the contract cannot be tampered with. Therefore, parties that have agreed to the smart contract can trust that the smart contract will remain unmodified. Additionally, if the smart contract writes records such as logs, records, and transactions to the distributed ledger, one can trust that the data produced by the smart contract is trustworthy and has not been tampered with.

7.2.5   Hyperledger Fabric

Hyperledger Fabric is an open-source implementation of a blockchain framework which includes a modular architecture such that blockchain developers/admins can use various different consensus protocols and membership options to deploy a blockchain network [14]. Hyperledger Fabric also includes a smart contract engine that is capable of executing smart contracts written in Java, JavaScript, and Go. Hyperledger Fabric allows the development and deployment of consortium blockchains by providing a set of tools that allows an administrator to generate various certificates and configuration files that are then used to deploy a blockchain network. Due to Fabrics plug-and-play architecture, it allows an administrator to select various database technologies to act as the data store such as 'LevelDB' and 'CouchDB' along with allowing the administer to specify membership policies and consensus protocols to use.

In Hyperledger Fabric, consensus is achieved in three stages which are the endorsement, ordering, and validation stages. Endorsement is achieved such that when a transaction is submitted, X out Y nodes must endorse the transaction in order for it to be accepted. Once the transaction has been endorsed, the ordering phase begins and accepts endorsed transactions and agrees to the order of transactions that should be committed. Lastly, once a block of transactions has been ordered, validation is carried out on the ordered block and validates the correctness of it. If the block is validated successfully, it is accepted and appended to the blockchain [15]. Hyperledger Fabric allows a blockchain administrator to specify various services to use for each of the three phases, allowing for a highly configurable consensus protocol. Hyperledger Fabric is therefore a highly configurable blockchain platform suitable for consortium use. It provides a high level of security and control over various access policies, allows administrators to specify which consensus protocols to use and allows for the deployment and execution of smart contracts written in many programming languages.

7.3   Related work

In their research, Aniello *et al.* propose a system called SLAVE (Service Level Agreement VErified) which recruits public blockchain technology to embed logs of a system that can be used to prove an SLA violation [3]. Aniello *et al.* argue that a TTP has drawbacks including performance overheads, single point of failure, and bottleneck issues and the use of blockchain technology could replace a TTP. While SLAVE is proposed to utilise public blockchain technology, however, the price of running the system in terms of transaction costs is not covered and is a suggested further work worth investigating. Aniello *et al.* also note that while blockchain may remove the possibility of false claims and accusations, a bottleneck issue still remains in their proposed system.

Alzubaidi *et al.* suggest a blockchain-based SLA management solution in the context of IoT monitoring and state that a single party should not be solely responsible for the control of the SLA and monitoring for violations [2]. Alzubaidi *et al.* argue that in a complex IoT system, it is difficult to determine who is responsible for a failure in the system due to multiple parties having influence over the functionalities. Therefore, it may not be possible for a single member to achieve a complete view of the system and possess all information. It is proposed that using a blockchain solution for SLA monitoring would remove issues from the current practices by providing automatic conflict resolution, remove of trust upon a single authority, and deliver complete awareness of the entire IoT system to all parties involved. Alzubaidi *et al.* consider consortium blockchains, suggesting that Hyperledger Fabric may be the best blockchain platform as opposed to public blockchains such as Ethereum due to not incurring transaction costs, providing a faster performance and scalable platform.

Neidhardt *et al.* propose an SLA solution that utilises smart contracts and the Ethereum blockchain platform for billing and detecting availability SLA violations [16]. The system proposed utilises a smart contract developed to detect when an acquired service is unavailable which results in a customer having coins deposited to their Ethereum wallet. At the end of each billing cycle, the coins credited to the customer is counted and if the number of coins exceeds a certain value, an availability SLA violation is determined. In this research, Neidhardt *et al.* propose that the user can pay for the services they have used using Ether, Ethereums currency. While only a prototype, it is argued that this research shows promise to achieve improvement in both the billing process of cloud-based services and checking for SLA violations. However, Neidhardt *et al.* also state that due to the volatility of the price of Ether, this may make it an impractical solution for billing and service prices. In their research, Scheid *et al.* propose that the compensation process of an SLA violation is complex due to the level of manual effort required and that a better solution may be to automate the compensation and payment process using blockchain technology and smart contracts [17]. Scheid *et al.* argue that there are potential issues for both the service consumer and the service provider as the consumer could refuse to pay for a service already used and a provider could refuse to compensate when a violation occurs. To overcome this issue, Scheid *et al.* develop a smart contract which is deployed to a blockchain platform (Ganache) to monitor a sample application for response time. If the response is too slow, a violation is captured and if the violation is severe enough, it automatically compensates the service consumer.

Uriarte *et al.* in their research explore the possibility of converting dynamic SLAs into smart contracts [2]. In their previous work, a formal SLA definition language called SLAC was developed to define SLA's and the goal of the research in [2] was to further this research by developing an SLA to smart contract conversion service which the resulting smart contract could be deployed to monitor a service being provided. The service and the prototype shown in their research convert an SLA defined using SLAC into a smart contract written in Solidity, targeting the Ethereum blockchain network. While the authors state that the prototype is still in development, a description of the system is provided. Uriarte *et al.* argue that their system could disrupt the cloud market by allowing for the notion of an open and distributed cloud, offering dynamic services to customers resulting in reduced cost and increased flexibility.

7.4 Design and implementation

This section focuses on the design and implementation of the smart contract generation library and aims to provide the reader a full understanding as to how the library generates a smart contract. The data model of the library created in this project is closely modelled on the JSON SLA document produced by the SLA generation tool used. Therefore, a brief description of the SLA schema is first provided and will allow the reader to more easily understand the inner workings of the library created.

7.4.1   SLA

Alqahtani *et al.* have created a tool that allows a user to easily define an end-to-end SLA of an IoT system [4]. This is achieved by allowing a user to specify the QoS metrics expected of the application along with the expected QoS of all other layers within the IoT system. There are a number of workflow activities that require services such as stream processing service as well as an infrastructure resource to host that service. There is a number of service level objectives (SLOs) associated with the required service and infrastructure resources. Along with these SLO's, there is other configuration requirements of the infrastructure resources and services for the involved workflow activities. Figure 7.3 shows the main concepts that has been considered within the SLA with some examples for clarification.

Figure 7.3 associates the concepts presented in the conceptual model with examples to illustrate the relation between infrastructure resources, services, configuration requirement, and SLO concepts. For example, 'capture event of interest' is a possible workflow activity, in RHMS, and it requires a sensing service. The sensing service has SLO constraints such as the required level of data timeliness. The sensing service will be deployed/hosted on an IoT device. Therefore, it is important to consider the requirements of the IoT device, such as its type (e.g., sensor or RFID), the mobility of the device (e.g., fixed or mobile), the communication mechanism (e.g., pushing data or pulling data), and the battery life. The same conditions will apply for the 'filter a captured event of interest' activity, which will be performed at the Edge of a network

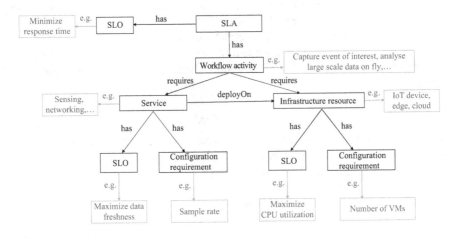

Figure 7.3   *Conceptual model with examples to illustrate the relationships among the key concepts of an SLA for the IoT*

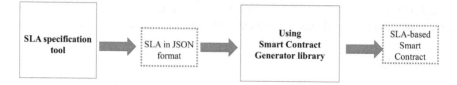

Figure 7.4   Abstracted generated smart contract from SLA specification steps

to filter data and utilise network bandwidth by neglecting uninteresting data; this task uses certain devices, such as a mobile phone or raspberry pi. Each of these devices has specific computational capabilities, such as a given CPU speed and memory size. Furthermore, to perform the 'real-time data analysis' activity, a stream processing service can be used with certain requirement constraints, such as low latency and certain configuration requirements, including the specification of the window type as a time-based window or event-based window. The stream processing service can be deployed on a Cloud, so certain requirements related to a Cloud resource can be specified, such as the number of VMs and the acceptable percentage of CPU utilisation. Therefore, in the next section, we identify the related vocabulary terms that can be used for specifying QoS and configuration parameters.

7.4.2   From SLA to smart contract Java library

Generating SLA in a machine-readable format simplifies the process of translating the SLA to Smart contracts. We aimed to translate the generated SLA to a smart contract and explore the use of blockchain technology to monitor IoT applications to record SLA violations.

A Java library* which we refer to as 'FromSLAToSmartContract' library. The library converts the generated SLAs for different IoT application use cases with different SLO constraints to a smart contract (see Figure 7.4).

Applying FromSLAToSmartContract library to the SLA can create a list of rules for each SLO constraint and configuration requirement related to each workflow activity.

7.4.3   FromSLAToSmartContract library

With the structure of the JSON SLA produced now in mind, the structure of the Java library created can be more easily understood. Since the library targets the SLA generation tools resulting SLA's, the data model of the library is heavily influenced by that of the SLA tool.

Figure 7.5 shows an abstract view of the components within the Java library along with the composition of these objects. Types in the diagram above such as ChaincodeBuilder and WorkflowActivity have been shown abstractly; however, there

---

*It is explained in Section 7.4.3.

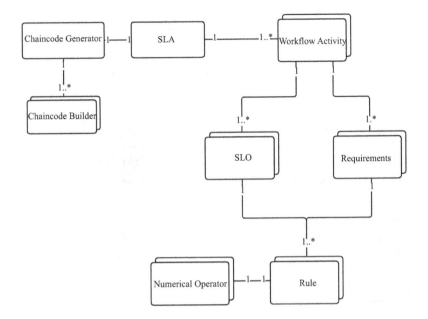

Figure 7.5   Entity-relationship diagram of the components in the library

is a concrete type for each workflow activity within the SLA generation tool and is shown in more detail in Section 7.5.2. The following is a very brief description of each component within the library:

- ChaincodeGenerator: The entry point of the library. A user of the library calls a static method within this class providing an SLA as either a file handle or JSON string and returns the generated chaincode.
- ChaincodeBuilder: Each workflow activity has an associated ChaincodeBuilder. It is the responsibility of the ChaincodeBuilder to convert the rules within a workflow activity into valid chaincode.
- SLA: The SLA type represents the SLA. It contains fields for the start and end dates along with the various workflow activities and application SLOs.
- WorkflowActivity: Represents a specific workflow activity within the SLA. Each workflow activity contains the various SLOs and configuration requirements for that activity.
- SLO: The service level objective of a specific service (e.g. batch processing, real-time analysis). It contains the QoS constraints.
- Requirements: Contains the constraints for various configuration requirements.
- Rule: Contains a numerical value of the expected QoS constraint along with a NumericalOperator. These two fields are used in conjunction to determine whether the rule is being violated when tested against a submitted value.

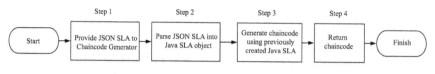

Figure 7.6   From JSON to Java Chaincode flow

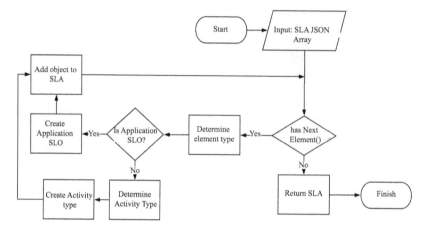

Figure 7.7   Creating each member of the SLA iteratively

- NumericalOperator: Operators (less than, greater than, etc.) which when given two values return a Boolean result. Provides an object-oriented approach to building Rules following the strategy design pattern.

As mentioned earlier, the ChaincodeGenerator class is the 'entry point' to the library. It is this class that a user will interact with by providing a JSON SLA document which then returns a smart contract capable of monitoring the IoT system for SLA violations. Figure 7.6 provides an abstract view of this process.

The major aspects of the library are steps 2 and 3, i.e. parsing the JSON into a Java object and then generating chaincode based on the object created. With these two tasks being somewhat complex, the following two subsections explain these processes.

7.4.3.1   Parsing a JSON SLA into a Java SLA

The Java SLA type contains a field for each of the possible workflow activities and application SLO defined by the SLA generation tool. This section explains how a JSON document is deserialised into a Java SLA object. As previously explained, the JSON SLA document produced by the SLA generation tool is a JSON array containing zero or more workflow activities and the application SLO. Therefore, to create a Java SLA object, each of the workflow activity types and application SLO must be determined and constructed. This process is illustrated in figure 7.7.

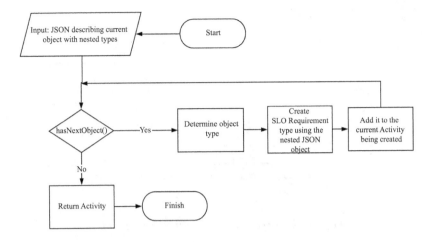

Figure 7.8   Creating a workflow activity process

With each workflow activity and the application SLO being an object within the array, each JSON element of the array is passed to the factory method of the respective workflow activity type. As shown previously, each workflow activity in the library contains members for each of the possible SLO's and Requirements types. When calling the factory method of a workflow activity and providing the JSON object for that activity, the process illustrated in Figure 7.8 is carried out.

The priority of the factory method of the activity type is to determine what SLO's and Requirement objects are within the JSON object provided, creating these objects in Java and setting them as a member of the workflow activity. An SLO/Requirement object is created by providing the JSON of the type discovered to the relevant SLO/Requirement static factory method which follows the process shown in Figure 7.9.

The static factory method of the SLO/Requirement type inspects the JSON provided for any rules relevant to the type being created and creates this Rule in Java by providing the JSON to the static factory method of the appropriate Java Rule class. A Rule is created by following the process shown in Figure 7.10.

As shown in the previous flow diagrams, creating a Java SLA is somewhat of a recursive and iterative process. Each workflow activity within the SLA must be created and is achieved by the calling factory method for that activity type and providing the JSON describing it. The workflow activity is constructed by creating all SLO/Requirement objects described in the JSON passed to the activity factory method. This is achieved by providing each nested JSON object describing the SLO/Requirements to the appropriate factory methods of each type. The factory method of the SLO/Requirement creates each Rule described in the JSON passed to its factory method. Once a Java SLA object has been created, the library progresses to the next step which generates chaincode based on the various objects defined in the SLA.

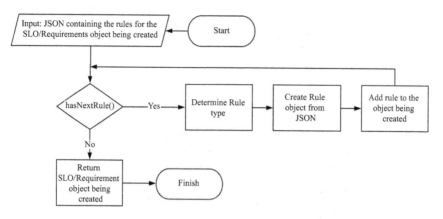

Figure 7.9   Creating an SLO/Requirement object

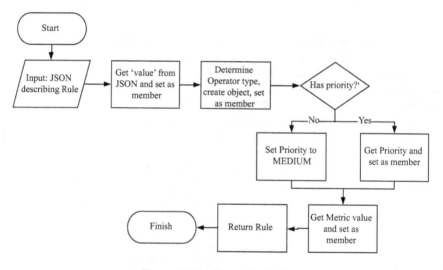

Figure 7.10   Create Rule flow

7.4.3.2   Generating Chaincode from Java SLA

As shown in the previous subsection, an SLA object within the smart contract generation library consists of zero or more workflow activities and an application SLO each containing Rules. It is these 'Rules' that express the required QoS metrics for the IoT system and are used to validate the state of a system being monitored.

Each workflow activity and application SLO type have an associated Chaincode-Builder class. A ChaincodeBuilder extracts each SLO/Requirement object from the provided workflow activity and then generates three chaincode methods for each of the SLO/Requirement types. The three methods generated for each SLO/Requirement objects are:

- *_update: The update method used to report the current state of the SLO/Requirement being captured in the IoT system. E.g. 'application_slo_update'.
- get_latest_*_update: Returns the latest state reported to the smart contract. For example, 'get_latest application_slo_update'.
- get_*_violations: Returns all recorded violations of the SLA for that specific SLO/Requirement.
  For example, 'get_application_slo_violations'.

Each ChaincodeBuilder generates these three methods for each SLO/Requirement object by following the process illustrated in figure 7.11 when the getMethods() method is called:

The update methods are created by extracting each of the QoS rules within the SLO/Requirement objects and creating if statements to check against submitted values. For example, if an SLO contains a rule for availability stating that it must be always greater than 99%, the if statement contained within the update method would read:

$$if\,(!(availability > 99)) * * * record_violation * * *$$

This is achieved with the assistance of the Java library 'JavaPoet' [18] to construct a method and add control statements using the Rule object values. For each rule in an SLO/Requirement object, a corresponding if statement is generated and contained within the same update method. The ChaincodeGenerator class is the entry point for the library and acts as the API. The ChaincodeGenerator class takes advantage of the

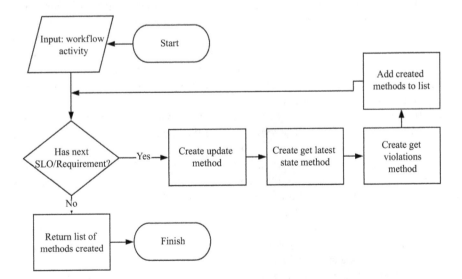

Figure 7.11   Constructing chaincode methods using a ChaincodeBuilder

ChaincodeBuilders described above by using these objects to generate a list of methods for all workflow activities within the Java SLA object. Once all methods have been generated, the ChaincodeGenerator class simply creates a Java class using the functionality provided by JavaPoet and appends these methods to the class. Finally, the ChaincodeGenerator returns a Chaincode object containing the Java class as a string and also documentation for the generated contract. A fully deployable Hyperledger Fabric smart contract project is also written to the file system, allowing the user to directly deploy the smart contract to the blockchain.

7.4.3.3 Chaincode

The smart contract generated by the library contains three methods for each SLO/Requirement objects and also three other methods which are 'init', 'invoke', and 'history'. The init method is called by Hyperledger Fabric when the smart contract is initialised and should contain any initialisation logic required for the contract. However, in the case of the monitoring contracts that are generated, there is no initialisation logic required and, therefore, this method is empty.

The invoke method is the external API of the smart contract and is the only method the end user will directly interact with. The invoke method expects two string parameters with the first being the name of the internal method to invoke e.g. 'batch processing slo update' and the JSON string containing the state of the batch processing SLO. The invoke method simply contains a switch statement containing a case for each method in the chaincode. When invoke is called, the method name submitted in the first parameter is evaluated by the switch statement and calls the relevant method providing the JSON string to it. If the method name is not recognised, an error is returned.

When an update method is called, the JSON string provided to it is converted into a Java JSON object, allowing for the values contained within the JSON to be extracted. Each update method expects the JSON to contain a key/value pair for each rule defined in the SLA along with an ID of the resource that produced it. The update method compares each value found within the JSON against the rules defined in the SLA for that type. If a value is missing, an error is recorded and is viewed as a violation for not being included.

If a value submitted to the update method violates a QoS rule, it is recorded as a violation on the blockchain. The violation record contains the rule that was violated, the value that caused the violation, the ID of the resource that produced the value and a timestamp. The record is stored under a composite key of both the SLO/Resource type and the ID of the resource that produced the state. For example, the violations recorded for a Gateway SLO produced by a device with ID 1 are a separate set from the violations produced by a Gateway SLO with the ID of 2.

After evaluating the submitted state for violations, the state is then stored in the ledger and can be read back using the get latest_*_update method. Similarly, a list of all violations for a specific SLO/Requirement associated with an object ID can be retrieved using the get_*_violations method. Listing 7.1 shows a simple example of the invoke method generated:

```
1  public org.hyperledger.fabric.shim.Chaincode.Response invoke(
       ChaincodeStub stub) {
2      String method = stub.getFunction();
3      List<String> params = stub.getParameters();
4  if (method.equalsIgnoreCase("examine_captured_eoi_gateway_slo_update"
       )) {
5          return examine_captured_eoi_gateway_slo_update(stub, params.get
              (0));
6      }
7      if (method.equalsIgnoreCase("
           get_latest_examine_captured_eoi_gateway_slo_update")) {
8          return get_latest_examine_captured_eoi_gateway_slo_update(stub,
               params.get(0));
9      }
10     if (method.equalsIgnoreCase("
           get_examine_captured_eoi_gateway_slo_violations")) {
11         return get_examine_captured_eoi_gateway_slo_violations(stub,
               params.get(0));
12     }
13 return newErrorResponse("ERROR", "Invalid function name".getBytes());
14     }
```

Listing 7.1   Generated invoke method.

In this example, only the code is shown for the gateway SLO belonging to the examiner captured EoI activity. When an update for this SLO is passed, the invoke method is executed.

In this example, only the code is shown the for gateway SLO belonging to the examine captured EoI activity. When an update for this SLO is passed to the invoke method, the code illustrated in Listing 7.2 is executed.

The Gateway SLO has one rule in this example which states that the availability should always be above 99.9%. The method exacts the gateway availability value from the JSON string submitted and compares it against the expected value. If the availability is recorded below 99.9%, a violation is recorded on the ledger. The update is added to the ledger regardless of violations and is returned to the caller.

Lastly, the entire history of updates for a specific SLO/Requirement can be read back by using the invoke method and providing the string 'history' and the name and ID of the SLO/Requirement to get the history for. When this occurs, a list of all historic updates is returned for that aspect of the system with each update containing the timestamp of when the update occurred.

7.5   Evaluation

In this section, a fictitious Remote Patient Monitoring (RPM) IoT system is presented along with a SLA defined for the system. A smart contract is generated using the smart contract generation library developed in this project which is then deployed to

```
1   private org.hyperledger.fabric.shim.Chaincode.Response
          application_slo_update(ChaincodeStub stub,
2            String jsonString) {
3       try{
4       JsonObject json = new JsonParser().parse(jsonString).
            getAsJsonObject();
5       byte[] state = stub.getState("APPLICATION_SLO_VIOLATION");
6       JsonArray arr;
7       if (state == null || state.length == 0) {
8         arr = new JsonArray();
9       }
10      else {
11        arr = new JsonParser().parse(new String(state)).getAsJsonArray
              ();
12      }
13  if (json.has("GATEWAY_AVAILABILITY")) {
14        double val = json.get("GATEWAY_AVAILABILITY").getAsDouble();
15        if (!(val >= 99.9)) {
16          String msg = "GATEWAY_AVAILABILITY rule violated. Offending
                value is: " + val + " at time " + new Date().toString();
17          arr.add(msg);
18        }
19      }
20      else {
21        String error = "GATEWAY_AVAILABILITY" + " missing at time " +
              new Date().toString();
22        return newErrorResponse("ERROR", error.getBytes());
23      }
24  stub.putState("EXAMINE_CAPTURED_EOI_GATEWAY_SLO_VIOLATIONS" + "_" +
      id, arr.toString().getBytes());
25      stub.putState("EXAMINE_CAPTURED_EOI_GATEWAY_SLO" + "_" + id,
          jsonString.getBytes());
26      return newSuccessResponse("
          EXAMINE_CAPTURED_EOI_GATEWAY_SLO_UPDATE", jsonString.getBytes
          ());
27      } catch (Exception e) {
28      return newErrorResponse("ERROR", e.getMessage().getBytes());
29      }
30  }
```

Listing 7.2   Generated smart contract update method

a Hyperledger Fabric network forming a consortium blockchain. The smart contract is then tested using an IoT emulation program developed to simulate various structures of the RPM IoT system and the results of these tests are presented.

7.5.1 Scenario

The example scenario presented in this section is in the form of a RPM IoT system that monitors the heart rate and blood pressure of patients due to some cardiovascular disease. The system is used to detect early signs of serious heart issues/defects and

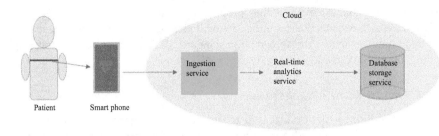

Figure 7.12   RPM IoT system

deploys emergency services in the case of heart failure. While the IoT system presented is fictitious with its purpose to demonstrate the usage of the smart contract generation library, it does, however, take inspiration from existing research in remote health monitoring such as [19].

Figure 7.12 illustrates the RPM IoT system responsible for monitoring and detecting heart failure and other serious cardiovascular health issues. The first layer (Patient) shown in the diagram is the sensor layer, which is responsible for reading the heart rate and blood pressure every 10 s of the patient. The edge device layer (smartphone) is a smartphone that collects heart rate and blood pressure readings from the sensors, filters this data, and aggregates it to the ingestion layer of the IoT system. The ingestion layer is responsible for receiving data from many patients, which is then processed and provided to the real-time data analytics service. The real-time data analytics service analyses the data provided looking for health issues and heart failure for each patient. If it detects some issue, it notifies healthcare professionals which may result in emergency services being deployed to those in need. Finally, from the real-time data analytics service, the data is stored in a database that can later be queried by medical staff. The IoT system consists of three organisational members including two service providers (SP1 and SP2) that are providing hardware infrastructure (e.g. sensors) along with services such as cloud-based data storage. The final organisational member is the healthcare provider (HCP) who uses the system to provide monitoring and health support for their patients.

7.5.2   SLA

With the IoT system being a type of smart-health application and is responsible for detecting serious health issues in real time, it is crucial that this system works correctly and to the desired level of service. If the system fails to meet the demanded quality of service, it may result in serious consequences such as deaths that could have been prevented along with lawsuits.

An SLA was created using the SLA generation tool [4] describing the required SLOs and resource requirements for each layer of the RPM IoT system. The SLA includes required QoS rules of the services used such as the required availability, accuracy, and cost. Each organisation that provides functionality (SP1, SP2) agree to the SLA stating that the services they provide meet this standard and is, therefore, safe to use. Failure to meet the required SLA will incur legal action against those who fail to provide services at the agreed upon standard. With all organisations agreeing to the defined SLA, the IoT system is deployed.

7.5.3   Smart contract generation

With an SLA defined, the next task is to generate a smart contract capable of monitoring the deployed system for SLA violations. Generating the smart contract is achieved by creating a simple Java program that references the smart contract generation library created in this project. This program simply calls the 'chaincodeFromFile' method within the smart contract generation library and provides a file reference to the JSON SLA produced by the SLA generation tool (previous step) and a path for where the generated smart contract project should be written to. After executing this program, the following files and folders were created resulting in a deployable smart contract project.

The chaincode folder (see Figure 7.13) contains all files required to form a deployable smart contract to a Hyperledger Fabric network. The Start.java class is the entry point for the smart contract that the Hyperledger Fabric platform will execute to start the chaincode application that then loads the Chaincode.java class. The Chaincode.java class is where the generated smart contract resides. This class contains all generated code which an end user/application will interact with to update various states and to read any violations. It is these update methods that will evaluate the submitted states to check whether the SLA is being violated and record these states and violations to the distributed ledger.

The ChaincodeTest.java file contains unit tests for the generated chaincode, however, these unit tests do not include any test logic for the smart contract and are instead provided if a user wishes to write their own tests. The 'build' and 'settings' gradle files are used by Hyperledger Fabric peers to build and deploy the chaincode project.

The chaincode generated from the RPM IoT SLA contained over 2,300 lines of code consisting of 57 methods. The chaincode was manually inspected and the validation logic generated was correct according to the defined SLA.

Figure 7.13   Generated smart contract project

7.5.4 Chaincode deployment

With a Hyperledger Fabric chaincode project generated, the next task was to deploy a Hyperledger Fabric network that would be used to monitor the deployed RPM IoT system. The network used in this example takes advantage of the 'first-network' [20] sample provided by Hyperledger Fabric to deploy a consortium blockchain consisting of three organisations (SP1, SP2, and HCP). The purpose of this network was to demonstrate the functionality of the smart contract generated and does not intend to accurately benchmark Hyperledger Fabric blockchain technology.

Therefore, this network is being used for testing the smart contract generated and all peers are deployed locally. In a production context, however, a network would be deployed to many machines with each organisation running their own peers on their own hardware. While this text briefly explains the deployment of the network used in this example along with installing and instantiating chaincode, the reader is encouraged to read [20]. The manual creation of Hyperledger Fabric networks is somewhat laborious and complex and is out of the scope of this text.

Hyperledger Fabric provides a project called 'fabric samples' which includes many tools and networks such that a user can easily deploy a prototype network on their local machine. One of these sample networks provided is called 'first-network' which a user can execute two scripts and deploy a Hyperledger Fabric consortium network consisting of three organisations. This process was carried out and after executing the 'byfn' and 'eyfn' scripts within the first-network project and providing a channel name of 'healthiot' along with the '-a' parameter as arguments to these scripts, the network was deployed.

Once the network was deployed, the smart contract was installed and instantiated on each of the peers for each organisation. This was achieved by first copying the generated smart contract project into the chaincode folder of the 'fabric-samples' project and then connecting to the Fabric CLI container that was deployed during the deployment of the network. After connecting to the fabric CLI container, appropriate commands were executed to install and instantiate the smart contract to each peer of each organisation in the network.

Figure 7.14 depicts the final network deployed and the process taken. The orderer node is responsible for ordering the transactions such that all peers in the network have executed the same transactions in the same order on their local ledger. While there are various distributed orderer protocols, the network deployed uses the solo ordering protocol. Also used is the 'goleveldb' database technology to store the recorded state of the ledger.

7.5.5 IoT emulation

With a Hyperledger Fabric network deployed and the smart contract generated running on each peer, the next step was to test the chaincode and network. Rather than actually deploying a real RPM IoT system, instead an emulator was developed such that it would submit transactions to the blockchain network for each layer of the proposed topology.

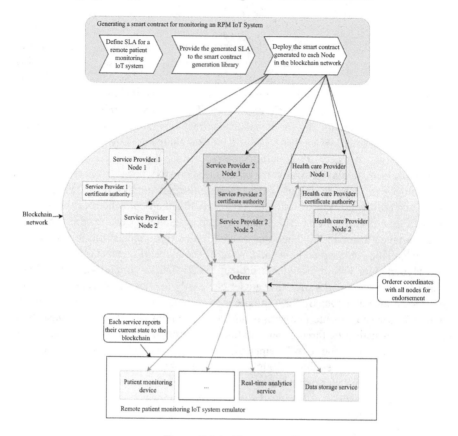

Figure 7.14   Test network

The emulator was developed using NodeJS and the JavaScript programming language. The emulator takes advantage of JavaScript's asynchronous programming model, allowing multiple transaction requests to be sent without blocking a response. This therefore allows the emulator to submit transactions to the blockchain network in fast succession in an attempt to simulate real-world transaction speeds.

The emulator contains fields configurable by the user to set the number of sensors, gateway devices, real-time analysis services, etc. allowing the user to simulate different structures of the IoT system with varying numbers of each service. The emulator would submit state update transactions for each element of the defined IoT system. For example, if the user configures the emulator to emulate an IoT system with 100 sensors at the sensor layer, 100 sensor state update transactions will be submitted to the Fabric network per iteration, thus emulating the deployed system.

Not only does the emulator include fields that allow the user to emulate different infrastructures but also contain another field 'VIOLATION RATIO'. This is a double value ranging from 0 to 1 that allows the user to control how many elements for all service layers will cause a violation. For example, if a user has configured the

Table 7.1 Performance of the generated smart contract with RPM IoT emulation

#Sensors	#Gateway	#Ingest	#RT analytics	#Storage	Avg. Time	#Trans. Performed	Violations Detected
2	1	1	1	1	2.5 s	18	17/17
20	10	1	1	1	3.32 s	72	21/21
100	50	1	1	1	6.95 s	317	29/29
200	100	2	2	1	20.23 s	620	42/42
500	250	3	3	2	39.58 s	1,532	89/89
1,000	500	5	5	4	71.54 s	3,056	162/162

emulator as 100 sensors at the sensor layer and a violation ratio of 0.05, 5 sensor states containing an SLA violation will be submitted per iteration.

The emulation logic is contained within a loop such that a user can configure the emulator to run X iterations. For each iteration, state transactions will be submitted for each defined element within the configured IoT topology in the emulator. For example, if the user has configured the emulator to contain 100 sensors, 50 gateway devices, 5 ingestion services, 3 real-time analytics services, and 2 storage services, SLO/Requirement state update transactions will be executed for all 160 elements of the IoT system per iteration. The total number of transactions submitted will depend on the number of SLO/Requirement updates for each device/service type. For example, at the sensor layer, there is only one update method; however, the gateway layer requires 4 update methods.

7.5.6 Results

Using the emulator described earlier, the network and smart contract deployed was tested using various emulated structures of the proposed RPM IoT system (see Table 7.1). Each test was performed using a violation ratio of 0.05 with at least one element of each layer producing a violation. Each test ran for three iterations, with the average time being recorded as the performance time. The tests were executed on a PC equipped with an i7-5820K CPU with 16 GB RAM running Debian 9 with the Hyperledger Fabric network deployed locally.

The purpose of these tests was to check that the deployed smart contract would detect all SLA violations produced by the emulator and that each submitted state was recorded to the ledger. While the average time is shown in the results, this is not an accurate representation of Hyperledger Fabrics transaction processing ability. It is also worth noting that no efforts were made to optimise the deployed network.

7.6 Discussion

The example scenario and results presented in the previous section represent a proof-of-concept by demonstrating the functionality of the auto-generated smart contract derived from an SLA. While the tests do show that the generated smart contract does in fact capture all violations and records them on the distributed ledger, it fails to demonstrate Hyperledger Fabric as being an optimal choice for IoT monitoring. However, this is not to say that Hyperledger Fabric is not suitable.

The tests shown previously illustrate that Hyperledger Fabric was slow in processing the transactions, especially as the emulated system was scaled. However, the Fabric network was deployed locally with all peers running on the same machine and did not fairly represent a production standard Fabric network. Therefore, the speed (transactions per second) in this case should not be seen as a reliable metric of the system.

With the project utilising the network sample provided by Hyperledger Fabric, there was no optimisation performed on the network. Research such as [21,22] suggest that various approaches can be taken to optimise a Fabric network, implying that it may be possible to achieve much higher transactions per second, possibly making Hyperledger Fabric an appropriate blockchain for IoT monitoring. Therefore, further research is required into optimising and benchmarking Hyperledger Fabric running the smart contracts generated by the library to determine the suitability of Hyperledger Fabric in a production setting.

The IoT emulator did function correctly and submitted the correct number of transactions for each element of the IoT system along with the correct number of violations. However, the emulator submitted these transactions sequentially per iteration as opposed to concurrently. While the emulator takes advantage of asynchronous programming, meaning that once the transaction is submitted, it is capable of submitting another without blocking, nevertheless, these transactions are not submitted concurrently and do not accurately emulate an IoT system. This is due to IoT systems consisting of many individual components each submitting transactions possibly at the same time, whereas the emulator is unable to do this. Despite not emulating the concurrent nature of an IoT system; however, the emulator does submit these transactions in very fast succession and does demonstrate the smart contracts ability to detect violations.

After each test performed on the example network and smart contract, the distributed ledger was examined to verify that all SLA violations were captured and recorded to the ledger along with the state updates for each SLO/Requirement type. During each test, the smart contract did capture all violations and recorded them along with recording all states submitted, thus demonstrating the correctness of the smart contract generated.

Consortium blockchains provide distributed ledger technology such that all members of the consortium have the same data. It is this distributed property along with the immutability of the ledger that makes it an attractive option when monitoring an IoT system for SLA violations with multiple parties. During the process of developing the smart contract library, however, some potential flaws in using blockchain technologies for this purpose were discovered.

The goal of the smart contract generated is to detect SLA violations which in turn may cause a member of the consortium to be penalised for not meeting the requirements of the SLA. Therefore, it is within members' interest for a violation they are committing to not be recorded on the distributed ledger. In some cases, it may be a requirement of a blockchain network that all members of the consortium accept a transaction for it to be recorded on the ledger. If this requirement is in place, it may be possible for the offending member to reject the transaction resulting in the violation not being recorded. While this rejection may be detectable by other members of the consortium with other means, nevertheless, the violation will not be recorded on the expected ledger. To solve this issue, the number of accepting members to allow a transaction to be committed to the ledger may be reduced; however, this may then lead to the next possible issue.

If the consortium requires less than the number of members within a consortium to validate and accept a transaction, it would then be possible for a group of members within the consortium to 'team up' on another member and record transactions suggesting that the victimised member did not meet the SLA. This, in turn, would defeat the purpose of using blockchain technology in this setting as it would allow a subset to gang up on a member and generate fictitious SLA violations and, therefore, requires some level of trust among peers. Another potential issue of using blockchain technology to monitor IoT systems relates to how the blockchain acquires the system state information of the IoT system. In this project, it was assumed that all services/devices would push their current state to the smart contract, thus placing implicit trust on these services/devices. This trust is required due to the possibility of the device reporting false/inaccurate state information, possibly programmed by a malicious member of a consortium wishing to hide their services true operational state. Therefore, a solution to the issue of determining the state of an IoT service in a trustworthy manner is required.

To the author's knowledge, there does not exist an API/standard definition for IoT metrics such that all IoT services/devices can publish their state in a standard way. For example, within the smart contract generation library, it is assumed a sensor or 'thing' will publish its availability under the JSON key AVAILABILITY. However, this places a strict requirement on the IoT device such that the availability must be reported under this key within a specific JSON format, resulting in a very specific API. A better approach would be to define an industry standard such that all services/devices will emit their state (if monitoring is enabled) in a standard way such that the smart contract generated by the library will be compatible with any service/device within any IoT system. This, in turn, would also solve the tight coupling issue between the smart contract generation library and the SLA generation tool.

7.6.1   Limitation

Although the smart contract generation library developed does generate valid smart contracts that accurately detects SLA violations, the structure of the library could be improved. The library developed is tightly coupled to the SLA generation tool along with the JSON SLAs that the tool produces. This can be attributed to the data model and SLA deserialization code.

The data model of the library is heavily influenced by that of the SLA generation tool. This was due to modelling the various domain objects such as workflow activities and SLO/Requirement objects based on the structure and information found within the graphical user interface (GUI) of the SLA generation tool. Therefore, the smart contract generation library expects certain workflow activities to have specific SLO/Requirements types and if, for example, the SLA generation tool was to be updated to include a new rule for the gateway SLO, these changes would need to be reflected in the smart contract generation library. This tight dependency on the SLA generation tool causes the smart contract generation library to be brittle, meaning that any changes to the SLA tool may cause the library to fail. Removing the tight coupling between the SLA generation tool and the smart contract generation library would improve the library and make it less brittle. Achieving this may require further research into defining SLA standards such as SLA keys so that it is safe to assume that they will rarely (if ever) change along with defining an industry standard for a JSON structured SLA.

7.7   Conclusion and future work

Monitoring IoT systems for SLA violations presents interesting challenges, especially when multiple organisations are involved and trust is difficult to achieve. This research project aimed to explore the possibility of using blockchain technology and smart contracts to monitor an IoT system to achieve implicit trust among all parties that are monitoring the system.

A Java library was developed that could convert an end-to-end IoT SLA into a smart contract that can be directly installed onto a Hyperledger Fabric consortium blockchain. The smart contracts generated by the library can detect any SLA violation and record the violation to the distributed ledger, thus making the data captured immutable. The smart contracts also record each reported state to the ledger such that a member of the consortium can view all updates recorded and can query the blockchain for all violations of a specific aspect of the IoT system.

An SLA was created to represent a remote patient monitoring system and the library developed was then used to generate a smart contract from this SLA. A Hyperledger Fabric blockchain network was deployed locally, consisting of three organisations that represented the consortium of the IoT system. Once the generated smart contract was installed onto the blockchain, a simple IoT emulator was developed using NodeJS that would submit state transactions to the blockchain with some containing SLA violations to test the smart contract functionality.

While testing the smart contract on a local blockchain network, multiple IoT system structures were emulated, testing how well the smart contract could handle a greater number of nodes in a system. It was noted that as the emulated system scaled up, the time to capture the state also increased with the final test taking over 70 s per full iteration. While this speed may be an issue for large-scale IoT systems, it is worth noting that the smart contract did detect and record all SLA violations that were generated during these tests.

Although the smart contract generated achieved the functional goal of detecting all SLA violations, further research was identified. First, the transaction throughput of the blockchain may not be fast enough for large IoT systems and, therefore, exploring ways to increase this speed or to reduce the number of transactions for monitoring is required. Research such as [21,22] have suggested that it could be possible to achieve a higher transaction throughput using Hyperledger Fabric with various parameters and optimisation techniques; however, this was not carried out in this research.

The Java library developed is also heavily dependent on the end-to-end IoT SLA generation tool such that it relies on the JSON output of the SLA generation tool. Removing this coupling issue is required and could be solved by defining an industry standard of keys/names for specific aspects of an IoT system such that all future IoT systems and SLA generation tools would report their state under the same keys.

The smart contract generation library only targets Hyperledger Fabric, producing smart contracts in the Java programming language. Due to the design of the library, support for other blockchain platforms and smart contract languages could be added, thus, catering for a wider audience. The smart contracts generated by the library developed have been demonstrated to capture all SLA violations and could be a step closer to achieving an IoT monitoring solution to increase trust and remove the possibility of foul play among organisations forming a consortium network.

As future work, currently the library created only generates smart contracts that detect SLA violations and records them to the ledger. However, having the smart contract automatically issue a penalty when a violation occurs would further increase the ability of the smart contract. With the current smart contracts generated by the library, human interaction is still required; however, it could be possible to have the library to generate smart contracts that also mediate SLA violation penalties.

The design of the library developed relies strictly upon JSON keys produced by the end-to-end IoT SLA generation tool along with defining its own API for IoT services to submit the current state of the service. Defining a standard that details specific JSON keys for specific values along with an industry standard API for reporting monitoring state would remove reliance upon specific tools. By creating a standard that all future services and tools developed would adopt would, therefore, remove any coupling issues.

Finally, the library created in this project currently only supports a single blockchain platform (Hyperledger Fabric) and only produces a smart contract in the Java programming language. Adapting the Java library to support other blockchain platforms such as Hyperledger Sawtooth and Ethereum may be beneficial to those who have strict requirements to use one of these alternative blockchain platforms.

References

[1] A. Botta, W. de Donato, V. Persico, and A. Pescapé. On the integration of cloud computing and Internet of Things. In *2014 International Conference on Future Internet of Things and Cloud*, pages 23–30, August 2014.

[2] R. B. Uriarte, R. de Nicola, and K. Kritikos. Towards distributed sla management with smart contracts and blockchain. In *2018 IEEE International Conference on Cloud Computing Technology and Science (CloudCom)*, pages 266–271, December 2018.

[3]   L. Aniello, R. Baldoni, and F. Lombardi. A blockchain-based solution for enabling log-based resolution of disputes in multi-party transactions. In *Proceedings of 5th International Conference in Software Engineering for Defence Applications*, pages 53–58, January 2018.

[4]   A. Alqahtani, Y. Li, P. Patel, E. Solaiman, and R. Ranjan. End-to-end service level agreement specification for IoT applications. In *2018 International Conference on High Performance Computing Simulation (HPCS)*, pages 926–935, July 2018.

[5]   J. Pan, J. Wang, A. Hester, I. Alqerm, Y. Liu, and Y. Zhao. Edgechain: an edge-IoT framework and prototype based on blockchain and smart contracts. *IEEE Internet of Things Journal*, 6(3):4719–4732, 2019.

[6]   J. M. Alcaraz Calero and J. G. Aguado. Comparative analysis of architectures for monitoring cloud computing infrastructures. *Future Generation Computer Systems*, 47:16–30, 2015. Special Section: Advanced Architectures for the Future Generation of Software-Intensive Systems.

[7]   G. Aceto, A. Botta, W. de Donato, and A. PescapÃš. Cloud monitoring: a survey. *Computer Networks*, 57(9):2093–2115, 2013.

[8]   J. M. Alcaraz Calero and J. G. Aguado. Monpaas: an adaptive monitoring platform as a service for cloud computing infrastructures and services. *IEEE Transactions on Services Computing*, 8(1):65–78, 2015.

[9]   S. Nakamoto. Bitcoin: a peer-to-peer electronic cash system. Cryptography Mailing list at https://metzdowd.com, March 2009.

[10]   P. Ekparinya, V. Gramoli, and G. Jourjon. "Double-spending risk quantification in private, consortium and public ethereum blockchains." arXiv preprint arXiv:1805.05004 (2018).

[11]   S. Zhang and J. Lee. Double-spending with a Sybil attack in the Bitcoin decentralized network. *IEEE Transactions on Industrial Informatics*, 10:1–1, 2019.

[12]   K. Christidis and M. Devetsikiotis. Blockchains and smart contracts for the Internet of Things. *IEEE Access*, 4:2292–2303, 2016.

[13]   C. Molina-Jimenez, I. Sfyrakis, E. Solaiman, *et al.* Implementation of smart contracts using hybrid architectures with on and off–blockchain components. In *2018 IEEE 8th International Symposium on Cloud and Service Computing (SC2)*, pages 83–90, November 2018.

[14]   Hyperledger Fabric: Hyperledger. https://www.hyperledger.org/wp-content/uploads/2017/08/HyperledgerArchWGPaper1Consensus.pdf. (Accessed on 17/08/2019).

[15]   Hyperledger Fabric: Hyperledger Architecture. https://www.hyperledger.org/projects/fabric. (Accessed on 19/08/2019).

[16]   N. Neidhardt, C. Köhler and M. Nüttgens *"Cloud service billing and service level agreement monitoring based on Blockchain,"* 2018, [ONLINE] https://dl.gi.de/server/api/core/bitstreams/ef2de851-d3fd-4fb3-895e-c4acf843e04f/content.

[17]   E. J. Scheid, B. B. Rodrigues, L. Z. Granville, and B. Stiller. Enabling dynamic sla compensation using blockchain-based smart contracts. In *2019*

IFIP/IEEE Symposium on Integrated Network and Service Management (IM), pages 53–61, April 2019.

[18]   Github – square/javapoet: a java api for generating .java source files. https:// github.com/square/javapoet. (Accessed on 09/17/2019).

[19]   J. Arora and P. Meumeu Yomsi. Wearable sensors based remote patient monitoring using IoT and data analytics. *U.Porto Journal of Engineering*, 5:34–45, 2019.

[20]   Building Your First Network – Hyperledger-Fabricdocs master Documentation. https://hyperledger-fabric.readthedocs.io/en/release-1.4/build_network. html. (Accessed on 09/17/2019).

[21]   C. Gorenflo, S. Lee, L. Golab, and S. Keshav. Fastfabric: scaling hyperledger fabric to 20,000 transactions per second, 2019. *arXiv preprint arXiv:1901.00910.*

[22]   P. Thakkar, S. Nathan, and B. Viswanathan. "Performance benchmarking and optimizing hyperledger fabric blockchain platform." In *2018 IEEE 26th international symposium on modeling, analysis, and simulation of computer and telecommunication systems (MASCOTS)*, pp. 264–276. IEEE, 2018.

Chapter 8

Intrusion detection and prevention in software-defined networks

Thomas Girdler[1], Celyn Birkinshaw[1], Wei Jie[2] and Vassilios Vassilakis[1]

8.1 Introduction

The latest generation of application-aware and programmable networks is a technology known as software-defined networking (SDN) [1]. A global network view is facilitated by SDN separating the data and control planes, which in turn increases network's overall performance and monitoring abilities. Current research indicates that the market for SDN is forecast to expand significantly, from $13.7 Bn in 2020 to $32.7 Bn in 2025 [2]. This is a Compound Annual Growth Rate (CAGR) of 19%. Factors driving the growth include increasing demand for cloud services, consolidation of data centres, virtualisation of servers, coupled with a reduction in capital expenses.

Since SDN can actively adjust itself to meet specific user requirements, it is particularly suited to cloud-based solutions and applications with real-time constraints [3]. These technologies are often based in distributed environments but require single overall control. Increasing network capacity will mean more services can be virtualised, with the distinction between local network and cloud likely to reduce. Although SDN allows for a greater virtualisation of network infrastructure, this can lead to an increase in the attack footprint for malicious actors. As SDN operation is solely orchestrated via a centralised controller, its compromise could result in the entire network becoming unavailable [4]. Due to this risk, cyber security researchers are now focusing on SDN security and are developing SDN-based security solutions [5,6]. Some of the most popular methods of infiltrating an SDN network include Man-in-the-Middle (MitM) attacks, Denial-of-Service (DoS) attacks and port-scanning [7]. These can allow networks to become modified or corrupted and traffic to be eavesdropped, which could then entail financial as well as reputational losses.

One such MitM attack is referred to as address resolution protocol (ARP) spoofing [8]. In this situation, an attacker sends false ARP messages across a network,

[1]Department of Computer Science, University of York, UK
[2]School of Computing and Engineering, University of West London, UK

which can result in the linking of their media access control (MAC) address to a genuine device's Internet Protocol (IP) address. Often, the method is utilised to 'poison' the ARP cache of a host machine, meaning the victim device sends all their packets to the attacker when communicating to another device. This may develop into further vulnerabilities or private data being exposed within the network. DoS attacks involve a series of fake packets being introduced into the SDN network [9]. These are often forwarded to the SDN controller where they occupy resources, which can impact the transmission of genuine packets to the controller. Large volumes of traffic can overload the controller, making it unreachable and jeopardising the entire network. Port-scanning is a technique whereby attackers scan remote hosts to determine which ports are sending and receiving data. Often, the attackers will focus on 'well-known' ports, which host popular services and may be easier to exploit.

To detect and mitigate network attacks, appropriate intrusion detection and prevention techniques could be utilised [10]. *Intrusion detection* is a process whereby networks are continuously monitored for threats or malicious activities. *Intrusion prevention* is a system whereby network configurations are adjusted to mitigate and prevent security threats. SDN offers the ability to dynamically adjust its operating parameters across all connected devices, therefore, making it possible to implement a network-wide intrusion detection and prevention system (IDPS). Our current work focuses on designing and developing an IDPS for SDN. We have also implemented associated tools and libraries to facilitate the security management and network monitoring. Our system can be utilised different scenarios to guard against adversaries. Thorough system testing and evaluation has taken place; with the results indicating that our proposed solutions could quickly detect and nullify malicious network traffic which attempts DoS or ARP spoofing attacks.

The rest of this chapter is organised as follows. In Section 8.2, we provide the basics of SDN. In Section 8.3, we review the SDN-based Cloud environments. In Section 8.4, we discuss SDN security. In Sections 8.5 and 8.6, we describe our proposed methods for the detection and mitigation of ARP spoofing, port-scanning, and DoS attacks in SDN. Finally, Section 8.7 concludes this chapter and considers possible future research directions.

8.2 Basics of SDN

Within this section, the necessary background information is provided to the reader. Relevant aspects are defined: a brief introduction to conventional computer networks, the development of programmable networks, followed by a discussion of SDN with its associated OpenFlow protocol.

8.2.1 Conventional networking vs. SDN

Network appliances have become ever more complex, requiring increased processing power on each device. Whilst standard network protocols exist, management standards are generally specific to each vendor [11]. These factors often result in limited

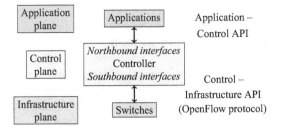

Figure 8.1   SDN network planes

interoperability between devices, meaning many prefer complex, vendor-specific hardware, rather than experiment with generic or open-source solutions. Networking technology has been gradually shifting towards applications developed by users. These users want the ability to fully customise their environment in terms of its services and applications. To facilitate this, the industry needed to change the way in which its products work.

As the SDN control and data planes are de-coupled, a secure link must established between them, usually with the OpenFlow protocol [12]. The SDN controller populates the forwarding devices with flow entries on a flow-table. Incoming packets are evaluated to find a matching flow, together with an associated action. Every flow-table has a table-miss entry which specifies the procedure for unmatched packets. These packets are sent back to the controller, dropped, or directed to a subsequent flow-table.

In conventional networks, routing choices are typically made for each individual packet, whereas with SDN, these decisions can be made on the first packet in a flow, then reused for a set amount of time. A flow can be generally described as a set of packet field values that determine a filter criterion with a set of instructions. A unified behaviour pattern within multiple network devices, including switches, routers, and firewalls, can then be constructed. This approach allows a considerable amount of flexibility in designing and implementing a network, limited only by the flow matching table capacity [1]. Figure 8.1 depicts the operation of an SDN network, together with the relationships between planes.

8.2.2 SDN components

The following are the key components within an SDN network [13].

Applications: Programs that directly communicate their requirements and desired behaviour to the SDN controller. This is done via one or more Northbound Interfaces (NBI). Applications may contain an abstracted view of the network for the purposes of their own decision making.

Controller: A centralised object in charge of translating requirements from application layer to the datapaths, as well as providing applications with an abstract view of the network. This could incorporate statistics and events.

Datapath: A logical network device that provides visibility and uncontested control over its advertised data processing and forwarding abilities. A logical representation may include all or a division of the physical substrate resources. The datapath comprises of a control to data plane interface (CDPI), one or more traffic forwarding engines with traffic processing functions. These may include forwarding between external interfaces of the datapath, internal traffic processing, or termination roles. A single (physical) network element may contain datapaths or defined amongst numerous physical network elements.

CDPI: The CDPI is an interface defined between controller and datapath. Programmatic control of every forwarding operation, advertisement of capabilities, statistics reporting, and event notification are provided by the CDPI. One advantage of SDN is that the CDPI is normally executed in a vendor-neutral open as well as interoperable manner, which provides greater flexibility for the user.

Northbound interfaces (NBI): These are interfaces between applications and controllers. They usually provide abstract views of the network and facilitate a direct expression of network requirements and behaviour. Again, SDN expects that these are realised in a vendor-neutral, open as well as interoperable manner.

Interface drivers and agents: Every interface is implemented by pair containing a driver and agent. The agent represents the 'southern', bottom side, which faces the infrastructure. In contrast, the 'driver' signifies the 'northern', top, or side that faces the application.

Management and admin: The management element covers tasks that are more suitably handled outside of the SDN planes.

8.2.3 SDN controller

SDN controllers maintain a global view of the entire network. They provide a northbound application programming interface (API) for communication with applications and a south-bound API to communicate with network elements. Together with the applications that make use of them, they apply choices regarding network routing, load balancing and redirecting. Often, the controllers are implemented in software and contain a set of standard applications, such as a learning switch, firewall, or router [14]. Core features of the controller incorporate discovery of end-user and network devices, for example desktop, laptops, switches, and routers. Furthermore, they record details of the network topology and associated interconnection details. The final key function of the controller is to manage the flow database and associate this with the forwarding devices.

To implement this view, there are two requirements that must be satisfied. First, all network devices (e.g., switches and routers) must be managed by an SDN controller, and present as a common logical architecture. As long as the SDN controller can recognise the devices as a uniform logical switch function, any vendor or type of network device can be employed. Second, a secure, standard protocol must be implemented between the SDN controller and all network devices. The most popular protocol is OpenFlow, outlined in Section 8.2.4.

One key advantage of SDN is the ability to enable a network-wide IDPS. In conventional networks, an IDPS is normally located in a specific network segment and has limited visibility beyond it. When compared with a conventional network, the IDPS in an SDN has significantly greater coverage and impact. Allocation as well as scheduling of resources is streamlined by the SDN controller having overall command of the datapaths and not contending with other elements of the control plane. This permits the overall network to run with exact policies, which in turn lead to greater resource utilisation and can guarantee quality of service [15]. For the purpose of detecting malicious network traffic, the SDN controller can analyse traffic statistics from all network devices.

8.2.4 OpenFlow protocol

In April 2008, a paper was published [16] which gave a background to research being conducted at Stanford University. This research centred around developing and innovating with new protocols using existing networks. The paper outlined the fundamental operation of an OpenFlow solution as being a controller populating a switch with entries on its flow table, the switch then evaluates incoming packet headers, a matching flow is then found, together with an associated action. The assessment begins at the layer two header, then conditional on the match criteria, continues to layer three header and, in a few cases, layer four header. When no matching flow entry is found, the switch forwards the packet to the controller, which provides instructions for dealing with the packet. Usually, when new flow entries are found, the switch will be updated by the controller, so the switch can deal with them locally, rather than having to rely on the controller for information. In addition, the controller can program wildcard rules into switches, these will govern many flows at a time. It can, therefore, be seen that OpenFlow networks allow traffic characteristics and features be configured as well as partitioning to take place [17].

8.3 SDN-based cloud

An ever-growing trend towards cloud computing brings both benefits and concerns. The main advantages include flexible resource allocation, simplified management, and increased availability. However, some issues still arise regarding the underlying network technologies and many aspects of user control. This section outlines how software-defined systems, together with SDN, can help mitigate these issues.

A family of solutions whereby the infrastructure is virtualised, managed by software, and delivered to the end-user as a service is known as Software-Defined Systems (SDSys). They have the ability to control a wide variety of computing resources in a unified manner. This is done by separating the control and work flow layer, allowing the controller to handle all independent devices using standard protocols. Virtualisation allows different devices or components to be integrated into a single function. To provide a comprehensive software-defined Cloud solution, SDN can be integrated with elements of SDSys, including Software Defined Data Centre (SDDC),

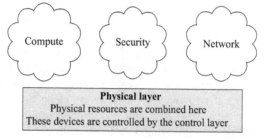

Application layer
Provides applications to End-users
and Northbound API to communicate with control layer

Control layer
Hosts the hypervisor, which controls and manages underlying devices
Rules and decisions are defined inside this layer
Communicates with physical layer using southbound API (OpenFlow)

Virtual pools
Resources are grouped together into specialised pools
These pools collaborate with one another to accomplish specific tasks

Compute   Security   Network

Physical layer
Physical resources are combined here
These devices are controlled by the control layer

Figure 8.2   SDSys architecture

Software-Defined Storage (SDStorage), Software-Defined Compute (SDCompute), and Software-Defined Security (SDSec) [18]. Figure 8.2 presents an overview of a general SDSys architecture.

Within the SDDC, a set of storage devices, servers, and networks are combined into a single asset or pool of resources. Many organisations have benefited from server virtualisation; SDDC expands this into all resource areas whilst providing a unified point of management. An SDDC-based architecture can provide both short- and long-term benefits. As software-based solutions take considerably less time to deploy than hardware-based ones, the time taken to provision new infrastructure can be reduced [19]. Tasks such as creating a new server, adding storage, or modifying network configuration take minutes or hours, as opposed to days and weeks. In the longer-term, SDDC reduces costs by better utilisation of infrastructure and a reduction in capital expenditure costs. In a similar manner to server virtualisation, SDStorage represents storage being pooled into an unified resource [18]. Like SDN, it has three layers: infrastructure, control, and application. Different types of storage devices can be combined into the infrastructure layer, including cloud, disk-based and flash. The control layer applies policies to the infrastructure layer, allowing end-users to interact with the storage via the application layer. SDCompute can be defined as a computing function which is virtualised then abstracted from the underlying hardware. A good example of SDCompute is VMWare's hypervisor, whereby a number of virtual servers can be created on the same hardware [20]. This provides the ability to isolate the virtual server from its host hardware, maximising resource utilisation which in turn can offer an adaptable, extensible infrastructure service.

To provide security to SDSys, SDSec operates in a manner unlike traditional mechanisms, by separating the forwarding and processing plane from the security control plane. This facilitates a security solution that can be scaled and distributed across multiple VMs, whilst being managed as a single, logical system. With SDSec, hardware devices such as firewalls, intrusion detection systems, and honeypots are implemented entirely in software [18]. The Cloud Security Alliance designed an architecture known as Software-Defined Parameter (SDP) that operates across all layers of the Open Systems Interconnection (OSI) model [21]. SDP operates on the principle of 'Zero-Trust' whereby any network access is withheld until comprehensively examined then authenticated; when finally authorised only the most restrictive permissions are granted.

8.4 SDN security

As with conventional networks, SDN can be vulnerable to security attacks. Table 8.1 outlines OpenFlow network attacks [1], based on STRIDE threat categories [22].

Here we summarise common SDN attacks; categorised by SDN plane targeted, together with possible rectifications [23].

8.4.1 Application plane

Poor or missing authentication protocols may allow unauthorised access to SDN, support the installation of malicious applications, that might discard or change control packets and disclose sensitive information. If the northbound API is misconfigured, this may disrupt the service or allow data sniffing between controller and target application. To mitigate these issues, the SDN controller must offer a reliable method for authorisation and authentication. Mattos *et al.* [24] advise that SDN devices use the Extensible Authentication Protocol (EAP), with the 802.1x standard and a Remote Authentication Dial-In User Service (RADIUS) server. Forwarding or discarding rules are sent to the SDN controller according to the RADIUS authentication process. Encryption between the SDN controller and data planes is critical to prevent unauthorised access, information disclosure or modification. Transport Layer Security (TLS), the default OpenFlow encryption protocol, is not mandatory and subject

Table 8.1   OpenFlow network attacks

Threat category	Security property	Attack
Spoofing	Authentication	IP/MAC address spoofing, MITM attacks
Tampering	Integrity	Modification of flow rules
Repudiation	Non-repudiation	Flow rule installation, forgery of source address
Information disclosure	Confidentiality	Attacks on the side-channel
Denial of service	Availability	Controller overloading
Elevation of privilege	Authorisation	Take-over of controller

to vulnerabilities. Sanchez *et al.* [25] suggest modifications to the protocol whereby client and server handshakes are compulsory, introduce status re-verification and communication termination upon handshake failure.

8.4.2   Control plane

Several weaknesses exist within the OpenFlow protocol and SDN controller, as outlined by Benton *et al.* [26]. A lack of authentication of incoming control messages means the switch table could be flooded with fake entries. DoS attacks could be launched against the controller, such as 'Packet-In' flooding, whereby adversaries broadcast a large number of malformed packets. These attacks have the effort of degenerating the controllers overall performance, which may lead to service disruption, or unauthorised disclosure of information. Sahay *et al.* [27] develop a solution to alleviate these vulnerabilities, with a policy management and enforcement framework, focused around a small Internet Service Provider (ISP) use-case. The proposed solution has a monitoring component, which extracts information about flows; this information is sent to the decision point. The latter chooses an appropriate action from the database, which is forwarded to the implementer. An enforcement point is selected and rules executed into the appropriate OpenFlow switches.

8.4.3   Data plane

On the SDN data plane, side-channel attacks are feasible which gather reconnaissance for further incursions. To gain configuration of an SDN network, Sonchack *et al.* [28], sent timing probes that compared the round-trip-time (RTT) to a set baseline. Their defense mechanism focusses around normalising the RTT of the attack probes with a timeout proxy placed between the switch and the control server. Experimental results indicated that the proxy did not impact non-attack network traffic, could apply a range of packet filters, and increases the control and data channel capacity. MitM attacks can take place, including ARP spoofing, whereby the controller identity is hijacked, forcing a switch connection to fake controller. The technique is depicted by Hong *et al.* [29] who put forward a countermeasure known as TopoGuard that provides automatic detection of poisoning attacks. TopoGuard validates network topology updates given by the PortManager and HostManager controller tracking services. Their system surveys OpenFlow messages to track switch port dynamics; this is stored in the Port Property Database. Together with a Host Probe module that probes host accessibility, the database can reason the trustworthiness of a topology update.

8.5   Detecting ARP spoofing attacks in SDN

In this section, we detail our SDN-based IDPS, with the associated configuration and testing tools. The IDPS was designed to defend against ARP spoofing and blacklisted MAC addresses. Specialised software was written to conduct the attacks and customise the IDPS. These were coupled to a specifically developed library to validate user input. Improvements were made to SDN in the area of attack detection, firewall and IPS, packet dropping, and shorter timeouts. Testing the IDPS involved four experiments – ARP Request Attack, ARP Reply Attack, ARP Reply Destination Attack, and Blacklisted MAC address.

8.5.1 Overview of ARP spoofing detection technique

Existing research into securing ARP within an SDN environment has focussed on utilising data from Dynamic Host Configuration Protocol (DHCP) servers, switch MAC to IP address mappings or 'sanitising' spoofed ARP requests with dummy values. Our motivation comes from the requirement to produce an SDN-based IDPS to detect and alleviate ARP spoofing attacks, which has minimal input from other network services or devices.

Our IDPS is designed to detect devices within the virtual SDN network performing ARP spoofing attacks [10]. The IDPS also identifies devices whose MAC address has previously been blacklisted using the IDPS Configuration Tool. After a packet is received on a switch port not meeting any existing flow-entry, a *PacketIn* event is sent from the Open Virtual Switch (OvS) [30] to the POX SDN controller [31]. The IDPS runs as an extension to the POX controller and listens for these *PacketIn* events. After the *PacketIn* event is received, it is then passed to the four separate functions: ARP Request Spoofing, ARP Reply Spoofing, ARP Reply Destination Spoofing, and Blacklisted MAC Addresses in turn. Packets meeting conditions set within each function are logged to screen and file. Any other packets are ignored. The attacker's IP address is obtained from the *PacketIn* event and used to generate a flow rule which prevents IPv4 network traffic to and from that specific address. This flow rule is active on the OvS switch for a set number of seconds, known as the flow hard timeout value, created by the IDPS Configuration Tool. If the flow hard timeout value is not available, a default value of 120 is set. Overall IDPS operation is represented by the flowchart of Figure 8.3.

8.5.2 IDPS

The IDPS functions were designed to recognise a separate type of network attack, as per Table 8.2. For example, a normal ARP reply has an Ethernet frame with an ARP payload packet encapsulated within it. The source MAC address is identical in the Ethernet frame and ARP *packet*, which verifies that it has been sent from the same physical device. The ARP payload in a spoofed ARP reply contains a different MAC address (the attacker) to that of the frame, so victim device sends packets to the attacker, not the intentional device.

These three ARP spoofing functions have the same fundamental design but differ upon the type of attack they intend to detect. Once the *PacketIn* event is received by the function, it is assigned to a variable called packet. Each packet has a field entitled EtherType that describes the type of data contained within it. The IDPS examines this field, to check if the type is ARP. The payload of the packet is assessed, which contains an ARP field entitled opcode. This can be set to either Request or Reply, depending on the type of ARP packet. The ARP Request Spoofing function considers if the opcode is set to Request, whereas the ARP Reply Spoofing function looks for Reply. Once

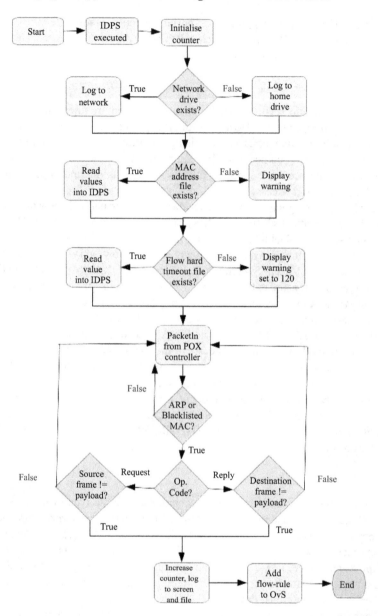

Figure 8.3   IDPS high-level operation

it has been ascertained that the received packet contains either an ARP Request or Reply the IDPS will then assess the content of the packet, as per the conditions in Table 8.2. If all of the conditions are matched, a variable called *counter* is increased by one. The counter references every packet detected by any IDPS function and set to zero upon IDPS initialisation.

Table 8.2   IDPS functions

Function	Packet conditions matched
ARP Request Spoofing	1. ARP Protocol 2. ARP Request 3. Source MAC Address in Ethernet frame or payload are not identical
ARP Reply Spoofing	1. ARP Protocol 2. ARP Reply 3. Source MAC Address in Ethernet frame or payload are not identical or
ARP Reply Destination Spoofing	4. Destination MAC Address in Ethernet frame or payload are not identical
Blacklisted MAC Addresses	1. IP Protocol 2. Source MAC Address of Ethernet frame contained within *blacklisted_mac_addresses.json* file

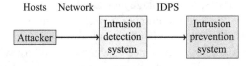

Figure 8.4   IDPS operation

The IDPS can also detect devices with Blacklisted MAC Addresses. A *PacketIn* event is transferred into the variable *packet*. The IDPS evaluates the EtherType field, to see if its type is IP. A JavaScript Object Notation (JSON) file containing the Blacklisted MAC Addresses is then read into the variable *blacklisted_mac_address_file*, which is compared to the source hardware address contained in the *packet* variable. An on-screen and file log of attacks is provided by the IDPS, written into a standard .xlsx spreadsheet file. Every row has the counter, time at which the packet was detected by the IDPS, type of attack, source IP or MAC address of attacker, and time when the flow-rule was installed. The IDPS Configuration Tool allows the IDPS flow timeout value and blacklisted MAC addresses to be configured. The IDPS Attacker Tool performs four separate ARP or TCP attacks. All user input into these tools is validated by the User Input Check Library. Figure 8.4 outlines operation of our IDPS. The *Hosts* send packets across the *Network*, these are initially received by the *Intrusion Detection System*. This passes them to the *Intrusion Prevention System*, which actively mitigates hostile packets.

8.5.3   Testbed

Our SDN testbed was based around Ubuntu Linux Virtual Machines (VM), with Virtual Box [32] as the hypervisor. Python-based POX [31] was deployed as the

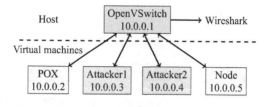

Figure 8.5　SDN testbed

SDN controller; this controls the OpenVSwitch (OvS) [30] virtual switch using the OpenFlow protocol. Figure 8.5 illustrates the SDN testbed.

The following metrics were used to assess the IDPS effectiveness and allow comparison to related systems. *Detection Time* is the time required to detect the attack. *Mitigation Time* is the time lapsed from attack detection to attacker being blocked. *False Positives* occur if the IDPS erroneously detects a benign packet as malicious. This is calculated by subtracting the number of attacker packets sent to those detected by the IDPS. A percentage indication of IDPS performance, *Detection Rate* is measured by dividing the number of packets sent by the attacker, to those detected by the IDPS, then multiplying the results by 100.

Our experiments employed the OpenVSwitch testbed host with POX controller and a combination of the other VMs, namely Attacker1, Attacker2, and Node. The IDPS Attacker tool had the following configuration: source IP address 10.0.0.3, destination IP address 10.0.0.4, source MAC address 11:11:11:11:11, each attack type sent 25 packets. All of our results recorded false positives as 0 and a detection rate of 100%. We used the network analyser software Wireshark to capture traffic on the switch.

8.5.4　Intrusion detection – ARP spoofing

The first experiment verifies intrusion detection operation, our software tools and network functionality. Attacker1 and POX VMs were utilised. Three separate attack types – Request, Reply, and Reply Destinations were employed. As depicted in Figure 8.6, the sender MAC address in the ARP payload is different to that of the source frame. The POX VM ARP cache was inspected to analyse attack success. Figure 8.7 establishes that the ARP cache was 'poisoned', as the host 10.0.0.3 was mapped to a spoofed MAC address – 11:11:11:11:11:11.

This experiment established an average detection time of 2.2 s across the three attack types. We examined Wireshark captures which indicated the IDPS Attacker Tool generated 'spoofed' ARP packets as we intended. Figure 8.8 and Table 8.3 summarise our results.

8.5.5　Intrusion detection – blacklisted MAC address

By employing a new type of attack from a different host, the second experiment built on the first. Using the IDPS Configuration Tool, we entered the enp0s3 interface

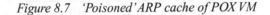

```
   77 10.0.0.2   62.20… TCP      66 54982 → 6633 [ACK] Seq=1593 Ack=369 Win=29312 Len=0 TSv…
   78 Broadcast  62.20… ARP      60 Who has 10.0.0.4? Tell 10.0.0.3
   79 Broadcast  62.20… OpenFl…  1… Type: OFPT_PACKET_IN
·Ethernet II, Src: PcsCompu_2c:f2:ef (08:00:27:2c:f2:ef), Dst: Broadcast (ff:ff:ff:ff:ff:ff)
 ·Destination: Broadcast (ff:ff:ff:ff:ff:ff)
 ·Source: PcsCompu_2c:f2:ef (08:00:27:2c:f2:ef)
  Type: ARP (0x0806)
  Padding: 000000000000000000000000000000000000
·Address Resolution Protocol (request)
  Hardware type: Ethernet (1)
  Protocol type: IPv4 (0x0800)
  Hardware size: 6
  Protocol size: 4
  Opcode: request (1)
  Sender MAC address: Private_11:11:11 (11:11:11:11:11:11)
  Sender IP address: 10.0.0.3 (10.0.0.3)
  Target MAC address: 00:00:00_00:00:00 (00:00:00:00:00:00)
  Target IP address: 10.0.0.4 (10.0.0.4)
```

Figure 8.6   Sender MAC address different to source frame

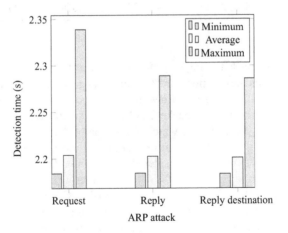

```
root@pox: /pox# arp -a
? (10.0.3.3) at 52:54:00:12:35:03 [ether] on enp0s3
openvswitch (10.0.0.1) at fa:10:4f:c5:12:4f [ether] on enp0s3
? (10.0.0.3) at 11:11:11:11:11:11 [ether] on enp0s3
```

Figure 8.7   'Poisoned' ARP cache of POX VM

Figure 8.8   Detection time – ARP Spoofing Attacks

MAC address of the Attacker2 VM. During the experiment, a repeating pattern of *Packet_In* and *Packet_Out* packets were noted, as per Figure 8.9.

We believe that this pattern was due to Attacker2 sending packets to the OvS switch, which are encapsulated with the OpenFlow protocol. These packets are directed to POX as *Packet_In* packet, inspecting this encapsulation contains an

Table 8.3   Detection time – ARP Spoofing Attacks

ARP Attack	Average	Minimum	Maximum
Request	02.203914	02.183804	02.338696
Reply	02.202416	02.184107	02.289039
Reply Destination	02.201044	02.183559	02.286205

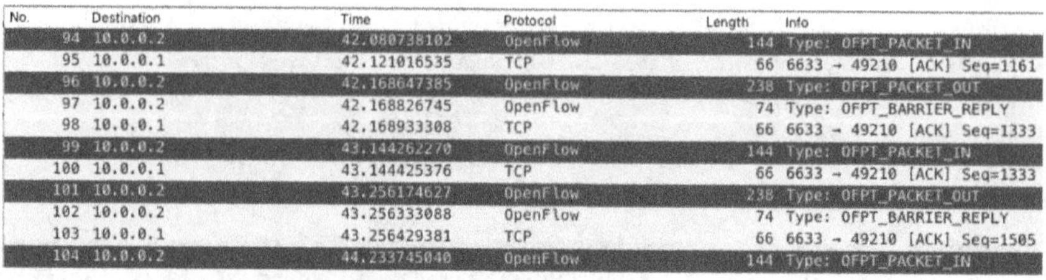

No.	Destination	Time	Protocol	Length	Info
94	10.0.0.2	42.080738102	OpenFlow	144	Type: OFPT_PACKET_IN
95	10.0.0.1	42.121016535	TCP	66	6633 → 49210 [ACK] Seq=1161
96	10.0.0.2	42.168647385	OpenFlow	238	Type: OFPT_PACKET_OUT
97	10.0.0.2	42.168826745	OpenFlow	74	Type: OFPT_BARRIER_REPLY
98	10.0.0.1	42.168933308	TCP	66	6633 → 49210 [ACK] Seq=1333
99	10.0.0.2	43.144262270	OpenFlow	144	Type: OFPT_PACKET_IN
100	10.0.0.1	43.144425376	TCP	66	6633 → 49210 [ACK] Seq=1333
101	10.0.0.2	43.256174627	OpenFlow	238	Type: OFPT_PACKET_OUT
102	10.0.0.2	43.256333088	OpenFlow	74	Type: OFPT_BARRIER_REPLY
103	10.0.0.1	43.256429381	TCP	66	6633 → 49210 [ACK] Seq=1505
104	10.0.0.2	44.233745040	OpenFlow	144	Type: OFPT_PACKET_IN

Figure 8.9   Repeating OpenFlow packets

Table 8.4   Detection time – Blacklisted MAC Address Attack

TCP Attack	Average	Minimum	Maximum
Blacklisted MAC Address	00.029930	00.068751	00.656727

explanation for the packet being sent 'Reason: No matching flow (table-miss flow entry)'. As source and destination ports are randomly generated in each packet sent by Attacker2, POX must create a new flow-entry, as none exist on the switch. To create the flow-entry, POX returns the packet header to the switch as a *Packet_Out* packet, containing an *Flow_Mod* packet, which allows the packet to reach its destination. Despite a delay being added to the packets, our IDPS was able to successfully detect the attacker. This delay might be considered as a potential flaw within an OpenFlow-based network. It was observed that the detection times were significantly lower than the first experiment. We believe that this was due to the TCP packets being transmitted at layer 3. An overhead involved in packet translation between layers could explain the higher response time for ARP packets, which are transmitted at layer 2. The second experiment asserted the operation of OpenFlow on our networking, including the insertion of flow rules. As with the first experiment, no false positives were recorded. Experimental results can be examined in Table 8.4 and Figure 8.10.

8.5.6   Intrusion prevention – ARP spoofing

The next experiment involved intrusion prevention, whereby we actively provide a countermeasure against attacks. Three ARP attack types were utilised – Request,

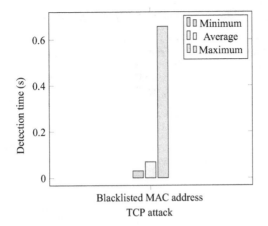

Figure 8.10   Detection Time – Blacklisted MAC address attack

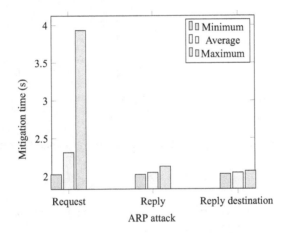

Figure 8.11   Mitigation time – ARP Spoofing Attacks

Reply, and Reply Destination, from the Attacker1 VM. After reviewing packets captured during the attack, we noted that the Sender MAC Address in the ARP payload was different to the Ethernet source in the Ethernet frame.

Our IDPS successfully detected the attack and installed a flow rule preventing network traffic from the attacker. We checked flow rule insertion by inputting *ovs-ofctl dump-flows ovs-br* on the OpenVSwitch host, this returned: *cookie=0x0, duration=0.700s, table=0, n_packets=0, hard_timeout=0, priority=1, ip, nw_src =10.0.0.3, nw_dst=10.0.0.4, actions=drop.* The output proved that a flow rule had been generated to block IP network traffic from the attacker. Further verification was carried out by sending a ping from the OvS host machine, resulting in 'Destination

Table 8.5   *Mitigation time – ARP Spoofing Attacks*

ARP Attack	Average	Minimum	Maximum
Request	02.314543	02.024589	03.933365
Reply	02.046977	02.021009	02.127211
Reply Destination	02.045087	02.028510	02.066943

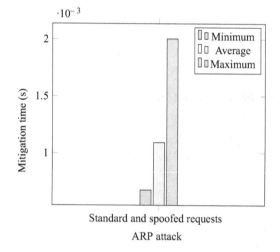

Figure 8.12   *Mitigation time – standard and spoofed Requests*

Host Unreachable'. This confirms that IP traffic cannot reach the attacker's IP address, before the attack this ping was successful.

We noted that the mitigation time was not significantly greater than in our previous experiments. Response times were similar to that of our first experiment, with an average of 2.2 s across all types of attacks. This establishes that intrusion prevention functionality does not add a significant overhead to our system. Figure 8.11 and Table 8.5 give a synopsis of our results.

8.5.7   *Intrusion prevention – standard and spoofed ARP requests*

Our final experiment involved 25 standard and spoofed ARP packets being simultaneously sent by the Node and Attacker1 VMs, respectively. The Node VM introduced a two-second gap between each packet, to mimic the network traffic an IDPS operates in. Our IDPS was successfully able to differentiate between spoofed as well as normal ARP requests and that mitigation times were roughly equivalent to the previous experiment. Figure 8.12 and Table 8.6 provide our results.

Table 8.6   Mitigation time – standard and spoofed requests

ARP attack	Average	Average	Maximum
Standard & Spoofed	0.001092	0.000674	0.002004

8.6   Detecting port-scanning and DoS attacks in SDN

This section outlines our work on defending against port-scanning and DoS attacks [9]. Note that the proposed design and detection methodology has the potential to be expanded to a wide range of other malicious activities. We have implemented and tested two connection-based techniques as part of the IDPS, namely the Credit-Based Threshold Random Walk (CB-TRW) and Rate Limiting (RL). As a mechanism to defend against port-scanning, we outline and test our Port Bingo (PB) algorithm. Furthermore, we include Quality of Service (QoS) as a DoS attack mitigation, which relies on flow-statistics from a network switch. We conducted extensive experiments in a purpose-built testbed environment. The experimental results show that the launched port-scanning and DoS attacks can be detected and stopped in real-time. Finally, the rate of false positives can be kept sufficiently low by tuning the threshold parameters of the detection algorithms.

8.6.1   Design

Our countermeasure against port-scanning is based on the principle that the attacker will send packets that are destined to a large number of different ports and that scans will typically prioritise the most valuable TCP port probes in descending order of accessibility. We monitor the TCP packet headers between pairs of network hosts and compare the packet destination ports with a list of 20 ports associated with portscanning. This is referred to as the PB algorithm. We define an anomaly as a series of communications within one tracking period in which one host sends packets to another, where the total number of matching destination ports is equal to the threshold value.

8.6.1.1   Rate limiting

RL is based on the premise that a benign host is unlikely to initiate many connections rapidly, whereas an attacker is more likely to do so. The same algorithm can be generalised to include connectionless protocols such as UDP. In the latter case, an anomaly is defined as an excessive number of UDP packets sent from one host to another. To mitigate against TCP-based attacks, the IDPS tracks TCP[SYN] packets sent by a host to a server, flagging an anomaly if the rate of connection-initiations exceeds the threshold value. After some predefined time (e.g., 1 min) if the RL threshold has not been exceeded, then the tracked connection is deleted. If an anomaly is detected, the IDPS generates a log at the controller and instructs the controller to create a flow-entry for the network switch to drop packets from the presumed attacker.

8.6.1.2   Credit-based threshold random walk

CB-TRW is based on the assumption that TCP connection requests made by a benign network host will generally be successful. If the host initiates a TCP connection with the server by transmitting a TCP[SYN] packet across the network via a switch, assuming the switch does not have a flow-entry to forward the packet, it will be sent to the controller and through the CB-TRW algorithm which will increase the tally of unsuccessful TCP connection by one. If the server replies to the host with a TCP[SYN,ACK] packet, then the TCP connection has turned out to be successful, and so the tally of unsuccessful connection initiations is decreased by one. An anomaly occurs when the tally exceeds a predefined threshold, which causes the IDPS to generate a log entry at the controller and a flow-entry at the network switch to drop packets from the presumed attacker.

8.6.1.3   Quality of Service

QoS is a network service which enables queuing on switch ports and can be applied to flow-entries. Our implementation of QoS is designed to detect flooding attacks, which is achieved by routinely checking the flow-entry statistics for anomalies. Specifically, we check for an excessive byte-count or an excessive packet-count in flow-entries that carry TCP packets between two hosts. If an anomaly is detected, the IDPS generates a flow-entry which can either enqueue or drop subsequent packets on the appropriate egress switch port.

8.6.2   Preparatory experiments

The SDN testbed is outlined in Figure 8.13. We used a Dell Inspiron with 8 GB RAM, an Intel Core i5-3337 CPU, 64-bit Ubuntu 16.04 Desktop with Ubuntu kernel 4.4. We installed OvS 2.7 which was used to set up an OvS bridge named 'ovs-br' and Wireshark was used to capture all packets received by ovs-br. For the controller, we used POX (Eel version) together with OpenFlow 1.0. The switch functionality was implemented via a module in the controller and we used the virtual Ethernet learning switch to connect the devices together.

We created four VMs in VirtualBox, each with 1,024 MB of memory, an Intel PRO/1,000 MT Desktop virtual network adapter and a bridged connection to the virtual network using virtual 10 Mbps cables. Each VM was running Ubuntu 16.04. The VMs were each assigned a static IP address and an MAC address.

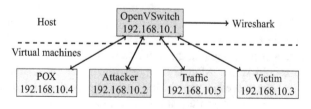

Figure 8.13   SDN testbed

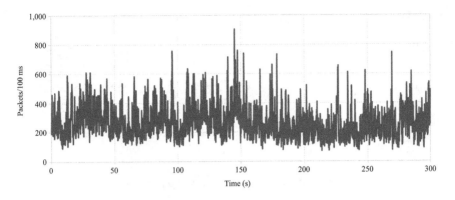

Figure 8.14 IO graph of background network traffic

The attacker was equipped with Nmap for network scanning and a range of DoS tools, including a DoS attack script which we created and named dos.py, a popular DoS script named Hammer.py and a DoS tool called Low Orbit Ion Cannon (LOIC). The victim VM was set up as a Web server. The traffic VM was used to generate benign network traffic, to make periodic Web requests to the victim while at the same time measuring response times and logging results. We created the network traffic by replaying a packet capture across the network using Tcpreplay. The packet capture file, named bigFlows.pcap, contained a sample of real network traffic from the access point of a busy private network to the Internet. The traffic included 133 unique Ethernet addresses, 132 different applications, an average throughput of 3 K packets per second (pps), and a peak throughput of 5 kpps. Figure 8.14 shows the IO-graph of the network traffic dataset. We also made regular requests to the Web server from the traffic VM and measured the time taken for a response to be able to gauge the impact of the attacks.

8.6.2.1 Characteristics of the attacks

Initially, we ran the attacks with the IDPS off on an otherwise quiet network, restarting the various network components for each new attack. Figure 8.15 shows the Nmap port scan as an IO graph. The associated packet capture file shows the scan was made up of TCP packets and the transmission peaked at a rate of 3 Kpps for a period of about 10 s. Over a number of similar scans, we observed the total scan time varied from about 15 s to about 220 s.

In the dos.py attack experiment, the attacker ran a TCP-based DoS attack using our Python script which attacked the Web server with 10 K packets, simply sending TCP[SYN] packets to the Web server one after another. The switch worked on twice as many packets as were sent from the attacker to the victim because the switch generated a new packet to the controller to request a new flow-entry for every packet from the attacker to the victim. Specifically, the switch requested additional forwarding information from the controller whenever the attacker's source port changed. Figure 8.16

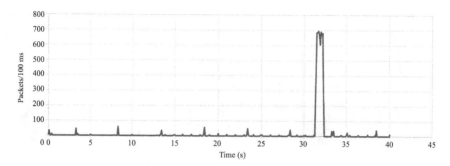

Figure 8.15   IO graph of Nmap port scan

No.	Source	Destination	Protocol	Source Port	Info
890	192.168.10.2	192.168.10.3	OpenFlow	57436,33680	Type: OFPT_PACKET_IN
892	192.168.10.2	192.168.10.3	OpenFlow	6633,33680	Type: OFPT_PACKET_OUT
898	192.168.10.2	192.168.10.3	OpenFlow	57436,33682	Type: OFPT_PACKET_IN
900	192.168.10.2	192.168.10.3	OpenFlow	6633,33682	Type: OFPT_PACKET_OUT
906	192.168.10.2	192.168.10.3	OpenFlow	57436,33684	Type: OFPT_PACKET_IN
908	192.168.10.2	192.168.10.3	OpenFlow	6633,33684	Type: OFPT_PACKET_OUT
914	192.168.10.2	192.168.10.3	OpenFlow	57436,33686	Type: OFPT_PACKET_IN
916	192.168.10.2	192.168.10.3	OpenFlow	6633,33686	Type: OFPT_PACKET_OUT
922	192.168.10.2	192.168.10.3	OpenFlow	57436,33688	Type: OFPT_PACKET_IN
924	192.168.10.2	192.168.10.3	OpenFlow	6633,33688	Type: OFPT_PACKET_OUT
930	192.168.10.2	192.168.10.3	OpenFlow	57436,33690	Type: OFPT_PACKET_IN
932	192.168.10.2	192.168.10.3	OpenFlow	6633,33690	Type: OFPT_PACKET_OUT

```
ip.src==192.168.10.2
```

```
> Internet Protocol Version 4, Src: 192.168.10.2, Dst: 192.168.10.3
v Transmission Control Protocol, Src Port: 33680, Dst Port: 80, Seq: 0, Len: 0
    Source Port: 33680
    Destination Port: 80
```

Figure 8.16   DoS attack causing excessive flow-entry creation

shows information from the packet capture and we see in the Source Port column that each packet from the attacker was sent from a different port, causing the number of flow-entries in the switch to build up quickly. Figure 8.17 shows the volume of attack traffic through the switch.

Figure 8.18 shows the IO graph for the Hammer DoS attack. The attack was formed of bursts of packets with a peak rate of about 8 Kpps. This attack caused the Web server to crash after about 20 s. After this time, the attack continued and the attacker was notified about the apparent downing of the server.

Figure 8.19 shows the IO graph for the LOIC DoS attack. The attack was formed of bursts of packets which peaked at a rate of about 0.5 Kpps. This attack caused a significant increase in the Web servers responses to our regular requests until after several minutes it stopped responding for the remainder of the attack without actually crashing.

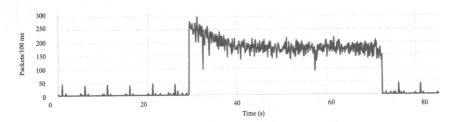

Figure 8.17 IO graph of our DoS attack

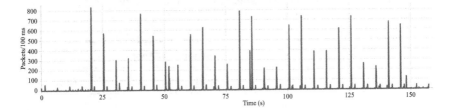

Figure 8.18 IO graph of hammer DoS attack

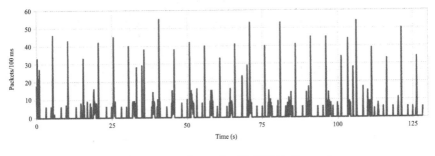

Figure 8.19 IO graph of LOIC DoS attack

Table 8.7 shows the breakdown of the different packet types which we recorded during each attack which can be contrasted with the row named bigFlows.pcap which describes the background benign network traffic which we used to set get appropriate algorithm thresholds for the IDPS and also as a source of noise to test the ability of the IDPS to mitigate attacks while allowing the network to function.

8.6.2.2 IDPS algorithm threshold settings

To determine appropriate IDPS algorithm threshold values, we ran the IDPS in a noisy network using our Background Network Traffic packet capture. We measured the number of false-positive alerts which were generated across a range of threshold values. Table 8.8 and Figure 8.20 show the results.

Table 8.7   Protocol hierarchy statistics – attacks

Packet capture	TCP %	UDP %	ICMP %
Our DoS attack	100	0	0
Hammer DoS attack	65	33	2
LOIC DoS attack	77	15	7
bigFlows.pcap	80	19	1

Table 8.8   IDPS number of false positive alerts across a range of threshold settings

Algorithm	Threshold setting			
	10	100	1 K	10 K
CB-TRW	548	72	4	0
RL	548	72	4	0
QoS	329	169	2	0
PB	0	0	0	0

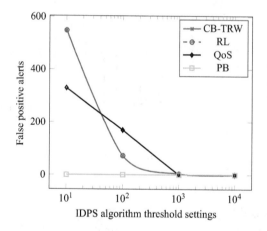

Figure 8.20   Dependency of false positive alerts on IDPS algorithm threshold settings

CB-TRW and RL resulted in identical false positive counts at every threshold setting with four FPs at a threshold setting of 1 K and no FPs at a threshold setting of 10 K. The PB algorithm generated the greatest number of FPs at threshold value of one (i.e. detect an attack every time a port is scanned) but did not generate any false positive alerts at higher order of magnitude higher threshold settings.

Table 8.9   Implemented IDPS algorithm threshold settings

Algorithm	Threshold setting
CB-TRW	10 K
RL	10 K
QoS (drop)*	10 K
QoS (enqueue)*	1 K
PB	10

* QoS was only partially implemented.

Table 8.10   IDPS algorithms used to block attacks

Attack	Detection and prevention
Dos.py	RL
Hammer.py	CB-TRW and/or RL
LOIC	CB-TRW and/or RL
Nmap port-scan	PB

In general, the setting of appropriate IDPS threshold values would depend on network security policy and should be adjusted to facilitate expected network activities and would also depend on the sensitivity of communications.

Table 8.9 includes the IDPS threshold settings which were used in our attack experiments.

8.6.3   Attack experiments and results

As shown in 8.10, all attacks were detected and then instantaneously blocked by the IDPS. The determining factor as to whether a DoS attack was blocked by RL or by CB-TRW was the responsiveness of the Web server. In the case of Hammer.py, the Web server crashed while the DoS attack continued, this meant that the number of unsuccessful connection attempts rapidly increased and the attack was detected by CB-TRW. Whereas for dos.py and LOIC, RL detected the quick succession of TCP connection attempts from the attacker and blocked the attacks.

CB-TRW was unable to detect the dos.py attack because the Web server responded to the attacker with TCP[SYN,ACK] packets. In the case of CB-TRW, every packet sent by the attacker resulted in a series of additional packets in the network. Initially, the attacker's TCP[SYN] packet to the switch caused the switch to request a flow-entry from the controller, to which the controller replied, enabling the switch to send the attacker's packet to the victim Web server. Then the same process happened in reverse for the Web server's TCP[SYN,ACK] packets. In summary, the CB-TRW algorithm was not effective because every response from the victim was effectively identified as a successful TCP connections and not part of an attack.

In the LOIC attack, CB-TRW would have blocked the attack, and we checked this by running the attack with RL switched off. The Web Server slowed down and became unresponsive for a period before Web requests to the server began to time out. At this stage, the number of unsuccessful connection attempts was greater than the CB-TRW algorithm threshold and so the attack was detected and blocked.

Toward our implementation of QoS, we made use of flow-statistics to set an appropriate threshold for the number of packets based on false positive testing using a dataset of benign network traffic. We also created queues on the OVS switch to be able to limit network traffic from the attacker. However, the full implementation of QoS was probably not possible with our testbed since OpenFlow 1.0 did not have functionality such as Set-Queue in OpenFlow 1.3 which can enqueue packets or drop them based on switch statistics. Our observations showed that DoS attacks tend to create many flow-entries which makes it difficult to handle an attack on a per-flow basis. By implementing QoS, an SDN-based IDPS can respond to an attack by controlling how traffic flows through a switch port used by an attacker.

For the Nmap network scan attack, the PB algorithm was used to monitor the attacker trying to check the state of different ports in a small period of time and blocked the attacker from the Web server.

8.7   Conclusion

Our work has shown the flexible nature of SDN and its capacity for customisation to meet user requirements. The IDPS systems developed demonstrated that SDN can satisfactorily detect and protect against network intrusions. The IDPS was proven to be successful in defending a network against ARP spoofing and blacklisted MAC address attacks, Nmap port-scans and DoS attacks. All sections of the SDN testbed, including the specifically designed software, were verified as fully operational. Our IDPS was able to send a log to the console as well as write to a spreadsheet file. The IDPS could dynamically defend the network against attacks by preventing the attacker's network traffic from entering the virtual network. Testing was carried out by using a variety of hostile and benign network traffic from assorted hosts.

Future work includes testing and developing an IDPS using SDN hardware-based switches and controllers. This would allow 'real-life' simulations to occur, giving an indication of the systems performance under normal operating conditions. Current SDN research is centred around IPv4, which is being replaced by IPv6. ARP functionality is delivered by a protocol entitled neighbour discovery protocol (NDP) within IPv6. We would also aim to develop an IPv6-based SDN IDPS, whilst providing backward compatibility with the existing solution.

There is also a scope to carry out further tests using the IDPS. We believe the IDPS could be improved by providing it with more benign network traffic datasets to minimize false positives and potentially auto-tune algorithm threshold settings. Additionally, by running more attacks we would identify limitations of the IDPS. For example, one feature of Nmap is its ability to perform scans in many different ways. It would be very difficult to detect a port-scan that was performed slowly, especially if it came via a range of different systems. In the case of such an attack, our PB algorithm could be extended to store network scanning probes over a longer period of time and from a range of sources. One potential use for this would be to identify a malicious network of attacker-controlled systems.

Acknowledgements

The authors wish to thank Elpida Rouka for sharing her virtual switch configuration, Dr Peter Reid and D. Helen Reid for supporting this research.

References

[1] Kreutz D., Ramos F.M.V., Verissimo P.E, Rothenberg C.E., Azodolmolky S., and Uhlig S. 'Software-defined networking: a comprehensive survey'. *Proceedings of the IEEE*. 2015, vol. 103, no. 1, pp. 14–76.

[2] MarketWatch, 'Software Defined Networking (SDN) Market 2021 Global Industry Demand Analysis'. [Online]. Available: https://www.market watch.com/press-release/software-defined-networking-sdn-market-2021-shar e-growth-trend-industry-analysis-and-forecast-to-2026-2021-02-09 [Access ed 25 June 2021].

[3] Zhang M., Ranjan R., Menzel M., Nepal S., Strazdins P., Jie W., and Wang L. 'An infrastructure service recommendation system for cloud applications with real-time QoS requirement constraints'. *IEEE Systems Journal*. 2015, vol. 11(4), pp. 2960–2970.

[4] Chica J., Cuatindioy J., and Botero J. 'Security in SDN: a comprehensive survey'. *Journal of Network and Computer Applications*. 2020, vol. 159, 102595, pp. 1–23.

[5] Alotaibi F.M. and Vassilakis V.G. 'SDN-based detection of self-propagating ransomware: the case of BadRabbit'. *IEEE Access*. 2021, vol. 9, pp. 28039–28058.

[6] Rouka E., Birkinshaw C., and Vassilakis V.G. 'SDN-based malware detection and mitigation: the case of ExPetr ransomware'. In *IEEE International Conference on Informatics, IoT, and Enabling Technologies (ICIoT)*, Doha, Qatar, 2020, pp. 150–155.

[7] Pradhan A. and Mathew R. 'Solutions to vulnerabilities and threats in software defined networking (SDN)'. *Procedia Computer Science*. 2020, vol. 171, pp. 2581–2589.

[8] Veracode, 'What is ARP spoofing?' 2019. [Online]. Available: https://www. veracode.com/security/arp-spoofing. [Accessed 25 June 2021].

[9] Birkinshaw C., Rouka E., and Vassilakis V. 'Implementing an intrusion detection and prevention system using software-defined networking: defending

against port-scanning and denial-of-service attacks'. *Journal of Network and Computer Applications.* 2019, vol. 136, pp. 71–85.

[10] Girdler T. and Vassilakis V. 'Implementing an intrusion detection and prevention system using software-defined networking: defending against ARP spoofing attacks and blacklisted MAC addresses'. *Computers and Electrical Engineering.* 2021, vol. 90, 106990, pp. 1–12.

[11] Feamster N., Rexford J., and Zegura E. 'The road to SDN: an intellectual history of programmable networks'. *SIGCOMM Computer Communication Review.* 2014, vol. 44, pp. 87–98.

[12] ONF, 'OpenFlow Switch Specification', April 2015. [Online]. Available: https://www.opennetworking.org/wp-content/uploads/2014/10/openflow-swit ch-v1.5.1.pdf. [Accessed 25 June 2021].

[13] ONF, 'SDN Architecture Overview', Dec. 2013. [Online]. Available: https:// opennetworking.org/wp-content/uploads/2013/02/TR_SDN_ARCH_1.0_060 62014.pdf [Accessed 25 June 2021].

[14] Göransson P., Black C., and Culver T. *Software Defined Networks – A Comprehensive Approach*, 2nd edn. Cambridge, MA: Morgan Kaufmann; 2016, p. 436.

[15] Dabbagh M., Hamdaoui B., Guizani M., and Rayes A. 'Software-defined networking security: pros and cons'. *IEEE Communications Magazine.* 2015, vol. 53, no. 6, pp. 73–79.

[16] McKeown N., Anderson T., Balakrishnan H., and Turner J.S., 'OpenFlow: enabling innovation in campus networks'. *SIGCOMM Computer Communication Review.* 2008, vol. 38, no. 2, pp. 69–74.

[17] Doherty J. *SDN and NFV Simplified: A Visual Guide to Understanding Software Defined Networks and Network Function Virtualization.* Addison-Wesley Professional; 2016, p. 143.

[18] Jararweh Y., Al-Ayyoub M., Darabseh A., Benkhelifa E., Vouk M., and Rindos A. 'Software defined cloud: survey, system and evaluation'. *Future Generation Computer Systems.* 2016, vol. 58, pp. 56–74.

[19] IBM Cloud Education. 'Software-Defined Data Centers'. [Online] Available: https://www.ibm.com/cloud/learn/software-defined-data-center [Accessed: 25 June 2021].

[20] VMWare. 'Software-Defined Data Center (SDDC) – In Depth'. [Online] Available: https://www.vmware.com/uk/solutions/software-defined-datacenter/in-depth.html [Accessed: 25 June 2021].

[21] Cloud Security Alliance. 'Software Defined Perimeter (SDP) and Zero Trust'. [Online] Available: https://cloudsecurityalliance.org/artifacts/software-defined-perimeter/ [Accessed: 25 June 2021].

[22] Microsoft. 'The STRIDE Threat Model'. [Online] Available: https://docs. microsoft.com/en-us/previous-versions/commerce-server/ee823878(v=cs.20)? redirectedfrom=MSDN [Accessed 25 June 2021].

[23] Correa-Chica J.C, Cuatindioy J., and Botero-Vega J.F. 'Security in SDN: a comprehensive survey'. *Journal of Network and Computer Applications.* 2020, vol. 159, 102595, pp. 1–23.

[24] Mattos D.M. and Duarte O.C. 'AuthFlow: authentication and access control mechanism for software defined networking'. *Annals of Telecommunications*. 2016, vol. 71, pp. 607–615.

[25] Belema A. and Sanchez-Velazqez E. 'OpenFlow communications and TLS security in software-defined networks'. In *IEEE Internatinal Conference on Internet of Things (iThings)*. 2017, Exeter, UK, pp. 560–566.

[26] Benton K., Jean Camp L., and Small C. 'OpenFlow vulnerability assessment'. In *2nd ACM SIGCOMM Workshop on Hot Topics in Software Defined Networking (HotSDN'13)*. 2013, New York, NY, USA, pp. 151–152.

[27] Sahay R., Blanc G., Zhang Z., Toumi K., and Hervé D. 'Adaptive policy-driven attack mitigation in SDN'. In *1st International Workshop on Security and Dependability of Multi-Domain Infrastructures*. 2017, Belgrade, Serbia, pp. 1–6.

[28] Sonchack J., Dubey A., Aviv A.J., Smith J.M., and Keller E. 'Timing-based reconnaissance and defense in software-defined networks'. In *32nd Annual Conference on Computer Security Applications (ACSAC'16)*. 2016, New York, NY, USA, pp. 89–100.

[29] Hong S., Xu L., Wang H., and Gu G. 'Poisoning network visibility in software-defined networks: new attacks and countermeasures'. *NDSS Symposium*. 2015, San Diego, CA, USA, p. 15.

[30] Open vSwitch, 'Production Quality, Multilayer Open Virtual Switch', 2019. [Online]. Available: http://www.openvswitch.org/ [Accessed 25 June 2021].

[31] McCauley J. 'Installing POX'. [Online]. Available: https://noxrepo. github.io/pox-doc/html/ [Accessed 25 June 2021].

[32] Oracle, 'VirtualBox'. [Online]. Available: https://www.virtualbox.org/. [Accessed 25 June 2021].

Chapter 9

Privacy challenges for Internet of Medical Things

Sabeen Tahir[1], Yinhao Li[1], Masoud Barati[2], Omer Rana[1],
Rajiv Ranjan[3], Gagangeet Singh Aujla[4] and
Kwabena Adu Duodu[3]

The Internet of Medical Things (IoMT) can be used to support the remote monitoring of patients using communication and sensing technologies. Security and privacy concerns in IoMT related to patient data are important issues for regulatory bodies, requiring the formulating and implementing laws that protect patients. The European General Data Protection Regulation (GDPR) provides a number of data protection rules that make it easier for citizens to know how their information is being used by external data processors. Citizens can raise complaints to the relevant legal authorities in case of a violation. GDPR Art. 5 imposes lawfulness, fairness, and transparency of data access as requirements that need to be met by a data processor. Medical data is sensitive and the existing healthcare ecosystem often lacks a secure architecture, that can lead to potential data breaches with consequences for both patients and healthcare providers. In this chapter, a multi-layered blockchain-based GDPR compliance verification technique is outlined as a solution for carrying out a privacy audit on how a patient's data has been handled. The multi-layer architecture includes medical sensors, gateways, edge devices, and cloud systems that need to work collectively to offer efficient and secure services to patients. To verify GDPR compliance, a blockchain-based provenance log is integrated with edge devices and cloud systems. A blockchain can be used to record various data activities at the different layers specified above and can be used to verify GDPR compliance.

9.1 Introduction

In the Internet of Things (IoT), physical objects ("things") can include sensors, software, and other technologies to connect and share information between systems and devices over the internet. IoT has a significant impact in every field of human life,

[1]School of Computer Science and Informatics, Cardiff University, UK
[2]School of Computing, Edinburgh Napier University, UK
[3]School of Computing, Newcastle University, UK
[4]Department of Computer Science, Durham University, UK

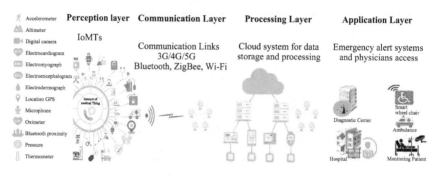

Figure 9.1 IoMT layers

especially in healthcare. For example, the Internet of Medical Things (IoMT) includes medical devices and applications can be used to monitor physical activities, body temperature, heart rate, glucose level, blood pressure, sleep, etc. IoMT devices collect, examine, and transmit information across the internet to support remote patient care [1]. IoMT enables medical staff to spend less time diagnosing diseases and healthcare delivery – and greater time on diagnosis and support of patients. For example, IoMT can provide real-time observations through a wireless body area network, enabling processing of this data using artificial intelligence and cloud-based analytics. IoMT can also be used to support an early warning system to control the spread of infection by using information gathering, storage, transfer and analysis [2–4].

IoMT layers and remote monitoring are illustrated in Figure 9.1. An IoMT remote healthcare monitoring architecture may consist of the following four layers – each with its own components.

- **Perception layer**: consists of devices with built-in medical sensors for collecting patient data and transferring this data to other devices without human intervention. IoMT devices can be categorized into three types: wearable devices, patchable devices, and implantable devices – examples include blood pressure monitors (Withings), body temperature monitoring systems (Temptraq), pulse monitoring systems (Wahoo device), daily physical activities monitor (Fitbit, Samsung Wearable, Garmin), heart rate monitor (EKG), an insulin pump (Animas Vibe), etc.
- **Connectivity layer**: responsible for end-to-end data transmission from IoMTs to a medical cloud system, using communication technologies like Bluetooth, Wi-Fi, NBIoT, LoRAWaN, 5G, etc. The communication technologies for IoMT can include both short- and medium-/long-range communication. Short-range communication technologies create links between devices within a limited geographical area, i.e. a connection between IoMTs and a gateway device. Medium-range technologies on the other hand support long-distance data exchange, e.g. a link between a gateway device and the cloud system [5]. Heart rate and impedance monitoring (e.g. from Libelium) often involve the use of specialist cables that have to be attached to a patient's body. This can be a practical challenge in many instances, as the number of cables and their distance to a capturing device (a hub)

is often limited. The accuracy and the efficiency of wireless (i.e. no-physical cables) are often limited at present.

- **Processing layer**: responsible for recording, storing, processing, and managing data and forwarding data to one or more cloud systems. For example, comparing patient's blood pressure readings to pre-defined thresholds, or correlating different data streams associated with a given individual.
- **Application layer**: responsible for device control and generating reports. It provides services to users through web-based dashboards and query application programming interfaces (APIs).

An increase in IoMT use also leads to additional security and privacy challenges [6]. According to a recent survey [7], around 95% of IoT data transmission is unencrypted, indicating that many IoT devices are vulnerable to security and privacy attacks revealing confidential data. An increase in the deployment of IoMT devices, especially during a pandemic to support remote monitoring of patients may increase privacy concerns. Therefore, protecting a patient's sensitive data becomes an even bigger concern. Furthermore, as security risks, attacks, and threats affect all IoMT architecture layers, an IoMT network must also follow stricter privacy and security specifications compared to other IoT devices [8,9]. Many existing IoMT devices are not designed with security and privacy features in mind, which makes them vulnerable. Protecting remote healthcare monitoring is paramount to secure medical staff, organizations and patients [10].

Due to the wide variety of wireless networking technologies and possible security and privacy threats against them, the whole system requires an audit of potential vulnerabilities related to data breaches [11]. Privacy vulnerabilities of remote health monitoring can make data during transit accessible to unauthorized parties. Securing remote health monitoring should begin with gaining trusted visibility and categorization of IoMT devices across endpoints e.g. remote hospitals, cloud systems, and hospital networks. IoMT device networks are often also heterogeneous, which can increase the potential attack surface against such networks. There are no existing efficient protocols that can mitigate against privacy issues caused by heterogeneous technologies – although recent work towards the Quic Protocol is attempting to address some of these limitations. IoMT is gradually increasing and replacing the traditional medical system. According to Goldman Sachs [12], it saves the medical industry US \$300B yearly through remote patient monitoring. Deloitte expects the market for IoMT devices to reach US \$52.2B in 2022 [13].

9.1.1 General data protection regulation (GDPR)

The GDPR was introduced in 2018 within European Union law to support data protection and privacy for all organizations having access to personal data. It is the main responsibility of IoMT providers to confirm that GDPR compliant data protection concepts are applied. For verification, healthcare providers using IoMT applications must conduct a data protection impact assessment as mentioned in the GDPR legislation and confirm that medical sensors do not gather unnecessary data. In addition, healthcare providers must follow the rules of data minimization and purpose limitations defined by GDPR. Therefore, devices must only collect the required amount of data for relevant purpose pre-agreed with the users of these devices.

It is obligatory that patients must provide up-to-date consent for remote data gathering, sharing, and analysis. After giving consent [14] patients expect their data to be treated confidentially across a complex set of systems – between IoMT manufacturers, communication systems, and medical IT systems. According to GDPR Article 30 [15], a medical system should include the information source for patient data, the purpose of storing and processing this information, a list of places/systems where personal data is stored, how data flows between these subsystems, and how long the system will keep this information.

The proposed approach described in this chapter considers a multi-layered architecture that includes IoMT devices, gateways, edge devices, and a medical cloud system. IoMT devices monitor patients' health and transmit information periodically to the relevant gateway devices that transmit the data to the edge and cloud system for processing. A blockchain can be used to record operations or events performed on patients' data and store them for subsequent analysis. When any data operations occur, an update will be added to the blockchain transaction and link to the medical record (kept off-chain) as a complete authenticated record. The blocks will be shared between authorized edge devices to run smart contracts and verify the new blocks. It is critical for medical systems to recognize the vulnerabilities of IoMT devices and how to protect them. Since the data is sensitive and personal, remote patient monitoring and IoMT applications bring new and critical challenges for data protection and patient's rights to know what information has been gathered about them and how it will be processed.

The rest of this chapter is structured as follows: Section 9.2 includes a description of related work and compares the proposed approach with other systems reported in literature. Section 9.3 describes a use case for an IoMT remote patient monitoring system. Our blockchain-based architecture along with its protocols are presented in Section 9.4, and finally Section 9.5 concludes the chapter and identifies directions for future work.

9.2 Related work

A number of research contributions describe the use of blockchain technologies to support healthcare, limiting access to healthcare data and giving patients more control over their private health information. For example, according to Samarin [16], medical records can be privately kept on the cloud (demonstrated for 175 patients) and a patient alone has access to these files – preventing the sharing of medical data with several entities. However, this work does not mention the process where a physician must keep non-disclosed healthcare information about the patient.

The use of cloud computing has transformed real-time healthcare monitoring. However, this also makes networks more vulnerable to malicious attacks that can cause mishandling of patient data. To protect IoMT networks, preventive measures must be adopted in the design phase of such a system. Since IoMT is a linked network of different devices connected to a server, any risks in security services of IoMT network can compromise patient privacy [5]. A web-based IoMT framework for security assessment [17] supports IoMT security features based on a specific scenario. The framework enables engagement with different stakeholders, supports operations at different granularity and compliances with standards. In general, system administrators formulate security and privacy-related decisions. Although the framework shows its effectiveness by assessing outcomes across a number of attributes – these assessment attributes were not easy to understand by medical staff, and patients who lack security and technical expertise.

A novel and secure scheme to share medical data based on private Blockchain technology and attribute-based encryption (MedSBA) is described in [18], as a practical and secure method for storing healthcare data. MedSBA is based on blockchain technology to ensure privacy and involves accessing patient data using attribute-based encryption (ABE) in compliance with the GDPR legislation. The use of a private blockchain to revoke direct access makes it very challenging in ABE. Security is verified through formal design, while functionality is verified using BAN logic. Furthermore, computational complexity and storage are demonstrated by implementing MedSBA using the OPNET simulator. A blockchain-based authentication key agreement technique BAKMP-IoMT [19] supports secure key management between servers (cloud and personal) and implantable medical sensors. This technique stores sensitive medical data into a blockchain, enabling secure access to sensitive medical data, and provides a mechanism to confirm that this data is retrieved only by authorized users. It also saves healthcare data in the blockchain stored in a cloud system. In addition, it conducts a formal security analysis by utilizing AVISPA, an automated tool that can be used to protect a system against potential attacks.

The efficiency of a blockchain, based on its properties of stability, security, decentralization, and non-modifiability is described in [20]. This work identifies that success of a blockchain is due to its consensus algorithm. It also describes features, performance, and system scenarios of various consensus algorithms. In [21,22], blockchain-based models were proposed for sharing medical data in IoT. The models were GDPR compliant by implementing smart contracts which verify data access, storage, and transfer obligations. Privacy requirements require that IoMT systems enforce confidentiality guidelines and allow users to access their data [23]. In addition, a collection of confidential medical data must follow ethical and legal privacy laws, such as Health Insurance Portability and Accountability Act (HIPAA) and GDPR [24]. These guidelines ensure the protection of a patient's personal and sensitive data from disclosure. They should keep the data for a limited time to meet GDPR requirements. Furthermore, the data should not disclose personal information of users during processing [25]. The use of wireless communications without supporting data privacy can lead to private and sensitive data being compromised [26].

In the last few years, a record number of cyberattacks have been reported on healthcare services – with approx. 418 attacks (in 2019) involving HIPAA security breaches. Existing computational healthcare infrastructures do not take efficient security measures against these attacks, which can raise questions on the security and privacy of healthcare data. In addition, systems for managing healthcare records show different challenges, i.e. healthcare organizations having patient data, leaving it at risk and causing ineffective data processing towards a patient's healthcare. For example, health information of a patient is not transmitted to the service providers on time, which can subsequently delay treatment. The limitations of electronic healthcare records can be overcome by using blockchain technology [27]. In [28], the authors formally defined how GDPR verification is undertaken on smart devices in IoT. They also proposed a container-based model on IoT gateways for monitoring and flagging GDPR violators. Remote healthcare monitoring based on IoMT collects data using medical sensors of remotely located individuals. Current research considers the use of blockchain for keeping patient records, managing, and sharing data. In [29], the authors support real-time monitoring and proposed a solution implemented on the Ethereum platform with smart contracts. However, it has been observed that this approach can only benefit smaller consortiums, due to the inherent latency in Ethereum's transaction processing over public networks. The techniques mentioned earlier are using advanced privacy-aware solutions to protect the patients' data. Still, none of the techniques shows implementing such a technique that combines blockchain and verification of GDPR obligations over data processing.

Based on this literature review, we conclude that the critical issues in current remote patient monitoring systems are patient privacy and secure transmission of healthcare data across the network. Furthermore, as healthcare services and devices rely on continuous availability, a Denial of Service (DoS) attack can lead to these devices and the services they support becoming unavailable. As a result, medical-related information is a lucrative target for cybercriminals. However, current research shows that blockchain technology has overcome the critical issues of data alteration and deletion, but there are still privacy-related issues that remain unresolved. To fulfill GDPR compliance, the approach proposed in this work will not save and transfer healthcare data through the blockchain; it involves keeping patient data confidential. Our proposed technique only records data operations (i.e. the type of operation carried out and not the data on which this operation was invoked) in the blockchain. An event is added to the blockchain whenever there is an operation on the data. Personal user data is kept off-chain – and only the outcome of a hash function is recorded in the blockchain.

9.3 GDPR compliance verification in IoMT

This section investigates the GDPR consequences on IoMT network design and implementation. Consider IoMT devices that monitor a remote patient to predict and treat various health conditions. These devices can monitor blood pressure, body temperature, oxygen saturation levels in the blood, glucose level, etc. Based on monitoring these parameters, IoMT devices can be used to diagnose and generate an alert message during an emergency. Such alert messages can be transmitted to both patients and healthcare providers. Critical variations of a patient's condition are sent to care

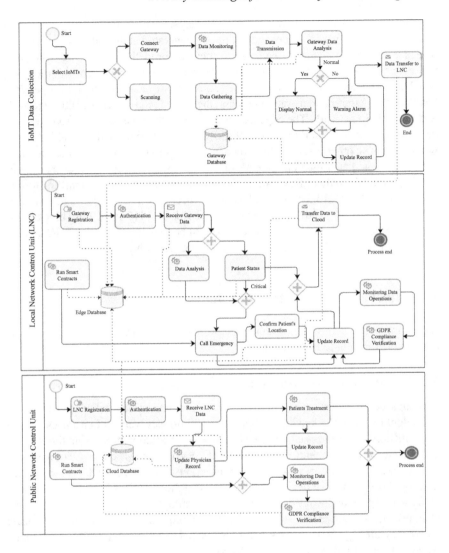

Figure 9.2   The business process model of IoMT remote patient monitoring

providers to enable them to respond. If there is a severe condition and cannot be remotely solved, it must provide enough information about what to do next.

The BPMN of remote patient monitoring is illustrated in Figure 9.2, describing the set of activities carried out over IoMT devices and gateways and their interactions. This business process model has three sections: IoMT data collection, Local Network Control (LNC) unit, and Public Network Control (PNC) unit. The first shows IoMT devices connected to their respective gateways using in-built communicators for data exchange across any wireless network interface. The IoMT devices monitor patients and transmit this data to gateway devices for analysis. Any initial alarms, due to data exceedings pre-defined thresholds, are directly generated at the gateway device. The data is then transmitted to the LNC, an edge device, for further processing – shown as the second block in Figure 9.2. All gateway devices must be registered with the LNC, which authenticates these devices before receiving any data and monitors a patient's health status. After the registration process, the edge device starts submitting records to a blockchain network. The edge device processes the received data from gateway devices and creates reports periodically, which are all encrypted and added to the blockchain. The other essential function of an LNC is to run smart contracts, monitor data operations performed on patient's data, and verify GDPR compliance. Finally, an LNC transmits only critical data to the PNC (a medical cloud system) for further processing – the third block of the business process model. All the LNCs must be registered with the PNC that is a medical cloud system. PNC is the third block of the business process model. First, all the LNCs must be registered with the PNC, as only pre-authenticated LNCs are allowed to submit data to a PNC.

9.4   Blockchain-based IoMT system

A description of IoMT system architecture, workflow, and implementation challenges are provided in subsequent sections.

9.4.1   Application requirements

This subsection presents application-level requirements based on the IoMT use case. The adoption of a blockchain to support IoMT privacy verification raises several non-functional challenges e.g. limited blockchain transaction processing throughput, and functional requirements e.g., sensitive patient data access control. For example, Ethereum can only process approx. 30 transactions per second – which can be very limiting if the number of devices or operations on these devices increase (influenced by network speed and workload on the server hosting the Blockchain). However, the response time of data processing tasks is a critical requirement in real-time healthcare emergency alert generation. A scalable blockchain network with high throughput, which can perform data processing tasks concurrently, is necessary to support IoMT-based data recording and analytics.

Placing openly visible data within a blockchain supports the audit process – i.e. identifying which operation was carried out on user data (and by whom), but can also expose private user data as every block in an open blockchain network (e.g. Ethereum) is visible to all other nodes in the network. All transactions stored in blockchain can be searched and traced. IoMT applications can utilize this transparency feature to allow any entities to track healthcare records and GDPR compliance verification. However, it is difficult to maintain patient data privacy along with transaction transparency in a single blockchain network. Encryption is one possible solution, especially if a Homomorphic encryption approach is adopted, which enables a limited number of operations to be carried out directly on encrypted data. However, this can be limiting in the types of operations that can be supported. Correspondingly, a multi-layered blockchain-based system which can carry out both privacy and transparency requirements needs to be considered. Such a multi-layered architecture can also be used as a basis for scaling a blockchain system.

9.4.2 System architecture

This section describes our blockchain-based IoMT architecture – proving an efficient solution for supporting secure medical data transmission, whilst still using a blockchain network to support auditing. The conceptual architecture is illustrated in Figure 9.3. A local network/edge layer consists of IoMTs (medical sensors), a gateway device, and an edge device. Medical sensors can carry out periodic measurements and transmit this data to the connected gateway device. A public network consists of gateway devices, edge devices, and a cloud system. The gateway devices transmit their data to the edge device known as the LNC unit. As the gateway devices transmit data periodically, they will transmit immediately if the data is critical.

For GDPR verification, the blockchain is integrated with the LNC unit to monitor patient activities. Personal data that has relevance for GDPR includes: patient name, identification number, location, physical address, email address, photograph, biometric data (eye retina, fingerprint, etc.). According to GDPR, a user should be consulted before their personal data is shared with other systems/parties and no operation can be performed on individuals' data without their consent. As blockchain supports tracking operations on data, it is used for GDPR compliance checking for IoMT networks – to audit if any operation was carried out on user data without consent. The records

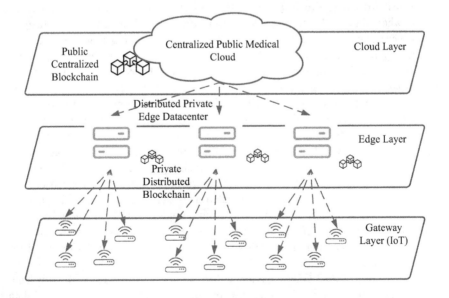

Figure 9.3 An overview of the multi-layer IoMTs architecture

in the blockchain can also be used to confirm which operation was performed on individual's data, through which cloud service operator and for what purpose. In the proposed system, as most of the data is stored in the databases of the LNC and PNC systems, it is essential to make these secure.

The IoMTs have limited processing and storage capabilities, and they can save their resources by using periodic monitoring mode. This technique can connect multiple gateways to one edge device, but it does not allow data sharing between all gateways. Gateways do not connect with each other; these are personal devices of patients. If data will be shared between gateways, it means data is available publicly and shared between patients. Blockchain technology has merged with the edge devices, and these are directly connected and sharing the data. An edge device will be a miner in a local blockchain-based network layer because it is the most powerful device. Each gateway device must authenticate before starting to transmit data by using specific public and private keys. The edge device will save all the keys in its database to quickly identify the authentic gateway devices. After the registration process, the edge device starts creating blocks. Once validated by the miner or edge device, blocks will be included in the local blockchain-based network. After this, the edge device processes the received data from gateway devices and creates reports periodically. In this layer, there will be an interaction between patients through their gateway devices and medical authorities. Moreover, there may also have interaction between different authorities through the edge devices. All the edge devices are linked with each other through a blockchain. We will have Proof of Work (PoW) and Proof of Stake (PoS), a necessary part of blockchain to enable trust. This layer consists of many miners to mine the blocks and authenticate them. The PoW ensures independent miners' security, whereas the PoS securely sequence the transaction history based on previous data and make it difficult to alter it. The edge devices transmit the updated data to the cloud device, where the cloud will create blocks about the received data and other data operations. The access control and user consent will be done by using contracts. The users can directly access their data from the edge and cloud system by using their accounts.

Due to GDPR compliance, no medical record will be stored on the Blockchain or in smart contracts. Patient records will be kept confidential; this technique only records data operations in the Blockchain. Medical staff perform these operations and updates are recorded and linked to medical records as a complete authenticated record of a patient. The authenticated medical record also helps to detect attacks on a patient's record. The blocks will be shared between the authorized edge devices that can run smart contracts and verify new blocks. This technique does not share blocks and patient data between gateway devices. This contract confirms a patient's consent and monitors data processing operations executed on patients' medical records. In addition, this contract verifies that data processing complies with GDPR requirements. According to Art. 5 of GDPR, medical centers are bound to explain the purpose of patient data processing. They will also explain the purpose of devices used for collecting data.

According to Art. 7 GDPR, patients' data cannot be processed with their legal consent. Data processing will be carried out based on patients' consent, and data controllers at medical centers shall verify that patients have consented to process their sensitive and personal data. Patients will also have the right to cancel their consent anytime. Hence, according to GDPR requirements, at the time of registration, the medical centers being processors demonstrate that a patient has consented to process their medical records indicating that a patient's received data has been reviewed by the authorized healthcare providers, advice or prescriptions have been written by authorized healthcare providers, patient's data has been deleted based on request, and transfer or sharing of patient data does not take place.

Based on Art. 25 of GDPR, medical centers will apply suitable measures to assure that only a patient's essential data, for a specific purpose, will be processed. This rule applies to a patient's collected data from IoMT sensors, level of processing, duration of data accessibility, and storage. These measures assure that patient data will not be accessible to anyone else without their consent. Art.5 of GDPR prevents data storage longer than the time required for data processing. According to Art. 32 of GDPR, medical centers should implement measures to assure the level of data security employed (e.g. encryption of data) and ensure the patient data confidentiality, availability, and integrity during data processing and storage. As medical data is considered critical data, there is a need to share it with other entities based on a patient's condition. For this purpose, GDPR requires medical centers to have patient consent and ensure that the patient has agreed to the proposed data sharing after being informed of possible risks. According to Art. 44-50 of GDPR, strict rules are implemented related to transferring of personal data to countries outside of the EU. This is the responsibility of medical cloud providers, to ensure that patient data is not migrated to a location that violates this requirement of GDPR.

9.4.3 System execution workflow

This subsection describes mutual authentication and run-time workflow stages during execution.

The first stage of execution involves Mutual Authentication (MA) – also known as two-way authentication. The MA requires both the client (Gateway) and the server (Edge) to provide digital certificates to verify their credentials. The certificates are exchanged between these two authentication entities using the Transport Layer Security (TLS) protocol. The main reason of this stage for to ensure that both entities only communicate with certificated clients and servers. The detailed steps of authenticating and the establishment of an encrypted channel are illustrated in Figure 9.4.

Before MA occurs, administrators need to identify a certificate authority (CA) to sign certificates on patient-owned sensor devices. The devices then deploy such CA chain to gateways. Once signed certificates have been registered, a gateway can connect to an Edge server by MQTT, HTTP, or WebSocket protocols and request access operation. Subsequently, the Edge server presents a server-side certificate to the gateway. After verification, a gateway certificate is sent to the Edge server to verify. If verification is successful, a secure channel is established for future communication.

9.4.3.1 System runtime workflow

The second stage involves a run-time workflow, identifying processing steps needed to complete the required processing, as illustrated in Figure 9.5. Patients can be equipped with multiple IoMTs that gather data and can send this concurrently to the

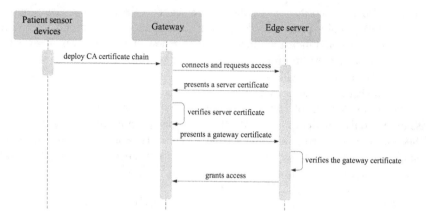

Figure 9.4   System mutual authentication diagram

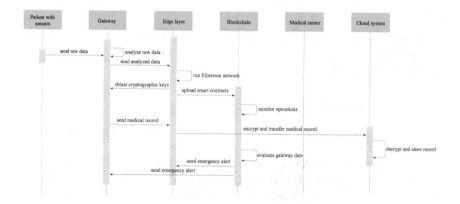

Figure 9.5   System workflow diagram

gateway device. The gateway device is responsible for analyzing the received data and forwarding the outcomes to the relevant edge device. The edge layer runs the Ethereum network and is responsible for creating smart contracts. For this purpose, gateway devices need to obtain the cryptographic keys from the edge layer. Subsequently, an edge device uploads smart contracts to the blockchain, to monitor operations on patient records in compliance with GDPR. The smart contract monitors several data processing operations, such as whether: consent for access to this data has been obtained, the identified purpose of data processing, security protocol used for the transfer of data, etc. When an edge device receives the medical record from the gateway device, it will encrypt it using a pre-shared key and transfer it to the cloud system. The cloud system decrypts the received medical encrypted record and stores it for further processing.

- All medical centers are connected through edge devices, hence if medical center A needs data from another medical center B, it will get it from the cloud-hosted system.
- An edge device from medical center A requests the cloud system for another medical center's record.
- The cloud system encrypts the record using a pre-shared secret key and sends it to medical center B.
- The edge device de-crypts the record and uploads the transactions to the blockchain. The transaction log includes the identity of gateway(s), edge device(s), timestamp, and their signatures.

9.4.4 Multi-layered architecture

This subsection describes a practical multi-layered blockchain architecture to address application-level requirements identified in previous sections. As shown in Figure 9.6, the multi-blockchain architecture consists of the following main entities: a patient or individual whose data has been captured using an IoMT device, edge gateway (and perhaps an additional edge datacenter) and a cloud datacenter. Each entity communicates with various data transformation protocols, such as MQTT, over a communication network. The data subject in this architecture is an individual wearing a smartwatch to monitor heart rate, temperature, etc. over a predefined time interval. After such readings are captured, the smartwatch will create a streaming time window to buffer data and then send it to a smartphone via Bluetooth automatically.

When an edge gateway devices receive this data from an IoT device, further data processing tasks can be carried out in smartphones (e.g., Android, iOS) or other connected devices – which may be realized using a Raspberry Pi or an Arduino board. Usually, edge gateway devices have limited computational power to execute complex data processing tasks, such as machine learning model training. Lightweight applications are designed for these devices to filter abnormal readings, or a pre-developed model developed at a cloud platform may be deployed at the edge gateway. In some instances, an edge gateway devices may also be treated as an actuator to carry out control actions based on the data analysis. An edge data center cooperates with a cloud data center to support a multi-layered blockchain system, to support both scale and adaptivity. A microservice-based orchestration engine can be used to process data from IoMT devices, enabling a number of services to be combined together. Each microservice may perform a single or several relevant functions on the captured data. As these services are located and hosted on different operating systems or virtual

Figure 9.6   A practical multi-blockchain architecture

machines/containers, it is easy to achieve maintainability with micro-service techniques, such as Docker and Kubernetes. To implement multi-blockchain architecture, Polkadot,* a network protocol that allows cross Blockchain data transfer is considered as a practical solution. Polkadot treats heterogeneous blockchains as parachains and proposes a relay chain to provide cross blockchain security and data sharing. Bridge is a network protocol provided by Polkadot to allow parachains to communicate with external public blockchain networks, such as Ethereum and Bitcoin. As Ethereum is the most popular public blockchain network for decentralized application development, a platform which can deploy Ethereum-based smart contracts to Polkadot network easily needs to be considered. Moonbeam† located at the edge datacenter offers Ethereum-compatible smart contracts implementation to attach to Polkadot as a parachain with minimized changes on Solidity codes.

9.5　Conclusion

There has been an increase in the use of IoMT for monitoring individuals, both for patients who already suffer from a known condition and to the general population interested in managing their general health and wellbeing. Increasingly, these devices can collect data that has implications for the GDPR legislation, as this data can expose particular characteristics of an individual often without their consent. IoMT can be combined with edge and cloud systems to carry out data collection, aggregation, storage, and processing – and increasingly, therefore, the requirements of GDPR need to be shared across this IoMT to Cloud continuum – often involving a variety of different systems operators.

Therefore, understanding what data is shared, with whom and over what period becomes a significant concern for ensuring GDPR compliance. We describe the use of a blockchain network to support this, using a combination of smart contracts that can be used to support key requirements of operations of interest – such as read, write, transfer, and profile/process – described in the GDPR legislation. We also describe a multi-layered blockchain architecture that can audit operations carried out by edge and cloud devices on user data, and how deploying blockchains across both edge and cloud resources can address scalability challenges inherent in the use of a blockchain system. Our future work involves practical deployment of this system and gaining user (and medical provider) confidence in its benefit and utility.

Acknowledgments

This work is supported by the Engineering and Physical Sciences Research Council (EPSRC) funded project PACE: Privacy-Aware Cloud Ecosystems (EP/ R033293/ 1 and EP/ R033439/ 1).

---

*https://polkadot.network/technology/
†https://moonbeam.network

References

[1]   Sharma D, Singh Aujla G, and Bajaj R. Evolution from ancient medication to human-centered Healthcare 4.0: a review on health care recommender systems. *International Journal of Communication Systems*. 2019;36:e4058.

[2]   Alabdulatif A, Khalil I, Forkan ARM, *et al.* Real-time secure health surveillance for smarter health communities. *IEEE Communications Magazine*. 2018;57(1):122–129.

[3]   Christaki E. New technologies in predicting, preventing and controlling emerging infectious diseases. *Virulence*. 2015;6(6):558–565.

[4]   Al-Dhief FT, Latiff NMA, Malik NNNA, *et al.* A survey of voice pathology surveillance systems based on internet of things and machine learning algorithms. *IEEE Access*. 2020;8:64514–64533.

[5]   Pradhan B, Bhattacharyya S, and Pal K. IoT-based applications in healthcare devices. *Journal of Healthcare Engineering*. 2021;2021.

[6]   Aujla GS, Chaudhary R, Kaur K, *et al.* SAFE: SDN-assisted framework for edge–cloud interplay in secure healthcare ecosystem. *IEEE Transactions on Industrial Informatics*. 2018;15(1):469–480.

[7]   https://www.globalxetfs.com/how-cybersecurity-will-accelerate-iots-growth;. Available from: https://www.globalxetfs.com/how-cybersecurity-will-accele rate-iots-growth.

[8]   Somasundaram R and Thirugnanam M. Review of security challenges in healthcare Internet of Things. *Wireless Networks*. 2020;27:1–7.

[9]   Yaqoob T, Abbas H, and Atiquzzaman M. Security vulnerabilities, attacks, countermeasures, and regulations of networked medical devices—a review. *IEEE Communications Surveys & Tutorials*. 2019;21(4):3723–3768.

[10] Chaudhary R, Jindal A, Aujla GS, *et al.* Lscsh: lattice-based secure cryptosystem for smart healthcare in smart cities environment. *IEEE Communications Magazine*. 2018;56(4):24–32.

[11] Aujla GS and Jindal A. A decoupled blockchain approach for edge-envisioned IoT-based healthcare monitoring. *IEEE Journal on Selected Areas in Communications*. 2020;39(2):491–499.

[12] https://healthtechmagazine.net/article/2020/02/what-makes-iomt-devices-so-difficult-secure-perfcon/. Available from: https://healthtechmagazine.net/article/2020/02/what-makes-iomt-devices-so-difficult-secure-perfcon/.

[13] https://www2.deloitte.com/uk/en/pages/life-sciences-and-healthcare/articles/medtech-and-the-internet-of-medical-things.html. Available from: https://www2.deloitte.com/uk/en/pages/life-sciences-and-healthcare/articles/medtech-and-the-internet-of-medical-things.html.

[14] Choi P and Walker R. Remote patient management: balancing patient privacy, data security, and clinical needs. In: *Remote Patient Management in Peritoneal Dialysis*. vol. 197. Karger Publishers; 2019. p. 35–43.

[15] https://www.privacy-regulation.eu/en/article-30-records-of-processing-activit ies-GDPR.htm. Available from: https://www.privacy-regulation.eu/en/article-30-records-of-processing-activities-GDPR.htm.

[16]   Milojkovic M. "Privacy-preserving framework for access control and inter-operability of electronic health records using blockchain technology," 2018, [ONLINE] https://digitalcommons.winthrop.edu/source/SOURCE_2018/posterpresentations/64/.

[17]   Alsubaei F, Abuhussein A, Shandilya V, *et al.* IoMT-SAF: Internet of medical things security assessment framework. *Internet of Things.* 2019;8:100123.

[18]   Pournaghi SM, Bayat M, and Farjami Y. MedSBA: a novel and secure scheme to share medical data based on blockchain technology and attribute-based encryption. *Journal of Ambient Intelligence and Humanized Computing.* 2020;11:1–29.

[19]   Garg N, Wazid M, Das AK, *et al.* BAKMP-IoMT: design of blockchain enabled authenticated key management protocol for Internet of medical things deployment. *IEEE Access.* 2020;8:95956–95977.

[20]   Mingxiao D, Xiaofeng M, Zhe Z, *et al.* A review on consensus algorithm of blockchain. In: *2017 IEEE International Conference on Systems, Man, and Cybernetics (SMC).* IEEE; 2017. p. 2567–2572.

[21]   Barati M, Petri I, and Rana O. Developing GDPR compliant user data policies for Internet of things. In: *12th IEEE/ACM International Conference on Utility and Cloud Computing.* IEEE/ACM; 2019. p. 133–141.

[22]   Barati M and Rana O. Enhancing user privacy in IoT: integration of GDPR and blockchain. In: Z. Zheng, HN. Dai, M. Tang, and X. Chen (Eds), *Blockchain and Trustworthy Systems. BlockSys 2019. Communications in Computer and Information Science.* Springer; 2019. p. 322–335.

[23]   Mosenia A and Jha NK. A comprehensive study of security of Internet-of-things. *IEEE Transactions on Emerging Topics in Computing.* 2016;5(4): 586–602.

[24]   Gupta S, Venugopal V, Mahajan V, *et al.* HIPAA, GDPR and best practice guidelines for preserving data security and privacy—what radiologists should know. In: *European Congress of Radiology—ECR 2020*; 2020.

[25]   Hassija V, Chamola V, Saxena V, *et al.* A survey on IoT security: application areas, security threats, and solution architectures. *IEEE Access.* 2019;7: 82721–82743.

[26]   Yaacoub JPA, Noura M, Noura HN, *et al.* Securing Internet of medical things systems: limitations, issues and recommendations. *Future Generation Computer Systems.* 2020;105:581–606.

[27]   Kshetri N. Blockchain and electronic healthcare records [cybertrust]. *Computer.* 2018;51(12):59–63.

[28]   Barati M, Rana O, Petri I, *et al.* GDPR compliance verification in Internet of things. *IEEE Access.* 2020;8:119697–119709.

[29]   Griggs KN, Ossipova O, Kohlios CP, *et al.* Healthcare blockchain system using smart contracts for secure automated remote patient monitoring. *Journal of Medical Systems.* 2018;42(7):1–7.

Chapter 10

Quality-aware Internet of Things applications

Kaneez Fizza[1], Abhik Banerjee[1] and
Prem Prakash Jayaraman[1]

As with other domains, quality in Internet of Things (IoT) applications has often been perceived as the Quality of Experience (QoE). However, as will be discussed in detail in this chapter, measuring the quality of IoT applications is characterized by unique challenges which cannot be encapsulated by QoE alone, arising due to the nature of IoT applications as well as how these applications are consumed by the end-user.

Quality in an IoT application is determined by the application outcomes and how these outcomes are often assessed. Depending on this, IoT application outcomes can be categorized as:

- *Human-in-the-loop IoT applications:* wherein the IoT application interacts directly with human users. Hence, humans can often be relied on to estimate/capture the quality of the IoT application. For example, quality can refer to accuracy in outcomes presented to the user in the form of insights, predictions or recommendations that aid in the decision-making by human users.
- *Autonomic IoT applications:* wherein all interactions are centered around machine-to-machine (M2M) communication, including the final application outcomes that are often interpreted and responded to (actuation) by non-humans entities (e.g., a machine in an industrial manufacturing facility). In such situations, the IoT application outcomes are consumed entitles that autonomously make decisions without any inputs from human users. Hence, such automatic IoT applications' quality must often be measured/computed without relying on human feedback.

While existing notions of QoE can easily be tuned to human-in-the-loop IoT applications, it is challenging to adapt them to autonomic IoT applications due to the absence of user perception. In addition to the above, IoT applications are distinguished by the fact that they are distributed and interconnected in nature, characterized by heterogenous systems, encompassing sensors, actuators, edge computers, servers, and cloud-based systems, along with the communication among these systems. The final application outcomes are often dependent on the outcomes of all these systems.

[1]Department of Computing Technologies, Swinburne University of Technology, Australia

Thus, a comprehensive evaluation of the IoT application quality depends on the quality of all the contributing systems.

In this chapter, we present an overview of quality in Internet of Things applications. In particular, we characterize the quality of IoT applications from the perspective of human-in-the-loop and autonomous IoT applications and identify the key factors impacting the quality of IoT applications. Finally, we examine how IoT applications can be made quality aware and propose a conceptual architecture for the same.

10.1 Human-in-the-loop vs. autonomic IoT applications – exemplary use case in smart parking

In this section, we use the example of a smart parking application to illustrate the differences between the quality of human-in-the-loop and autonomic IoT applications. Parking management and smart parking have seen significant interest in smart city initiatives. Let us consider a smart parking IoT application which incorporates IoT with data analytics to recommend vacant parking spots. The application takes the destination address as input and provides the parking spot recommendation available at or near the destination. To achieve this outcome, the smart parking IoT application collects data from the (1) moving cars (such as car's current location, and license plate number); (2) sensors and actuators installed in the parking garage (e.g., cameras, ultra-sonic sensors, etc.); and (3) parking garage information (e.g., location, availability). Using this data, it performs data analytics to recommend a vacant parking spot. Figure 10.1 depicts such a smart parking IoT application deployment, which includes a cloud-based component that collects data from moving cars, such as their location, destination, and license plate along with parking availability data from parking garages which include data from cameras and ultra-sonic sensors. Through the application of data analytics techniques on this collected data, the smart parking IoT application generates recommendations of suitable parking spots for the moving cars and communicates the recommendation outcomes back to the moving cars.

The smart parking IoT application described above may be implemented either as a human-in-the-loop or autonomic IoT application, based on which the application quality is defined, as discussed below:

(A)   An example of a *human-in-the-loop smart parking IoT application* is one in which multiple parking spot recommendations close to the destination are presented to a human user, such as the driver, who decides on one of the recommended parking spots to use. The human user can then provide feedback on the suitability of the recommended spots, using which the IoT application quality can be measured, e.g., the average rating provided by all users.

(B)   An example of an *autonomic smart parking IoT application* is one in which a single parking spot recommendation is selected and provided to an autonomous vehicle, autonomously navigates to the parking spot. The selection of the parking spot is based on multiple factors such as the exact location of the vehicle and traffic conditions. The quality of such an application can be measured using a

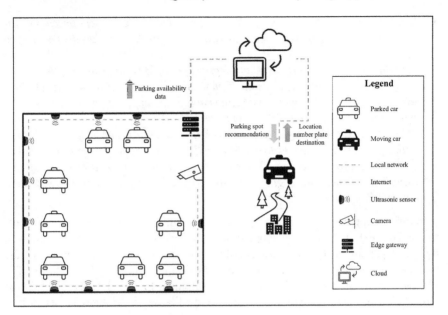

Figure 10.1   Smart parking IoT application

combination of metrics including the time taken to generate a spot and distance from the intended destination.

While the quality of the smart parking IoT application discussed above is subjective in (A) and objective in (B), they are both impacted by the quality of the application components, i.e., sensing, data transmission, and data analytics, which are measured using the IoT quality metrics (described in Section 10.4).

10.2   Quality of experience – background

Various organizations and researchers have proposed definitions of QoE. We discuss how these existing definitions are adapted for applications which have human-in-the-loop to provide their feedback on the experience provided by the application but do not account for autonomic IoT. Organizations like International Telecommunication Union ITU-T (ITU-T) and The European Telecommunications Standard Institute (ETSI) have defined QoE. Such QoE definitions proposed by standard organizations and researchers are listed below.

- *"The overall acceptability of an application or service, as perceived subjectively by the end-user"* [1].

- *"QoE is a method for measuring performance according to users based on subjective and objective psychological measurement, for the use of product or service ICT"* [2].
- *"Quality of Experience (QoE) is the degree of delight or annoyance of the user of an application or service. It results from the fulfillment of his or her expectations with respect to the utility and / or enjoyment of the application or service in the light of the user's personality and current state"* [3].
- *"Quality of experience (QoE) is a metric that depends on the underlying QoS along with a person's preferences towards a particular object or service where his/her preferences are defined by his/her personal attributes related to expectations, experiences, behaviour, cognitive abilities, object's attributes and the environment surrounding that person"* [4].

Various application domains such as video conferencing, mobile applications, multimedia IoT, and IoT have adopted these QoE definitions. The definition given by ITU-T [1] has a subjective measure of an application or a service received by the end-user. In contrast to the definition from ITU-T, the definition of QoE from ETSI [2] includes a subjective and objective measurement to complete the blueprint of QoE definition. Subjective human factors are qualitative and include factors such as usefulness, usability, need, availability, feelings, happiness, boredom, expectations, desires, social influences, brand image, and satisfaction. On the contrary, objective human factors such as reaction time are quantitative. While subjective evaluation is commonly used to obtain user opinions, it is unsuitable for real-time applications. The majority of the existing QoE definitions focus on the understanding and measuring the quality of an application or a service received by end-users (humans), and typically focus on multimedia applications. Such QoE measurements primarily rely on the subjective feedback provided by humans, which makes them unsuitable for IoT, especially IoT applications which require objective measurement of quality metrics.

10.3   Quality in IoT applications – a view of existing literature

In the existing literature, the QoE paradigm has been used to measure the overall experience of a user in using an application or a service. QoE has been defined as a metric to quantify the experience of an end-user. QoE measures the user experience both objectively and subjectively. It aims at assessing user experience with all the human-dependent variables.

There are different types of models used for measuring the quality of IoT applications. Broadly, there are three types of models discussed as follows.

- **Conceptual models:** Several researchers [5–10] have proposed QoE models to identify the metrics and relationship among them. For example, Pal *et al.* in [5] proposed a QoE taxonomy for IoT. They identify various factors which can impact QoE in IoT from three different perspectives i.e., technical, user, and context, which includes both subjective (user) and objective factors (technical and context). However, it is a conceptual taxonomy which does not provide any methods for quantitative measurement. The authors in [6] also proposed a conceptual QoE model for context aware health services. In this chapter, the authors have two broad abstractions for QoE management i.e., user experience and factors influencing user experience. The factors influencing user experience are mainly human, content, context, and quality.

Shin *et al.* [8] identified a series of factors which can impact QoE, including satisfaction, involvement, affordance, coolness, enjoyment, and hedonicity, as well as application factors which can impact these identified QoE factors. These application factors are information quality, system quality, and service quality. Based on human–computer interaction (HCI), they identified a relationship between QoE factors and application factors. The results show that a high value of application factors leads to high level of customer satisfaction (coolness and affordances) which provide strong cues for IoT. The major limitation of their model is that it is based on HCI assuming that an application customer is always a human which does not include machine-to-machine interactions in IoT.

- **Statistical models:** QoE can be modeled using various statistical methods, such as regression analysis. Li *et al.* in their work [11] exploited multiple regression analysis to model QoE for IoT applications. To do so, the authors identified the network parameters of the QoE and collected sample data, which they analyzed using principal component analysis (PCA). Subsequently, the authors associated QoE with the principal components using multiple regression analysis and built the regression equation between QoE and principal components. Finally, they modeled QoE and network parameters based on the regression equation.

  Similarly, Floris *et al.* [12] computed a linear (l) and a logarithmic (nonlinear (nl)) regression between inputs (Quality of Data and Quality of Service) and output data (QoE).

  While these statistical models [11,12] are derived through statistical mapping between QoE and network factors, they do not account for the addition of new metrics.

- **ML/AI-based models:** The recent boom in AI and ML-based methods has paved a pathway for predicting QoE in IoT. IoT being an interconnection of devices leverages the power of AI and ML to predict the quality of the application before the application is deployed and used. Techniques such as Decision Trees (DT), Recurrent Neural Networks (RNN), and Deep Neural Networks (DNN) are used to predict QoE [13,14]. These models are more reliable and less prone to uncertainty. However, the accuracy of these models is highly dependent on the training data set.

While the above-mentioned approaches have been proposed for modeling QoE of IoT applications, comprehensive measurement of the quality of IoT applications is challenging due to multiple reasons, primary among which are the following:

- *IoT applications have a diverse range of experiences, which vary based on the type of application.*

  IoT is growing rapidly and is finding substantial applications in domains like transportation, healthcare, manufacturing, retail, etc. Considering the plethora of IoT applications in each of these domains with different characteristics in terms of requirements, heterogeneity among connected devices and network, application criticality, every application has its own experience to provide to its users. For example, the applications in the transportation domain while the applications in healthcare domain such as e-health monitoring applications require accurate data. Such variations in application requirements exist not only in applications belonging to different domains but also between the applications belonging to the same domain.

- *IoT applications are typically distributed in nature, consisting of multiple devices, because of which QoE metrics can be difficult to derive.*

  IoT applications are characterized by diverse requirements and purposes are populated by many devices. Such devices adopt heterogeneous technologies and standards in view of their varying capabilities in terms of processing power, communication technologies, and energy availability. Such heterogeneity makes IoT deployments comprised of complex networks. In such scenarios, it is extremely difficult to provide some generic model to measure QoE in IoT.

- *IoT application outcomes are often consumed by machines, as opposed to users, which invalidates existing QoE measurement approaches.*

  Another challenge with measuring QoE of IoT applications is that often the end user of the application is a machine. Since machines are not supposed to experience or have views, the existing QoE measurement approaches cannot be directly applied to measure QoE of IoT applications. This lays down the basis for reconsidering the existing QoE measurement approaches from IoT perspective.

10.3.1   Quality in human-in-the-loop IoT applications

Given the challenges associated with defining and measuring QoE for IoT, various approaches have been developed in the existing literature. We first examine the existing approaches to subjective measurement of the QoE of IoT applications and services.

A conceptual framework for measuring the QoE of IoT services and applications was proposed by Shin in [8]. The author identified various factors influencing QoE encompassing IoT systems and user perception. A broad assessment of factors driving QoE in smart cities was done in [15], where the authors assessed the impact of QoE on different smart city verticals. A generic framework for QoE measurement was proposed in [16], which is based on obtaining mean opinion scores (MOS) from user surveys.

While the above approaches are focused on subjective measurement of QoE, objective QoE measurement is challenging in IoT due to the diversity of IoT applications. In [7], the authors propose using indicators obtained from application data usage for QoE measurement, as an approach to go beyond Subjective Quality Assessments (SQAs). Objective methods of QoE measurement have been explored within the context of multimedia IoT, often referred to as MIoT [12]. Floris and Atzori proposed a layered design for QoE management in [12], which is used for QoE evaluation based on network QoS metrics computed by the framework. An example of an MIoT application is used to show how network QoS metrics such as network delay can be combined with multimedia characteristics such as video bitrate for QoE evaluation. A quantitative QoE measure for fitness tracking wearables was presented in [17] as a weighted combination of quality of data, measured as the accuracy and precision of step count and heart rate monitoring, and quality of information, which comprises of multiple factors such as the perceived usefulness of information provided by the wearables. It is noted, however, that each of the individual factors is obtained based on user feedback.

10.3.2 Quality in autonomic IoT applications

While the above approaches have sought to measure the quality perceived by end-users of IoT applications, they are not suitable for autonomic IoT applications that do not involve any human interactions. Because of this, other approaches in the literature have looked at quality measurement focusing only on devices.

In [10], Karaadi *et al.* propose the concept of Quality of Things (QoT) for multimedia IoT applications, which they term as MIoT. As part of the proposed architecture, QoT is defined as a composite measure which incorporates QoS factors, device factors, environmental factors, and application-specific factors. A network perspective of IoT performance assessment has been presented in [18], where the authors present the Ericsson's framework for prediction of IoT subscriber's QoE, which is termed as Machine QoE (M-QoE). The framework comprises of a list of KPIs that are computed for each device and subscriber and based on the IoT vertical that the application belongs to. Minovski *et al.* [19] defined Quality of Machine Experience (QoME) to measure the performance of intelligent machines, which is an objective metric comprising of three components, namely the physical, network, and logical aspects of machines. Here, the physical component is obtained from hardware-related data, network component from QoS metrics, and logical component related to autonomous decision-making. Subsequently, the authors define the Quality of IoT (QoIoT) as a composite metric comprising of QoE, which measures the performance as perceived by end-users, and QoME, which measures machine behavior. A case study of autonomous mining vehicles was used in [20] to illustrate QoIoT measurement, including both QoE and QoME.

Despite the various approaches proposed in the literature for measuring QoE of IoT applications, comprehensive performance evaluation of autonomic IoT applications remains an open problem [21].

10.4 Establishing the key factors impacting quality in IoT applications

The IoT application lifecycle broadly consists of three stages [21], as shown in Figure 10.2. Human-in-the-loop and autonomic IoT applications are primarily distinguished in the final stage of the IoT application lifecycle, with autonomic IoT applications being characterized by automated decision-making and actuation [22], whereas for human-in-the-loop IoT applications, the decision-making is typically left

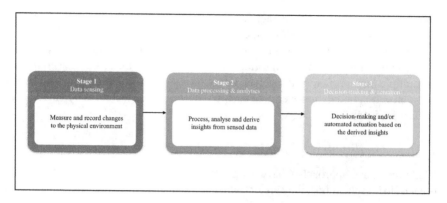

Figure 10.2 Stages of an IoT application lifecycle

to a human user. It is necessary to have objective quality measurement at all stages of the application lifecycle. This problem of holistic quality evaluation of IoT applications was also explored in [23] where the authors proposed a multi-dimensional quality measurement approach for IoT applications. Further, in [24], the authors categorized the metrics impacting IoT application quality into two broad categories physical metrics and metaphysical metrics. Physical metrics correspond to IoT architecture while metaphysical metrics correspond to application requirements. To organize the quality metrics corresponding to IoT architecture, functions of IoT architecture are coordinated into four different layers and the quality metrics are defined for each layer, which are device, network, computing, and user interface. In the device layer, metrics related to IoT devices that generate data are considered such as GPS accuracy of sensor devices or the resolution of camera devices along with the time duration for which the sensor is sensing. A taxonomy of influential metrics for QoE in IoT was presented in [5], which categorized them into three categories such as technical, user, and context.

In this section, we discuss the factors impacting the overall IoT application quality, which we term IoT quality metrics, and which include subjective metrics, targeting non-autonomic IoT applications, as well as objective ones, which can be used to evaluate the performance of both autonomic and non-autonomic IoT applications. We categorize IoT quality metrics as:

1. Quality of Data (QoD): QoD measures characteristics of data, primarily captured during the sensing stage, including accuracy, truthfulness, completeness, timeliness, and integrity.
2. Quality of Service (QoS): QoS measures network quality including jitter, latency, and throughput, pertaining to data transmission among distributed application components.
3. Quality of Processing (QoP): QoP measures the efficiency of processing sensed data, typically as part of the data analytics stage of the application.

4. Quality of Device (QoDe): The QoDe refers to the quality of physical devices such as sensors, IoT cameras, and e-health devices.
5. Quality of Context (QoC): The QoC refers to the external factors that impact the decision-making of the application, typically as part of the data analytics stage, along with any processing that takes place here.
6. Quality of User Interface (QoU): The quality of interface through which a user interacts with the application.
7. Quality of Information (QoI): QoI measures the usefulness and relevance of the analyzed data, with respect to the application objectives.

10.4.1 Quality of data

Considering that an IoT application collects data in a variety of contexts, the QoD metric includes different factors such as accuracy, completeness, truthfulness, and up-to-dateness. In [25], authors have proposed to evaluate the QoE for IoT applications in two dimensions, profit and cost. QoD is classified under the profit dimension, which comprises of the metrics affecting analytics and the result of cognitive IoT. In the data layer of profit dimension, the quality of sensed data, and the process of acquiring the data is evaluated. It also checks for the quality of sensors and keeps a track that the sensed data is accurate and complete.

In [7], the authors posited that good quality can be ensured at the time of the application design and proposed a method to design an IoT application which focuses on the collection of user data and information. QoD further depends on data accuracy, truthfulness, completeness, and up-to-dateness. Each of these metrics can be defined as:

- Data accuracy refers to the precision of the collected data.
- Data truthfulness is related to the reliability of the IoT device from which data is collected.
- Data completeness is the ratio of the amount of data collected to the total amount of data required.
- Data up-to-dateness is, how valid the collected data is for decision-making.

In [12], the authors used a layered IoT architecture to analyze and determine the factors impacting QoE of IoT applications, wherein the QoD is a measure of the content acquired from the real world by physical devices. In a similar vein, the accuracy and precision of step count and heart rate measurements obtained from smart wearables were correlated with the subjective measure of QoE in [17].

Minovski *et al.*, in [20], defined QoD as metrics pertaining to data generated by physical devices. Measuring the accuracy and integrity of such data can help identify anomalies in the hardware or software or both. In [26], the authors have provided a comprehensive review of key metrics for prescriptive analytics in smart manufacturing. They have focused on the quality of data and the way it is acquired, as real-time information is necessary for data analytics and production control on industry floors in smart manufacturing.

10.4.2   Quality of Service

Because of the highly distributed nature of most IoT applications, ensuring good network quality is crucial, which has been explored extensively in the literature with QoS metrics such as throughput, latency, jitter, etc. In [20], authors consider QoS as a significant metric contributing to the overall QoE of the application. It focuses on network monitoring, techniques for pattern recognition, role of virtualization, and prediction algorithms. As part of the QoE for Industrial Internet of Things (IIoT) defined in [27], QoS is deemed to be an important quality metric to measure QoE in Industrial applications. QoS is an important metric in not only manufacturing industry but also health care [28], such as to solve doubts between patients and medical staff in e-health services, communication services are incorporated. Such an application for healthcare, Psiconnect, proposed in [29], provides video conferencing services through Skype, discussion forum, chat, etc., for which QoS metrics plays a significant role in determining the performance.

10.4.3   Quality of Processing

Quality of Processing is the efficiency or accuracy of the data processing algorithm. In [24], authors considered QoP to be mainly the intelligent processing required for IoT applications such as in autonomous vehicles, video analysis is required for detecting surrounding situations. In such applications, the accuracy of video analysis is needed to achieve good QoE of the vehicle navigation applications. In another work [26], authors have provided a review of key metrics for prescriptive analytics in smart manufacturing, wherein they explored the significant role of prescriptive analytics in decision making on factory shop floor. For such applications, QoP is an important metric which measures the quality of the analytics obtained from machine data, which can impact manufacturing operations and productivity.

10.4.4   Quality of Device

QoDe covers the quality of physical devices used in the application. According to the taxonomy of metrics proposed by authors in [24], they classified QoDe in the physical layer. Authors considered QoDe metrics as GPS accuracy of sensor devices, resolution of camera devices, or even the battery consumption of the device. Authors in [30] explained the importance of physical devices in measuring QoE by stating that QoDe impacts QoD and QoS. For example, the quality of the image captured (QoD) depends on the resolution of the camera (QoDe). The importance of the quality of physical devices in the healthcare domain was explored in [9,28], the latter of which looked at the use of healthcare applications involving wearables. The QoDe of such wearables critically impacts the success of the healthcare applications involving them.

10.4.5   Quality of Context

The context in this chapter refers to the external factors which can impact QoE of the IoT application. For example, in [20], authors consider context in an autonomous service from two major perspectives: humans and machines. In this direction, the objective KPIs such as productivity, safety, and efficiency in autonomous vehicles in mining are context situations.

In [31], where authors proposed a monitoring system to monitor beach conditions, the contextual data includes temperature, humidity, wind speed, along with social data, all of which impact the performance of the application significantly. Therefore, it is necessary to measure the quality of context. In another paper [10], QoC refers to environmental factors such as temperature which affect the Quality of Things (QoT), which the authors use to measure the application quality.

10.4.6 Quality of User Interface

For human-in-the-loop IoT applications, the quality of interface is an important metric to decide the performance of the application. In [24], where quality metrics are classified as physical and metaphysical, authors have highlighted the significance of user interface. QoU is a physical metric that accounts for functions which exists between application and user. For example, in a navigation system, the quality of other metrics such as data can be satisfactory, but the overall performance of the application is likely to be impeded significantly if the user interface of the navigation system is not usable. In [17], QoU is classified in the application layer such as a web portal.

10.4.7 Quality of Information

While QoD deals primarily with the sensed data, Quality of Information (QoI) concerns with the quality of insights obtained from such sensed data as a result of processing and analytics. Terming IoT characterized by intelligent decision-making as cognitive IoT, the authors in [25] defined QoI as a measure of the effectiveness of the inputs for decision making. They define QoI metric as a composition of sub-metrics such as quantity, precision, recall, accuracy, detail, timeliness, and validity.

A similar approach for measuring QoI was explored in [7]. The authors identify multiple IoT quality indicators, with QoI being the metric used to measure the effectiveness of information used for decision making. The authors define QoI as a product of multiple sub-metrics including information quantity, precision, recall, accuracy, detail, timeliness, and validity where information quantity relates to the quantity of useful information obtained. Precision is the proportion of relevant information obtained to the total information gathered from sensors, networking devices, and services. On the contrary, recall is the proportion of relevant information gathered without the involvement of sensors, networks, or services. Accuracy is related to the degree of accuracy of the information concerning the requirements of the end-users. The detail is the complete degree of information required for making a decision. Timeliness refers to the timeframe within which the information must be utilized. Validity is a measure of how true the information is.

10.5 IoT platforms for developing quality-aware IoT applications

Having covered the different approaches to measuring factors impacting IoT application quality, we now discuss how IoT applications can be designed and developed to make decisions that ensure application quality requirements are met. We first explore existing literature on adapting IoT applications to quality requirements. Subsequently, we present a conceptual framework for quality-awareness in IoT applications.

With the objective of achieving QoE targets for IoT applications, existing research has looked at the correlation between IoT quality metrics and QoE. A generic method for resource estimation in fog computing environments was presented in [32], to enhance QoS based on previous QoE measurements. The authors built upon this model in [33], a QoE Ratio (QoER) model is proposed for the estimation of the QoS requirements based on QoE. The correlation between QoS and QoE was explored in [11] through principal component and linear regression analyses. Going beyond just network quality metrics, the authors in [17] used QoD and QoI to measure the QoE of smart wearables. Using a companion app installed on a smartphone, a subjective experiment comprising of 40 participants and 5 wearable devices is performed to create the QoE model. The results were used to provide appropriate recommendations smart-wearable vendors to improve their products.

Given that IoT applications are distributed with a high degree of heterogeneity, a critical aspect has been adapting IoT architectures based on QoE requirements. A holistic study of QoS, QoE, and IoT architectures has been defined as a part of the International Telecommunication Union's (ITU) study group on Smart Cities and Communities [34]. A method for dynamic service selection and aggregation based on QoE constraints was proposed in [35], which was evaluated on an open dataset and shown to match QoE requirements with high accuracy. In [36], the authors addressed the problem of task offloading in IoT environments consisting of devices with varying computation constraints. In the system proposed in the paper, task offloading and scheduling were performed based on application QoE constraints, and shown to reduce latency by more than 50% compared to state-of-the-art systems.

10.5.1 Conceptual framework to develop quality-aware IoT applications

While automatic adaptation exists in domains such as video streaming, e.g., video bitrate adaptation based on network conditions [37], and cloud applications [38], it is challenging to use similar solutions IoT applications because IoT application quality depends on multiple factors in different stages of the application life cycle presented in Section 10.4.

We propose a conceptual platform for developing quality-aware IoT applications shown in Figure 10.3. In the figure, the top layer (1) shows the generic stages of IoT application, (2) shows the IoT quality awareness framework which computes the quality metrics, and (3) gives the measured quality of each metric. At every stage, the IoT Quality Awareness Framework computes the quality at that corresponding stage of the application. For example, during the data sensing stage of the IoT application, the framework uses the sensed data to compute metrics such as the quality of the sensed data. Similarly, for other stages of the application lifecycle, the framework computes the appropriate quality metrics in real time.

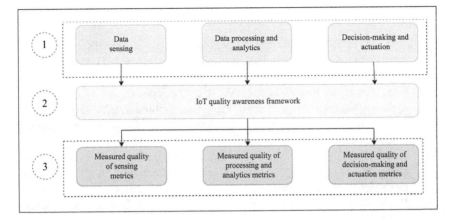

Figure 10.3   Conceptual framework for quality awareness in IoT applications

Quality-aware IoT applications make use of quality metrics computed by the IoT Quality Awareness Framework to adapt to uncertainties in underlying application quality. For instance, taking the example of the autonomic smart parking IoT application introduced earlier in Section 10.1, a parking spot with high quality of sensed data can be selected over one with lower quality, even if the latter is closer to the destination.

10.6   Conclusion

This chapter presented a discussion on the measurement and evaluation of the quality of IoT applications. We noted that IoT applications may be human-in-the-loop or autonomic, depending on how the application outcomes are consumed, which influences the quality measurement. We identified the key challenges with quality measurement of IoT applications, and subsequently presented a discussion on existing approaches for quality measurement of human-in-the-loop and autonomic applications. Further, we characterized the factors impacting the quality of IoT applications, which we term IoT quality metrics, and also looked at how IoT architectures can adapt based on quality. Finally, we proposed a conceptual framework for quality-aware IoT applications, to enable IoT applications to adapt, in real-time, to uncertainties in underlying quality.

We envisage that IoT application quality is a research area demanding increased attention from the academic community, especially as IoT becomes enmeshed in multiple domains, such as manufacturing, cities, transport, and healthcare, among others. The IoT applications in these domains are increasingly autonomic in nature, because of which comprehensive quality measurement and evaluation are both critical to the operation of such applications. Further, we envision that autonomic IoT applications would need to be quality aware, to ensure that they recognize and adapt to quality variations.

References

[1]   Rec, ITUT, "P. 10: Vocabulary for performance and quality of service, Amendment 2: New definitions for inclusion in Recommendation ITU-T P. 10/G. 100," *Int. Telecomm. Union, Geneva*, p. 10, 2008.

[2]   ETSI Technical Report 102643 V1. 0.2, "Human factors (HF); quality of experience (QoE) requirements for real-time communication services," 2010.

[3]   K. Brunnström, S.A. Beker, K.D. Moor, *et al.*, "Qualinet white paper on definitions of quality of experience," 2013.

[4]   K. Mitra, A. Zaslavsky, and C. Åhlund, "Context-aware QoE modelling, measurement, and prediction in mobile computing systems," *IEEE Transactions on Mobile Computing*, vol. 14, no. 5, pp. 920–936, 2013.

[5]   D. Pal, V. Vanijja, and V. Varadarajan, "Quality provisioning in the Internet of Things era: current state and future directions," in *Proceedings of the 10th International Conference on Advances in Information Technology*, 2018.

[6]   M.P. da Silva, A. Leopoldo Gonçalves, and M. Antônio Ribeiro Dantas, "A conceptual model for quality of experience management to provide context-aware eHealth services," *Future Generation Computer Systems*, vol. 101, pp. 1041–1061, 2019.

[7]   A. Floris and L. Atzori, "Towards the evaluation of quality of experience of Internet of Things applications," *IEEE Internet Things J*, vol. 25, pp. 567–590, 2017.

[8]   D.-H. Shin, "Conceptualizing and measuring quality of experience of the Internet of Things: exploring how quality is perceived by users," *Information & Management*, pp. 998–1011, 2017.

[9]   T. Banerjee and A. Sheth, "IoT quality control for data and application needs," *IEEE Intelligent Systems*, vol. 32, no. 2, pp. 68–873, 2017.

[10] A. Karaadi, L. Sun, and I.-H. Mkwawa, "Multimedia communications in internet of things QoT or QoE?," in *2017 IEEE International Conference on Internet of Things (iThings) and IEEE Green Computing and Communications (Green-Com) and IEEE Cyber, Physical and Social Computing (CPSCom) and IEEE Smart Data (SmartData)*, 2017.

[11] L. Li, M. Rong, and G. Zhang, "An Internet of Things QoE evaluation method based on multiple linear regression analysis," in *2015 10th International Conference on Computer Science Education (ICCSE)*, 2015.

[12] A. Floris and L. Atzori, "Managing the quality of experience in the multimedia Internet of Things: a layered-based approach," *Sensors*, vol. 16, no. 12, p. 1747–1752, 2016.

[13] M. Lopez-Martin, B. Carro, J. Lloret, S. Egea, and A. Sanchez-Esguevillas, "Deep learning model for multimedia quality of experience prediction based on network flow packets," *IEEE Communications Magazine*, vol. 56, no. 9, pp. 110–117, 2018.

[14] X. He, K. Wang, and W. Xu, "QoE-driven content-centric caching with deep reinforcement learning in edge-enabled IoT," *IEEE Computational Intelligence Magazine*, vol. 14, no. 4, pp. 12–20, 2019.

[15] L.G.M. Ballesteros, O. Alvarez, and J. Markendahl, "Quality of Experience (QoE) in the smart cities context: an initial analysis," in *2015 IEEE First International Smart Cities Conference (ISC2)*, 2015.

[16] M. Suryanegara, D.A. Prasetyo, F. Andriyanto, and N. Hayati, "A 5-step framework for measuring the quality of experience (QoE) of Internet of Things (IoT) services," *IEEE Access*, vol. 7, pp. 175779–175792, 2019.

[17] D. Pal, V. Vanijja, C. Arpnikanondt, X. Zhang, and B. Papasratorn, "A quantitative approach for evaluating the quality of experience of smart-wearables from the quality of data and quality of information: an end user perspective," *IEEE Access,* vol. 7, pp. 64266–64278, 2019.

[18] C.W. Tchouati and S.a.G.S. Rochefort, "Monitoring IoT application performance with machine QoE," *Ericsson Technology Review*, vol. 2020, pp. 2–11, 2020.

[19] D. Minovski, C. Åhlund, K. Mitra, and R. Zhohov, "Defining quality of experience for the Internet of Things," *IT Professional*, vol. 22, no. 5, pp. 62–70, 2020.

[20] D. Minovski, C. Åhlund, and K. Mitra, "Modeling quality of IoT experience in autonomous vehicles," *IEEE Internet of Things Journal,* vol. 7, no. 5, pp. 3833–3849, 2020.

[21] K. Fizza, A. Banerjee, K. Mitra, *et al.*, "QoE in IoT: a vision, survey and future directions," *Discover Internet of Things*, vol. 1, no. 1, pp. 1–14, 2021.

[22] K. Fizza, P.P. Jayaraman, A. Banerjee, D. Georgakopoulos, and R. Ranjan, "Evaluating sensor data quality in Internet of Things smart agriculture applications," *IEEE Micro,* vol. 42, no. 1, pp. 51–60, 2021.

[23] J.-M. Martinez-Caro and M.-D. Cano, "A novel holistic approach for performance evaluation in Internet of Things," *International Journal of Communication Systems,* vol. 34, no. 2, p. e4454, 2021.

[24] Y. Ikeda, S. Kouno, A. Shiozu, and K. Noritake, "A framework of scalable QoE modeling for application explosion in the Internet of Things," in *2016 IEEE 3rd World Forum on Internet of Things (WF-IoT)*, 2016.

[25] Q. Wu, G. Ding, Y. Xu, *et al.*, "Cognitive Internet of Things: a new paradigm beyond connection," *IEEE Internet of Things journal*, vol. 1, no. 2, pp. 129–143, 2014.

[26] J. Vater, L. Harscheidt, and A. Knoll, "Smart manufacturing with prescriptive analytics," in *2019 8th International Conference on Industrial Technology and Management (ICITM)*, 2019.

[27] R. Zhohov, "*Evaluating Quality of Experience and real-time performance of industrial Internet of Things*," thesis, Luleå tekniska universitet, Institutionen för system- och rymdteknik, 2018. http://urn.kb.se/resolve?urn= urn:nbn:se:ltu:diva-71357.

[28] I.d.l.T. Díez, S.G. Alonso, E.M. Cruz, and M.A. Franco, "Measuring QoE of a teleconsultation app in mental health using a pentagram model," *Journal of Medical Systems,* vol. 43, no. 7, pp. 1–5, 2019.

[29] D. Velasco-Morejón, B. Martínez-Pérez, I. de la Torre-Díez, and M. López-Coronado, "PSICONNECT: a platform for communication between medical

staff, caregivers and patients with psychiatric problems," *e-Society,* p. 101, 2014.

[30]   A. Floris and L. Atzori, "Quality of experience in the multimedia Internet of Things: definition and practical use-cases," in *2015 IEEE International Conference on Communication Workshop (ICCW)*, 2015.

[31]   R.a.A.M. Girau, M. Fadda, M. Farina, A. Floris, M. Sole, and D. Giusto, "Coastal monitoring system based on social Internet of Things platform," *IEEE Internet of Things Journal,* vol. 7, no. 2, pp. 1260–1272, 2019.

[32]   M. Aazam, M. St-Hilaire, C.-H. Lung, and I. Lambadaris, "MeFoRE: QoE based resource estimation at Fog to enhance QoS in IoT," in *2016 23rd International Conference on Telecommunications (ICT)*, 2016.

[33]   M. Aazam and K.A. Harras, "Mapping QoE with resource estimation in IoT," in *2019 IEEE 5th World Forum on Internet of Things (WF-IoT)*, 2019.

[34]   International Telecommunication Union (ITU), "IoT and SC&C architectures, protocols and QoS/QoE," [Online]. Available: https://www.itu.int/en/ITU-T/studygroups/2017-2020/20/Pages/q3.aspx. [Accessed 2 September 2021].

[35]   B. Jia, L. Hao, C. Zhang, H. Zhao, and M. Khan, "An IoT service aggregation method based on dynamic planning for QoE restraints," *Mobile Networks and Applications,* vol. 24, no. 1, pp. 25–33, 2019.

[36]   B. Li, W. Dong, G. Guan, *et al.*, "Queec: QoE-aware edge computing for IoT devices under dynamic workloads," *ACM Transactions on Sensor Networks (TOSN),* vol. 17, no. 3, pp. 1–23, 2021.

[37]   Y. Qin, S. Hao, K.R. Pattipati, *et al.*, "Quality-aware strategies for optimizing ABR video streaming QoE and reducing data usage," in *Proceedings of the 10th ACM Multimedia Systems Conference*, Amherst, Massachusetts, 2019.

[38]   D.C. Nascimento, C.E. Pires, and D.G. Mestre, "A data quality-aware cloud service based on metaheuristic and machine learning provisioning algorithms," in *Proceedings of the 30th Annual ACM Symposium on Applied Computing*, Salamanca, Spain, 2015.

Chapter 11

IoT deployment and management in the smart grid

Dilara Acarali[1], Sunny Chugh[1], K. Rajesh Rao[2] and Muttukrishnan Rajarajan[1]

As a result of society's ever-increasing reliance on technology, energy infrastructures have been under growing strain. To cope, the traditional power grid has gone through a technological evolution to become the smart grid, integrating the existing power infrastructure with information and communication technology. This enables the transmission of performance and usage data, as well as commands, so that management can become more automated and decentralised. IoT technologies can be deployed in a variety of settings and are equipped with the ability to sense their surroundings to generate data that is then communicated with management. When integrated into the smart grid, and coupled with cloud or edge technologies, IoT can offer new operational paradigms for more efficient energy production. In this chapter, the role of IoT within the smart grid will be discussed, including networks, management, and devices, as well as the cybersecurity threats that must be considered.

11.1 Smart grid infrastructure

To date, conventional power grids have been highly centralised and hierarchical with central power generation hubs pushing electricity to end users [1]. This constituted a unidirectional flow from source to consumer. To improve efficiency and resiliency, the smart grid was designed to dismantle this rigid hierarchy by decentralising production and using distributed management [2], where the latter facilitates the former. Historic and modern technologies are amalgamated so that a cyber network of sensing and computing devices can monitor the grid, creating a bidirectional flow of power and data [3] amongst producers, consumers, and sensors. This section provides an overview of the smart grid's core requirements and structure.

[1] School of Mathematics, Computer Science and Engineering, University of London, UK
[2] Department of Information and Communication Technology, Manipal Institute of Technology, MAHE, India

11.1.1   Key concepts

11.1.1.1   Functional requirements

The nature of electrical energy means that the power grid has unique functional requirements. Electricity is created by converting energy from primary sources and is difficult to store effectively, especially at large scale or for long periods [4,5]. Therefore, to avoid waste whilst satisfying demand, energy generation must be continuous. Meanwhile, grid stability requires a high level of synchronisation in frequency, phase angle and voltage, as well as a steady balance between supply and demand [4]. If the supply is greater or lower than the energy available, the grid will become unsynchronised, potentially leading to outages. Wide-scale dependence on power for daily activities means that there is little tolerance for service drops amongst large and small-scale consumers alike.

11.1.1.2   Interoperability and interdependency

A grid consists of many individual components working together. In smart grids, inter-connectivity exists between cyber networks and the traditional grid, with interoperability as a core requirement [2,6]. In the former, information technology (IT) devices monitor power operations and communicate their data. In the latter, operational technology (OT) devices handle the day-to-day functioning of grid components. IT and OT devices, both of which may be IoT-enabled, must be able to interface with each other for real-time monitoring and control, and interdependencies are born as a result. The smart grid is, therefore, significantly more complex than traditional power grids. Also, any failures on one side can propagate throughout and into the other. Similarly, disruptions caused by cyber-attacks will likely have a ripple effect on other parts of the system. Furthermore, individual grids are often interconnected to create systems covering larger geographic areas [4], adding even more complexity. The nature and impact of propagating or cascading failures is most commonly modelled with interconnected graphs, using percolation to mimic failures [7,8].

11.1.2   Grid architecture

11.1.2.1   Functional domains

To delineate between the different composite functions, NIST [2] created a conceptual model that divides the smart grid into domains (and sub-domains), each housing application, personnel, networks, and equipment that serve common service goals [2]. Domains can be roughly divided into power- and data-centric. The former are *Generation, Transmission, Distribution*, and *Customer*, and the latter include *Operations, Service Providers*, and *Markets*. As the name suggests, *Generation* contains generators situated in power plants that act as central hubs of electrical power production. It may also include the sub-domain of distributed energy resources (DER) [2]. In *Transmission*, high-voltage electricity is loaded onto heavy-duty power lines and carried to different geographic areas, handled by regional sub-stations. Within *Distribution*, electricity is delivered to the *Customers*, who (if using DER) may also generate and store power themselves [2]. IoT devices are most commonly seen in the *Distribution*

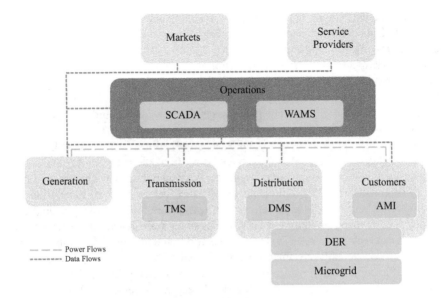

Figure 11.1   Functional domains of the smart grid as defined by NIST [2]

domain, with growing numbers now permeating the others for the purposes of sensing and control.

Grid management sits in *Operations*, where systems like supervisory control and data acquisition (SCADA), wide area monitoring system (WAMS), and energy management systems (EMS) are found [2], and receive the data generated by other domains' sensors. This domain, along with *Customers*, connects to *Service Providers* to enable billing and service provision. Finally, *Markets* handle the business side of energy, connecting to both *Operations* and *Generation* [2]. Despite the clear organisation of this framework, it should be noted that domains do not necessarily map to particular geographic locations, meaning that the components of each domain may be widely distributed. Figure 11.1 provides a depiction of the domains and their relationships.

11.1.2.2   Modern sub-systems

The smart grid uses IoT to deconstruct the traditional centralised structure of old grids to create a more distributed network. Hence, there are multiple sub-systems, enabling different applications and contributing to grid management. Alongside the inherited ones, like transmission management systems (TMS) and distribution management systems (DMS), modernisation has introduced several newer sub-systems, which are discussed here.

One component system is the advanced metering infrastructure (AMI), which is used for applications like demand response. Specialised sensors known as smart meters [1] sit within customer premises and monitor energy consumption. They also interact with smart appliances to learn about their behaviours and require-ments [9]. Data collected is then shared to facilitate various functions, generalised as distribution-, market-, and customer-based [10]. For distribution, data is sent to *Operations* for demand response, fault detection and resource optimisation, improving overall performance [1,10]. Data sent to *Service Providers* affects *Markets* by enabling automatic readings, accurate and responsive billing, and dynamic tariffs [1,10]. Finally, data shared with customers increases their awareness and empowers them to make informed decisions, increasing overall satisfaction [1,10].

Another component system is DER, where distributed generators (DGs) and energy storage systems (ESSs) are situated outside of the main power plants [11]. When this location is on customer premises, customers become 'prosumers' rather than just consumers [3]. Minimising the distance between power generation and consumption helps to reduce power lost during transmission, improving overall effi-ciency [11,12]. In addition to this, DER allows small-scale generators to make use of renewable energy sources (RES) [12] like solar or wind power, contributing towards a more environmentally sustainable energy system.

DER is commonly considered in the context of a microgrid [12]. This mini grid uses local energy generation to serve a small geographic region [10]. If connected to the main grid – typically to the distribution network via a point of common cou-pling (PCC) – excess power can be transferred. Additionally, if local generation is insufficient, demand may be supplemented. This is often necessary due to natural fluc-tuations in RES. Otherwise, the microgrid may decouple itself to work independently, stopping it from being impacted by disruptions or faults in the main grid [12]. As such, the decentralisation provided by DER also contributes to overall grid resiliency [13].

Component systems of the smart grid make use of ESSs to further help sta-bilise power supply. Despite limitations in volume and duration, energy storage is a necessary buffer against fluctuations [14], especially with the increasing applica-tion of RES. Due to its natural properties, electricity must typically be stored in an alternative form. Some common ESS examples include batteries (storing chemical energy), hydro-pumps and flywheels (kinetic energy), and capacitors (electrostatic energy) [14,15]. In recent times, electric vehicles (EVs) have also been introduced as potential storage systems. These operate in two modes: grid-to-vehicle (G2V) and vehicle-to-grid (V2G). The former is when an EV receives power from the grid via a typical charging station. The latter is when a non-operational EV is used for remote power storage [16,17].

11.1.3   Network architecture

11.1.3.1   Area networks

The domains of the smart grid have differing requirements when it comes to com-munications. Meanwhile, both smart grids and IoT are relatively young technologies which are in active development. Industry standards and best practices are still being defined and refined, such that multiple types of network and a range of protocols may be present to facilitate different applications. At a high level, communications can be considered in three parts: at the customer-side, in the field, and in the wider

Table 11.1 IoT-based communication protocols used in smart grids

Protocol	Frequency	Max rates	Coverage	Use
Bluetooth	2.4 GHz[1]	1 Mbps[1]	10 m	CPNs
Bluetooth LE	2.4 GHz[1]	125 Kbps[1]	10 m	CPNs
Zigbee	2.4 GHz	250 Kbps	100 m	CPNs
Z-Wave	800–900 MHz	100 kbps	100 m	CPNs
Z-Wave LR	800–900 MHz	100 kbps	1.6 km	CPNs
Wi-Fi	2.4/5.6 GHz	600 Mbps	100 m	CPNs, FANs

[1][20]

network [3,18]. Customer-side communications roughly align with the *Distribution* domain, field communications with the *Transmission* domain, and the wider network then connects them to all of the other domains.

Residential customer premises are served by a type of local area network (LAN) called a home area network (HAN). This enables interaction between smart meters, smart appliances, and home energy management systems (HEMSs), whilst also facilitating customer-tier DER and G2V/V2G for EVs [3,10]. These networks are, therefore, characterised by short-range communications between low-power devices. HANs typically cover up to 100 m, and transmit at a rate up to 100 kpbs [18]. Multiple HANs may be connected to form a neighbourhood area network (NAN) [10]. A similar setup in a large building (e.g. an office block) may be referred to as a Building or business area network (BAN), and in a factory may be called an industrial area network (IAN) [18,19]. Customer-side networks are often referred to collectively as customer premise networks (CPNs). Substations in the *Distribution* and *Transmission* domains will likely run their own private LANs.

In the field, field area networks (FANs) support component systems like the AMI and distribution-tier DER-ESS, providing an interface between the customers and the main grid [3]. With a coverage range between 100 m and 10 km, and a data rate range of 100 kbps–10 Mbps, NAN and FAN definitions can sometimes overlap in the literature [18]. To enable full end-to-end functionality and grid monitoring, the wide area network (WAN) will connect the disparate LANs and FANs with control systems in *Operations*, and analysis systems in *Service Providers* and *Markets*. To support this, WAN can transmit between 10 Mbps and 1 Gbps over distances of up to 100 km [18]. At various points, the Internet may also be used for remote access or to connect to the corporate networks of energy companies. An high-level view of these networks is given in Figure 11.2.

11.1.3.2 Communication protocols

Different communication protocols exist for different areas of the smart grid. For example, management systems such as SCADA use industrial protocols like MODBUS and DNP3, which were developed before the present level of cyber integration

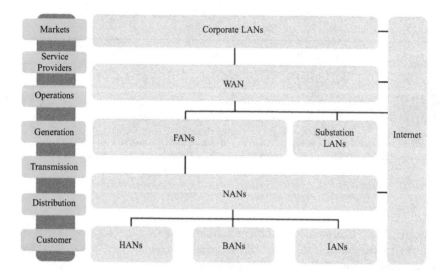

Figure 11.2   Hierarchy in the smart grid communication (IT) network

existed and, as a result, do not have robust security mechanisms [21]. At the distribution end, power line communication (PLC) has been used for wired access to customer premises alongside Ethernet, the ubiquitous TCP/IP wired protocol. Meanwhile, to accommodate the huge (and growing) number of IoT endpoints, IPv6 needs to be deployed at the network layer. With the addition of IoT into the smart grid, IoT-based wireless protocols are now increasingly prevalent and the most popular are discussed here.

Bluetooth is a wireless protocol characterised by short-range, high-rate data exchange between devices. Within an average coverage range of 10 m, it transmits over the 2.4 GHz frequency band [22] at rates of around 1–2 Mbps. Up to eight devices can be connected in a controller/agent architecture to form Personal Area Networks (PANs) [23], also known as piconets. A lightweight version called Bluetooth low energy (BLE) is also available and is used for power-restricted mobile devices [24]. In the smart grid, Bluetooth is well-suited for customer premise networks like HANs and BANs where many consumer-grade smart appliances now have Bluetooth capability. IEEE Standard 802.15.1 provides definitions for this protocol [23].

An alternative short-range wireless protocol is Zigbee, which offers a larger coverage range of up to 100 m in exchange for lower data rates of around 250 kbps [24]. Also operating on the 2.4 GHz band, Zigbee creates mesh, star, or cluster tree networks amongst low-power devices, where a single node behaves as a coordinator for the remaining edge devices [23]. This protocol is a popular choice for smart meters, street lights, sensors, and BANs where devices may be physically more distanced and data exchanges are small and periodic [22–24]. IEEE Standard 802.15.4 defines

Zigbee's physical and data link layers [23], whilst 6LoWPAN (IPv6 over low-power wireless personal networks) enables IPv6 routing over 802.15.4 networks [22].

Another popular short-distance, low-rate protocol is Z-Wave. This operates on the 800–900 MHz frequency band, and so can avoid noise interference that may be suffered by protocols sharing the 2.4 GHz band [23]. Thanks to its low power consumption, Z-Wave is mainly used within HANs for EMS, smart appliances, and home automation [22]. A mesh network is formed by a central controller through which end devices communicate with other Z-Wave networks and with the Internet [22,23], supporting up to 232 devices [25]. Z-Wave long range (LR) is an updated specification which extends the supported device count up to 4,000, arranged in a star topology and able to operate at distances of reportedly up to a mile [25].

For longer range communication, Wi-Fi can be used to create wireless LANs (WLANs). For coverage areas of up to 100 m, the latest version, Wi-Fi 6, can work on either the 2.4 GHz (ultra-high frequency) band or the 5.8 GHz (super high frequency) band, with theoretical data rates of up 9.6 Gbps [23]. Wi-Fi-enabled devices will connect to the WLAN via an access point, often in the form of a wireless router which will then transmit their data through the network. Multiple devices can communicate simultaneously thanks to TDMA multiplexing with CSMS/CA [23]. Whilst higher data rates allow for more frequent transfers, this protocol is not designed to be power saving [22], limiting its usability in sensor networks. Therefore, Wi-Fi is best suited for longer range and more bulky communications between high-power devices in FANs and within the WAN. IEEE Standard 802.11 defines Wi-Fi at the physical and data link layers [23].

11.2 Smart grid management

The central requirement for the smart grid's functionality is that power input and output be balanced to avoid disruption that may lead to brownouts (i.e. partially diminished capacity) or blackouts (i.e. total outage). To achieve this, management needs to be able to collectively handle heterogeneous applications and geographically dispersed devices, whilst monitoring and regulating both electro-mechanical and digital processes. Furthermore, it needs to be able to interface with electrical power and energy systems (EPES) personnel and various other stakeholders. Modern industrial control systems are highly digitised and increasingly integrate IoT at multiple levels. This section will describe how smart grid management systems work before presenting some of the ways in which cloud and edge technologies are now being applied.

11.2.1 Management systems

11.2.1.1 EMS

Traditionally, the power grid's main sources of supply were the generators within power plants. These would likely run on fossil fuels and so energy production would be largely predictable. Now, with the advent of RES, DER, and microgrids, there is an increased number of energy input points, and their capacities are less predictable. To maintain supply-and-demand balance, an EMS monitors and regulates energy input and consumption. This improves life expectancy for equipment, minimises outages, and helps to maximise profit thanks to better overall performance [26]. This is achieved using sensors to monitor energy flows and actuators to convert control signals into mechanical actions.

Architectures may be centralised, with a single central controller, or decentralised, with numerous local controllers and P2P communications [26]. The term EMS can refer to either a grid-wide system or smaller-scale localised systems such as home EMS (HEMS), building EMS (BEMS), or plant EMS (PEMS) [26]. The EMS also facilitates energy markets by interfacing with suppliers, distribution and transmission system operators (DSOs and TSOs, respectively), and aggregators [26,27].

11.2.1.2   SCADA

An EMS often works in tandem with the SCADA system, which manages the overall operation of the smart grid. Typically arranged with a centralised architecture, a set of control servers sit within the Operations domain and regularly receive data from distributed field equipment. Incoming data is logged and analysed to determine the current status of the grid. The control software then issues command signals back to the field devices for optimisation and adjustment as needed, making the grid 'self-healing'. Human–machine interfaces (HMIs) [28] will provide visualisations and intelligence to operations personnel for advanced decision-making, whilst logged data may be added to historical records [28] and used to derive operational baselines and optimal performance ranges. Due to the geographically distributed nature of smart grid equipment, regional sub-control centres may be created to report back to the main control system. This aligns well with the HAN–FAN–WAN network hierarchy discussed previously and can reduce load on central servers [28], thereby improving performance.

SCADA field equipment consists of intelligent electronic devices (IEDs), programmable logic controllers (PLCs), and remote telemetry units (RTUs) [28], the definitions of which can sometimes overlap. IED is a general term used to describe any device that is equipped with a microprocessor, allowing it to participate in digital processes like communication [29]. It is typically a specific piece of low-level smart grid equipment (e.g. a sensor, actuator, or transformer) which serves a specific function and reports to a PLC or an RTU [29].

A PLC is a remote field device used for automation. It is characterised as highly specialised, receiving particular inputs, responding with specific outputs, and running proprietary or bespoke operating systems [29]. PLCs communicate with SCADA central control to receive and execute commands for applications requiring real-time response. Finally, an RTU is a remote field sensor, often found in substations, used to record measurements from different grid processes. It is connected directly or indirectly to the WAN, through which it relays its readings to an master telemetry unit (MTU) within central control [29].

11.2.1.3 WAMS

A complementary approach to SCADA is the WAMS. The phasor synchronisation or synchrophasor system contains specialised sensors in the form of phasor measurement units (PMUs). These devices are placed at distributed points around the grid to observe power flows and take phasor measurements with regular, coordinated periodicity [10]. Hence, using this system, the WAMS can measure the grid state more directly. All PMUs are synchronised via GPS so that readings can be universally time-stamped, removing the need for estimations of grid state based on local data [30,31]. Synchrophasor data is aggregated by regional phasor data concentrators (PDCs) in substations, responsible for many local PMUs. They will then relay this data up to a master PDC within the central control centre [30].

As with SCADA, an HMI will then present this information to operations personnel, and the data will be used to generate and distribute control signals to the grid. As a result, WAMS facilitates more granular monitoring and fine-tuning of smart grid devices. PMU locations must be carefully considered because installation in legacy infrastructure can be difficult and expensive, and placement points must provide adequate visibility of the grid [32]. Furthermore, average PMUs may not be able to detect very small differences. For these reasons, they have mostly been deployed in the *Transmission* domain [33]. Recently, highly sensitive micro PMUs (μPMUs) have emerged for use in the *Distribution* domain, where shorter distances result in much smaller variations [34].

11.2.2 Grid management using the cloud

Cloud computing (CC) allows geographically distributed users to access, via the Internet, a common pool of resources for data processing and storage. A management provider handles incoming requests and assigns them to the available resources without exposing this process to users so that access appears seamless [35]. A cloud environment essentially consists of the underlying infrastructure (i.e. network and hardware), applications (i.e. software for data processing), and platforms (i.e. tools operating on the infrastructure that facilitate applications) [35]. Users subscribe to the cloud in one of a number of possible service models, the most common being infrastructure-as-a-service (IaaS), platform-as-a-service (PaaS), and software-as-a-service (SaaS). SaaS provides access to a piece of software, installed and executed remotely, on a pay-per-use basis. An example is weather prediction applications, as weather can impact energy supply and demand [36]. PaaS provides access to tools that can be used to build or run user-side applications or services. IaaS uses virtualisation to provide servers, databases, and networks for things like storage, backups, and hosting [35,36].

Cloud services can be deployed at the management tier to provide data storage and processing for the smart grid's distributed population of devices, supporting SCADA or WAMS control systems. Deployment may be public or private, where the former allows access for many users, and the latter restricts access to a select few via individual data centres for different utilities [37]. A hybrid approach, where the cloud is partially public whilst sensitive resources are secured, is arguably the most suitable approach for smart grids thanks to its balance between security and accessibility. This prevents third-party data exposure and provides a degree of visibility for grid operators so that data can be more easily retrieved for disaster recovery [37].

A number of CC characteristics align well with the requirements of the smart grid. First, the cloud enhances resiliency for data applications thanks to the availability and distribution of resources [37]. This means that data flows can continue despite partial failures or outages, and cascading failures between the IT and OT may be mitigated. CC also improves scalability so that any expansion to grid applications or growth in the data they generate can be met with additional cloud resources instead of requiring intervention at lower levels [37]. However, specialised or proprietary APIs may need to be developed and may not compatible across providers [37]. Given the size of smart grids and the proliferation of data-generating sensors, the volume of the data to be processed will be very large. The cloud can speed up processing times by running multiple instances of applications in parallel to spread the load [36,37]. This in turn will accelerate response times, which is vital to service continuity.

11.2.3 Grid management using edge computing

The cloud is a remote computation and data storage hub serving a large number of geographically distributed devices. Whilst this provides centralisation and access to resources, repeated transmissions with the cloud can be costly and slow. Bandwidth limitations and heavy loads on cloud resources can result in latencies which can hinder the performance of real-time smart grid applications [33]. An alternative approach is edge computing (EC). This paradigm is designed to balance the remote with the local by allowing data processing to happen closer to the data's point of origin, at the so-called 'edge' located between data sources and the cloud. Dependence on the cloud is reduced, and shorter transmission distances result in reduced latency. Data gravity (defined as the cost of moving large volumes of data) is also improved through savings on energy, money, and resource consumption [38]. Local processing can identify noise in data more quickly, further minimising load on cloud services [38]. Additionally, grid- or consumer-generated data does not need to leave the trusted network, providing greater privacy [33].

Placed between 'things' and the cloud in a 3-tiered architecture, EC forms part of the continuous flow of communications between data sources and the cloud known as the cloud-to-things (C2T) continuum [33]. The things tier consists of the OT equipment responsible for basic grid operations and IoT-enabled devices that sense (i.e. monitor) those operations. However, due to the conceptual nature of the edge, a device with sensing capabilities may be considered an edge node if it is also capable of computation [33]. Data may be pushed to the edge from the cloud, pulled to the edge from IoT, or a combination of the two [33]. The actual implementation of a smart grid edge application will depend on its requirements. If fast feedback is needed and data loads are reasonably small, edge offloading will be ideal. However, if data volume is very large or complex, there may be cases where direct access to the cloud is preferable. Therefore, data size, sampling frequency, queuing strategies,

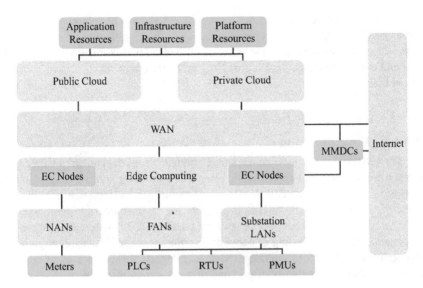

Figure 11.3   Smart grid management network architecture with cloud and edge technologies

and latency allowances must all be considered to satisfy the trade-off between speed and capacity [33] (Figure 11.3).

Like the cloud, the edge is a logical entity rather than a physical location, which makes it difficult to derive blanket definitions [38]. For critical infrastructure, the edge will typically exist within or close to the last-mile network [38]. On the infrastructure side, this may include micro-modular data centres (MMDCs), whilst the device side will consist of (mostly low-power) IoT machines, including consumer objects (e.g. smartphones, home appliances, EVs) and end-point equipment [38]. Within the smart grid, the edge should sit close to OT equipment and EPES personnel, but thanks to the proliferation of IoT throughout the grid domains, will not be limited to the last-mile (i.e. distribution and customer domains) [33]. Given the rapid growth in distributed electrical devices, energy resources, and energy consumers, EC use in smart grids is likely to expand [33]. Combined with CC, this decentralising of data processing can again enhance the smart grid's resiliency against cascading failures caused by IT-OT inter-dependencies.

11.3   Smart grid cybersecurity

In the past, the power grid was isolated. The modern integration of IT systems has opened up new possibilities, but has also expanded the threat of cybersecurity compromise. This is confounded by aging grid infrastructures that require upgrading, as well as the wide geographic distribution of grid sub-systems and devices. Furthermore, relatively young technologies like IoT, cloud, and EC are still evolving, with standards and best practices in active development. Lastly, cyber-physical systems are increasingly being targeted in cyber-attacks due to the high likelihood of wide-scale disruption, if successful [39]. This section outlines the main threats against devices, data, and control systems, before providing an overview of the defensive measures against them.

11.3.1 Attacks in the field

11.3.1.1 Eavesdropping

As discussed throughout this chapter, smart grid operations depend on rich data flows between components and applications, often transmitted through wireless channels. Wireless networking is inherently less secure than wired equivalents due to the exposed nature of the medium. This makes it possible for eavesdroppers to gain access to unsecured channels for snooping or sniffing attacks. Data is passively observed for either user behaviour profiling or network reconnaissance, with the aim of gathering intelligence for later, more sophisticated attacks. Hence, this is a breach of both user privacy and the confidentiality of grid and network structures.

11.3.1.2 False data injection

For correct functionality, data flows must be accurate. This core requirement is exploited by false data injection (FDI), which takes place as part of Man-in-the-Middle or replay attacks. Communications are intercepted and implanted with fake data before being forwarded on to the intended destination. The result of FDI attacks depends on which data streams are targeted. For AMI traffic from smart meters, it could give a false view of demand and consumption, influencing prices or manipulating customer bills (with the latter playing a role in energy theft campaigns [40]). For telemetry readings from PLCs or phasor measurements from PMUs in the field, FDI could cause desynchronisation or the generation of erroneous control signals, both of which could escalate into damage to equipment or outages if the grid becomes unbalanced.

11.3.1.3 Denial-of-service

A relatively simple but effective attack is denial-of-service (DoS). This targets availability and reliability and can render component systems nonfunctional and cause latencies in data transfers. A typical DoS attack consists of a large influx of packets directed towards an exposed interface on a device with the aim of overwhelming its processing capacity. DoS attacks with more participating nodes have a larger impact and are often referred to distributed DoS (DDoS). These are typically launched using botnets, a well-documented example of which is Mirai [41,42]. DoS attacks can also be smaller scale and consist of specially crafted packets with instructions designed to consume maximum resources. Jamming is another attack method against availability and can be considered a type of DoS specifically targeting wireless access channels. The attacker identifies the frequency band of the legitimate signals and transmits opposing signals on the same band to cause noise and interference. As with FDI, the impact of DoS will depend on which part of the smart grid is targeted. For example, if web-facing servers within the AMI or WAMS are attacked, remote access could be prevented. Attacks against field devices like PLCs, RTUs, or PMUs could overwhelm them and prevent data sharing. Similarly, flooding channels with junk data can increase latencies and disrupt real-time applications.

11.3.1.4 Device compromise

IoT devices are open to compromise because they are often not powerful or sophisticated enough to support complex cybersecurity mechanisms. In addition to this, manufacturers tend to prioritise functionality over defence in order to get devices into deployment as soon as possible. Devices which are closer to the logical grid perimeter (i.e. easier to access) should be considered the most vulnerable. An example is in the AMI, where smart meters sitting within customer premises interact with consumer-grade smart appliances. Furthermore, due to a lack of sufficient cybersecurity awareness in IoT device owners, combined with high-levels of interconnection, malware infections can achieve rapid lateral spread. For example, Mirai was able to exploit the use of default login credentials to recruit a huge population of IoT bots, including IoT cameras and routers [42]. Malware such as Mirai and its many variants are known for their DDoS capabilities and, hence, pose a dual threat to the smart grid.

11.3.2 Attacks on management

11.3.2.1 APTS and insiders

An advanced persistent threat (APT) is a special type of attack characterised by a high level of sophistication, complexity, and a long execution period. Commonly believed to be the work of nation-states, an APT consists of a multi-stage process and often encompasses several of the previously defined attack types [43], A malicious entity slowly builds up knowledge of the grid via methods like eavesdropping and phishing, and then uses this knowledge to establish a presence within the network. They can then carefully plan and execute their attack for maximum impact. A key component in APTs is often a malicious insider, which refers to anyone who has legitimate access to internal processes and systems and who can abuse this privileged position to divest critical or sensitive information. However, an insider might also be a careless employee who leaves systems exposed by not following procedures [43].

11.3.2.2 Attacks on the cloud and edge

Cloud service providers may also be targeted by DDoS, and a successful attack can cause disruption for a large number of cloud customers. Meanwhile, CC has its own set of cybersecurity vulnerabilities. Whilst services appear unified and seamless to customers, data shared with the cloud is physically processed and stored on whatever resources are currently available. This can make it difficult to guarantee data confidentiality and integrity [44]. Meanwhile, thanks to its large user base, the cloud is increasingly being exploited as a vector for the delivery of malware, and phishing campaigns to steal cloud access credentials are also on the rise [45]. Additional vulnerabilities may exist in hardware and network virtualisations as well as in APIs [44,46] which can expose both the cloud and the grid applications using it.

EC can suffer from device compromise as a result of both weak IoT and the proximity of edge components to the grid perimeter, making them more easily accessible than the cloud. EC nodes serve many IoT devices at once [47] and can be targeted by fake sensors maliciously inserted to either create noise and diminish service quality or availability, or to disrupt edge-based data processing. Any access control systems also need to protect the identities of legitimate devices or users from being hijacked [47]. Exposure and manipulation of data is also possible for edge-to-things or things-to-edge streams if communication channels are not sufficiently secured. Hence, attacks on the edge threaten processes in both the field and within management.

11.3.3 Defence mechanisms

11.3.3.1 Key principles

Cyber-physical systems such as the smart grid require sophisticated defences to protect against the targeted (and equally sophisticated) attacks against them. The continuity of power generation and delivery is the top priority, followed by the privacy and confidentiality of customer information [48]. NIST defines cybersecurity as one of nine key areas for the development of smart grid standards [2] and highlights defence-in-depth and defense-in-breadth as two recommended approaches [48]. The former refers to a scheme bringing together people, technology, and processes [48] to apply security in layers, such that the most critical assets are simultaneously protected in several ways. The latter refers to a holistic approach, encompassing entire component lifecycles across hardware, software, and networks.

11.3.3.2 Intrusion detection

If a compromise takes places, quick response is vital to mitigate the damage. An intrusion detection system (IDS) monitors devices and networks for suspicious activity. Signature-based detection creates templates of known attack patterns used by the IDS in its search [39]. If a match is found, the alarm will be raised. For unknown or new attack types, anomaly-based detection is more effective. Based on profiling or modelling of normal grid or application behaviour, AI or machine learning is used to identify anomalous patterns and issue alerts [39]. IDSs can be strengthened with real-time data analytics, made possible by both EC and the availability of large volumes of up-to-date data, which is prepared, cleansed, and visualised as soon as it is available. This type of analysis can also facilitate predictive maintenance and fault detection [49]. Sophisticated intrusion or anomaly detection systems can also protect against APTs and insider attacks [43].

11.3.3.3 Network security

Alongside IDS, traditional network security approaches can also be adapted and applied. For instance, firewalls should be placed at the ingress points of all LANs and the WAN, as well as in front of any facilities where data is stored. This will help to prevent illegitimate access, whilst providing logging facilities for repudiation purposes. With the addition of reverse proxy servers and load balancing, this approach could also improve general performance and mitigate the impact of DDoS attacks on Internet-facing servers. Another method against DDoS is IP hopping, where the server IPs are continuously switched (at both server and client ends) to obfuscate them and ensure continuity [39]. Smart grid entities may use virtual private networks (VPNs) to protect remote access channels, and simple measures like the securing of Wi-Fi access points will also help to mitigate risks.

11.3.3.4 IoT security

Attacks against IoT devices can be mitigated using authentication, which refers to the verification of device or user identities as they access or participate in the grid [50]. This would defend against the interception of data, protecting it from eavesdropping and FDI attacks. If authentication is combined with encryption, end-to-end data privacy can be ensured. As encryption is traditionally a costly process, lightweight solutions are currently being researched and developed. Examples include elliptic curve cryptography (ECC) [51] and the use of physical unclonable function (PUF) [52,53]. Another recommended approach is trust management, where data on the characteristics or behaviours of an IoT device are used to assess its trustworthiness. Actual definitions of trust can vary, but serve the overall aim of ensuring that only legitimate devices can access or communicate with grid systems [50]. For consumer-grade smart devices, compromises can be mitigated with greater awareness of simple measures such as the disabling of unused services and changing the default logins.

11.3.3.5 Cloud and edge security

To protect the cloud, security should be considered at the host, network, and the application levels [54]. This requires a clear definition of trust boundaries that is understood by providers and customers [54]. At the network-level, critical infrastructures like the smart grid benefit from using a private cloud setup combined with network security measures as described earlier. At the host-level, security is offloaded to providers for the SaaS and PaaS models as applications and tools are implemented on the cloud itself [54]. For the IaaS model, virtualisation programs need to be secured on the customer side. Finally, at the application level, customers need to apply their own application security frameworks to the software they build and deploy within the cloud [54]. Defence of IoT devices overlaps with defence of the edge network. Encryption should be used to ensure privacy and confidentiality of data, with authentication to prevent illegitimate users, devices, or services from accessing edge resources [33,47].

11.4 Current challenges and future research

At present, there is a range of possible protocols for IoT communications and cross-protocol integration is difficult to achieve. To better meet the interoperability needs of the smart grid, and for easier integration in general, formalised IoT communication and deployment standards need to be agreed upon by the industry and the energy sector [39]. Furthermore, the communication protocols used by IoT and industrial control systems need to have security mechanisms, providing features like authentication, repudiation, and encryption, built into them to better protect data streams. Given the vast population of endpoints, IoT needs to use IPv6 at the network layer, whilst much of the defensive approaches currently in place were developed for IPv4 networks. As a result, the protection of critical infrastructure also depends on a wider redefinition of cybersecurity approaches to meet the challenges of IPv6 deployment.

Cybersecurity generally remains an ongoing challenge both for the smart grid as a whole and for the individual technologies it utilises. As with the protocols, IoT manufacturers need to move towards security-by-design, whereby device vulnerabilities are minimised at the design and development phase instead being considered after deployment. Better regulatory standards are needed to ensure that IoT devices manufactured for and used within critical infrastructure are sufficiently secure [39]. As an extension of this, consumers need to be better informed about the IoT capabilities of their smart appliances and the data generated by them. Although data laws like General Data Protection Regulation (GDPR) now provide some guidance around the use of customer data, there is also still a need for greater clarity in how the vast pools of data collected by infrastructure systems like the smart grid should be handled.

The sheer volume of the information to be processed can be defined as a big data challenge. However, there are several open issues hindering effective big data processing in the smart grid. First, processing capacity and resources will need to expand very rapidly to keep up with the growing volume of grid data being collected [55]. Hence, any big data models need to be highly scalable. Second, incoming data will typically be in many different formats given the lack of standardisation. This means that a large amount of cleansing, consolidating, and synchronising will need to be performed [55], making the development of efficient parallel processing schemes necessary. Data accuracy is also a concern as noise added during transmission or by inaccurate equipment is likely [55]. Standard data privacy and confidentiality issues will also apply.

Lastly, the smart grid has a central role to play in the fight against climate change. There are ongoing investigations into the most effective types of RES and how they can be safely integrated into the energy system via DER and microgrids. This may require predictive applications that use AI to estimate energy generation based on weather or other relevant factors, and the improvement or renewal of distribution networks so that the load of prosumer-generated power can be handled safely and efficiently [56]. At the larger scale, interoperability with legacy infrastructure, and reliability of new systems during upgrade procedures, need to be considered as well. Meanwhile, an increase in the active involvement of customers in power operations presents an opportunity to encourage behavioural shifts and a change in attitudes to energy consumption for a more sustainable and environmentally-friendly society.

11.5 Conclusions

The smart grid is the combination of the power generation and distribution network and cyber communication technologies that enable remote monitoring and control.

The addition of IoT devices (such as smart meters, PLCs, RTUs, and PMUs), which are capable of sensing and communicating, has made it possible to observe grid operations in real-time, to respond quickly, and to balance supply and demand more efficiently. This makes the smart grid resilient, because issues are quickly detected and rectified, and more environmentally-friendly because less energy is wasted. Advances in technology have also enabled greater integration of RES and the prosumer user model via microgrids.

Smart grid control systems like SCADA and WAMS operate in a distributed manner by communicating with grid devices within each functional domain and network tier to gather data, issue automatic commands, and provide intelligence to EPES personnel. Modern iterations of these control systems can use cloud computing to assist in the running of grid applications or to add additional computing capabilities, combined with EC to mitigate latencies and privacy issues.

Smart grids can be targeted in cyber-attacks such as eavesdropping, FDI, and DDoS, or they may be victim to large-scale campaigns launched by hostile nation states. For protection against these threats, a holistic security approach should be followed. This includes the securing of end devices, including consumer-grade smart appliances, protection of data channels, system-wide intrusion detection, and better cybersecurity awareness amongst end users, suppliers, and others involved in energy markets. Open issues for further research include standardisation of protocols and best practices, improvements to cybersecurity, efficient handling of the grid's big data, and improvements to grid efficiency and sustainability to combat climate change. The smart grid will continue to develop and play a central role for society in the coming years.

References

[1]   J. F. Martins, A. G. Pronto, V. Delgado-Gomes, and M. Sanduleac, "Smart Meters and Advanced Metering Infrastructure," in *Pathways to a Smarter Power System*, A. Taşcıkaraoğlu and O. Erdinç, Eds. Boston, MA: Academic Press, 2019, pp. 89–114.

[2]   C. Greer, D. A. Wollman, D. E. Prochaska, *et al.*, "NIST Framework and Roadmap for Smart Grid Interoperability Standards, Release 3.0," 2014, accessed 29-06-2021. Available: https://www.nist.gov/el/smart-grid/smart-grid-framework/framework-and-road-map-smart-grid-interoperability.

[3]   L. Tightiz and H. Yang, "A Comprehensive Review on IoT Protocols' Features in Smart Grid Communication," *Energies*, vol. 13, no. 11, p. 2762, 2020.

[4]   Z. Liu, "Grid Development and Voltage Upgrade," in *Ultra-High Voltage AC/DC Grids*, Z. Liu, Ed. Boston, MA: Academic Press, 2015, pp. 1–33.

[5]   A. G. Ter-Gazarian, "Introduction," in *Energy Storage for Power Systems (3rd ed.)*. Institution of Engineering and Technology, 2020.

[6]   Standards Committee, "IEEE P2030 – Guide for Smart Grid Interoperability of Energy Technology and Information Technology Operation with the Electric

Power System (EPS), End-Use Applications, and Loads," 2020, accessed 29-06-2021. Available: https://standards.ieee.org/project/2030.html.

[7]   S. V. Buldyrev, R. Parshani, G. Paul, H. E. Stanley, and S. Havlin, "Catastrophic Cascade of Failures in Interdependent Networks," *Nature*, vol. 464, no. 7291, pp. 1025–1028, 2010.

[8]   C. D. Brummitt, R. M. D'Souza, and E. A. Leicht, "Suppressing Cascades of Load in Interdependent Networks," *Proceedings of the National Academy of Sciences*, vol. 109, no. 12, pp. E680–E689, 2012.

[9]   M. R. Asghar, G. Dán, D. Miorandi, and I. Chlamtac, "Smart Meter Data Privacy: A Survey," *IEEE Communications Surveys & Tutorials*, vol. 19, no. 4, pp. 2820–2835, 2017.

[10] J. Momoh, "Smart Grid Communications and Measurement Technology," in *Smart Grid: Fundamentals of Design and Analysis*. New York, NY: John Wiley & Sons, Ltd, 2012, Chapter 2, pp. 16–28.

[11] E. Raju P and T. Jain, "Distributed Energy Resources and Control," in *Distributed Energy Resources in Microgrids*, R. K. Chauhan and K. Chauhan, Eds. Boston, MA: Academic Press, 2019, pp. 33–56.

[12] V. K. Sood and H. Abdelgawad, "Microgrids Architectures," in *Distributed Energy Resources in Microgrids*, R. K. Chauhan and K. Chauhan, Eds. Boston, MA: Academic Press, 2019, pp. 1–31.

[13] M. Ouaissa and M. Ouaissa, "Cyber Security Issues for IoT Based Smart Grid Infrastructure," in *IOP Conference Series: Materials Science and Engineering*, vol. 937, no. 1. IOP Publishing, 2020, p. 012001.

[14] A. G. Ter-Gazarian, "Energy Storage as a Structural Unit of a Power System," in *Energy Storage for Power Systems (3rd Edition)*. Institution of Engineering and Technology, 2020.

[15] X. Tan, Q. Li, and H. Wang, "Advances and Trends of Energy Storage Technology in Microgrid," *International Journal of Electrical Power & Energy Systems*, vol. 44, no. 1, pp. 179–191, 2013.

[16] D. Kolokotsa, N. Kampelis, A. Mavrigiannaki, M. Gentilozzi, F. Paredes, F. Montagnino, and L. Venezia, "On the Integration of the Energy Storage in Smart Grids: Technologies and Applications," *Energy Storage*, vol. 1, no. 1, p. e50, 2019.

[17] A. G. Ter-Gazarian, "Electric Vehicles as Distributed Energy Sources and Storage," in *Energy Storage for Power Systems (3rd ed.)*. Institution of Engineering and Technology, 2020.

[18] M. Kuzlu, M. Pipattanasomporn, and S. Rahman, "Communication Network Requirements for Major Smart Grid Applications in HAN, NAN and WAN," *Computer Networks*, vol. 67, pp. 74–88, 2014.

[19] E. Kabalci and Y. Kabalci, "Smart Grid Network Architectures," in *From Smart Grid to Internet of Energy*, E. Kabalci and Y. Kabalci, Eds. Boston, MA: Academic Press, 2019, pp. 97–118.

[20] Bluetooth, "Bluetooth Wireless Technology," 2021, accessed 29-06-2021. Available: https://www.bluetooth.com/learn-about-bluetooth/tech-overview/.

[21] A. Almalawi, Z. Tari, A. Fahad, and X. Yi, "Introduction," in *SCADA Security: Machine Learning Concepts for Intrusion Detection and Prevention*. New York, NY: John Wiley & Sons, 2021, Chapter 1, pp. 1–13.

[22] T. Gupta and R. Bhatia, "Communication Technologies in Smart Grid at Different Network Layers: An Overview," in *2020 International Conference on Intelligent Engineering and Management (ICIEM)*. IEEE, 2020, pp. 177–182.

[23] S. Misra, A. Mukherjee, and A. Roy, "IoT Connectivity Technologies," in *Introduction to IoT*. New York, NY: Cambridge University Press, 2021, p. 128–162.

[24] P. Manoj, Y. B. Kumar, M. Gowtham, D. Vishwas, and A. Ajay, "Internet of Things for Smart Grid Applications," in *Advances in Smart Grid Power System*, A. Tomar and R. Kandari, Eds. Boston, MA: Academic Press, 2021, pp. 159–190.

[25] Z. Alliance, "What is Z-Wave Long Range and How Does it Differ from Z-Wave?" 2020, accessed 29-06-2021. Available: https://z-wavealliance.org/what-is-z-wave-long-range-and-how-does-it-differ-from-z-wave/.

[26] S. K. Rathor and D. Saxena, "Energy Management system for smart grid: An overview and key issues," *International Journal of Energy Research*, vol. 44, no. 6, pp. 4067–4109, 2020.

[27] K. Poplavskaya and L. de Vries, "Aggregators Today and Tomorrow: From Intermediaries to Local Orchestrators?" in *Behind and Beyond the Meter*, F. Sioshansi, Ed. Boston, MA: Academic Press, 2020, pp. 105–135.

[28] D. Upadhyay and S. Sampalli, "SCADA (Supervisory Control and Data Acquisition) Systems: Vulnerability Assessment and Security Recommendations," *Computers & Security*, vol. 89, p. 101666, 2020.

[29] E. Knapp, "How Industrial Networks Operate," in *Industrial Network Security*, E. Knapp, Ed. Boston, MA: Syngress, 2011, pp. 89–110.

[30] R. N. Gore and S. P. Valsan, "Wireless Communication Technologies for Smart Grid (WAMS) Deployment," in *2018 IEEE International Conference on Industrial Technology (ICIT)*. IEEE, 2018, pp. 1326–1331.

[31] A. Sundararajan, T. Khan, A. Moghadasi, and A. I. Sarwat, "Survey on Synchrophasor Data Quality and Cybersecurity Challenges, and Evaluation of Their Interdependencies," *Journal of Modern Power Systems and Clean Energy*, vol. 7, no. 3, pp. 449–467, 2019.

[32] B. Appasani and D. K. Mohanta, "Uncertainty Analysis and Risk Assessment for Effective Decision-Making Using Wide-Area Synchrophasor Measurement System," in *Decision Making Applications in Modern Power Systems*, S. H. Abdel Aleem, A. Y. Abdelaziz, A. F. Zobaa, and R. Bansal, Eds. Boston, MA: Academic Press, 2020, pp. 63–88.

[33] C. Feng, Y. Wang, Q. Chen, G. Strbac, and C. Kang, "Smart Grid Encounters Edge Computing: Opportunities and Applications." *Advances in Applied Energy*, vol. 1, p. 100006, 2020.

[34] E. Dusabimana and S.-G. Yoon, "A Survey on the Micro-Phasor Measurement Unit in Distribution Networks," *Electronics*, vol. 9, no. 2, p. 305, 2020.

[35]　S. Misra and S. Bera, *Introduction to Cloud Computing*. New York, NY: Cambridge University Press, 2018, p. 18–37.

[36]　G. Dileep, "A Survey on Smart Grid Technologies and Applications," *Renewable Energy*, vol. 146, pp. 2589–2625, 2020.

[37]　M. Yigit, V. C. Gungor, and S. Baktir, "Cloud Computing for Smart Grid Applications," *Computer Networks*, vol. 70, pp. 312–329, 2014.

[38]　A. Marcham, "What Is Edge Computing?" in *Understanding Infrastructure Edge Computing*. New York, NY: John Wiley & Sons, Ltd, 2021, Chapter 2, pp. 3–19.

[39]　K. Kimani, V. Oduol, and K. Langat, "Cyber Security Challenges for IoT-Based Smart Grid Networks," *International Journal of Critical Infrastructure Protection*, vol. 25, pp. 36–49, 2019.

[40]　A. Jindal, A. Schaeffer-Filho, A. K. Marnerides, P. Smith, A. Mauthe, and L. Granville, "Tackling Energy Theft in Smart Grids Through Data-Driven Analysis," in *2020 International Conference on Computing, Networking and Communications (ICNC)*. IEEE, 2020, pp. 410–414.

[41]　C. Kolias, G. Kambourakis, A. Stavrou, and J. Voas, "DDoS in the IoT: Mirai and Other Botnets," *Computer*, vol. 50, no. 7, pp. 80–84, 2017.

[42]　M. Antonakakis, T. April, M. Bailey, *et al.*, "Understanding the Mirai Botnet," in *26th USENIX Security Symposium USENIX Security 17)*, 2017, pp. 1093–1110.

[43]　B. Li, R. Lu, G. Xiao, H. Bao, and A. A. Ghorbani, "Towards Insider Threats Detection in Smart Grid Communication Systems," *IET Communications*, vol. 13, no. 12, pp. 1728–1736, 2019.

[44]　A. Aljumah and T. A. Ahanger, "Cyber Security Threats, Challenges and Defence Mechanisms in Cloud Computing," *IET Communications*, vol. 14, no. 7, pp. 1185–1191, 2020.

[45]　Netskope Threat Labs, "Cloudy With A Chance of Malice: Forecasting the New Era of Cloud-Enabled Threats," 2021, accessed 29-06-2021. Available: https://www.netskope.com/typ-cloud-and-threat-report-feb-2021.

[46]　A. Singh and K. Chatterjee, "Cloud Security Issues and Challenges: A Survey," *Journal of Network and Computer Applications*, vol. 79, pp. 88–115, 2017.

[47]　H. Zeyu, X. Geming, W. Zhaohang, and Y. Sen, "Survey on Edge Computing Security," in *2020 International Conference on Big Data, Artificial Intelligence and Internet of Things Engineering (ICBAIE)*. IEEE, 2020, pp. 96–105.

[48]　P. Pritzker, "NIST Guidelines for Smart Grid Cybersecurity, Revision 1," 2014, accessed 29-06-2021. Available: https://www.nist.gov/el/smart-grid/smart-grid-framework/cybersecurity.

[49]　C. Tu, X. He, Z. Shuai, and F. Jiang, "Big Data Issues in Smart Grid – A Review," *Renewable and Sustainable Energy Reviews*, vol. 79, pp. 1099–1107, 2017.

[50]　M. b. Mohamad Noor and W. H. Hassan, "Current Research on Internet of Things (IoT) Security: A Survey," *Computer Networks*, vol. 148, pp. 283–294, 2019.

[51]   M. A. Khan, M. T. Quasim, N. S. Alghamdi, and M. Y. Khan, "A Secure Framework for Authentication and Encryption Using Improved ECC for IoT-Based Medical Sensor Data," *IEEE Access*, vol. 8, pp. 52018–52027, 2020.

[52]   T. A. Idriss, H. A. Idriss, and M. A. Bayoumi, "A Lightweight PUF-Based Authentication Protocol Using Secret Pattern Recognition for Constrained IoT Devices," *IEEE Access*, vol. 9, pp. 80546–80558, 2021.

[53]   B. Zhao, P. Zhao, and P. Fan, "ePUF: A Lightweight Double Identity Verification in IoT," *Tsinghua Science and Technology*, vol. 25, no. 5, pp. 625–635, 2020.

[54]   M. GhasemiGol, *Cloud Infrastructure Security*. New York, NY: John Wiley & Sons, Ltd, 2019, Chapter 2, pp. 23–50.

[55]   B. P. Bhattarai, S. Paudyal, Y. Luo, *et al.*, "Big Data Analytics in Smart Grids: State-of-the-Art, Challenges, Opportunities, and Future Directions," *IET Smart Grid*, vol. 2, no. 2, pp. 141–154, 2019.

[56]   Y. Yoldaş, A. Önen, S. Muyeen, A. V. Vasilakos, and İ. Alan, "Enhancing Smart Grid with Microgrids: Challenges and Opportunities," *Renewable and Sustainable Energy Reviews*, vol. 72, pp. 205–214, 2017.

Chapter 12

Consensus algorithm for energy applications: case study on P2P energy trading scenario

Vidya Krishnan Mololoth[1], Saguna Saguna[1] and Christer Åhlund[1]

Blockchain technology is being widely used in energy applications for P2P energy trading, demand management, electric vehicle charging, and scheduling. Moving towards a decentralized and secure grid has gained the acceptance with the adoption of blockchain. However, researchers face certain challenges when implementing blockchain technology in the energy sector, the primary challenge being the choice of consensus mechanism. Even though PoW is the commonly used consensus algorithm, it is inefficient in nature and not applicable for energy applications. This chapter aims to compare energy efficiency and complexity of PoW and PoA consensus algorithm in terms of computation time within the context of energy applications. To give more insight into blockchain application in energy sector, we present a simple case of blockchain-based P2P energy trading and analyze the complexity of applying PoW and PoA algorithms. Further, a discussion on advantages of PoA for energy sector is presented.

12.1 Introduction

The idea of blockchain was first introduced by Satoshi Nakamoto as an underlying structure behind the most popular cryptocurrency Bitcoin [1]. Blockchain was initially designed for cryptocurrencies. However, later on, due to its critical properties, it gained acceptance in other fields, namely, health sector, supply chain management, markets, and energy sector [2]. The main properties of blockchain include immutability, decentralization, indestructibility, security, and distributed. Blockchain uses cryptographic techniques and consensus mechanisms to achieve these properties. As the name implies, blockchain is a chain of blocks that is linked using hashes. Each block contains a block id, nonce, several transactions, timestamp, hash of the block, and hash of the previous block. The hash of the previous block added in the

[1]Department of Computer Science, Electrical and Space Engineering, Luleå University of Technology, Sweden

current block makes the blockchain immutable, i.e., when there is a small change in the input, hash value changes rapidly, so if some malicious activity occurs in the block, hash value changes and creates a mismatch, then the attacker needs to change all the previous hashes which is not easily possible. Consensus algorithms in blockchain are used to decide on which blocks to add [3]. The participating nodes will participate in a mining process to get the chance to add a block and get the reward. The method for adding a block can vary depending on the type of consensus algorithm. Out of various consensus algorithms, proof of work (PoW) is the most popular which is used in bitcoin. Consensus algorithms decide several characteristics of blockchain network like scalability, energy efficiency, transaction speed, and so on.

In the energy sector, blockchain is being mainly used for energy trading, demand management, and electric vehicle charging. The main aim here is to move towards a decentralized system using blockchain rather than using a centralized system [2]. However, the development of a blockchain network for energy applications requires careful consideration in the choice of consensus algorithms. From the review done by authors in [4], we can see the different blockchain application areas and commonly used consensus mechanisms in the energy sector. Due to the popularity, PoW is being widely used despite its drawbacks. Even though PoW is secure and popular, it is computationally complex and energy consuming. There are several other energy-efficient consensus mechanisms like proof of stake (PoS), proof of authority (PoA), proof of elapsed time (PoEt), etc. In this chapter, we discuss proof-based consensus algorithms PoW and PoA by comparing their properties. The main reason to choose PoA as an alternative is because of its high scalability and energy-efficient property. Nowadays, PoA is being widely used by industries and other communities due to its improved performance and better finality [5]. Next, we present an energy trading scenario to demonstrate the complexity of applying PoW and PoA algorithms for energy applications. Finally, we discuss the advantages of using PoA in the energy sector. The main contributions include:

1. We compare proof-based consensus algorithms PoW and PoA.
2. We present an energy trading use case, to compare and analyze the complexity of applying PoW and PoA algorithms.
3. We present insights regarding the best choice of consensus algorithm for energy applications.

12.2   Consensus mechanisms

Consensus mechanisms in blockchain are used to reach to a common agreement regarding the state of the blockchain. It helps to decide on which block has to be appended to the chain of blocks. These algorithms prevent any malicious activities of the nodes and determine the performance characteristics such as scalability, transaction speed, security, etc. of the blockchain network [3]. Like this, consensus mechanisms ensure trust in any type of blockchain network. Consensus algorithms are mainly of two types: proof based and Byzantine fault tolerance based [6]. In proof-based algorithms, nodes have to prove themselves to add a block. Some of the proof-based consensus algorithms are PoW, PoS, delegated PoS (DPoS), PoA, PoEt, and so on. Byzantine fault tolerance-based algorithms address the Byzantine fault tolerance problem in the distributed computing. Examples are practical Byzantine fault tolerance (PBFT), federated Byzantine agreement (FBA), and delegated Byzantine fault tolerance (DBFT). Here we intend to discuss PoW and PoA in detail.

12.2.0.1 Proof of work

PoW is the most commonly used consensus algorithm. In PoW, nodes compete using their computational power to add a new block in each round of consensus. Node that first solves the complex cryptographic puzzle will get the right to create the new block. A nonce value is concatenated with the hash value and hashed again repeatedly until an acceptable hash is obtained. The acceptable hash condition may be that hash should precede with a predefined number of zeros which decide the difficulty level of the network. This is achieved only through continuous guessing of nonce value and nodes use their computational power, i.e., nodes perform some work to add a block, hence, the name proof of work [6]. The winning node will get reward for successful mining. PoW is used by the popular cryptocurrency bitcoin. However, the main concern regarding PoW algorithm is the need for high computational power and time.

12.2.0.2 Proof of authority

PoA is the modified version of PoS or DPoS algorithm. PoA is designed for permissioned blockchain networks and it is different from other consensus mechanisms. Here the identity of the node is used as an entity to add a new block. In PoS, nodes stake their coins whereas in PoA, nodes use their own reputation. PoA relies on certain number of trusted validators/nodes who act as moderators in the system [8]. This makes it a highly scalable system. However, it deviates from the decentralization property of blockchain but can achieve high scalability and throughput. PoA is considered as an emerging blockchain solution which is suitable for private blockchain applications.

12.2.1 Analysis of algorithms

12.2.1.1 Energy efficiency

PoW is well known for its security; however, its massive energy consumption makes it unsuitable for many critical applications. The involved mining process to add a block makes it secure but also complex. The most popular cryptocurrency bitcoin uses PoW and studies say that the electricity consumption of bitcoin is quite high when compared with the consumption of several countries [7]. PoW is generally used with public blockchain networks and is completely decentralized.

PoA algorithms are easy to run and maintain compared to PoW. It is based on a set of trusted validators and does not involve any mining which allows the network to reach consensus more faster, i.e., transactions are confirmed at less than 1 s [8]. This makes PoA systems more scalable. However, since it relies on certain number

Table 12.1   Comparison of PoW and PoA

PoW	PoA
Complex mining process	No Mining
High computational power required	Less power required
Energy inefficient	Energy efficient
Based on miners computational power	Based on validators reputation
Few transactions per second	Thousands of transactions per second
Decentralized	Not completely decentralized
Less scalable	Highly scalable

of validating nodes, PoA networks are slightly centralized. As it does not involve any complex mining process as PoW, it is an energy-efficient consensus algorithm.

12.2.1.2   Network security

PoW algorithm presents many vulnerabilities. They are mainly categorised as double-spending attacks, network attacks, and 51% attacks [9]. Double spending occurs when the same input is used for two or more transactions. Digital currencies can be easily replicated as compared to physical currencies and because of this, there is a chance of using same currency multiple times. However, bitcoin has some mechanisms to prevent this double-spending issues. 51% attack is common in PoW public blockchains. Here, attacker tries to do a double spending by acquiring more than 50% of the networks hash rate. Another type of an attack that exploits consensus convergence in PoW is selfish mining attack. Here, a selfish miner will keep on mining the blocks without broadcasting it and publish many mined blocks at a later time. Other innocent miners will waste their energy. Sybil attack is a type of network attack where attackers try to manipulate the network by creating fake accounts.

An attacker needs to acquire 51% of computational power in PoW. In the case of PoA, an attacker needs to obtain the control of 51% of the validator nodes for 51% attack. Getting the control of the network nodes in blockchain network is very difficult than achieving the computational power. For example, in PoW, attacker can increase the performance or computational power of the network. In the case of PoA, this makes no sense, because for network decisions, there is no effect for the computational power of node. This makes PoA more resilient to 51% attack. DDoS attacks can occur in PoA networks; however, there are mechanisms to defend against this attack [8].

12.3   An energy trading scenario

Blockchain-based energy trading model provides an open, efficient, secure, and trustworthy trading platform [11]. In this section, we intend to discuss blockchain-based energy trading scenario and analyze the complexity of applying PoW and PoA consensus algorithm.

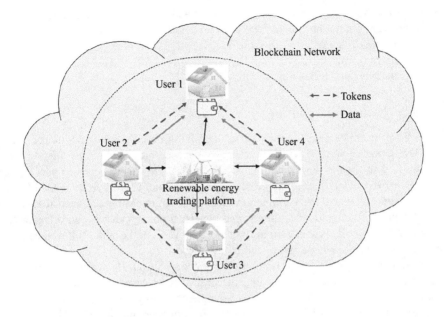

Figure 12.1   Energy trading using blockchain

Consider a group of houses that have installed solar panels and are connected to blockchain network. Figure 12.1 shows an example of four houses connected using blockchain network. Let us assume that each house is equipped with smart meters that can record energy usage and energy transfers. With the installed solar panels, users can generate their own energy as well as trade excess energy to other users. Consider a case where user 1 has excess energy and user 3 is in need of energy. User 1 can trade its energy to user 3 and receive the payment for the transfer. Blockchain can be used for secure energy trading in this case. However, the selection of suitable consensus algorithm is important.

To analyze the computational complexity, a similar prototype using PoW and PoA consensus was implemented using Python 3 and HTML. Python was used as a back end for blockchain process and HTML was used as a front end to create user interacting web pages. We used a Macbook Pro with 32GB RAM and 2.6 GHz Intel Core i7 CPU for conducting the study. A python module emulates the smart meter and records the energy transfers. Energy trading transactions are created and mined using PoW and PoA algorithms separately. We varied the difficulty level for PoW and number of transactions per block. The difficulty value of the PoW algorithm determines the number of preceding zeros to be added to the hash to solve the cryptographic puzzle. It can be any integer value depending on how complex system one needs [12]. For demo, the difficulty level was set to 4, 5, 6, and the number of transactions was varied from 1 to 5. The nonce value and time taken to complete the mining process for PoW and time taken for PoA were recorded. Nonce is an integer value that is concatenated with the hash to get a hash preceding with predefined number of zeros to solve the puzzle. The main objective to vary difficulty level and number of transactions is to analyze the performance of PoW and PoA algorithms and to find the relation between these parameters and block mining time.

12.3.1 Using PoW consensus algorithm

In PoW, all users or nodes participate in the mining process. Involved miners have to solve a puzzle and the winning node will get the chance to add the new block. Figure 12.2 shows the flow of mining process in PoW. Nodes will create a new block and to add the block to the chain, they have to (1) calculate the hash of the block, (2) compare calculated hash with target hash, (3) if target hash is achieved, that node get the chance to create a new block, and (4) else a nonce value is concatenated to block hash and hashed again until the target is achieved. All the nodes follow the same process to solve the puzzle and to get mining reward.

Mining process for PoW is to solve the cryptographic puzzle by finding the nonce value that satisfies the condition i.e., the hash that precedes with difficulty value number of zeros. Figure 12.3 shows an example of mining process, for difficulty of 4. Here, the original hash is concatenated with an integer and hashed again until the targeted hash that precedes with 4 zeros is obtained. For the particular example, the nonce value that satisfied the condition is 15,799. Nonce is initially set to zero and incremented in each iteration until the 64 bit hash precedes with the required number of zeros. Like this, miners solve the PoW cryptographic puzzle.

Figures 12.4 and 12.6 show the observed results. In Figure 12.4, the number of transactions is plotted against the nonce value. In Figure 12.6, the number of transactions is plotted against the time taken to complete the mining process. Here in our experiment, we set difficulty values as 4, 5, 6 and, for values above that, the system was not responding after some time. For difficulty = 4, during the mining, the miner has to hash an integer (nonce) along with the original hash until a hash value that starts with 4 zeros is found. As difficulty value increases, solving the

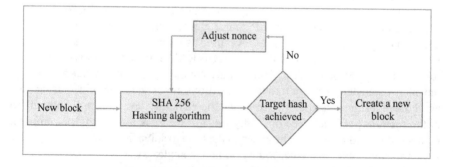

Figure 12.2   Mining process in PoW

Figure 12.3   *An example of Hash calculation*

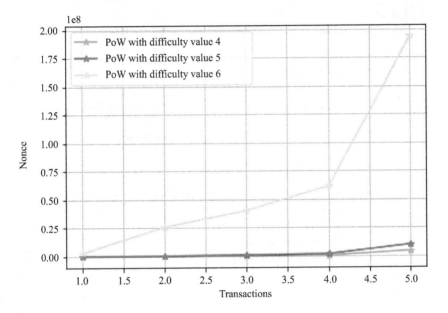

Figure 12.4   *Number of transactions vs. nonce value for PoW*

puzzle by finding suitable nonce value becomes difficult and uses significant time and resources. From the observed values, as the difficulty value increases, the time taken to mine a transaction was increasing. The same was the case with multiple transactions adding to a block, i.e., as difficulty increases, the nonce value increases and time taken to mine transaction increases in PoW. For normal systems, this process can consume more time and resources which is not recommendable. However, high difficulty indicates that the system is difficult to attack.

Figure 12.4 clearly explains the relation between difficulty value and mining process. The process of adding nonce value to hash to solve the puzzle becomes more complex as the difficulty value is more. However, high difficulty indicates that the system is difficult to attack [12]. This means that a fully distributed blockchain system

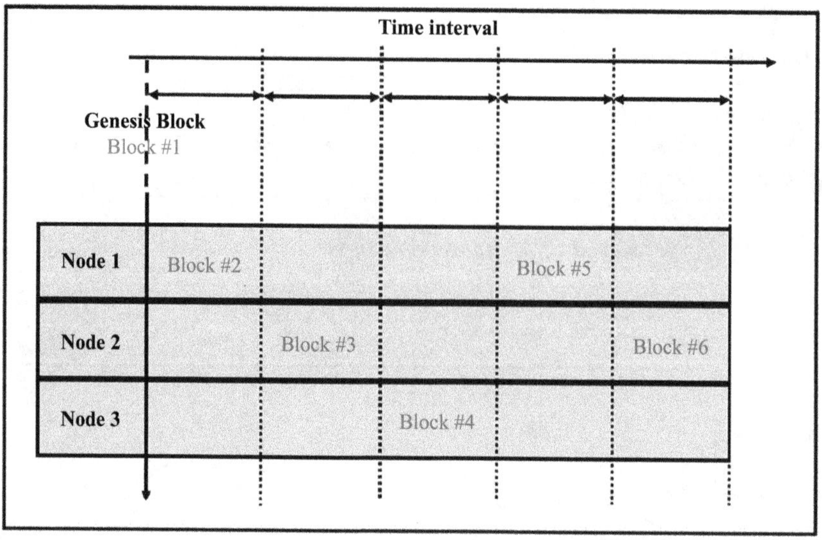

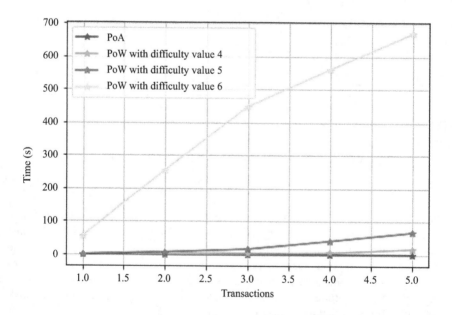

Figure 12.5   Validation process in PoA

Figure 12.6   Number of transactions vs. time to complete mining process (seconds) for PoW and PoA

with PoW is difficult to attack but computational complexity increases i.e., with PoW, system security is more but with the cost of computational power and time.

12.3.2   Using PoA consensus algorithm

With PoA, the involved complex mining process can be eliminated. Out of all available users, some users will become the trusted validator nodes and perform the consensus. Instead of all the available users participating in the mining process as in PoW, here only selected trusted users become the validators. A leader node from the trusted set of validators will generate the new block at one time interval and the leader role is passed to the next validating node in the next time interval. Figure 12.5 depicts the validation process in PoA. Here, out of all the nodes, only three nodes participate in the consensus. Initially, node 1 is the leader node which creates the block and other validators verify the block. In the next round, node 2 becomes the leader node and the process continues.

The observed results with PoA consensus algorithm can be seen in Figure 12.6. The time taken to complete the consensus process increases with the number of transactions; however, it is very low compared to PoW. This is because the computational power of nodes is not a criteria to perform consensus in PoA. Since nodes use their identity to become part of the consensus, the chance for malicious activity will also be less. Computational time infers to energy consumption of the system and hence PoA is energy efficient. The involved block validation process in PoA is much simpler and faster compared to PoW.

12.4   Discussion

As seen in Section 12.2, many consensus algorithms exist and each algorithm has its own advantages and limitations. It is practically impossible to choose a specific algorithm as the best one. The choice of algorithm critically depends on the field of use. However, for energy applications, timing is critically important and the energy consumption should be minimum. To manage all the energy customers, a scalable and secure system is required. While integrating with blockchain, appropriate consensus algorithm should be chosen. As PoW is not energy efficient and scalable, it is not a good choice of consensus algorithm when dealing with energy applications and being in regulated trading markets. Hence, PoA is more suitable, where nodes stake their reputation to become validators and any malicious activity will destroy their reputation which was earned over time. This makes it less vulnerable and ensures integrity. Also, it is highly scalable, can process thousands of transactions per second and the validation process is less costly considering time and energy perspective. Here, the question that arises is about the decentralization of PoA. PoA is not completely decentralized, but it is distributed and makes the blockchain systems more efficient. PoA is mainly geared towards private organizations as it is a centralized consensus model in the blockchain network. Hence, it can be seen that while comparing the two proof based consensus mechanisms, PoW is energy expensive and less scalable;

PoA is energy efficient, secure, and highly scalable. Thus, PoA is an ideal choice of consensus algorithm while dealing with energy application.

12.5   Conclusion

Consensus protocols ensure the stable operation of blockchain systems. To make a decision regarding the best choice of consensus algorithm, factors like energy efficiency, scalability, transaction time, and security have to be considered. When it comes to energy applications, transaction speed and energy usage are critical factors. PoW is highly secure and decentralized, but due to its high energy consumption and less scalability, it is not a good choice for large-scale energy applications. PoA is gaining popularity in the energy industry and many private organizations are adopting it because of its advantages. However, we highlight through the discussion in this chapter that PoA is an ideal choice to energy applications as it is energy efficient, requires less transaction time, and highly scalable.

References

[1]   S. Nakamoto, *Bitcoin: A Peer-to-Peer Electronic Cash System*, www.bitcoin. org. Accessed: Jun 15, 2021.

[2]   M. B. Mollah, J. Zhao, D. Niyato, *et al.*, "Blockchain for future smart grid: a comprehensive survey," in *IEEE Internet of Things Journal*, vol. 8, pp. 18–43, 2021, https://doi.org/10.1109/JIOT.2020.2993601

[3]   S. Zhang and J. H. Lee, "Analysis of the main consensus protocols of blockchain," in *ICT Express* 6, June 2020, pp. 93–97, https://doi.org/10.1016/j.icte.2019.08.001.

[4]   M. Andoni, V. Robu, D. Flynn, *et al.*, "Blockchain technology in the energy sector: a systematic review of challenges and opportunities," in *Renewable and Sustainable Energy Reviews*, vol. 100, pp. 143–174, 2019. https://doi.org/10.1016/j.rser.2018.10.014.

[5]   Changelly, *A Complete Guide to the Proof of Authority Algorithm*, https://www.changelly.com/blog/what-is-proof-of-authority-poa/, Accessed: May 16, 2022.

[6]   M. R. Comans, O. N. de Haas, R. Jongerius, D. A. J. Oudejans, and E. de Smidt, *Stop Boiling the Oceans: A Review on Energy Efficient Proof of Work Alternatives*, 2019, http://resolver.tudelft.nl/uuid:f1378204-cfcb-4ab6-84cc-b7249c0c3868.

[7]   BBC News, https://www.bbc.com/news/technology-56012952 Accessed: May 10, 2022.

[8]   Apla Blockchain Platform Guide, *Proof-of-Authority Consensus*, https://apla. readthedocs.io/en/latest/concepts/consensus.html, Accessed: May 16, 2022.

[9]   G. Antonio, F. Rebello, G. Camilo, *et al.*, *A Security and Performance Analysis of Proof-Based Consensus Protocols*, https://www.gta.ufrj.br/ftp/gta/TechReports/RCG21.pdf.

[10]   M. Saad, J. Spaulding, L. Njilla, *et al.*, "Exploring the attack surface of blockchain: a systematic overview," in *IEEE Communications, Surveys & Tutorials*, vol. 22, no. 3, pp. 1977–2008, 2020, doi:10.1109/COMST.2020.29 75999.

[11]   J. Wu and N. K. Tran, "Application of blockchain technology in sustainable energy systems: an overview," in *Sustainability*, vol. 10, p. 3067, 2018, https:// doi.org/10.3390/su10093067.

[12]   C. Gupta and A. Mahajan, "Evaluation of proof-of-work consensus algorithm for blockchain networks," in *2020 11th International Conference on Computing, Communication and Networking Technologies (ICCCNT)*, 2020, pp. 1–7, doi:10.1109/ICCCNT49239.2020.9225676.

Chapter 13

Streamed gaming

Dale Whinham[1], Yiang Lu[1], Zhaoran Wang[1],
Jiaming Zhang[1], Richard Davison[1], Gary Ushaw[1]
and Graham Morgan[1]

13.1 Introduction

Streamed gaming is the ability to deliver video games to players through the use of cloud and edge-based technologies [1]. The centralised resources of cloud computing are used to offset local resource requirements to allow players to participate in video games on a wider variety of lower-powered devices. Edge technologies are utilised to lower latency to levels suitable for modelling real-time player interaction in modern video games.

Traditionally, costly consoles and PCs incorporating significant resource capabilities are required to play many video games. For example, graphics processing units (GPUs) can easily cost as much as the rest of the local machine put together and are a key requirement to unlock the gaming experience expected by players of today's video games. Therefore, streamed gaming can be viewed, commercially, as removing this financial barrier for the player, thereby potentially expanding the consumer market for video game publishers.

Streamed gaming requires a sequence of events to be repeated to deliver video games to players:

- The cloud server updates the video game application based on the latest player input.
- The screen image and sound produced by the game are rendered into video format at the server.
- The video is streamed to the remote player across the Internet, to be viewed on the client hardware.
- The input from the player is sent from the client hardware to the cloud server to be used in the next update of the game state.

Although closely related to streamed video services, streamed gaming requires two distinct additional functions that video streaming services lack:

[1]School of Computing, Newcastle University, UK

- A need for real-time (or near real-time) reaction to ongoing player input.
- A need to facilitate, if required, multiple-player participatory scenarios.

These two additional requirements pose significant technical challenges in the ability to deliver video games in an economically efficient manner. The primary reason for this is that there is a significant resource requirement in generating a streamed video game for play over the Internet while ensuring timely requirements are satisfied. Generating the required video format suitable for streaming is, in itself, a significant resource cost. By comparison, a streamed video service simply streams existent video files, whereas the streamed gaming service must generate the video content in real time. Further to this, the hardware costs at the server are significantly greater than that required at the client, which requires comparatively little processing power (e.g. a thin client console).

When employing edge technology, the cloud server assumes responsibility for instantiating and managing the life-cycle of the video game using edge technology that is physically closer to the player and so lowers interactive latency, a key requirement to deliver fast-paced gaming scenarios [2].

Fundamentally, the resources required to deliver streamed gaming outstrip those required for local gaming (i.e., purchasing a title, downloading it, and playing it on a player's machine). The power of cloud server, and/or edge device, must be greater than the expected target machine of a player. This indicates that streamed gaming itself is less economically viable and substantially more environmentally harming than the existing approach to traditional downloaded, locally executed, video games [3]. In fact, per-game played has a dramatically increased resource footprint over locally executed titles, making streamed gaming a less than green consideration primarily due to the need to maintain the timely interaction requirement.

Reducing resource requirements while delivering a quality gaming experience is imperative if streamed gaming is to grow commercially [1]. There is no doubt that streamed gaming is potentially the future cloud-enabled service that consumes most power per-user/player. Therefore, a significant research investment is required to ensure a greener approach to such technologies.

One may wonder just why the streamed gaming model is rapidly increasing in favour of commercial enterprises given the significant resource consumption and the complexity of technology required. This is easily answered by the desire to establish a business model of general stable growth of revenue rather than that based on creative risk (i.e., a single title selling). In the creative industries, the risk of product/franchise failure is high when there is a direct link between unit sales and an identifiable product (i.e., a single video game and its associated sales). However, if one could move to a business model of subscription, then two benefits emerge:

- A predictable revenue stream – the shelf-life unit sales of video games are not steady and tend to drift downwards significantly after initial release. However, subscriber numbers do not witness the same degree of fluctuation. In essence, once subscribed, the decision to unsubscribe is less likely than the decision not to buy an unpopular video game.

- Increased shelf-life and revenue – to generate unit sales of video games that are past their maximum sales point requires price-point adjustment. However, such games on a streaming service will be played more and add to the overall quantity of availability of titles on a game streaming platform. In essence, subscribers are more likely to play an older video game on a streamed platform than actually purchase it as a unit sale.

This commercial drive to generate revenue from subscription-based gaming (as opposed to unit sales) has seen significant commercial activity in streamed gaming in recent years. This has even included companies that are not known for video game titles entering the market place [4].

The streaming of video games is a significant, yet relatively new in commercial terms, cloud/edge-enabled service. However, the commercial growth potential of such services may be considered greater than video on-demand streaming services. The video game market in terms of sales is larger than that of movies with suggestions that the pandemic of 2020 has increased this difference in favour of video games more rapidly [5].

In this chapter, we introduce the reader to the area of streamed gaming. First, through consideration of the origins of streamed gaming. These are firmly placed in the original development and distribution of online gaming. However, consideration of streamed media is presented to clearly identify the differences (and commonalities) of these two services. We then highlight the requirements of streamed gaming which in turn provides a basis on which to describe the technology surrounding streamed gaming. We then explore the latest challenges in streamed gaming in the context of multi-player, resource sharing, possibilities. A future for streamed gaming is envisaged that departs from the single-player experience while creating expansive virtual worlds of shared gaming experiences. We then draw out conclusions that reflect on the discussions presented in this chapter.

13.2 Streaming video games

To better understand streamed gaming one must clearly understand the differences and similarities between distributed gaming, online gaming, and streamed media. In addition, we focus on delivering an experience in terms of player expectations as well as quality in terms of measurable resource usage.

13.2.1 Origins

Commercial streamed gaming may still be in its infancy but the origins of streamed gaming can be traced to the earliest developments in online simulations. Of particular note is the military-funded work for graphical simulations in the 1980s and early 1990s. In fact, one of the earliest requirements for military simulations from this era was for remote devices (e.g., aircraft simulators) that could not be moved to communicate with each other through a shared 'theatre of war' (a scenario not too dissimilar to many of the games streamed to players today).

Early pioneering work on SIMNET [6] delivered a wide-area network management of interacting graphical simulations. In essence, the key technical challenge was the requirement to share the progression of a graphical simulation across numerous recipients. These simulations evolved over a number of years to include techniques such as dead reckoning [7], spatial sub-division [8], and eventually attempted standardisation for interconnecting simulations [9].

Commercial endeavours in online gaming started with text-based adventures sold as part of a package by Internet service providers (ISPs) (e.g., Island of Kesmai [10]). These types of games evolved rapidly through a number of developments due to the introduction of increasingly powerful graphically capable home computers and consoles. This rapid evolution has delivered worldwide popular titles such as Everquest [11] and World of Warcraft [12], which are still played today.

Distributed simulation, online gaming, and multiplayer networked gaming are concerned with sharing content, either from a server, or across player machines or both. Such content may be the location and behaviour of a player, or an item in the playing area, a sum of money paid for a virtual item, or a line of text typed by a player. However, streamed gaming is primarily concerned with executing the video game in its entirety in the cloud while delivering the resultant output to a remote player. The majority of resource requirements is placed in the cloud. Streamed gaming may or may not support multiplayer scenarios. The streaming of the game content itself (in the form of a video) while gathering user input remotely is the main difference from the aforementioned non-streaming online gaming scenarios.

As early as 2004, streamed gaming (may be termed online gaming, cloud gaming, and server-streamed gaming), as defined as a streamed realisation of a video game played remotely by players, was demonstrated. The phrase, gaming-on-demand, was coined not too long after this date and the business model based on subscription rather than unit sales suggested [13].

The two commercial forerunners of streamed gaming provided public facing services from 2010 (OnLive and Gaika) [14]. They were subsequently acquired by Sony Online Entertainment. However, the services were soon terminated, primarily due to the significant infrastructure required to reach large populations and the limited penetration of high-speed broadband at the time [15]. More recently, with the advent of increased home broadband capability, coupled with technological advancement in cloud and edge technologies (primarily for non-gaming service requirements), there is now a commercial imperative to deliver subscription-based gaming. Google, Apple, NVIDIA, Microsoft, and Netflix are just a few of the multinational organisations that have released, or expect to release, streaming gaming platforms (e.g., [16–19]).

13.2.2   Streamed media

Our discussion on the origins of streamed gaming from the perspective of online gaming provides an insight into the development of distributed real-time graphical simulations. However, the fundamental difference is the need to stream a video game in its entirety so as to alleviate the local install (and resource) requirements of a player's machine. As such, streamed gaming is closely related to existing services that provision streamed media services. In fact, the techniques used in streamed media services are reemployed in streamed gaming infrastructures.

Streamed media refers to the delivery of any media consumed by a user over the Internet. Primarily, the term refers to such media that is readied for consumption at the user's machine as soon as technologically possible. This usually means that such media is readied and displayed to users prior to its complete delivery. For example, a streamed video may start playing to a user prior to being completely received by the user's machine. The user expects streamed media services to deliver in real-time or near real-time and waiting for data streams to start, or their pausing, is a detrimental outcome and deters their use. The term is often prescribed to services that are delivering video, and premium quality video-streamed media services usually employ a subscription-based business model.

Streaming media first originated in 1974 [20] but did not attain commercial success until networking technology could deliver speeds in excess of 1 Mbit/s (broadband) into the home. A modern-streamed media system consists of three components: encoder, server, and player. The encoder is used to convert the original audio and video into a suitable format for streaming, the server sends the encoded media stream to the client, and the client decodes and plays the received media.

The function of the encoder is to compress and encode the input raw audio and video data. Different streaming services have different performance requirements for the encoder. The commonly used video encoding schemes are MPEG-4, H.264, and AC-1 [21]. The additional technologies for governing networked streaming fulfil the intermediary step of getting the data across the network. These technologies are employed on many of the popular video streaming services and the protocols governing them may be proprietary, standard, or derived into a standard from an initial proprietary solution [22]. For example, a popular choice is MPEG-DASH [23] for over HTTP delivery. Irrespective of protocol, services fundamentally derive their solutions from origins that combine sliding window style message re-sending coupled with forward error recovery (e.g., [24]).

As there are many parameters to consider in terms of available resources at both the client and the server side, streamed media requires a degree of variability in rate control. This is not fixed throughout a streamed session as it must accommodate real-time variances in resource availability. Therefore, employing protocols that may manage such variance (in addition to actually getting the streamed data sent) are an integral part of any streaming platform. For example, RTSP [25] was developed to accommodate the control of media servers to enable variability of streamed data in the context of resource availability.

Encoding, streaming, and rate control provide the fundamental building blocks to deliver streamed media services. Simply stated, the quality of the video is manipulated in collaboration with the rate of dissemination to more closely align with resources available at the server side, client side, and the network itself. This relies on the manipulation of the quantisation parameter (QP) which governs streamed quality.

To reduce bitrate, the value of QP can be increased, but at the cost of distortion or loss of detail. Since each frame of the video is different, using the same QP in compressing an entire video can result in bitrate fluctuations (as some frames and

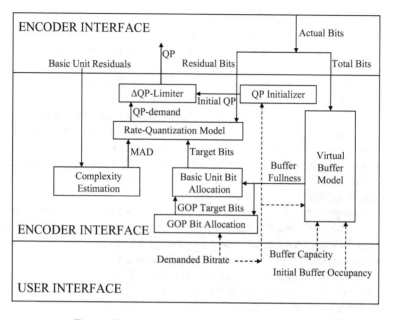

Figure 13.1   Elements of H.264 rate controller

the progression of one frame to another exhibit variable complications). Therefore, rate control allows the dynamic adjustment of QP to attempt video compression at a constant rate. A rate control algorithm adjusts encoding parameters according to the characteristics of the actual video frames to achieve a target bit rate and to allocate a budget for bits to each group of pictures (GOP) or a single picture or sub-picture in the video. Figure 13.1 shows the main elements for H.264 rate control [26].

Using *constant bitrate (CBR) encoding* provides a constant bitrate which allows determined resource usage and prediction given available bandwidth. However, this results in fluctuations in streamed quality (due to variance in complexity in the encoding process). Using *variable bitrate (VBR)* results in variance in bandwidth requirement but does provision a standard quality in the stream. *Constrained variable bitrate (CVBR)* provides an accommodation between the steadiness of bit rate in CBR and the steadiness of streamed quality in VBR, saving bandwidth when required. For example, when streaming a movie in 4K fidelity, the server may buffer as much of the movie as possible into the client machine at opportunistic points in the streaming process (i.e., when images are particular still and encoding and resultant bandwidth requirements are minimal).

Considering employing existing streamed infrastructure support in the context of streamed gaming may, at first glance, appear straightforward. However, the requirement of real-time or near real-time interaction indicates that buffering of future content is meaningless if such content is subject to change constantly. Unlike our example of a 4K movie that is buffered for future viewing, how can you buffer such a movie when the course of events that take place in such a movie are constantly susceptible to user-directed change? This is, fundamentally, the challenge in streamed gaming.

13.2.3   Gaming requirements

Streamed gaming, although a commercial concern for a number of organisations, is still technologically immature. Service delivery requires significant resources to provide a typically limited number of titles, and the subscription cost, when including premium titles, is far higher than traditional streaming services for standard video and audio. The requirement for exhibiting user influence on the screen in near real-time requires significant bandwidth and low latency. Reviews of resource consumption for such services (e.g., [27]) indicate bandwidth usage of up to 45 Mbit/s. However, there is an indication that PSNow (Sony's streamed gaming offering) requires much less bandwidth (possibly related to its acquisitions of earlier technology and associated patents).

As with any cloud-enabled service, a reduction in resource requirements while maintaining quality of service (QoS) can be measured in financial savings. Considering the size of the video game market and the reach of the Internet, even small reductions in resource requirements in streamed gaming platforms can translate to substantial financial savings. Furthermore, the current threshold of 25–45 Mbit/s requirement for home broadband access rules out a large number of the global Internet users. Even if this broadband is generally available, non-cable access (e.g., home Wi-Fi, telephony 4G/5G) will have a detrimental effect on QoS at the players home.

Bandwidth requirements are stated by all commercial suppliers of streamed gaming services, however, latency can be an issue [1,28]. A substantial infrastructure is required to deliver streamed gaming, typically involving edge technologies [29,30], to ensure that latency remains low enough for near real-time player interaction. However, latency increases not only for network delay, but processing overheads. As streamed gaming relies on processing tasks that take time to accomplish (e.g., transposing output to a video stream), a significant investment in high-performing technology is required [31]. Any video game player knows that, even with the most powerful PCs running a video game locally, jitter and freeze frame may still happen due to excessive resource usage [32].

The extra latency in a streamed video game compared to the traditional online video game (wherein the video stream is generated at the client) is primarily due to the downstream network load for transmitting the game video. In a streamed game single-server situation, a 1080p 60FPS game video needs over 3 Mbit/s for one client device [31]. As the number of players grows, the cloud provider must invest further in network bandwidth. Physical distance is also a significant problem for the remote server model. The cloud provider cannot give all users an acceptable streamed gaming experience when some users are too far away from the server [32].

The edge computing model was introduced to address heavy network load in cloud services for distributed clients [29,30]. In fact, the edge computing topology was primarily introduced to serve media with a high-bandwidth requirement (at the time in the 1990s) (e.g., [33]). In the context of streamed gaming today, a simple view could be to place the rendering and physics calculation to be deployed in the edge node, which then sends the game video to the player for presentation on their device/console. In reality, the game must be streamed from edge technologies due to the low latency requirement to enable player interaction in most games [34]. Even for buffered media, such an approach is advocated, although intermediary buffering is possible from central servers to edge devices [2].

This model reduces the physical distance from game video sender to end user device and reduces the requirement for network bandwidth of the main server. Consequently, the streamed game service will benefit from edge computing with a reduction in network fluctuations and latency. Employing such scenarios in the future can also make advanced predictions based on big data analytics to further enhance the dynamic deployment capabilities of edge servers [35].

13.2.4   Platform expectations

As most video games require high interactivity to satisfy the player experience, latency must be maintained in a stable and acceptable range. A player is likely to abandon playing streamed games if unacceptable interactivity delays are experienced, or the latency varies across a wide range, resulting in the player feeling unable to control the game [1,32]. Both upstream and downstream are important for the streamed gaming user experience. The upstream is required to send the player inputs to the server, and the downstream is required to transmit the game video and audio back to the client device.

Cloud server hardware specifications can vary greatly depending on their intended workloads. The specifications of a web server, for example, may be designed for energy and cost efficiency rather than raw compute performance, and may have no GPU capabilities at all. However, GPU-equipped cloud servers are now commonplace, especially with the rise of embarrassingly parallel compute workloads such as deep learning that can be accelerated by GPUs. Therefore, the underlying hardware available in datacentres today can certainly accommodate video games. For example, the NVIDIA Tesla P40 and NVIDIA RTX T10-8 – two models of datacentre GPU used by streamed gaming service *GeForce Now* – can be configured to deliver similar performance to desktop PC GPUs, the GTX 1080 and RTX 2060 [36]. Server hardware specifically aimed at streamed gaming is also now available, featuring several GPU nodes and the ability to run many concurrent game instances [37]. Meeting the performance requirements of a typical console or PC video game, therefore, poses no issue for appropriate datacentre hardware configurations.

Providing a streamed gaming service incurs additional overheads. The game software needs to receive input from the player via the Internet. Real-time transmission and reception of game controller, mouse, and keyboard input should not pose a significant computational cost. More significantly, the video output of the game must be captured, encoded, and transmitted to the player as quickly as possible, and each stage of this process has a measurable cost in terms of CPU and GPU processing power depending on implementation and choice of video codec. Therefore, the performance

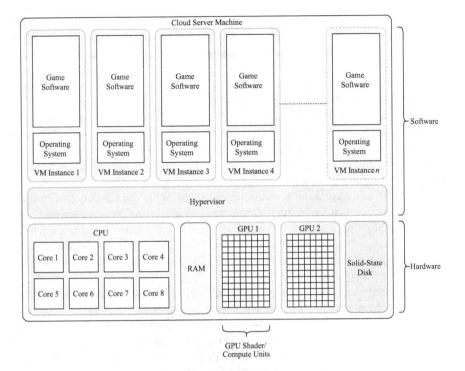

Figure 13.2 Streamed gaming utilising hypervisor approach

of the cloud platform running the game software needs to be greater than a local platform to account for this [38].

The effective performance of a cloud server available to the application depends on the service agreement between the cloud provider and the client. To save on running costs and maximise profits, the hardware may be shared between multiple clients on-demand using virtualisation, which means that by using hypervisor technologies, a single cloud server can appear as multiple virtual machines and, therefore, host multiple clients (Figure 13.2). This means that effective performance may be artificially limited, or vary depending on demand.

Additional cloud infrastructure will also be needed for content delivery, i.e. providing a browsable catalogue of software to the consumer and distributing it to server nodes. Session management and load-balancing tasks also need to be accommodated, such as allocation of the most suitable cloud server instance for running the consumer's chosen title and monitoring session performance.

13.2.5 Handling legacy titles

Previous generations of video game console often used custom hardware, with bespoke graphics chipsets and CPU architectures not found elsewhere. Video game software would be written specifically for these hardware platforms and it would not be possible to directly run the software on typical x86/AMD64 hardware (as is often used in the cloud). Source code re-engineering, i.e. a 'port', would be required – which could incur significant development costs. Alternatively, software emulation of the original platform could be used, as long as the emulation is performant enough to deliver an acceptable player experience.

The hardware used by the current and previous generations of video games consoles (such as the Xbox One, Series X or PlayStation 5) now closely resembles that of commodity desktop PCs [39,40]. These consoles share the same x86/AMD64 CPU architectures and use integrated GPUs which are based on the same fundamental designs as PC graphics cards. This means that video game console vendors are now able to shift the execution of recent titles onto typical GPU-equipped cloud server hardware without requiring a significant amount of adaptation. Vendors can make use of lightweight virtualisation technologies and implement a software runtime environment in the cloud that provides the same functionality as the console. In this way, the same runtime environment can be used for all game titles, and the game software itself can potentially run unmodified.

One of the more subtle problems with this strategy is that, given the fixed specifications of the platform, video game software originally programmed for a console may make assumptions about the resources available to it and the overall performance of the system. For example, slow disk I/O may be hidden by 'loading screens' which provide hints and tips, or show a cutscene to the player as they wait for the game to start. A cloud deployment may benefit from I/O performance many magnitudes faster than a console due to the availability of virtualised storage backed by large arrays of high-performance solid-state disks. Whilst the player may therefore enjoy much quicker entry into a game, they may never see a 'loading' screen, and, therefore, never benefit from the hints and tips, or miss out on some storyline. These kinds of assumptions may require careful consideration in case the gameplay experience is significantly altered and could pose an engineering challenge. Software workarounds may need to be implemented at the vendor or the developers' expense, to ensure that the overall game experience is preserved as it makes its transition to the cloud.

13.2.6   Genre and timeliness

Video games present many different types of genres. Such genres allow players to participate in gaming scenarios ranging from replicating traditional board games through to real-time simulations involving players exploring immersive 3D worlds. The number, range, and classification of gaming genres is considerable and debatable; however, literature has identified, primarily in terms of online gaming, genres in the context of their message delivery requirements [41]. Unlike streamed video services (e.g., movies, TV), adaptation of the technology to gaming genre as well as available technical resource can result in significant financial savings, so understanding genre considerations is a fundamental part of delivering fiscally sustainable streamed gaming services [42].

Considering the required message exchange rate to enable player interaction in streamed gaming, any input latency presented to players can degrade human performance and detract from the gaming experience [43]. Studies have shown that high amounts of latency and jitter can result in a measurably poor experience for the player, introducing error into their actions and contributing to a less enjoyable and more frustrating experience [44,45].

A clear observation to anyone who has played fast-paced video games is that the effect of latency and jitter on the overall quality of the gaming experience is genre dependent. Fast-paced first-person shooters require constant input from the player and quick reactions in order for them to succeed competitively, therefore, high amounts of latency are unacceptable. This is not only reflected in the graphical representation [46] but also the immersion requirement for the surround sound of modern video games [47]. Studies measuring the effects of latency on players' performance across various genres of games have shown that player performance in first-person shooter games sharply decreases after only 100 ms of latency, whereas a real-time strategy game fares much better, remaining playable up to a latency of 1,000 ms [48]. In those games that do not require fast-paced gaming (e.g., turn-based), latency and jitter may not adversely affect the player's performance.

To reinforce the impact of genre on gaming platform requirements we now consider three genre examples: turn-based, partially real time, and real-time interaction.

Turn-based games
- Board games (e.g. chess, Go).
- Card games (e.g. Hearthstone).
- Turn-based role-playing games.

A *turn-based game* can be described as a game in which user interaction is only permitted at specific times. The flow of the game is often halted until the user confirms their action. Individual interactions may be started and finished within a single frame. For example, in a chess game, the user may play their next move by using direction buttons to move a cursor between squares, and a selection button to choose their chess piece and confirm its destination. Cursor movement and selection actions can each be acted upon to change the game state within individual frames. In a turn-based game, the user does not need to provide an instantaneous, real-time response to events within the game, and, therefore, there is ample time for the new game state to be made visible on their client device so that they can decide on their next action. Therefore, turn-based games are not impacted by input latency or jitter.

Turn-based gaming is a popular genre, with many of the players transferring their gameplay from physical cards to the digital medium of video games [49]. On current commercial platforms, the lack of consideration for delivering such titles is a strong indication that such titles, although popular, are not the gameplay demographic commercial organisations are targeting. This is primarily due to price point associated business model of such games [50] combined with the relatively low technical requirement to run such games on local devices. As such, the traditional turn-based game, at the moment, is not a concern for streamed gaming platforms.

Partially real-time games
- Sports games (e.g. golf, billiards, bowling).
- Puzzle games.
- Real-time strategy games (RTS).

A *partially real-time game* is similar to a turn-based game in that user interactions are only permitted at specific times, but a complete action may span several frames of media presented to a player depending on whether the game is expecting a real-time interaction in its current state or not. For example, in a golf game, the user typically inputs their intent to hit the ball by holding a button or key for a few seconds to determine the amount of power that goes into their golf swing. The success of the user's shot may depend on a precise release time, introducing an element of skill into the game. As the release time is a real-time interaction, a large amount of input latency could lead to game inconsistency and, therefore, impact the game experience negatively.

In a streamed gaming context, inconsistency may occur during this type of game. Using the golf game example, the user begins to hold the button or key to start accumulating power for hitting the ball, and this interaction is transmitted to the server. At the time, the cloud server receives the command and begins to increase the power frame by frame. For each game state transition (and new video frame generated), the server streams the new frames back to the user's device. As this is a precise action sensitive to timely consideration of when to release the button, any latency will inevitably alter the server's perception of what the player actually did. This threshold of consistency can, if too large, render this type of game unplayable.

This type of genre can accommodate predictive resource assignment to increase the likelihood that player interaction is handled appropriately. This is similar to predictive interest management suggested to alleviate this problem in non-cloud-hosted online games [51].

Real-time interaction games
- Shooter games (e.g. first-person/third-person shooters [FPS/TPS], top-down shooter games, space shooters).
- Action games.
- Racing games.
- Sports games (e.g. basketball, soccer).

A *real-time interaction game* can be described as a game where user interaction primarily depends on the current game state and commands can be sent at any time during the play session. In other words, the game requires constant input from the player as they react to events occurring in real-time. For example, in a first person shooter game, the user will be constantly sending commands to control the camera to look around the environment and aim at opponents. The 'shoot' command will be sent when the player thinks they are aiming at an opponent, and the choice of when to press that button depends entirely on the game state that is visible on the client device. This means that any sort of input latency with this genre of game is more likely to lead to game inconsistency and a less enjoyable game experience.

These genres of video games are the most difficult to support, yet the most popular on streamed gaming platforms. Employing edge-based technology to enable such games is commonplace (required) [52], as any jitter or latency, or loss issues in message delivery will quickly deteriorate player experience [53].

13.2.7 Experience

The relationship between the QoS and the Quality of Experience (QoE) of a video game is defined in the expectation, and then realisation, of gameplay. In traditional media streaming services, there has been a recognition of a difference between QoS and QoE, defining QoE as a measure of consumer satisfaction of the presented media whereas QoS defines the technically measurable presentation of such media [54]. For example, QoS may measure timeliness and throughput of message delivery whereas QoE attempts, with user consideration and the context of the media in question, the quality of received media [54]. This is easily understood if we consider a video that contains a relatively static background and a moving character in the centre of the screen. A viewer will probably not notice deviations in background quality, but will notice deviations in character presentation. A QoS description will not take into account such differences but QoE will accommodate this subtle, yet important, difference.

Although work differentiating QoS and QoE can be traced back to any work that seeks to represent improved delivery of perceived quality for data (e.g., practical forward error correction engineering techniques developed as early as 1950s [55]), many assimilate the phrase with Web (Internet) delivered content and many assume this to be only video [56], although significant work has occurred in Voice over IP services [57].

Genres of video games do present an additional challenge in measuring QoE as opposed to QoS. It could be said that the difference between QoE and QoS is made significantly more complicated in video games rather than non-interactive streamed media as genre dictates QoE. As many modern video games mix genres within their presentation to players (to present complex virtual environments), QoE may be highly variable throughout a single gameplay session.

The genres based solely on message exchange do not compromise the entirety of expectation of QoE, and simply indicate a measurable QoS. Earlier works often present such work as a description in consideration of message ordering and consistency [58]. However, the challenges of any gaming scenario delivered over any network do have a context depending on genre [59].

In the consideration of streamed gaming and the advancement of the field academically, a lack of published statistics from commercial providers makes it difficult to quantifying QoS in terms of QoE [1,60]. However, due to known requirements associated with video game execution, streamed media bitrate management, encoding and decoding video, and the timeliness of player interaction, we can infer that these are the main factors influencing QoS [61] which in turn dictate QoE [1,62].

13.2.8 Summary

The advent of streamed gaming has the potential to be highly disruptive to the video game industry providing a completely different profit model for game publishers and developers. Rather than expecting customers to invest heavily in hardware to be used in the home, the streamed gaming model concentrates the processing power at the cloud server, with the customer only requiring a relatively low-cost thin client. The game is executed on the cloud in response to the user's inputs, and the game image and audio are streamed over the Internet to the user. The finance model is then based on frequent consumption through a subscription-based service.

The overall costs associated with transferring video game processing to the cloud can be greater than those associated with traditional means. This additional cost includes an increase in computational requirements, which has consequences for green computing and sustainability. The cloud gaming service operator, therefore, needs to consider the costs of meeting the minimum performance requirements for delivering a high-quality gaming experience and ensure that streaming overheads and additional infrastructure requirements are accounted for. The use of shared servers may significantly reduce running costs, but result in less deterministic levels of performance. Software compatibility may also pose a problem, especially if the software makes assumptions about hardware behaviour or performance due to being written for a fixed-specification console platform. The greater concern for the player is the expected experience of play. The player is expecting a fidelity of service that is similar, if not better, than they would expect from a downloaded game instance on a console or local PC. Game genres are highly influential in determining this QoE and manipulation of the QoS at the resource level must take into account. In simple terms, genre may dictate how a player may focus on the gaming arena and the relationship of this focus to the expected player interactivity of the video game itself. These areas are minimally explored at the moment, but will provide the most savings in terms of resource usage while promoting player QoE.

13.3 Multiplayer streamed gaming

We have discussed many of the issues pertaining to the remote execution and delivery of video game software via cloud-based streaming services. However, the cloud also presents additional opportunities for lifting some of the restrictions imposed by traditional video game engineering patterns concerning the implementation of multiplayer experiences.

13.3.1 Distributed virtual environments

Some of the most successful video games offer rich multiplayer experiences where several players can participate in a shared virtual world simultaneously, and interact with the world, and each other, in real-time. These are known as *distributed virtual environments* (DVEs). Traditionally, a DVE uses a client–server architecture where a server with a high-bandwidth network connection hosts the session and maintains the state of the world. Remote clients then connect to the server and exchange messages with the server about the user's interactions, whilst also presenting a graphical representation of the state of the DVE to the user.

The scale and complexity of a DVE can vary greatly; a small session with 4–16 players in an environment the size of 2–3 buildings (e.g. a small-scale first-person shooter game) could be a fairly trivial scenario hosted by a single server, but an environment spanning hundreds of kilometres hosting thousands of players (e.g. an MMORPG such as World of Warcraft) may be distributed across many servers, posing a significant engineering challenge. A DVE must ensure mutual consistency, such that all participants perceive the state of the world to be the same. This is achieved via message passing; users' client software periodically receives network packets containing updated positions, velocities, and other state information about objects and other users within the world. In a real-time simulation, the frequency of these messages must be great enough such that interactions appear to execute smoothly and consistency is maintained.

Given that a user's network connection quality can vary greatly, a video game may impose limitations on its own design to ensure correct operation of the DVE given a wide range of user network connection qualities. Users can connect to the Internet in a variety of ways; ADSL, cable, Wi-Fi, and cellular connections for example each have their own benefits and drawbacks in terms of cost, convenience, bandwidth, and latency.

13.3.2 Interest management

A large-scale DVE with large numbers of users and interactive objects can be problematic to successfully implement when the network connection quality (i.e. frequency of lost packets) and latency varies on a per-user basis, as it would over the Internet. Some of these problems can be mitigated by *interest management*, which limits the passing of messages such that users will only receive high-frequency updates about entities that lie within their area of influence. A pair of users geographically distant enough from one another such that they are invisible may exchange messages about their activities at a greatly reduced frequency, or the messages may be omitted completely. This strategy reduces demands on network infrastructure and increases overall efficiency, which especially benefits users on bandwidth-limited connections.

Basic implementations of interest management may use fixed geographical regions determined at the time of world initialisation – users will then only receive messages related to other entities within their region. Alternatively, spheres of influence, or 'auras', attached to each entity can be used – an intersection of two or more auras would determine that messages should be exchanged between the associated entities. More advanced implementations may attempt to predict potential future interactions and ensure that the frequency of exchanged messages is increased before a high-fidelity interaction actually occurs, improving the overall consistency of each user's perception of the world [51].

13.3.3 Cloud-based game clients

In a multiplayer streamed gaming scenario, the DVE client runs in the cloud, and the user is simply receiving the video stream produced by the client. The DVE client can, therefore, benefit from running within the same network as the DVE servers, on high-performance cloud infrastructure. Given that a cluster of cloud servers co-located on the same local area network within a datacentre can benefit from very high-speed, low latency network connections with high reliability, there is less of a requirement for constraining bandwidth usage between DVE clients and servers. Interest management strategies would still be relevant, but areas of interest could be expanded to far greater volumes. The quality of the user's network connection can then only affect the timeliness of their controller inputs and quality of their received video frames – the simulation of the DVE itself and the networking logic that maintains state and consistency of the DVE need not concern itself with poor quality connections. This opens up possibilities for higher-fidelity interactions between greater numbers of users in larger environments.

Two users competing against one another in a traditional DVE may be unfairly matched if one user has a network connection to the server with a significantly lower latency than the other. For example, in a first-person shooter game, the low-latency user may be able to see, shoot, and defeat the high-latency user before the high-latency user has a chance to see their opponent. Edge computing nodes located geographically close to the user could offer a more efficient network route to a cloud-based server with less hops than if the user were to make their own connection to the cloud server via the Internet [63]. Therefore, a streamed gaming service running a DVE client on an edge node, with the edge node streaming the video output to the user, has the potential to improve competitive fairness and overall game experience for the user in spite of the additional latency associated with video and input streaming.

13.3.4 Distributed physics

Modern video games often leverage real-time physics engines to offer convincing interactions between players and simulated objects within the game environment. These engines are responsible for simulating forces being applied to objects (e.g. gravity), collision detection and resolution, and resolving constraints such as hinges and ball-and-socket joints. The fast pacing and high degree of realism players expect from modern titles demands a physics engine that can resolve its per-frame calculations in a very timely manner (in the order of milliseconds) such that real-time interactivity is maintained and an accurate, convincing simulation is delivered.

The scale and complexity of simulated real-time physics environments is often designed for local execution within the processing power limitations of the target platform, which is usually a commodity video games console or PC. These constraints can also have an impact on the accuracy of the physics simulation itself, whose implementers may also choose to sacrifice mathematical accuracy in favour of responsiveness or to meet tight frame-time deadlines. Traditional implementations are therefore not scalable and video games must be designed to work within these restrictions.

In multiplayer scenarios, physics interactions are often of reduced quality due to the challenges of network bandwidth and latency. Some types of interactions that do not inherently affect gameplay are often simulated on the DVE client, but not synchronised with the server. For example, a player may shoot down a tapestry from a wall and enjoy a realistic cloth simulation as it falls to the ground, but this may not be witnessed by other players in the vicinity.

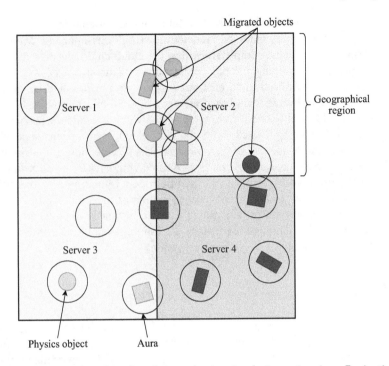

Figure 13.3   *A distributed real-time physics simulation using Aura Projection*

Aura Projection is a novel approach to distributed physics which aims to facilitate scalability without reducing the fidelity of the simulation, by ensuring that objects which could potentially collide (and therefore require a collision response) are co-located on the same server [64]. This approach is fundamental to ensuring a high-fidelity simulation, as the 'narrow phase' (object intersection tests) of the collision detection is then immune to network phenomenon such as latency and jitter, which would otherwise negatively affect the perceived accuracy and stability of the simulation.

In Aura Projection, servers participating in the distributed simulation each manage their own geographical regions, or partitions, within the environment, and simulated objects situated within these regions are simulated by the associated server. Regions are non-overlapping and can be placed adjacent to one another in various layout configurations (e.g. side-by-side, three-way 'T-junction', or four-way 'cross'). Figure 13.3 shows an example of a simulation distributed across four servers. The objects are coloured according to which server is responsible for simulating them. Objects transmit their auras to adjacent servers when close to geographical boundaries. If an aura intersects with a remote object's aura, that object may be migrated to the remote server to ensure that any possible collisions are resolved within a single simulation instance, ensuring a stable and consistent collision response.

Aura Projection demonstrates the feasibility of scaling real-time physics using cloud computing resources and fixed, predetermined region assignments. Multiplayer games designed to execute completely within the cloud could leverage distributed physics to provide convincing real-time interactions on a massive scale; a convincing large-scale destructible battlefield or a busy city environment could be simulated accurately in across several cloud-based servers. The DVE client providing the user's view of the world would benefit from a high-bandwidth, low-latency connection to the physics workers being located within the same cloud, or on an edge node with an efficient connection to the cloud, therefore, the user's perception of the simulation would not suffer from consistency issues associated with latency or bandwidth.

Further work could bring dynamic partition reconfiguration and load balancing, which would enable on-demand reconfiguration of the simulation in response to changes in the environment. For example, cloud instances could be added to or removed from the simulation to redistribute the computational workload in response to additional players joining or leaving the session.

13.4   Conclusions

In this chapter, we have examined many aspects of streamed gaming, the issues it faces, and its potential to change how video games are consumed in the future. Streamed gaming can still be considered an emerging technology with many research challenges to overcome in order to reach its full potential and achieve widespread adoption. Increased service delivery costs compared to traditional audio and video streaming services (e.g., hardware provisioning) translate into higher subscription costs to the user. Higher network bandwidth requirements (as well as the need for low latency) may mean that many users' home Internet connections, especially those in rural areas, are not capable of receiving an acceptable QoS.

The adoption of edge technologies within geographically acceptable distances to distant communities will not be economically viable without substantial advances in economising resource usage while maintaining player expectations of QoE. Unlike streaming services, streamed gaming faces significant economic challenges in reaching a wider audience. This will, without political consideration, result in streamed gaming focused on wealthy nations with higher population concentrations (e.g., towns and cities).

The imperative of lowering resource requirements is simply not just an economic one, but a question of inclusiveness.

Understanding the fundamental differences between QoS and QoE are critical to gaining the greatest potential for effective management of resources. When developing models for content delivery, a more efficient use of resources may be realised by considering the user's perception of the service – their QoE – compared to when a model is based solely on technically measurable performance metrics (QoS) [54]. The interactive nature of video games and the wide variety of genres used in modern titles presents additional challenges in how we may determine QoE compared to non-interactive media. There is a clear understanding that genre will play a significant role in achieving near-optimum resource savings in bringing streamed gaming to the widest possible audience.

In the first instance, we can expect to see a reduction in resource requirements through the adoption of edge computing models, which would move the most latency-critical computing tasks physically closer to the user. Further efforts to change how video games themselves are engineered may enable more efficient use of distributed computing to lower provisioning costs (e.g., allowing the video game's subsystems to be broken up and executed across a varying number of virtual machines depending on the workload). This could also open up the possibility of a 'hybrid' model, in which some of the game subsystems are executed locally, and, some in the cloud, depending on the capabilities of the user's client device [65].

Overall, there is no doubt that streamed gaming is placing significant technical demands on existing cloud/edge-enabled services. The reuse of existing technologies, primarily developed for media streaming services augmented with know–how from distributed, multiplayer, gaming is resulting in an environmentally damaging, financially inhibiting approach with limited audience reach. The existence of commercial activity in this area is, in one sense, misleading in that it is clearly only undertaken at great initial investment. This financial barrier to entering the market will stifle innovation and flexibility in the market place if academic research does not contribute to the advances of this relatively new technology.

References

[1] Rossi HS, Ögren N, Mitra K, *et al.* Subjective quality of experience assessment in mobile cloud games. In: *GLOBECOM 2022 – 2022 IEEE Global Communications Conference*; 2022. p. 1918–1923.

[2] Bilal K and Erbad A. Edge computing for interactive media and video streaming. In: *2017 Second International Conference on Fog and Mobile Edge Computing (FMEC)*. IEEE; 2017. p. 68–73.

[3] Marsden M, Hazas M, and Broadbent M. From one edge to the other: exploring gaming's rising presence on the network. In: *Proceedings of the 7th International Conference on ICT for Sustainability*; 2020. p. 247–254.

[4] Shaw L and Gurman M. Netflix Plans to Offer Video Games in Push Beyond Films, TV; 2021. https://www.bloomberg.com/news/articles/2021-07-14/netflix-plans-to-offer-video-games-in-expansion-beyond-films-tv.

[5] Witkowski W. Videogames are a bigger industry than movies and North American sports combined, thanks to the pandemic; 2021. https://www.marketwatch.com/story/videogames-are-a-bigger-industry-than-sports-and-movies-combined-thanks-to-the-pandemic-11608654990.

[6] Thorpe JA, Bloedorn GW, Taylor R, *et al. The SIMNET Network and Protocol.* Cambridge, MA: BBN Labs Inc.; 1987.

[7] Cheung S and Loper M. Synchronizing simulations in distributed interactive simulation. In: *Proceedings of Winter Simulation Conference*. IEEE; 1994. p. 1316–1323.

[8]   Zeswitz SR. *NPSNET: Integration of Distributed Interactive Simulation (DIS) Protocol for Communication Architecture and Information Interchange.* Monterey, CA: Department of Computer Science, Naval Postgraduate School; 1993.

[9]   Dahmann JS, Fujimoto RM, and Weatherly RM. The department of defense high level architecture. In: *Proceedings of the 29th conference on Winter Simulation*; 1997. p. 142–149.

[10] Kesmai Company. Island of Kesmai. CompuServe; 1996 [Online Resource].

[11] Verant Interactive. *Everquest.* NA: Sony Online Entertainment, EU: UbiSoft; 1999 [Online Resource].

[12] Blizzard Entertainment. *World of Warcraft.* Blizzard Entertainment; 2004 [Online Resource].

[13] Ojala A and Tyrvainen P. Developing cloud business models: a case study on cloud gaming. *IEEE Software.* 2011;28(4):42–47.

[14] Finkel D, Claypool M, Jaffe S, *et al.* Assignment of games to servers in the OnLive cloud game system. In: *2014 13th Annual Workshop on Network and Systems Support for Games*; 2014. p. 1–3.

[15] Huang CY, Chen KT, Chen DY, *et al.* GamingAnywhere: the first open source cloud gaming system. *ACM Transactions on Multimedia Computing, Communications, and Applications (TOMM).* 2014;10(1s):1–25.

[16] Newsroom N. *Tencent Games Partners with NVIDIA to Launch START Cloud Gaming Service.* NVIDIA; 2021. Accessed: 15/07/2021. Available from: https://nvidianews.nvidia.com/news/tencent-games-partners-with-nvidia-to-launch-start-cloud-gaming-service.

[17] Riungu-Kalliosaari L, Kasurinen J, and Smolander K. Cloud services and cloud gaming in game development. *Proceedings of the IADIS Game and Entertainment Technologies.* 2013;22(24.7):2013.

[18] Hood V. *Sony is Working on a Cloud Gaming Strategy that is 'Unique and only on PlayStation'.* TechRadar; 2021. Accessed: 15/07/2021. Available from: https://www.techradar.com/news/sony-is-working-on-a-cloud-gaming-strategy-that-is-unique-and-only-on-playstation.

[19] Asia MS. *SK Telecom and Microsoft Announce Plans for Joint 5G-Based Cloud Gaming.* Microsoft; 2019. Accessed: 15/07/2021. Available from: https://news.microsoft.com/apac/2019/09/04/sk-telecom-and-microsoft-announce-plans-for-joint-5g-based-cloud-gaming/.

[20] Ahmed N, Natarajan T, and Rao KR. Discrete cosine transform. *IEEE Transactions on Computers.* 1974;C-23(1):90–93.

[21] Seeling P, Fitzek FH, Ertli G, *et al.* Video network traffic and quality comparison of VP8 and H. 264 SVC. In: *Proceedings of the 3rd Workshop on Mobile Video Delivery*; 2010. p. 33–38.

[22] Fecheyr-Lippens A. "A review of http live streaming." [ONLINE] https://citeseerx.ist.psu.edu/document?repid=rep1&type=pdf&doi=57d33cda30c2d497b694470aaa8b502613851fa5, 1–37.

[23] Sodagar I. The mpeg-dash standard for multimedia streaming over the internet. *IEEE Multimedia.* 2011;18(4):62–67.

[24] Nguyen T and Zakhor A. Distributed video streaming with forward error correction. In: *Packet Video Workshop*, vol. 2002; 2002.

[25] Schulzrinne H, Rao A, and Lanphier R. *RFC2326: Real Time Streaming Protocol (RTSP)*. RFC Editor; 1998.

[26] All rights reserved copyright 2012 PC. Comprehensive Solutions and Products for Video Compressionists. Accessed: 30/07/2021. Available from: https://www.pixeltools.com/rate_control_paper.html.

[27] Di Domenico A, Perna G, Trevisan M, *et al.* A network analysis on cloud gaming: Stadia, GeForce Now and PSNow; 2020. arXiv preprint arXiv: 201206774.

[28] Sabet SS, Schmidt S, Griwodz C, *et al.* Towards the impact of gamers' adaptation to delay variation on gaming quality of experience. In: *2019 Eleventh International Conference on Quality of Multimedia Experience (QoMEX)*; 2019. p. 1–6.

[29] Satyanarayanan M. Edge computing. *Computer*. 2017;50(10):36–38.

[30] Ai Y, Peng M, and Zhang K. Edge computing technologies for Internet of Things: a primer. *Digital Communications and Networks*. 2018;4(2):77–86. Available from: https://doi.org/10.1016/j.dcan.2017.07.001.

[31] Huang CY, Chen KT, Chen DY, *et al.* GamingAnywhere: the first open source cloud gaming system. *ACM Transactions on Multimedia Computing, Communications, and Applications (TOMM)*. 2014;10(1s):1–25.

[32] Chen H, Zhang X, Xu Y, *et al.* T-gaming: a cost-efficient cloud gaming system at scale. *IEEE Transactions on Parallel and Distributed Systems*. 2019;30(12):2849–2865.

[33] Laursen A, Olkin J, and Porter M. Oracle media server: providing consumer based interactive access to multimedia data. In: *Proceedings of the 1994 ACM SIGMOD International Conference on Management of Data*; 1994. p. 470–477.

[34] Tsipis A, Oikonomou K, Komianos V, *et al.* Performance evaluation in cloud-edge hybrid gaming systems. In: *Third International Balkan Conference on Communications and Networking 2019 (BalkanCom'19)*. Skopje, North Macedonia; 2019.

[35] Elliott G. *The Future of Cloud Gaming is on the Edge*; 2020. Accessed: 27/07/2021. Available from: https://www.datacenterdynamics.com/en/opinions/future-cloud-gaming-edge/.

[36] NVIDIA. GeForce Now Community-Owned FAQ (2021 Edition); 2021. Accessed: 05/07/2021. https://www.nvidia.com/en-us/geforce/forums/gfn-tech-support/46/329285/geforce-now-community-owned-faq/.

[37] NVIDIA. NVIDIA RTX Server; 2021. Accessed: 05/07/2021. https://www.nvidia.com/en-us/data-center/rtx-server-gaming/.

[38] Shea R, Liu J, Ngai ECH, *et al.* Cloud gaming: architecture and performance. *IEEE Network*. 2013;27(4):16–21.

[39] Microsoft. Xbox Series X; 2020. Accessed: 05/07/2020. https://www.xbox.com/en-GB/consoles/xbox-series-x#specs.

[40]   Sony. Unveiling New Details of PlayStation 5: Hardware Technical Specs; 2020. Accessed: 05/07/2020. https://blog.playstation.com/2020/03/18/unveiling-new-details-of-playstation-5-hardware-technical-specs/.

[41]   Lakkakorpi J, Heiner A, and Ruutu J. Measurement and characterization of Internet gaming traffic. In: *Research Seminar on Networking*, Helsinki University of Technology, Networking Laboratory; 2002.

[42]   Suznjevic M, Beyer J, Skorin-Kapov L, *et al.* Towards understanding the relationship between game type and network traffic for cloud gaming. In: *2014 IEEE International Conference on Multimedia and Expo Workshops (ICMEW)*. IEEE; 2014. p. 1–6.

[43]   MacKenzie IS and Ware C. Lag as a determinant of human performance in interactive systems. In: *Proceedings of the INTERACT'93 and CHI'93 Conference on Human Factors in Computing Systems*; 1993. p. 488–493.

[44]   Pavlovych A and Gutwin C. Assessing target acquisition and tracking performance for complex moving targets in the presence of latency and jitter. In: *Proceedings of Graphics Interface 2012*. Citeseer; 2012. p. 109–116.

[45]   Normoyle A, Guerrero G, and Jörg S. Player perception of delays and jitter in character responsiveness. In: *Proceedings of the ACM Symposium on Applied Perception*; 2014. p. 117–124.

[46]   Nacke L and Lindley CA. Flow and immersion in first-person shooters: measuring the player's gameplay experience. In: *Proceedings of the 2008 Conference on Future Play: Research, Play, Share*; 2008. p. 81–88.

[47]   Mark G and Gareth S. Situating gaming as a sonic experience: the acoustic ecology of first-person shooters. In: *DiGRA &#3907 – Proceedings of the 2007 DiGRA International Conference: Situated Play*. The University of Tokyo; 2007. Available from: http://www.digra.org/wp-content/uploads/digital-library/07311.06195.pdf.

[48]   Claypool M and Claypool K. Latency and player actions in online games. *Communications of the ACM*. 2006;49(11):40–45.

[49]   Ito M. Technologies of the childhood imagination: Yugioh, media mixes, and everyday cultural production. In: *Structures of Participation in Digital Culture*. Durham, NC: Duke University Press; 2005. p. 88–111.

[50]   Rayna T and Striukova L. 'Few to Many': change of business model paradigm in the video game industry. *Digiworld Economic Journal*. 2014;94:61.

[51]   Morgan G and Lu F. *Predictive Interest Management: An Approach to Managing Message Dissemination for Distributed Virtual Environments*. Richmedia2003, Switzerland. 2003.

[52]   Bhojan A, Ng SP, Ng J, *et al.* CloudyGame: enabling cloud gaming on the edge with dynamic asset streaming and shared game instances. *Multimedia Tools and Applications*. 2020;79(43):32503–32523.

[53]   Wahab A, Ahmad N, and Schormans J. Variation in QoE of passive gaming video streaming for different packet loss ratios. In: *2020 Twelfth International Conference on Quality of Multimedia Experience (QoMEX)*. IEEE; 2020. p. 1–4.

[54] Mitra K, Zaslavsky A, and Åhlund C. Context-aware QoE modelling, measurement, and prediction in mobile computing systems. *IEEE Transactions on Mobile Computing.* 2015;14(5):920–936.

[55] Hamming RW. Error detecting and error correcting codes. *The Bell System Technical Journal.* 1950;29(2):147–160.

[56] Chen Z, Tan SM, Campbell RH, *et al.* Real time video and audio in the world wide web. In: *Fourth International World Wide Web Conference.* Citeseer; 1995. p. 333–348.

[57] Chujo VHVCV. Policy-based management for enterprise and carrier IP networking. *Fujitsu Scientific and Technical Journal.* 2000;36(2):128–139.

[58] Morgan G. Highly interactive scalable online worlds. *Advances in Computers.* 2009;76:75–120.

[59] Morgan G. Challenges of online game development: a review. *Simulation & Gaming.* 2009;40(5):688–710.

[60] Shea R, Liu J, Ngai ECH, *et al.* Cloud gaming: architecture and performance. *IEEE Network.* 2013;27(4):16–21.

[61] Chen KT, Chang YC, Hsu HJ, *et al.* On the quality of service of cloud gaming systems. *IEEE Transactions on Multimedia.* 2014;16(2):480–495.

[62] Laghari AA, He H, Memon KA, *et al.* Quality of experience (QoE) in cloud gaming models: a review. *Multiagent and Grid Systems.* 2019;15:289–304. Available from: https://doi.org/10.3233/MGS-190313.

[63] Bilal K and Erbad A. Edge computing for interactive media and video streaming. In: *2017 Second International Conference on Fog and Mobile Edge Computing (FMEC)*; 2017. p. 68–73.

[64] Brown A, Ushaw G, and Morgan G. Aura projection for scalable real-time physics. In: *Proceedings of the ACM SIGGRAPH Symposium on Interactive 3D Graphics and Games.* ACM; 2019. p. 1.

[65] Zhao Z, Hwang K, and Villeta J. Game cloud design with virtualized CPU/GPU servers and initial performance results. In: *Proceedings of the 3rd workshop on Scientific Cloud Computing*; 2012. p. 23–30.

Index